Got shade?

Got Shade?

A "Take It Easy" Approach for Today's Gardener

CAROLYN HARSTAD

PHOTOGRAPHS BY CAROLYN HARSTAD

DRAWINGS BY JEAN VIETOR

INDIANA University Press

Bloomington & Indianapolis

This book is a publication of
Indiana University Press
601 North Morton Street
Bloomington, IN 47404-3797 USA

http://iupress.indiana.edu

Telephone orders   800-842-6796
Fax orders   812-855-7931
Orders by e-mail iuporder@indiana.edu

Library of Congress Cataloging-in-Publication Data
Harstad, Carolyn.
Got shade? : a "take it easy" approach for today's gardener / Carolyn Harstad ; photographs
by Carolyn Harstad ; drawings by Jean Vietor.
    p. cm.
Includes bibliographical references and index.
ISBN 0-253-21625-7 (pbk. : alk. paper)
1. Gardening in the shade. 2. Shade-tolerant plants. 3. Low maintenance gardening.   I. Title.
SB434.7.H36 2003
635.9'543—dc21   2003005391
1 2 3 4 5 08 07 06 05 04 03

Indiana University Press gratefully acknowledges the generous support of the following sponsors:

Dr. and Mrs. Gilbert Daniels
Bobbi and Jim Diehl
Dawn Fazli
Steve and Elaine Fess
Mark M. Holeman, Inc.
Dr. and Mrs. Willis Peelle
Dr. and Mrs. Robert L. Rudesill
Ann R. Strong

Publication of this book was also assisted
by the Friends of Indiana University Press.

A gardener is
a dreamer,
an artist,
a laborer,
a philosopher
and an optimist.

—Unknown

Dedicated to the memory of
my friend
Jeanette Wong Ming
1936–2002

Contents

Careful selection of plants and proper garden site preparation will do much to bring beauty to your shaded garden. —*Shady Oaks Nursery*

Preface: Using This Book

Got Shade? describes a variety of low-maintenance plants, both native and exotic. Shade tolerance is the main criterion for inclusion. All will thrive in some degree of shade, from a few hours to no direct sunlight at all. Are these plants really low maintenance? It depends on how you use them. The key to low maintenance is choosing the right plant for the right place. This premise sounds simplistic, but it works.

Many plants have a host of common names. For accuracy and ease of identification, descriptions appear in alphabetical order by scientific name. Just as a Social Security number narrows down the multitudes to one individual, scientific names narrow down multitudes of plants to just one species. Cultivar names appear within single quotation marks and are not in italics. The arbiter of nomenclature is *Hortus Third: A Concise Dictionary of Plants Cultivated in the United States and Canada* by Liberty Hyde Bailey and Ethel Zoe Bailey. Plant names constantly change. When there are two or more legitimate names for the same plant, they are separated by aka ("also known as").

Most plants listed in this book are hardy to Zone 4 and will tolerate winter temperatures of −20° to −30°F or lower. Plants listed as hardy only to Zone 5 will probably succumb if temperatures dip below −10° to −20°F. Savvy gardeners push these by one zone by creating a microclimate for particular plants, but this book is about how to reduce maintenance—not increase it. Parentheses (4) indicate marginal hardiness.

Some plants reach their mature height quickly while others take 20 to 30 years or more. Climatic conditions directly impact the growth rate.

Using all caps indicates someone is shouting to get your attention! AGGRESSIVE plants are recommended for specific tasks, primarily as a

Preface

ground cover or for erosion control in difficult environments. Use these plants with caution or they may become environmental problems. Personal responsibility is the key. Deer Resistant means just that. Resistant. It does not mean Deer Proof, but resistant plants should be the last to go.

Plants that have proven themselves troublesome in the environment are identified as "not recommended." I urge you *not* to use these. Ever.

Most of the plants are readily available; some are so new or so unusual that finding a ready source may prove frustrating. Less than a decade ago, the only way to acquire native wildflowers was to rescue them from construction sites. Now many are tissue cultured or propagated by specialty nurseries and can be ordered from their catalogs, or even found at local garden centers. In the fall of 2002, my daughter purchased Wood Poppy at her nearby Wal-Mart in Minneapolis. Because it all harkens back to the laws of supply and demand, I have included a number of nifty plants that may seem impossible to locate—not to frustrate you, but to encourage nurserymen to get some of these beauties into their regular stock. If enough people keep hunting, ordering, asking, squeaking, or recommending, eventually rare treasures will become as readily available as Purple Coneflowers and Zonal Geraniums!

The items in the Bibliography proved immensely helpful to me as I read, researched, and learned. After working on this book, I feel as if I know all of these garden writers. I wish I did.

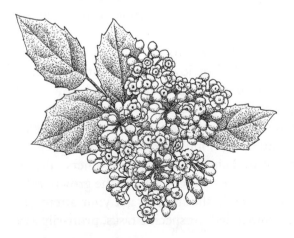

Oregon Grape Holly

Friends are flowers in the garden of life.
—*Anonymous*

Acknowledgments

My editor, Bobbi Diehl, is an expert gardener. She is also my friend. And what a great editor. I am blessed with the best of the best. Thanks, Bobbi!

Kudos to Matt Williamson, IU Press designer, who did the layout. I love his creativity and his style.

Thanks also to those expert friends who gave of their time and talent to ensure the accuracy of this book. Jo Ellen Meyers Sharp (annuals); Mike Homoya (grasses); George and Kay Yatskievych (ferns); Terri Parks (conifers); Randy Goodwin (hostas); Marge Soules (hostas/daylilies); Chris Wilhoite (aroids). Special thanks to Dr. Rebecca Dolan, Professor of Botany and Director of the Friesner Herbarium at Butler University; and Dr. Gilbert Daniels, both of whom critiqued the entire manuscript.

Nursery owners were very kind and their catalogs proved to be great sources of information. I especially thank the folks at Shady Oaks Nursery and Doug and Lynna Spence of Spence Restoration Nursery. I loved the catalog descriptions written by Tony Avent of Plant Delights and Bob Stewart of Arrowhead Alpines. Their plant humor kept me chuckling.

I want to acknowledge the incredible resource works of Allan Armitage, Cole Burrell, Michael Dirr, Harrison Flint, Liberty Hyde Bailey, Adrian Bloom, Sandra McLean Cutler, Charles Deam, Ken Druse, Barbara Ellis, Peter Loewer, Robert Mohlenbrock, Robert Obrizok, Leon Snyder, Floyd Swink, and Gerould Wilhelm, all of which helped me learn so much along my journey.

I send love and a hug to my dear friend Jean Vietor, an excellent artist of repute in the Midwest, who completed the exquisite botanical drawings for this book. They are truly works of art. Thank you, Jean.

Thanks to my five children—Linda, Karen, Mark, Kristen, Dave—

Acknowledgments

and their families; my sister Joan and brother Dave; and my fantastic dad, Walt Schneider, who at 96 still goes to work Monday–Saturday from 9 to 4:30 P.M. and sends me daily e-mails, jokes, and philosophical tidbits. He is my inspiration.

Another inspiration was my high school friend, Jeanette Wong Ming, who visited the Brooklyn Botanic Garden to sketch plants even as she was feeling the first effects of the pancreatic cancer that eventually took her life. I miss her.

And last, but never least, thanks to my wonderful husband who has been my best friend and confidant since our marriage in the summer of 1957. After 17 years as Executive Director of the Indiana Historical Society, Peter retired in 2001 and in his newfound freedom willingly fixed meals, cleaned, read my manuscript, made suggestions to tighten it up, and was always there for support. He often said, "Only one person in a household can write full time." Now it is his turn.

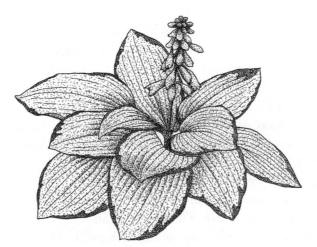

Hosta 'Gold Standard'

Got
shade?

No occupation is so delightful to me as the culture of the earth, and no culture comparable to that of the garden.
—*Thomas Jefferson*

1.

My Garden— Wild, but Civilized

Garden visitors often ask if I have to spend "all day every day" working in the garden. I suppose I did when I first began. And I still could—if I wanted to do that. But I don't. I don't have to anymore.

The most commonly observed natural shade is found in woodland areas. This is not to say that you cannot have a shady formal garden, but formality generally requires more maintenance. Meander through a natural area to observe plants providing erosion control. Small trees and shrubs dominate the landscape, providing seasonal interest and leafy refuges for birds and wildlife. Spring ephemerals appear en masse or as specimen plants, blooming before the leaf canopy emerges. Vines scramble up trees and walls; ferns and herbaceous perennials combine with assorted ground covers to fill blank spaces, and yet there are spaces between plants so air can readily circulate. Sounds of nature are all around.

Hosta 'June'

My Garden

It may not be possible to duplicate this kind of idyllic space on every typical shaded suburban lot, but when we moved to Indianapolis in the summer of 1984, I decided to try.

Because we all spend more time indoors than outdoors, the first thing I did was to go into the house. All too many gardens are located in the space surrounding the foundation of the house or at the base of the mailbox. Who sees them? Your neighbors! Dig your gardens where *you* can easily enjoy them from indoors.

Our home, situated on a heavily shaded, one-acre wooded lot, is about seven miles from downtown Indianapolis. Unfortunately, construction had destroyed much of the loamy soil of the original natural woodland. When I first started gardening, I learned, as Ann Lovejoy so aptly observed, that "the secret to having a thriving, healthy garden is to make beautiful dirt. Instead of feeding your plants, feed your soil with compost." Over the years, I have added ground-up leaves, wood chips, peat moss, and even bales of animal bedding chips to my gardens to create loamy soil—beautiful dirt—one of the primary ingredients of a successful low-maintenance landscape. If you are fortunate enough to live in a city that sells or gives away compost created from yard waste such as grass clippings, branches, leaves, and even Christmas trees, then beg, borrow, or rent a pickup or hire a dump truck to haul as much of this black gold to your property as possible. It is far better than purchasing topsoil. Plants love it and your maintenance chores will be greatly reduced. Unlike topsoil, weed seeds have been "cooked" in the composting process and are virtually nonexistent. If I had just built a new home, I would spread a minimum of 4 to 6 inches of this wonderful compost over the entire property before planting a single thing—turf grass seed or sod included.

I mark and mulch paths that wind and turn through many "rooms" of gardens and plant more foliage than flowering plants. As Daniel Foley puts it, "Flowers, at best, are of fleeting beauty, but it is the quality, the texture, and particularly the endurance of the foliage that counts"—ensuring low-maintenance gardening.

Small and medium-sized shrubs anchor my perennial beds, giving a solidity and sense of permanence. Conifers, as well as deciduous trees and shrubs with exfoliating bark, architectural branching, or persistent berries provide winter interest. A variety of ground covers cut maintenance; I try to use color where it has the most impact; I often use a curving path or a large plant to hide what is "just beyond," creating an element of surprise. A deciduous vine disguises the chain-link fence near the property line that used to be part of a dog run.

Spring is the busy time in my garden, the only high-maintenance time of the year. One of the most effective soil conditioners has been the multiple truckloads of wood chips delivered free by the power company or local tree trimming firms that we still apply annually between November 1 and March 1 when trees are leafless and plants are dormant. Because I do not have room to compost the wood chips, I apply them to the garden immediately. And no, my plants do not suffer from this immediate application. To counteract the loss of nitrogen, I sometimes broadcast a balanced fertilizer over the entire gardening space in early spring—but not always. My gardens are lush and green. I may have more slugs and other insects than fellow gardeners who elect to have bare dirt. However, the 2 to 3 inch layer of mulch helps retain moisture, deters weed germination, and gives the garden a cohesive appearance, so there are trade-offs. And sometimes you just have to "share."

I apply a granular pre-emergent containing Treflan on the paths in February before plant seeds begin to germinate. Broadcasting pre-emergent over all of the gardens would cut down on maintenance even more, but I don't do that because I want to encourage wildflower seedlings. And through experience, I have found that Treflan can distort the foliage of bulbs, Virginia bluebells, and some of the other midseason spring ephemerals. Being heavy-handed can actually kill the spring wildlings. So I hand-weed those areas, giving in to this bit of high maintenance for the sake of my spring wildflowers and bulbs. I do a thorough weeding in the spring, generally before May Day, and then, for the rest of the growing season, go on a weekly weed patrol, pulling up stray culprits to add to the compost heap. Once every 2 or 3 years I sprinkle a light dusting of urea (46-0-0) around the base of each hosta when the pips first emerge to encourage larger leaf growth. I time this application with an impending shower. I also apply slug bait, particularly around prize hostas.

I water precious plants during severe drought, but the rest have to survive on their own. I have incorporated many drought-resistant plants into my gardens because I hate dragging hoses. For precious moisture-lovers I follow my friend Jean's advice and poke small holes in the bottoms of gallon plastic milk jugs. Filled with water, these unsightly caretakers deliver an entire gallon of water to treasured plants during drought. The water drips out slowly over about 1½ to 2 hours, depending on the size of the holes, and goes directly to the roots. You can even bury a punctured plastic jug to its neck in the soil next to a moisture lover, filling it regularly with water. But low-maintenance wannabes who have a whole gardenful of moisture-loving plants in locations that are not naturally moist should consider investing in an underground drip irrigation system. Or choose other plants.

Gardening is recognized as one of the top leisure pastimes in the United States. In *The Natural Habitat Garden*, Ken Druse writes, "If even a fraction of America's 38 million gardeners turned a quarter of their landscape into a wild garden (only one tenth of an acre each) there would be a measurable impact . . . a tremendously positive gain for America's, and the world's, ecology." Consider certifying your property as a Backyard Wildlife Habitat. Sponsored by the National Wildlife Federation in Washington, D.C., this program encourages homeowners to create a wildlife-friendly environment by providing the four essential habitat requirements: food, water, cover, and safe spaces to raise young—obvious necessities for wildlife and humans alike.

Anyone can certify property—individuals, schools, or businesses—and the size of the property is not an issue. You can order a starter kit, or simply sign on to www.nwf.org/backyardwildlifehabitat and print the application from the website. Next, take a notebook, walk your property, and make a rough sketch, listing all existing plants and available water sources. A small pond or even a birdbath can fill the latter niche. Fruit or seed-bearing shrubs and trees, conifers, some bird feeders, perhaps a few ornamental grasses, annuals, perennials—in other words, whatever will delight both the wildlife *and* the homeowner. The requirements are neither difficult nor impossible to fulfill. In fact, you may already have most or all of these components in place. If not, ask a knowledgeable friend to help you figure out what you will need to qualify. Using your notes, complete the application form and send it, along with a check payable to the National Wildlife Federation, to NWF, P.O. Box 975, Newark, NY 14513-3092. In a few weeks, you will receive a handsome personalized certificate. Metal signs are also available for purchase.

Because there is generally less turf grass, and the trees and shrubs are allowed to maintain their natural shape, maintenance of a Backyard Wildlife Habitat is generally less intensive than that of property with a "normal" lawn. A realtor told me that Backyard Wildlife Habitat certification can positively influence buyers. So it is a win-win proposition. Besides, it is fun.

Not long ago, I offered to help a friend get her typical suburban yard certified, expounding on all the positive aspects of the program. Her property has wall-to-wall turf grass and neatly trimmed hedges. She expressed concern about installing and encouraging plantings that might "get out of control." She stopped by recently when I was working in the front yard. After wandering my winding paths, exclaiming over the presence of so many birds, butterflies, and squirrels, and appreciating the peace and repose, she commented, "I love what you have done to your property. It is wild but it is civilized. I want to welcome nature into our yard too."

Being natural does not mean being a mess. The best part about our yard is that, regardless of the multitudes of plants, it *is* low maintenance. But I am sure you already know that low-maintenance landscapes do not happen overnight or without work. In fact it took at least five years just to get things established, because unless you have a ready source of mature plants, the first thing you have to realize is that plants need time to grow. And yes, every garden needs *some* ongoing maintenance. But through the years I have learned both methods and plants that can save time and energy. As I work with nature, I try to understand each plant's individual needs, pay attention to what grows where, incorporate many native plants, and try not to fight the site. Other than my annual spring applications of slug bait around the hostas and Treflan on the paths, I seldom use chemicals and have resolved to share with any pests that disdain my "natural" controls such as slug-pubs and sticky yellow cards to catch errant insects.

A few of my neighbors have begun to emulate our "wild but civilized" look. Others still maintain their typical wall-to-wall grassy suburban lots. Our property, anything but typical, is calm, restful and best of all, about as low maintenance as a one-acre lot filled with multiple gardens can be.

Plants are like people—put them in the right place and they thrive.
—*Daniel J. Foley*

2.

How to "Take It Easy" and Still Make It Zing!

Mountain Laurel

Time is something all of us can use more of. Whether we are young professionals, working people, stay-at-home moms, or retirees, in this fast-paced world there is little time to "take it easy" and even less to spend in the garden. We spend more time cleaning the patio chairs than sitting in them, but we long for time to relax. Each of us needs the natural healing of body and spirit that occurs when we tune in to nature. Wallace Stegner calls it our "geography of hope." Being in the out-of-doors helps us forget the cares of the world. Sometimes it is just more relaxing to sit and do nothing. And what better place to sit and relax than in your own calm, cool, shady garden?

Some gardeners bemoan the shadiness of their gardening space and insist that shade creates problems. Problems? No. A challenge perhaps, but seldom a problem. In *Plants for Shade*, Allen Paterson suggests thinking "potential" rather than "problem" when considering that shady spot. Shady spots are, by their very nature, easier to maintain than their sunny counterparts. Think about it. Which do you prefer? Working in cooling shade or feeling the sweat roll down your back in the grueling sun? Limited amounts of weeding, or fighting that continual barrage of weeds that springs up in a sunny yard? Since weed seeds need ample light in order to germinate, weeding tasks in a shady garden are reduced. Shade cools the gardener and the plants. Moisture does not dissipate as quickly from shaded soil. Mulch slows the process even more. If you have a shady spot to plant a garden, then you are fortunate indeed.

The foliage of plants grown in shade is often larger and showier than of the same plant located in full sun. Variegated foliage effectively lights up dark spaces, and plants marked with white or cream seldom burn in the shade. There may not be as many flowers in a shady spot, but those blossoms tend to be more vibrantly colored and retain their freshness longer than their siblings in the sun. And while you don't have the profusion of blooms, that also means less deadheading. So content yourself with tradeoffs.

I hear the protest, "Oh, but gardening is so much work." Granted, if a shady garden triggers thoughts of "weed, deadhead, divide, mulch," then the very idea will signal a hasty retreat to the TV. And yes, gardening requires work—at least initially. But with careful planning, it *is* possible to create a low- rather than a high-maintenance garden.

Before we go on, let me stress . . . there is no such thing as a *no-maintenance* garden. Even concrete requires a certain amount of maintenance to keep it neat and tidy, so let's face it. You are going to have to do a little work to create this haven on your property, especially at the outset. And yes, weeding and watering will be necessary from time to time. But choosing the right plants for the right site and mulching your gardens can help alleviate both those problems. Light, soil, moisture, and pH requirements must be considered if the garden is truly to be low-maintenance. Initial assessment and preparation of the site are very important, and if done correctly at the very beginning, should not have to be redone. So don't skimp on these steps.

This book identifies and describes a variety of plants, both native and exotic, that will flourish in several degrees of shade, from a few hours to almost total shade. Most are hardy in zones 4–8. Some require an acidic home. A few prefer alkaline soil. Some demand a consistently moist environment. Once established, several will tolerate dry shade, while others are not fussy and will accept a variety of planting conditions. There are descriptions of plants that grow slowly, others that seem to double in size while you take your afternoon power nap.

So with all this variation, how can all these plants be considered low maintenance? Consider the well-known maxim of the realtor—location, location, location. Light, soil, moisture, pH, and winter hardiness need to match each plant. Why does a particular plant thrive in one spot and languish in another? Location. Don't just buy a plant before considering its needs. Study a plant's growth habit, its environmental preferences, and with whom it combines forces. Aggressive plants can be a nightmare unless they are used as a ground cover. Then their aggressiveness is welcomed and even encouraged. Companion plants must be compatible, just like people. If one needs a moist, acid site and its companion prefers a hot, dry location there is going to be trouble—both for the plants and for the gardener. Your life will be much simpler if you choose plants that thrive in similar environments. If we put the right plant in the right place, other gardening tasks become minimal or even unnecessary and can spell the difference between success and failure.

Light in the Garden

Living things require light to survive, so even though we are addressing shade in this book, it is crucial to determine what kind of shade each plant will accept. Trees and shrubs, hedges, buildings, and walls create different types of shade in our landscape. Think about it. The shade under a Locust Tree is different from that under a Sugar Maple. An evergreen tree casts different shade than a deciduous one. Natural shade is different than the man-made shade next to a building or a high wall. Man-made shade is often more difficult to garden with than natural shade and the direction of that shade is important for plant selection. Southern exposure is the hottest and brightest, while a northern exposure often provides full or even dense shade that is also dry. An eastern exposure is more forgiving than a western one. Morning sun/afternoon shade is better for shade-lovers than morning shade/afternoon sun.

Some shade-tolerant plants, particularly flowering varieties, demand more sun than others. Some will thrive as long as there is at least an hour or more of direct sunlight each day, but are not fussy about when that occurs. And many foliage plants actually prefer shade.

So how do we get a handle on the meaning of shade? Most gardeners describe full sun as a site that receives at least 6 hours of direct sunlight daily. Conversely, if the spot gets sun less than 6 hours per day, it is considered shady. Commonly used terms include part, light, full, and dense shade.

Part shade is the most open type of shade and the easiest term to understand. The terms partial shade, semi-shade, and half-shade all imply that a given location receives sunlight for at least *part* of the day—usually 3–6 hours in either the morning or afternoon. Plant selection for morning or afternoon shade is very important.

Morning sun/afternoon shade is the best combination for most shade-loving plants. They love it because it gives them the best of both worlds—gentle warmth, plenty of light in the morning for photosynthesis and flowering, and a welcome respite from the harsh, relentless heat of the midday or afternoon sun. In the morning, plants are turgid and the cool earth retains moisture. Small trees and shrubs welcome the morning light. Hosta foliage grows larger and stronger with morning sun. Vines become more vigorous, and even ferns will flourish in part shade if the planting site has enough moisture. To achieve this kind of shade, choose an eastern exposure.

Morning shade/afternoon sun is hard on most shade loving plants. Their cool, shaded environment suddenly heats up, as the hottest sun of the day dries out both plants and soil. Choose sun-loving plants, or else shade-tolerant plants that will tolerate some drought, for these harsh locations, usually found on a western exposure. Consider adding more loam to the planting bed to help retain moisture. If you insist on growing moisture-lovers, it may be necessary to install an underground drip irrigation system at the outset to lower your maintenance.

Light shade is often called thin, moving, or dappled shade. These terms imply a fleeting combination of sun, light, and shadow. Light shade has less light than part shade, but it is not as dark as full shade. It is that ideal "middle-of-the-road" where shade lovers thrive. A garden may be bright and have as little as 1–2 hours of actual sunlight. Or the planting site can actually be in full shade for 2–3 hours, as long as it is bright the rest of the day. There are several ways to create light shade. Sunlight filtered through the gentle movements of small deciduous leaves creates dappled shade. Trees that have been limbed up can provide light shade, or bright light. Reflective white building walls give enough light for some plants. A canopy of woven mesh fabric or a lath house can create light or dappled shade.

Full shade means that the garden is nearly always in substantial shade during the growing season. Many woodland plants prefer full shade during the heat of summer, but need bright light in early spring, before the trees leaves emerge, in order to carry out their life cycles. There are several ways to lighten up full shade. Use reflected light to good advantage with white walls or fences; install light-colored stones for paths; plant trees with small rather than coarse leaves; limb up tree branches 20–35 feet, or selectively remove some of the canopy.

Dense shade is that difficult kind of dry, inhospitable shade that occurs under decks, under low-growing evergreens, or next to north walls in close urban environments. Few plants will survive in really dense shade, other than overly aggressive ground covers like Yellow Archangel. Densely shaded areas are good candidates for hardscape features like brick walkways, patios, or mulch. It is usually easier to rotate potted plants in and out of densely shaded spaces if you want to attempt to grow living plant material there.

Identify Your Soil Type

After you understand the kind of shade in your prospective garden space, the next step is to identify the soil type—clay, sand, silt, or loam. The composition, moisture, and drainage of your soil are probably the single most important factors to consider in the initial preparation of a garden. Plants that meet an early demise are often drowned in poorly drained soil or wilted to death in soil without moisture.

Clay is composed of sticky sheets of soil. A handful of lightly moistened clay soil will make a tight ball when you mold it. Break the ball apart and there will be small clods on the ground rather than crumbled earth. It holds moisture, yet can dry rock hard during droughts, becoming "concrete" in the heat of summer. Clay soil usually drains poorly, or slowly at best. This is great for those few plant that prefer wet feet, but spells doom and gloom for the rest.

A handful of moistened *sandy* soil feels gritty. Try to make it into a ball and sandy soil will crumble and refuse to hold its shape regardless of how hard you squeeze. It is always well drained—in fact often *too* well drained, so that nutrients leach away and necessary moisture dissipates.

Silt lies somewhere between clay and sandy soil. Its particles are larger than clay particles, but smaller than sandy ones. If you rub silty soil between your fingers, it feels slightly rough, unlike clay, which feels smooth. It does not feel as gritty as sand. Like clay, silt holds water and nutrients better than sand, but also tends to dry out.

Loam is as perfect as it gets. I'll bet that Adam, the world's first shade gardener, tilled loamy soil! Gardeners covet loam because it is that "moist, well-drained" soil that so many plants require. A moistened handful of loamy soil can be compressed into a loose ball that will easily break into crumbly dirt. Loam is moisture retentive, full of nutrients and because of its light, fluffy nature, it welcomes digging and planting. Plant roots spread out easily and delve deeply into the earth. In *The Natural Shade Garden*, Ken Druse insists that the soil in a shade garden must be rich in organic matter. He writes, "There should be a layer of humus equal to the soil's sand and clay in volume, as there would be on the woodland floor." There is no better "black gold" than a deep planting bed of loamy soil. However, I have found that even 4–8 inches of loam will suffice. If there are surface tree roots, add 4–6 inches of loam over the top of them. Don't get carried away and add more, however, or you may kill the tree.

Under *Planting requirements* for each plant, you will often read "average soil." Average soil has a neutral pH, neither too acid nor too alkaline. It is not quite as optimal as loamy soil, but is better than heavy clay or total sand. In other words, it is average—or what gardeners term "ordinary garden soil."

Some sources discourage doing any amending, encouraging gardeners to plant whatever will grow in their existing soil. That works if you live in a natural area, but unfortunately the soil left around modern homes after construction is usually pretty poor. Amending with compost and other materials will loosen soil, improve drainage, and eventually turn it into loam—a process I highly recommend. An ongoing process, to be sure, and certainly not low maintenance at the outset, but crucial for the long term. Beautiful dirt is important for success.

If a planting area is just so large that amending the whole space is impossible, choose plants that will thrive in that particular site, and do some long-term amending. My grass-free front yard is filled with Sugar Maples that snatch most available moisture and nutrients away from anything I plant under them. Over the years I have added an annual layer of wood chips. In a year or two, the wood chips break down, becoming soil. Autumn leaves are another easy source of humus. Most people rake, bag and send off this treasure to the landfill. Instead, after all have fallen, my husband grinds them up with our mulching mower, letting most lie where they are. They decompose into soil by the following spring. I would estimate three to five years passed before I began to notice any appreciable difference from this kind of amending. But now the soil in my front "woodland" yard is friable and loose. Yard wastes are recycled in my own yard instead of at the city landfill. Plants thrive and the trees are doing well too.

What Is the pH?

pH is a measure of acidity or alkalinity of the soil. Values range from 0 to 14 with 7.0 as neutral. Less than 7.0 is acidic and more than 7.0 is alkaline. As a general rule, clay soil is usually alkaline, sandy soil is neutral, and loamy soil tends to be slightly acidic. To acidify the soil, one must add soil sulfur, sphagnum peat moss, sawdust, or composted oak leaves. To raise the pH and produce a more alkaline soil, add lime, wood ashes, or bone meal. Organic matter, manure, and compost tend to neutralize the pH, raising it in acid soils and lowering it in alkaline soils.

It is often possible to have the county extension agency test the pH for a small fee. "Do-it-yourself" kits are also available. Higher priced kits do not necessarily produce better readings. In the 1998 issue of *Fine Gardening* magazine, Keith Davitt wrote, "Regardless of the test, the most important things that you can do are to use the same test on a regular basis, to note the effects on your plants of applying the recommended amounts of fertilizer, and to keep track of those results so you have a history to refer to."

Let me stress that for low-maintenance gardening, it is crucial to identify pH, especially for acid-lovers, before even thinking about ordering plants. Yes, you can amend your existing soil to alter the pH, but this is a long, expensive, time-consuming project. If you are truly into low-maintenance gardening, this is *not* the way to go. Most gardeners have lists of plants they yearn to grow, but if the available planting sites do not meet the pH requirements, they would be well advised to enjoy them in someone else's yard, or in a botanical garden. For example, if you have clay soil with a high pH, just skip the descriptions of plants that need moist, acid soil. In the long run, you'll be glad you did!

Is There Adequate Moisture?

Most plants dislike too much or too little moisture. As in "Goldilocks," the key to success is to provide moisture that is "just right" for a particular plant. Is the site consistently moist? Moist in spring, but very dry in the heat of summer? Always dry unless you water it? Of all the causes of plant failure, improper moisture and bad drainage are probably the two biggest culprits. More shade-tolerant plants succumb from moisture problems than from any other cause. And yes, you may occasionally need to provide the plants with additional water during dry spells.

Like people, each plant has specific requirements, so when you are mixing and matching, be sure to choose compatible plant companions. Be kind to yourself and select plants that enjoy the amount of moisture available in your gardening location. Otherwise you must either install an underground drip irrigation system or resort to dragging hoses.

Drought tolerance is noted under *Planting requirements*. Note: Drought tolerance also carries the caveat "when well established." This is probably the most important point that I can make about the ability of any given plant to withstand dry conditions. You cannot just plunk a plant into a dry, shady area and expect it to survive. It takes at least one full growing season for it to become established, and even during the second growing season it may need at least some additional moisture.

Some plants tolerate drought better than others, but don't expect any to perform like desert plants. Prolonged drought can take its toll. In a dry season you can expect a variety of responses from fully established drought-tolerant plants. Many may not look like first-prize winners for the remainder of the summer. Some will go dormant. Others may get brown-edged leaves, fail to flower, or fall over, but at least they will survive . . . unlike those plants that demand consistent moisture all the time. Drought-tolerant does not mean drought-loving. There are relatively few plants that really enjoy dry shade and even fewer that thrive in it.

Choosing the Plants

Finally, as you begin planning your garden in the shade, ask yourself what qualities in a plant suggest "low maintenance."

1. Is this plant hardy in your zone? Will you have to protect it from the elements of nature? Or cover it in winter?

2. What are its cultural needs—light, soil type, pH, moisture—and can you duplicate those needs without a lot of ongoing work?

3. How often does it need to be divided to retain its vigor?

4. Is it aggressive or even invasive? Will you have to pull out multiple seedlings? Or can you use those aggressive tendencies to good advantage?

5. Is it susceptible to disease or to insect damage?

6. Will it survive the growing season without becoming ratty-looking or going dormant? And if not, is there a companion plant that can be interplanted to mask that tendency?

7. Does it require staking, or can it stand on its own?

Final Notes . . .

1. Prepare the planting bed before ever installing a single plant.

2. Choose plants that will thrive in your particular site. Remember "location, location, location."

3. Learn about plants native to your area and use them. They are the survivors.

4. Think about using shrubs and ground covers as an alternative to extensive perennial beds.

5. Species plants are often hardier and less demanding than their cultivars, so choose cultivars with your eyes wide open.

In *Ground Covers for Easier Gardening*, Daniel J. Foley writes, "There is no garden without some maintenance, and planting what will grow in difficult areas, in difficult soils, in difficult weather and in generally difficult exposure is the answer to making gardens and gardening easier. Finding the plants that fit the place and then meeting their requirements is, in essence, what takes the drudgery out of gardening."

Make It Zing! Landscape Planning and Hardscape

Begin your low-maintenance shade garden by making a master plan. In addition to planning beautiful gardens, don't forget to include such things as user needs and priorities for day-to-day living. Preplanning helps to create a unified and functional landscape design, so analyze your lot first and then choose the plants. Note: Your financial budget should always dictate the specific *phasing* of the landscape plan, not the design.

1. DRAW A ROUGH SKETCH OF THE PROPERTY

Include street and property lines, the "footprint" of the house, existing sidewalks, driveways, and off-street parking pads, major trees, walls, fences, and any other large feature that will remain, such as a boulder, rock garden, or storage shed.

2. FIGURE OUT YOUR FAMILY'S NEEDS AND DESIRES

As with the interior of your home, on every property there are logical parts of the yard more suitable for one function or another. Plan both plantings and functions accordingly. The front yard, like the living room and front entry, is where you greet the public. Generally this should be relatively neat and tidy. Family activities often take place in the back of the house—the private, casual "family room of the yard." The side yards are usually used as corridors or hallways. Try to group all utility functions in one specific area, likely near the entrance to the garage.

3. CONSIDER THE VIEW

Determine where the main viewing windows are located in the house. What good are gardens if you cannot see them from inside? Identify lovely views and vistas that may be enhanced by plantings as well as features that need to be hidden or camouflaged. Views are important.

4. WIND AND SUN

Finally, on your Master Plan take time to figure out and record where the summer and winter sun rises and sets. Also note the prevailing direction of the wind in both winter and summer if possible, and indicate these on the plan with arrows pointing to the house. These observations will help to determine the availability of sunlight during the growing season as well as to identify areas that may need to be planted with species undaunted by windy conditions.

As you design your gardens try to let both gardens and plants flow. My hosta friend Randy Goodwin uses masses of all-one-type of hosta to sweep through his gardens, setting off a few specimen plants. A velvety green carpet of turf grass sets off jewel-like compositions undulating about the perimeter of his yard. Gardens within the turf area are connected by paths, stepping stones, and swishes of small hostas. Rather than several unconnected gardens and island beds floating about the yard, Randy's gardens are an artistic, unified whole.

Gardeners with turf grass expect to mow regularly. Sharp and jagged garden edges can be difficult to maneuver, causing starting, stopping, backing up, and generally painful maintenance. Instead, design planting edges that are lawn-mower-operator friendly. As Graham Rose writes in *The Low Maintenance Garden*, "The principal goal . . . is to reduce potentially time-consuming chores to a minimum, and to build these factors into your design."

Hardscape

Hardscape features are a vital component of any low-maintenance landscape. By this I mean pavement, stepping stones, pre-formed concrete slabs, gravel of all sorts and sizes, sidewalks and paths, decks and patios—in other words, permanent components designed to satisfy functional and aesthetic needs. Many gardeners find attractive hardscape more inviting and user-friendly than turf grass. It certainly takes less maintenance. Gardeners in cold climates are advised to choose materials that are resistant to frost. Water features can easily be incorporated, adding visual, auditory, and even tactile sensations close at hand.

Used bricks are my favorite hardscape materials. They are often readily accessible, relatively inexpensive (or even free) and if you decide you want them somewhere else, they are not that difficult to relocate. Concrete pavers give a similar effect, but are harder and sturdier. A young couple I know built a deck and extended their outdoor living space by adding a large pad of broken and whole concrete slabs that stops only at the edge of the woods surrounding the property. Retired friends transformed their entire back yard into a haven of stepping-stones and hostas.

Their fabulous collection snakes through the back yard in either raised or lowered beds that add additional interest to an otherwise flat landscape. I have seen entire yards covered with pea gravel and stepping-stones. I don't find this as appealing as my used bricks, but to each his own.

And of course decks and concrete patios are the outdoor hardscape of choice for most homeowners. A deck can be just a plain, unimaginative rectangular platform or it can be an exciting design element, complementing the house. Our son-in-law changed the entire feeling of his deck by interrupting the traditional balustrades with a sunburst pattern made of the same material. Use 3 rows of straight cedar boards to outline diagonally cut center boards. Incorporate a checkerboard pattern, reminiscent of a huge parquet floor, into a new deck. Cut a hole in the deck and plant a slow-growing shade tree in the space. Incorporate a huge square concrete slab partway into the deck to hold a heavy houseplant in the summer and provide design interest as well.

Even concrete patios can be made more interesting by adding gravel just before the cement sets. There are artisans who can stamp interesting designs into concrete, creating what looks like fancy stone or a mass of unique patterns.

Study photographs and drawings in books and magazines and visit (and photograph) private homes and commercial establishments to figure out what you really like.

Hardscape is often the only medium that will "survive" in deeply shaded spaces where rain seldom penetrates the ground. It can effectively keep out weeds under a raised deck, providing a clean, dry spot to store lawn equipment and used flowerpots. Possibilities for hardscape are endless. Just do a little research and use your imagination to make it zing.

3.

Garden Jewels

Small Trees for Shade

Small trees provide interesting patterns of
light, shadow, and texture as they fill in
the middle-story layer that is so often
missing in the landscape. They can be
used as focal points, or to screen off undesirable views. Plant them singly or in
groups of 3 to 5, tuck them under huge
shade trees, put them at the edge of a
woodland garden, or combine with shrubs
to create a privacy screen. By planting a
variety of small trees and shrubs of different shapes and sizes you create a biohedge
(described in chapter 4) which can offer
cover, nesting sites, and food to wildlife
as well as multiseasonal interest for
the homeowner. But how-
ever you use small trees, try to
plant them where you can see
them from inside the house.

I do not address large trees
in this book, because I assume the
reason your garden is shady is because these big fellows are doing their
job. Small trees, commonly referred to as
understory trees, mature at 10 to 30 feet.
Some can also be grown as large shrubs.

Japanese Maple

They may have single or multiple trunks. All enjoy, or will at least tolerate, some degree of shade. Most are hardy in zones 4–8; those with specific requirements are noted.

Many of these trees will tolerate dry sites *once established*. A newly planted tree must have adequate moisture for 2 to 3 years until it is fully established and able to cope with a lack of moisture. I have a simple, foolproof suggestion: every Monday from May 1–October 31, fill a five-gallon bucket with water and pour the contents over the roots of any newly planted tree or shrub. Choosing a specific day ensures adequate deep watering will be done weekly.

Planting a Tree or Shrub

Midwestern gardens, moist in spring, often dry up in the heat of summer. In such planting sites, the following small trees can be depended upon to survive—once they are established:

Downy Serviceberry (*Amelanchier arborea*)

Allegheny Serviceberry, Smooth Juneberry (*Amelanchier laevis*)

Apple Serviceberry (*Amelanchier × grandiflora*)

American Hornbeam (*Carpinus caroliniana*)

Roughleaf Dogwood (*Cornus drummondii*)

Gray Dogwood (*Cornus racemosa*)

American Smoke Tree (*Cotinus obovatus*)

American Hop Hornbeam (*Ostrya virginiana*)

Persian Parrotia (*Parrotia persica*)

Hoptree (*Ptelea trifoliate*)

Dig the planting hole 2 to 3 times as wide but no deeper than the existing root ball, so that the root ball can be set on solid, undisturbed soil. Gently slant the sides of the hole and score the dirt with a trowel or knife rather than leaving the sides smooth. Set the tree at the same depth level or even a little higher than it was growing in the nursery or in the pot. There is usually a soil mark on the trunk. Pay attention to it.

After the tree is situated in the hole, fill the hole with water and let it drain away. Only then should the soil be replaced. Some authorities discourage amending the soil and recommend using the same dirt that comes out of the hole. I agree that overamending can create a bathtub effect and drown the tree, but to do absolutely no amending seems to be the opposite extreme. Besides, most trees have nursery soil clinging to their roots which may not be the same as the soil from the planting site. So I recommend adding 1 to 3 large ice cream pails of compost to any planting site to give the roots a better chance. After replacing the soil, tamp it down lightly and add about a 20-inch ring of mulch. The mulch ring will help keep mowers and weed whackers from getting too close and damaging the trunk. It is important to keep the mulch pulled at least 2 inches away from the trunk to prevent insect and disease problems. Finally, either dig a small trench or install a little berm around the outside of the mulch ring to keep those Monday watering efforts from draining away too quickly.

If staking is necessary, encase the supporting wire in an old bicycle inner tube or garden hose so the wire does not cut into the trunk. Stakes should be removed the following year. Install a tightly woven mesh ring around the trunk to deter rabbits, deer, or beavers from gnawing on the bark during the winter. Place this protection 6–8 inches from the trunk.

Prune crossed, rubbing, or damaged branches at the collar. Black tree paint is unnecessary and undesirable. Study the silhouette to shape the tree properly, and remove branches before they get too large. If you are not sure if a branch is alive or dead, scratch the bark. Live branches will show green under the scratch.

Most of the small trees in this chapter can safely be planted near walkways, driveways, or the foundation of your house because their roots are not nearly as powerful or as invasive as those of their bigger brothers.

Small trees add a necessary dimension to the landscape and help provide the framework for a garden, acting as a foil for shrubs and lower plantings. Granted, most landscapes do not require an army of small trees, so select them with care. They are the jewels whose addition complements and completes the entire ensemble.

Small Trees for Shade

Fullmoon Maple (*Acer japonicum*)
Japanese Maple (*Acer palmatum*)
Zones 5–7
20–30 (40) feet

Japan
Deer Resistant

Japanese Maples, as a group, can generally be found at the beginning of any book on trees and shrubs. Now, it may be simply because its scientific name—*Acer*—falls at the beginning of the alphabet. But I prefer to believe that it is because this particular genus deserves star billing.

This slow-growing tree is worth pampering. And most of the time, it doesn't need any special attention other than rich, well-drained soil and adequate moisture. The color, size, shape, and "laciness" of the leaves vary widely from one species or cultivar to the next. There is even a yellow-leaf cultivar called 'Sunglow' that changes to shades of red and gold in the fall.

These elegant small trees or shrubs lend that sought-after Oriental look to a garden. Site them near a pond so their finely divided leaves can be reflected in the water. Place them near a patio to enjoy as you sit and sip your tea. Plant two or three where they will be in full view from an indoor window, or tuck one under a towering deciduous tree. As long as your planting area is favorable to Japanese Maples, plant one . . . any one. Anywhere.

PLANTING REQUIREMENTS

Japanese Maples require humus-rich, moist, well-drained soil. Most prefer part to light shade, particularly in the afternoon, or full sun. Mulch the soil to help retain soil moisture. Give them some shelter in colder regions.

PROPAGATION

Purchase container-grown or balled and burlapped plants early in the spring. Adventurous experimenters may plant freshly ripened seed immediately, before it has a chance to dry out. Some gardeners have success taking 6–7-inch cuttings from new branches early on a May morning. To root these softwood cuttings, immediately immerse the cut ends in water so they do not dry out. Rooted cuttings will need extra winter protection.

Paperbark Maple (*Acer griseum*)
Zones 4–8
18–30 feet tall
China

Garden Jewels

I have always admired trees with exfoliating bark, but Paperbark Maple has to be the most exquisite of them all. You can plant several of these stunning individuals because no two are alike. The unusual trifoliate leaves are deep bluish-green but usually change to shades of red in the fall. Provide good drainage and this lovely tree will glow happily in your landscape, beautiful in every season. Threeflower Maple (*A. triflorum*) is similar. It also has red fall foliage, but the exfoliating bark is gray-brown rather than cinnamon.

PLANTING REQUIREMENTS
Plant in well-drained, average garden soil in sun or part to light shade.

PROPAGATION
Difficult to root from cuttings or grow from seed. Because of this, it is harder to find in the nursery trade than most Acer species. But it is worth the hunt.

Red Buckeye (*Aesculus pavia*)

Zones 4–8
15–20 feet tall
Native to U.S.
REQUIRES MOIST SOIL

Anyone who sees the rich rosy-red flowering panicles of this small tree in the spring immediately falls in love with it. Each opposite, compound leaf has five glossy dark green leaflets, spread out just like oval-shaped fingers on a hand. Red Buckeye's smooth gray-brown bark begins flaking off with age, creating winter textural interest.

PLANTING REQUIREMENTS
Red Buckeye will not tolerate a dry planting site and must have rich, moist, well-drained soil in sun or part to light shade.

PROPAGATION
Plant the interesting smooth shiny seed in fall or purchase young potted seedlings or balled and burlapped specimens at the nursery.

Downy Serviceberry (*Amelanchier arborea*)
Zones 4–9
15 to 25 feet
Native to U.S.

If you spot a small tree in early to mid-April, covered with masses of creamy white flowers, and peeking out from the woods or growing near a road, it is probably one of the Amelanchiers. Downy Serviceberry, which blooms just before the Redbud puts on its spring show, is also known as Shadbush, Juneberry, and Service Tree, or, as you may hear it pronounced in parts of the Midwest, "sarvis-tree." These common names reveal much about this tree. The leaves of Downy Serviceberry are covered with soft downy hairs. It is called Shadbush, because it blooms when the shad fish began their run up rivers to spawn. Early settlers, birds, and wildlife sought out Juneberry to gather its small, blackish purple fruits, the first ripe fruits of the season.

And it is called Serviceberry or Service Tree because it blooms about the time people were able to conduct the service to bury their dead after a long, cold winter. The white branches were also used in wedding services. Many a spring bride carried a bouquet of Serviceberry blossoms, since not much else was available.

PLANTING REQUIREMENTS
Plant in part or light shade, or full sun. Amelanchiers prefer moist soil, but, once established, will tolerate dry soil as long as the planting site is well-drained. This native tree is often found growing near Red Maples, Red and White Oaks, and American Hop Hornbeam.

PROPAGATION
Plant fresh seed immediately, or cold-stratified seed in the fall. It can be propagated by softwood cuttings. Transplant young trees or rooted suckers. Amelanchier is readily available in the nursery trade.

Allegheny Serviceberry (*Amelanchier laevis*)
Zones 4–8
15–25 feet
Native to U.S.

Delicate racemes of creamy white flowers dangle above the gray-streaked trunk of Allegheny Serviceberry in early spring. If you want a fast-growing early bloomer with luscious sweet fruit, this is the tree to choose. Also called Smooth Juneberry, it is a hardy, reliable native.

Just as the flowers begin to fade, smooth new leaves emerge with a bronze-purple hue, a color characteristic that distinguishes Allegheny Serviceberry from most of its siblings. The 1½–2½-inch leaves change to dark green in summer, turning bright yellow or yellow-orange in autumn.

The sweet, juicy, purple-black drooping fruits sometimes take up to two weeks to mature, extending the "eating season." These fruits are favorites of many birds and small animals.

Apple Serviceberry (*Amelanchier* × *grandiflora*), a hybrid of Allegheny and Downy Serviceberry, is hardy in Zones 5–8, and marginally hardy in Zone 4. Hybridizers have developed more cultivars from this natural hybrid than from any other native Amelanchier. 'Autumn Brilliance' probably has the most outstanding red fall color. Other cultivars include 'Cumulus', 'Forest Prince', and 'Rubescens'. Planting requirements are the same as for those of its parents.

PLANTING REQUIREMENTS

Will grow in full sun, part, or light shade, and although it prefers moist soil, it does fine in either moist or dry soil as long as the planting site is well drained. It will also grow in full shade, but the flowering and fall color will not be as spectacular. These little trees are not fussy about pH.

PROPAGATION

Plant fresh seed immediately or propagate by softwood cuttings taken in July. Young plants or rooted suckers are easy to transplant. Amelanchier is readily available in the nursery trade.

Pawpaw (*Asimina triloba*)
Zones 5–9
8–20 feet
Native to U.S.

When garden writers describe the leaves of the Pawpaw, they use adjectives such as droopy, tropical, or sleepy, but to me they look like floppy dog's ears. The thick green skin darkens with age, enclosing soft, mushy fruit resembling custard or a *very* overripe banana. Buried in the custard are two or three large, flattened, glossy dark brown seeds.

The fruits on our tree are creamy-white and bland. I am told that yellow fruits are more palatable. However, they are all adored by wildlife.

Odd, three-parted brownish-purple flowers appear in late spring. Pawpaws, which are nearly always found in the company of Tulip Trees in the wild, have bright yellow foliage in the fall. They are disease and pest free.

Some people have an allergic reaction to all parts of the Pawpaw, including its fruit, and develop a rash and intense itching.

PLANTING REQUIREMENTS

This attractive little tree prefers the moist, humus-rich soil of typical woodlands, but is really quite adaptable. In the wild it seeks the shade of the understory, but will also tolerate sun.

PROPAGATION

Pawpaws sucker heavily, creating massive stands in the wild, but in my yard I find only an occasional clone. I have tried to dig these for friends, but unless the suckers are young and very small, they seldom survive the amputation. The seeds are extremely hard and can take up to two years to germinate without intentional stratification and scarification. Small young seedlings must be ordered from specialty nurseries, because the Pawpaw is not regularly stocked at most local garden stores.

Woolly Bumelia (*Bumelia lanuginosa*)

Zones 5–9
20–40 feet
Native to U.S.

Adjectives like "sturdy, prickly, adaptable, interesting" all describe Woolly Bumelia, a relatively unfamiliar native tree. Also known as Gum Bumelia, Gum Elastic, Woolly Buckthorn, False Buckthorn, and Chittamwood, this tough fellow scoffs at heat and drought, and can even survive in wet sites. It may be a good option for that impossible planting space.

The undersides of its smooth, dark-green, wedge-shaped leaves are covered with dense woolly hairs, which distinguishes it from southern

Bumelia species. The sap is milky or gummy. The flowers are of no ornamental value, but wildlife and people both enjoy the dark blue-black oval fruits. It can be grown as a shrub or small tree. Even though it is often referred to as False or Woolly Buckthorn, it is not related to the invasive exotic Buckthorns.

PLANTING REQUIREMENTS
Woolly Bumelia will grow in just about any soil and moisture conditions. It is not fussy about pH or light and can tolerate road salt.

PROPAGATION
Plant ripened seed in the fall.

American Hornbeam (*Carpinus caroliniana*)
Zones 3–9
10–30 feet
Native to U.S.

My grandson thinks the Hornbeams growing in the woods behind his house are the greatest of all climbing trees. The common name, Ironwood, describes the extremely strong wood, which is still used to make axe handles. The trunk with its birch-like, bluish-gray bark gives the appearance of convoluted and tensed muscles, explaining another of its common names—Musclewood. It is also called Blue Beech and Water Beech.

Very slow growing and pollution tolerant, the American Hornbeam makes a fine ornamental and a good street tree. It thrives as a multi-trunked specimen, or can be sheared as a hedge. The 2½–4½-inch dark bluish-green leaves with pale undersides turn a brilliant orange or scarlet in fall.

In the wild, it is generally found in shady, woodland environments, growing as an understory tree with Red or White Oaks, Sugar Maples, or Sassafras. These disease-resistant trees generally have a somewhat bushy or rounded appearance. For a narrower, more upright form, purchase 'Fastigiata'.

PLANTING REQUIREMENTS

Prefers moist, well-drained, humus-rich soil. It can survive in areas that flood, or are continually wet, yet will tolerate dry sites as long as the soil is not compacted.

PROPAGATION

Curious, nut-like fruits, attractive to squirrels, can be planted and will germinate the following spring. Transplant young trees, but be sure to dig wide enough to get all of the shallow roots.

Eastern Redbud (*Cercis canadensis*)
Zones 5–9
15–25 feet
Native to U.S.

Tiny rosy-lavender, pea-like flowers cover the naked branches of the Eastern Redbud in early spring, giving the woods a veritable fairyland appearance. Plant as single specimens or in groups. They can be incorporated into a naturalistic site, a mixed shrub border, or a biohedge. Young trees will begin to bloom after 4–5 years. Pointed on each end, the 3-inch-long seedpods clatter in the wind in midsummer. Seeds germinate readily the following spring.

Redbuds have pretty dark-green, heart-shaped leaves that turn bright yellow in the fall. The handsome bark is nearly black. There are several white-flowering cultivars, including 'Alba', 'Royal White', and 'Texas White'. White-variegated leaf cultivars, like 'Silver Cloud', do not flower as profusely. A few cultivars have been hybridized for deeper rosy flowers ('Oklahoma') or leaves that emerge reddish-purple ('Forest Pansy').

PLANTING REQUIREMENTS

Redbud is very adaptable and will grow in either moist or dry well-drained soil. It will not tolerate wet locations. It is not particular about pH. A woodland tree, it prefers part or light shade, but accepts full sun. In full shade, it will not flower so heavily. Trees found in the wild usually grow close to the edge of the woods.

PROPAGATION

Plant fresh or cold-stratified seed in the fall to germinate the following spring. Because of their long taproot, bare-root Redbuds do not transplant easily except when very young. Large balled and burlapped specimens purchased from a nursery should be planted when the tree is dormant. Or dig up seedlings from a friend's yard; mature trees are quite prolific.

Fringe Tree (*Chionanthus virginicus*)
Zones 4–9
10–20 feet
Native to U.S.

The common and scientific names—Fringe Tree, Old Man's Beard, and *Chionanthus*—refer to the abundance of long, thin, fringe-like snow-white flowers that emerge with the unfurling soft green leaves and cover the tree in late May or early June. *Chionanthus* comes from the Greek meaning snow and flowers. Fringe Tree is also known as Flowering Ash. It is dioecious (= "two houses"), which means it needs both a male and female tree to set fruit. If you plant a male cultivar such as 'Floyd', an upright form of Fringe Tree, he will make sure the feathery flowers on all your female trees are pollinated and produce the deep blue grape-like drupes, enjoyed by wildlife.

Typical of a slow grower, Fringe Tree awakens late in spring and goes to bed early in fall, losing its clear yellow leaves before most other trees have even begun to think about going dormant. For this reason, it is wise to plant a Fringe Tree as part of a mixed hedge, or in a sheltered spot where its late appearance won't be mistaken for winterkill. Fringe Tree can also be grown as a large, multistemmed shrub.

PLANTING REQUIREMENTS

If given a choice, this adaptable little tree would opt for slightly acidic, moist, well-drained soil. However, it will grow happily in most sites. Fringe Trees take a bit of time to settle in and may need to be babied at the outset. In northern climates, their chance of survival is greater in a sheltered spot. They begin to bloom when they are about 3–4 years old.

PROPAGATION
Like Trillium, the seeds of the Fringe Tree take two years to germinate. Michael Dirr advises, "3 months warm/3 months cold stratification is ideal." Experiment if you wish, but for faster results, purchase trees at a nursery.

Pagoda Dogwood (*Cornus alternifolia*)
Zones 4–8
12–25 feet
Native to U.S.
REQUIRES MOIST SOIL
The architectural form of the Pagoda Dogwood resembles a classic Oriental pagoda. Horizontal branches hold the 2–5-inch, alternate, rich green leaves. In the spring, clusters of white flowers rise above the foliage on sturdy stalks. As the season progresses these stalks transform into an eye-catching rosy red. They hold the bitter, small purplish-black fruits that ripen in midsummer and are consumed by birds and wildlife. The leaves turn deep magenta in fall.

This disease-resistant tree is ideal for nesting birds. Pagoda Dogwood makes a good specimen tree, or blends into a shrub border or biohedge. It can also be grown as a multistemmed tree. The variegated forms 'Variegata' and 'Argentea' have creamy white-edged leaves.

Giant Variegated Pagoda Dogwood (*C. controversa* 'Variegata'), hardy in zones 4–8, is a bit larger. From Asia, it is reputed to be more disease and stress resistant but, as Dirr writes, "it has not lived up to the press clippings."

PLANTING REQUIREMENTS
Requires moist, humus-rich soil and a pleasant, lightly shaded spot to remain at its healthiest. Mulch the soil to keep the roots moist.

PROPAGATION
This tree is readily available in the nursery trade. Young seedlings transplant easily. To grow from seed, plant the fresh seed immediately after it ripens in midsummer.

Roughleaf Dogwood (*Cornus drummondii* aka *C. asperifolia*)
Gray Dogwood (*C. racemosa*)
Zones 4–8
10–15 feet
Native to U.S.

The Indiana Native Plant and Wildflower Society planted Roughleaf Dogwood, transplanted from a member's woods, in a demonstration garden at the Indiana Historical Society in downtown Indianapolis in 1999. That first year it looked like death warmed over. We were surprised when it covered itself with flat-topped clusters of white flowers the following spring. Later, white fruits on red stalks hung like decorations and in the fall the leaves turned a deep wine-red. Roughleaf Dogwood is often confused with Gray Dogwood. The flower clusters are a little different—Roughleaf's are flatter and larger. Both are fast-growing trees.

Gray Dogwood is covered with small pyramidal clusters of white flowers in mid-spring. The white fruit, relished by birds and wildlife, is borne on red stalks and ripens in late summer or early fall. The red and white color combination is stunning against the dark green leaves. As autumn progresses, the small leaves turn deep wine color. The silhouette of the tree and its handsome reddish-gray bark lend winter interest.

PLANTING REQUIREMENTS
Both Gray and Roughleaf tolerate a much drier site than most other dogwoods. It prefers a slightly acidic soil and performs well in sun or part shade.

PROPAGATION
These dogwoods tend to sucker and create clumps, so if a specimen is desired it will require a little maintenance. Plant ripened seed in the fall, or dig rooted suckers. Dogwoods transplant easily.

Flowering Dogwood (*Cornus florida*)
Zones 5–9
10–20 feet
Native to U.S.
Deer Resistant

I can think of no other small tree that can rival the American Flowering Dogwood. Perfect in every part, it heralds spring with grace and charm. Generally blooming just after serviceberries, it overlaps with the bloom of the redbud. This pink and white combination transforms woodlands into enchanted fairylands. Flowering Dogwoods prefer to be at the edge of the woods, rather than in the middle of a lawn.

The notched white flowers are bracts, and the tiny yellow centers are the actual flowers. These flowers become the shiny bright red fruits that provide a reliable source of energy for migrating songbirds. Gorgeous shades of red makes the Flowering Dogwood an outstanding tree in autumn, and even in winter, its dark bark, prominent flower buds, and interesting skeleton proclaim its innate beauty.

Several cultivars are available, including double-flowered 'Pluribracteata'. Our pink dogwood is 'Rubra'; reliable red 'Cherokee Chief' has been in the trade for years. Variegated leaf cultivars include 'Cherokee Daybreak' (white margins) and 'Gold Nugget' (gold margins).

Dogwood has been attacked by Anthracnose (*Gnomonia quercina*) in recent years. This organism has killed many wild trees. Cut diseased trees to the ground and destroy them to avoid further spread. When purchasing trees, make sure that they are certified Anthracnose-free. A prolific bloomer, 'Appalachian Spring' is reputedly the best Anthracnose-resistant cultivar to date.

PLANTING REQUIREMENTS

Needs humus-rich, slightly acid, moist, well-drained soil, like that found in natural woodlands. It prefers part or light shade, but accepts full sun as long as the roots are well mulched to keep them cool. Good air circulation will help to deter Anthracnose. During drought, apply adequate water to keep the tree healthy. Weakened trees are more susceptible to borer and disease damage.

PROPAGATION

Dogwood seeds planted in fall should germinate the following spring. Softwood cuttings taken in midsummer root quite easily. Try to plant the seeds or rooted cuttings where you want the tree to grow, because they resent being transplanted. Purchase potted or balled and burlapped specimens from the nursery.

Garden Jewels

Kousa Dogwood (*Cornus kousa*)
Zones 5–8
15–25 feet
Japan, China
Deer Resistant

Nurserymen often recommend substituting the Kousa Dogwood for native Flowering Dogwood (*C. florida*) because of its resistance to Anthracnose. If this disease is prevalent in your area, it may be a wise trade. Or just plant them both and extend the bloom season on your property. Kousa Dogwood covers itself with sharply pointed, starry white flowers (actually bracts) a couple of weeks after the native. These appear bright white in contrast to the glossy dark green leaves. In late summer or early fall, strawberry-red fruits create a striking picture against the pretty leaves. They are edible, but not very tasty. Leave them for the birds. Kousa Dogwood's fall color tends to favor varying shades of orange and red, rather than the deep scarlet-red of the Flowering Dogwood. It has handsome, exfoliating patchwork-quilt bark in shades of browns and tans.

Pink cultivars include 'Satomi' (aka 'Rosabella'), 'Stellar Pink', and 'Heart-throb'. 'Snowboy' and 'Samaritan' both have white-edged leaves.

PLANTING REQUIREMENTS
Plant in moist, humus-rich, well-drained soil in part shade, or full sun. Kousa Dogwood is not as fussy about pH as Flowering Dogwood, and is also somewhat more drought resistant, although it does not like to be dry. It is also more heat tolerant.

PROPAGATION
Fall-planted ripe seeds germinate readily. Softwood cutting are relatively easy to root, and potted seedlings are available as well as larger balled and burlapped specimens.

Corneliancherry Dogwood (*Cornus mas*)
Zones 4–8
20–25 feet

Asia and Europe
Deer Resistant

Generally grown as a multistemmed small tree or large shrub, Corneliancherry Dogwood puts on one of the earliest spring shows with tiny, bright yellow flowers thickly covering the naked branches. Be sure to locate where it can be admired from inside the house on dreary March days. It shouts "Think spring!" 2–4-inch glossy green leaves follow the early flowers, and in July edible, tart, shiny deep-red fruits abound. They are relished by the birds.

Because of its suckering tendency, this plant is often used to create a hedge or privacy screen. It is a great plant to include in a biohedge with other small shade-tolerant shrubs and trees that have a variety of bloom times. Limbing up the lower branches shows off the interesting exfoliating bark to good advantage.

There is no appreciable fall color in the species, but the cultivar 'Aurea' boasts bright yellow leaves in autumn. 'Golden Glory' is an excellent choice for colder climates. Its pyramidal form seldom exceeds 15 feet in height. Variegated cultivars include yellow-edged 'Elegantissima' or white-edged 'Variegata' and var. 'Argenteo-marginata'.

PLANTING REQUIREMENTS
Prefers full sun, but many gardeners feel that it is more handsome in part to light shade. Also prefers a moist, humus-rich, well-drained planting site, but is very adaptable and will grow just about anywhere.

PROPAGATION
Transplants easily. Dig small rooted suckers, or plant fresh or stratified seed immediately to germinate the following spring.

American Smoke Tree (*Cotinus obovatus*)
Zones 4–8
20–30 feet tall
Native to U.S.

The common name comes from the pinkish-gray hairs that surround the insignificant yellow flowers that emerge in May or June. It is these long, hairy, feathery panicles that, for several weeks, make the tree appear as if it is covered with a haze of purple smoke. Smoke Trees are dioecious and, like the birds that nest in its branches, the males are reputedly showier than the females.

Bronze-colored leaves emerge in spring, quickly changing to blue-green. The fall leaf color is variable but always spectacular. Dark brownish-gray "overlapping fish scale" bark lends winter interest to this unique native.

American Smoke Tree is pest and disease resistant, and a good choice for a street or urban tree. Several cultivars, offering a variety of flower and leaf color, have been introduced including 'Royal Purple', which has deep purple, nearly black, leaves, and 'Grace', with a more upright form. The Eurasian Smoke Tree (*C. coggygria*) has a more spectacular floral display, but its fall color is not as intense. It is also not as cold tolerant as the native, and must annually resprout from the ground in Zone 4.

PLANTING REQUIREMENTS
In the wild, American Smoke Tree is generally found growing in alkaline soil. This adaptable tree prefers moist, well-drained soil but, once established, is extremely drought tolerant. Sun or light shade.

PROPAGATION
Plant ripened seed immediately, or purchase from a nursery.

Wahoo (*Euonymus atropurpureus*)
Zones 3–8
8–15 feet
Native to U.S.
REQUIRES MOIST SOIL

Wahoo is also known as Strawberry Tree because of the clusters of strawberry-red fruits that adorn this dainty little tree in late summer. The fascinating four-parted fruits combine with intense shades of red and scarlet leaves to make it a knockout for the fall landscape. As autumn progresses, each fruit splits apart, much like Bittersweet, revealing a shiny red seed. These provide long-lasting "decorations" until they fall or are eaten by birds and wildlife.

Relatively insignificant flowers appear in June, nearly hidden by the chartreuse-green leaves.

PLANTING REQUIREMENTS
Wahoo prefers moist, humus-rich soil and will perform well in shade or sun. Because it is tolerant of pollution, it makes a good urban tree, as well as a stunning addition to any landscape.

PROPAGATION
Seedlings of this small, shallow-rooted tree are easy to transplant. Plant ripe seeds in the fall, root softwood cuttings, or dig rooted suckers.

Silverbell (*Halesia diptera*)
Carolina Silverbell (*H. tetraptera* aka *H. carolina*)
Zones 5–9
20–30 (40) feet
Native to U.S.

One of the main differences between Silverbell and Carolina Silverbell is the number of wings on the greenish fruit. Silverbell fruit has two wings, Carolina Silverbell four. Both have hanging clusters of picturesque small bell-like flowers in late spring just before the leaves emerge. Either can be grown as a small tree or large shrub.

Carolina Silverbell or Snowdrop Tree is larger than *H. diptera*, but has smaller flowers and leaves. It is also slightly more cold tolerant. For pink bells, plant 'Rosea', the pink-flowering form.

PLANTING REQUIREMENTS
Both trees prefer moist, humus-rich, well-drained soil that is slightly acidic. Alkaline soil can cause chlorosis. Silverbells will prosper in shade or full sun.

PROPAGATION
Greenwood cuttings root quite easily and are probably the most successful method of propagation. Plant ripened seed immediately for best results. Purchase potted container plants or balled and burlapped specimens to plant in early spring so they can get established before winter.

Magnolia (*Magnolia* spp.)
Zones 5–9
10–30 feet tall
Native to U.S.
Deer Resistant

Most Magnolias are not hardy in northern zones, but both Sweetbay (*M. virginiana*) and the hybrid Saucer Magnolia (*M. × soulangiana*) flourish in colder realms. In good years the well-known Saucer Magnolia is a glorious sight and a true herald of spring. However, an unexpected frost can turn the flowers to limp brown rags. The cultivar 'Verbanica' may be better for northern gardeners since its deep magenta-red flowers emerge a little later. The 3–6-inch, dark green leaves seldom produce any memorable fall coloration.

Sweetbay Magnolia's dark green leaves are conspicuously whitened on the underside and flash in the sun on a breezy day. They complement the fragrant creamy-white flowers that open in late spring or early summer. Birds relish the scarlet seeds. Sweetbay remains a smaller tree in colder regions, seldom exceeding 20 feet.

Two unusual natives, Bigleaf Magnolia (*M. macrophylla*) and Umbrella Tree (*M. tripetala*), both have exceedingly large leaves that may overpower small properties. Give these two trees enough space and they make striking additions to the landscape. Either can grow to 30 feet tall.

PLANTING REQUIREMENTS
Plant in part or light shade, or in full sun. Magnolias prefer humus-rich, moist, well-drained soil. Saucer and Sweetbay magnolias are fairly tolerant of the pH, but Bigleaf and Umbrella magnolias need slightly acidic soil.

PROPAGATION
Gather freshly ripened seed to plant immediately in the fall. Purchase container-grown seedlings or balled and burlapped specimens from a nursery. Provenance is important; seedlings from trees growing in your area have a better chance of survival.

Star Magnolia (*Magnolia stellata*)
Zones 4–8
15–20 feet
Japan
Magnolias are fussy about cold weather, especially when flowering. Remarkably, the Star Magnolia is both cold and heat tolerant. However, gardeners in zones 4 and 5 may want to consider planting this little tree in a sheltered location. Or plant it in a spot that does not warm up too early, to delay the bloom time. Beautiful multipetaled, large 3-inch creamy white

flowers open over a period of 10 days to two weeks. Be sure you can appreciate its beauty from indoors! It can flower as a youngster, even when it is barely two feet tall.

This handsome tree has dark green, 2–4-inch-long oblong leaves and lovely silvery gray bark. Dirr lists the most reliable cultivar as 'Centennial', saying that it is "the most vigorous of all *Magnolia stellata* types . . . cold hardy to at least −30°F."

PLANTING REQUIREMENTS
This adaptable tree prefers part to light shade, moist, well-drained, and slightly acidic soil, but will tolerate most soils. Pruning is generally unnecessary. Any pruning should be done immediately after blooming.

PROPAGATION
Readily available. Purchase balled and burlapped specimens or potted plants. Cuttings from young branches in early summer can be successfully rooted, or raise seedlings from fresh or cold stratified seeds.

American Hop Hornbeam (*Ostrya virginiana*)
Zones 3–9
20–30 feet tall
Native to U.S.

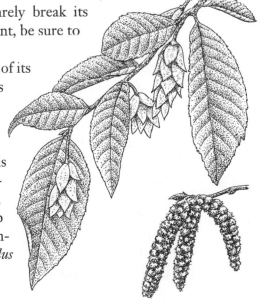

The Hop Hornbeam is handsome, sturdy, disease resistant, and extremely slow growing. Ice storms rarely break its strong branches. During property development, be sure to spare these natives from the bulldozer.

Gardeners often choose this tree because of its bright green, finely textured foliage that turns a bright, clear yellow in the fall. However, Hop Hornbeam's primary claim to fame is its fruit. Curious light green inflated "cones" enclose a smooth, spindle-shaped nutlet that is relished by wildlife. These bladder-like oddities are created by an inflated circle of bracts, which surrounds the seed. The bracts overlap like shingles on a roof to form a "cone" resembling the fruit of the Hop plant (*Humulus lupulus*).

Hop Hornbeam has both male and female flowers. In early spring, the long greenish male catkins are notice-able amid emerging downy leaves, while the tiny green female flowers are very inconspicuous. Large, pointed buds and striking exfoliating dark reddish gray-brown bark give interest to the winter landscape.

Like the Hornbeam (*Carpinus caroliniana*), Hop Hornbeam is also commonly called Ironwood because of its extremely heavy, tough, close-grained wood.

PLANTING REQUIREMENTS

Grows in full shade to full sun. Dislikes wet sites, but will tolerate dry and exposed locations and just about any type of pH or soil. An excellent choice for an urban area or near the street. However, it is sensitive to road salt. Unfortunately, it is also a favorite larval food source of the Gypsy Moth.

PROPAGATION

This tree is tough to propagate, difficult to transplant, and its stubborn seeds need both warm and cold stratification in order to germinate. Ordering a balled and burlapped specimen from the local nursery to plant in early spring may be the best plan.

Sourwood (*Oxydendrum arboreum*)
Zones 5–9
25–30 feet
Native to U.S.

Feathery white flower sprays hang from the tips of the weeping branches of Sourwood in June and July to create a stunning picture. As autumn arrives, its long, narrow bright green leaves are transformed into shades of scarlet, orange, and gold. Also known as Sorrel Tree, it has deeply fissured, blocky bark. This slow-growing tree naturalizes well, blending into a biohedge or shrub border or flourishing in the woods.

Swink and Wilhelm report finding three Sourwoods growing "in a quaking aspen thicket at the north end of Sweet Woods Forest Preserve south of Thornton, Cook County" not far from Chicago, so perhaps gardeners in Zone 4b could successfully grow this beautiful tree.

PLANTING REQUIREMENTS

Sourwood can be planted in shade or full sun in any moderately decent, slightly acidic soil. It will languish if the soil is too alkaline. It prefers a moist planting site but, once established, will tolerate drought.

PROPAGATION

Plant fully ripened seeds immediately. For faster results, purchase container-grown or balled and burlapped specimens.

Persian Parrotia (*Parrotia persica*)
Zones (4)5–8
15–40 feet
Iran

Small bundles of deep red blooms cover the bare branches in early spring, and the unique exfoliating bark, mottled in shades of brown, cream, and silvery greenish-gray, provides still more visual interest. Its strong, close-grained wood makes this yet another tree bearing the common name of Ironwood. Its 3–4-inch, rich green alternate leaves emerge with a bronze cast in the spring and change to lush shades of burgundy, orange, and gold in the fall. It is disease and insect resistant. Its pollution tolerance makes it a good choice for a street or urban planting site. It can be grown as a single or multibranched specimen.

For those who seek unusual trees, few can compare with the drooping cultivar called 'Pendula'. However, Dirr warns that there is some confusion in the trade, so try to get a guarantee from your nursery that yours is a weeping, rather than horizontally branched, specimen.

PLANTING REQUIREMENTS

Will grow in sun or shade. Prefers moist, well-drained soil, but once established, is drought tolerant. Dislikes wet sites. Not fussy about pH. Some references list this handsome tree as hardy to Zone 5, but only marginally hardy in Zone 4. To be on the safe side in northern gardens, provide a sheltered spot and adequate mulch for this tree.

PROPAGATION

Purchase young trees from a nursery, plant balled and burlapped specimens in the spring, or propagate greenwood cuttings taken in early summer.

Hoptree (*Ptelea trifoliata*)
Northern Prickly Ash (*Zanthoxylum americanum*)
Zones 4–8
6–20 feet
Native to U.S.

Hoptree is also known as Wafer Ash, Stinking Ash, or Quinine Tree. It gets its scientific name (*Ptelea*) from the Greek word for elm because of its round-winged, elm-like seeds. The seeds are dispersed when winter winds prevail, which helps this little understory tree perpetuate itself in the wild. The crushed or bruised bark and foliage gives off the strong odor of hops. In fact, the fruit was occasionally used as a substitute for hops.

Hoptree can be grown as a small tree or large shrub. Its alternate, compound leaves each have 3 leaflets, hence *trifoliata*. The top of each leaf is a lustrous dark green, while the underside is lighter in color. The greenish flowers bloom in May or June and are monoecious (meaning "one house"), having both male and female parts in each flower. It has smooth dark gray bark that sometimes gets a few warts! In the wild, it can be found with companions like American Bittersweet, Yellowtwig Dogwood, Dwarf Sand Cherry, and wild grape vines.

Cultivars include 'Aurea', with bright yellow fall foliage, and 'Glauca', with slightly downy, grayish green leaves.

Prickly Ash is in the same family as the Hoptree and has similar cultural requirements. It has pairs of thorny prickles on the branches. Small clusters of yellow-green flowers emerge in mid-spring, followed by dark green leaves. These compound, opposite leaves look like typical ash tree leaves. The bark is about the color of fireplace ashes. This aromatic tree gives off a lemony smell when bruised.

PLANTING REQUIREMENTS
These trees prefer slightly moist soil, but will tolerate drought. No specific pH requirements. As woodland understory trees, they thrive in all degrees of shade, but can also be grown in sun.

PROPAGATION
Plant freshly ripened seed immediately, or cold stratified seed in fall to germinate in the spring. Root greenwood cuttings or order seedlings from specialty tree nurseries.

Bladdernut (*Staphylea trifolia*)
Zones 3–8
6–20 feet
Native to U.S.
REQUIRES MOIST SOIL

Bladdernut loves TLC. Trees in the landscape become more attractive than those found in the wild. This small understory tree is often used as a large shrub. Bladdernut has greenish-gray bark with white-fissured stripes, and three-parted leaves like the Hoptree. Dainty hanging bell-shaped flower clusters bloom in May or June. The flowers become larger and showier in cultivation. Inflated papery seed capsules, resembling tan Japanese Lanterns, contain a few hard, shiny brown seeds that loosen inside the capsule and rattle on windy days. A European species (*S. colchica*) with similar growth habits matures at about 15 feet.

PLANTING REQUIREMENTS
Bladdernut prefers a moist, well-drained site in full shade to full sun.

PROPAGATION
Plant the stone-like seeds in fall for spring germination, transplant rooted suckers, divide when dormant, or order from a specialty nursery.

Japanese Stewartia (*Stewartia pseudocamellia*)
Zones 5–7
20–40 feet
Japan
Deer Resistant

Huge camellia-like white flowers with large yellow centers burst forth in midsummer, and the show goes on for nearly three weeks. Each flower lasts a day, then falls to the ground. If these spent flowers bother your sense of neatness, then picking them up will require extra maintenance during July. But the tradeoff is definitely worth it.

Bright green leaves emerge in spring with a bronze cast and turn shades of intense scarlet, orange, and magenta in the fall. The bark is unusually ornamental too; long strips flake off the smooth red trunk, revealing a variety of autumnal shades.

PLANTING REQUIREMENTS

Site in a place of honor—preferably in afternoon shade so that the leaf edges do not burn. Provide with humus-rich, moist, slightly acidic soil and then just sit back and enjoy. Relatively pest-resistant and slow-growing but cannot tolerate drought, so supplemental water may be necessary during dry spells. Providing ample mulch over the roots will help to retain soil moisture.

PROPAGATION

Collect seed capsules when they change from green to brown in early fall and plant seed immediately. Seeds may take up to two years to germinate. Purchase potted seedlings, or balled and burlapped specimens from a retail nursery. Or order seedlings from a specialty nursery to plant in early spring.

Fragrant Snowbell (*Styrax obassia*)
Japanese Snowbell (*S. japonicus*)
Zones (4)5–8
20–30 feet high
China, Korea, Japan
Deer Resistant

Glistening white bells hang from this elegant little tree in late spring, a clue that Snowbells are related to the Silverbells. The masses of dainty flowers open in waves, and the fat white buds are nearly as delightful as the flowers. A superb focal point for any landscape, this fast-growing tree is marginally hardy in Zone 4 (to −25°F) but needs some shelter in colder regions. Its long leaves are hairy on the underside. The stark beauty of smooth gray branches contrasts with dark backgrounds or glistening snow to create a winter feast for the eyes.

Japanese Snowbell (*S. japonicus*) is neither as cold nor as heat tolerant. Architecturally beautiful, it boasts similar nodding white bell-like flowers and small, glossy green leaves. The cultivar 'Pink Chimes' has soft rosy-pink flowers. Dirr praises 'Emerald Pagoda' for its "larger, more leathery, lustrous dark green leaves and heavy textured, waxy, 1-in.-wide flowers."

Although American Snowbell (*S. americanus*) can be grown in a sheltered spot in Zone 5, it is generally only considered hardy to Zone 6. This native has white flowers and is useful for naturalizing.

PLANTING REQUIREMENTS

Snowbells prefer humus-rich, moist, acidic soils in part shade or full sun. They do not appreciate drought, so be sure to apply additional water during dry periods.

PROPAGATION

Propagate from softwood cuttings taken in early summer. Snowbells are profuse seed producers. Plant freshly ripened seeds in the fall. Dirr suggests three months each of warm and cold stratification for best results.

Black Haw (*Viburnum prunifolium*)
Zones 3–8
12–15 feet
Native to U.S.

Mildew-resistant Black Haw is one of the best viburnums to grow as a small tree; it is likely a better choice than Nannyberry (*V. lentago*). Also known as Stagbush and Sweet Haw, it has scaly, reddish-brown bark. It has outstanding foliage and a nice, stiffly branched form. The leaves emerge in spring tinged with red. They quickly take on their dark green color and then in fall change to a show-stopping brilliant scarlet and burgundy red. The large creamy-white, flat-topped flower clusters are 3–4 inches in diameter. In October, the fruit ripens to a dark blue-black, and hangs on until winter. After the first frost, the fruit is edible.

Viburnums are among the most desirable shade-tolerant trees and shrubs. They can give the gardener a wide variety of flowers, fragrances, sizes, shapes, and forms. Black Haw is commonly found in the wild in moist woods, growing with Wild Geranium, Spicebush, Sugar Maples, Ash, and Red Oaks.

PLANTING REQUIREMENTS

Black Haw likes moist, well-drained soil with a neutral pH. More drought tolerant than Nannyberry. Enjoys shade.

PROPAGATION

Plant the broad oval seeds in fall, try rooting cuttings in early summer, or just purchase this great little tree at the nursery and get a head start! It is easily available.

Rusty Black Haw (*Viburnum rufidulum*)
Zones 5–9
10–20 feet tall
Native to U.S.
Deer Resistant

Birds love the fleshy bright blue olive-shaped fruits of Rusty Black Haw. In the spring, soft, flat-topped clusters of creamy-white flowers cover the dark green foliage. Its fall foliage is an exquisite shade of wine. Also known as Rusty Nannyberry, Blue Haw, and Southern Black Haw, this resilient shrub gets some of its common names from the rusty haired undersides of the thick, leathery leaves. It can be grown as a shrub or small tree and is tolerant of heat and humidity.

PLANTING REQUIREMENTS

Will tolerate dry shade, although it prefers moist, well-drained soil. Often found in the wild in light to full shade, but flowers more profusely with some sunlight.

PROPAGATION

Plant freshly ripened seeds immediately, or root softwood cuttings in midsummer.

Not Recommended

Amur Maple (*Acer ginnala*)
Zones 3–8
12–18 feet
China, Japan

Although Amur Maple has a nice shape, interesting fruit, handsome winged fruit, and rich red and orange autumn color, I do *not* recommend it. Unfortunately, it has proven very invasive, shading out native species and grabbing moisture and nutrients from more desirable trees. Resist temptation and choose a better-behaved tree.

Common or European Buckthorn (*Rhamnus cathartica*)
Smooth or Glossy Buckthorn (*R. frangula*)
Zones 2–7
10–12 feet
Europe, Asia

The "Buckthorn twins," warmly recommended by nurseries and landscapers alike for their ability to quickly screen property, are taking over woodlands and wetlands in many Midwestern states. Birds love the tasty seeds and so these invasive plants are now widely disseminated, creating dense thickets where little else is allowed to survive.

Tamarisk (*Tamarix ramoisissima, T. chinensis, T. parviflora*)
10–15 feet
Zones 2–8
Mediterranean, China, Japan

All three of these Tamarisk species resemble cedars. In early summer long, feathery panicles of lovely rosy-lavender flowers burst forth. These last for over a month and often reappear throughout the summer. There are major infestations of Tamarisk in nearly every western state. Let's not give it a toehold in the Midwest.

Shrubs are the low-maintenance gardener's best friends.
—*Bobbi Diehl*

4.

Best Friends

Shrubs for Shade

Shrubs are usually shorter than trees, seldom exceeding 20 feet. Some are only a foot or two tall. Most are multistemmed, rather than rising from a single or multiple trunk like a tree. In this chapter you will find shrubs of all sizes, ranging from low-growing ground huggers to tall shrubs that can even provide shade. Some flower; some fruit; some have special foliage.

Shrubs will effectively define the outer limits of a planting space. Landscape architects often recommend designing outdoor "rooms" using shrubs as the walls. Plant shrubs as a focal point a striking mass, or a privacy hedge. Use to frame attractive views or to camouflage unsightly ones. Site them where you can smell their fragrance or hear their leaves rustle as they sway in the breeze. Massed shrubs can also mask odors and muffle traffic sounds on a busy street. Plant shrubs with beautiful foliage as a restful green backdrop to a flower garden. Small flowering shrubs incorporated and

Black Chokeberry

repeated throughout the perennial border can knit the entire design together into a unified whole. Unlike herbaceous perennials, evergreen and deciduous shrubs continue to maintain a presence in the stark landscape of winter. Well-placed shrubs can help buffer strong winter winds, creating a friendlier climate near the house. You can even grow a shrub in a pot, as long as you keep the soil well watered. Once established, shrubs need minimal maintenance.

For a variation on a theme, consider combining shrubs. Mix in some evergreens and a few small trees. Select species that enjoy a similar planting site, planting them in a random zigzag pattern. Let them retain their natural shapes and sizes as they weave together, and voila! you have created a biohedge. I believe it was Ken Druse who first proposed this concept. Many homeowners reduce the amount of lawn by covering more of the property with herbaceous and woody plants, but soon complain of having "too many gardens." By planting shrubs and trees fairly close together, much is accomplished. In addition to mowing less area, with a biohedge or two you can create privacy without the labor of maintaining a formal, clipped hedge. And variety, known as the spice of life, is certainly more interesting than a monoculture of matching shrubs. Planting ground cover under the biohedge creates more habitat and requires less weeding. You can also plant annuals to fill in blank spaces until the ground cover is well established, if that suits your fancy. Perhaps in time you will even relax enough to allow leaves to fall and decompose where they land.

A biohedge is tailor-made for any homeowner interested in certifying his property as a Backyard Wildlife Habitat. And just imagine the seasonal extravaganzas possible! With careful choices, you can have masses of flowers about any time, restful as well as colorful foliage, fragrance, size, shape—and the list goes on. What a wonderful way to bring interest and diversity into a small space.

As you make out your "wish list," determine the mature size and shape of each shrub you want to include. Before purchasing even one, study your property to determine the available spaces for planting. If you measure carefully, you will not be as apt to face an overgrown-shrub problem down the road. Shrubs that mature at 8 feet tall and wide are wonderful at the back of the property, providing privacy for you and refuge for wildlife, but they have no place next to the sidewalk or front door.

You are often better off choosing smaller, less expensive shrubs at the nursery rather than big ones unless you need a mature look immediately. Younger shrubs are easier to transplant and will catch up to the older ones sooner than you think.

When planting shrubs, dig the hole 2 to 3 times wider than the root ball but no deeper. Water thoroughly and continue to water deeply at least once a week if there is not adequate rainfall.

Unlike trees, shrubs generally carry their foliage from the ground to the top, leading the eye from earth to sky as they tie the entire landscape into a unified package. Shrubs can add character to your garden as they create a sustainable, low-maintenance landscape.

Shrubs for Shade

Bottlebrush Buckeye (*Aesculus parviflora*)
Zones 4–8
8–15 feet tall/wide
Native to U.S.

In full bloom, this puts on a spectacular show! Long, tapering, creamy-white bottlebrush flowers cover the plant. There are 5–7 leaflets on each large dark green palmate leaf. Bottlebrush Buckeye suckers readily, quickly filling in large spaces. It is not particular about light, and flowers as dramatically in full shade as in full sun. The clusters of var. *serotina* open as late as three weeks after the species. 'Rogers', a cultivar with larger flower clusters, blooms midway between *A. parviflora* and *serotina*. Try alternating all three in a hedge to extend the bloom period.

PLANTING REQUIREMENTS

Needs a moist, well-drained planting environment when first planted, but once established can tolerate nearly any growing conditions, including a wide range of pH. Give it room to spread.

PROPAGATION

Can be propagated by division, seed, root, or sucker cuttings, but it is probably best to purchase potted or balled and burlapped specimens from the nursery. Give it a good deep planting bed so the roots have plenty of room to roam.

Shadblow Serviceberry (*Amelanchier canadensis*)
Zones 4–8
6–25 feet tall/wide
Native to U.S.
MOIST SOIL REQUIRED

Shadblow Serviceberry has an upright habit and often forms thickets. It is usually grown as a large shrub, but can be pruned to create a multi-stemmed small tree. It resembles *A. arborea* but its flower clusters are more upright. Downy hairs cover both sides of the early emerging leaves. As the leaves mature, they become smooth. The cultivar 'Prince William' was developed in Wisconsin.

While excellent pies and preserves can be made from the fruit of most serviceberries, the fruit of Shadblow Serviceberry can best be described as "dry and insipid," although wildlife relish it all the same.

PLANTING REQUIREMENTS
Plant in moist, well-drained soil part shade or full sun.

PROPAGATION
Seed planted immediately after ripening, or cold stratified.

Running Serviceberry (*Amelanchier stolonifera*)
Zones 4–8
3–6 feet tall
Native to U.S.

Running Serviceberry is the "short cousin" of the better-known Amelanchiers. Its thicket-forming ability makes it a good cover for dry hillsides. It produces abundant flowers and sweet, delicious fruits.

PLANTING REQUIREMENTS
Give this hardy stoloniferous shrub space to run. It prefers average, well-drained soil and once established tolerates drought. Part shade or sun.

PROPAGATION
Division or seed.

Red Chokeberry (*Aronia arbutifolia*)
Zones 4–8
6–10 feet tall
Native to U.S.

This shrub can be a vigorous colonizer, and needs plenty of room. The light-colored undersides of its leaves are covered with downy hairs. Clusters of small white flowers in late spring are followed by pretty red berries that ripen in the fall and hang on for most of the winter. The fruit is unpalatable, hence the common name. Even birds avoid chokeberries unless there are no other options available. But that flaw is an asset for the home landscape, because these clusters of bright red berries fairly sparkle on a wintry day.

'Brilliantissima' (also known as 'Brilliant') is particularly showy, with shiny red berries and intense red fall foliage. It is a good substitute for Burning Bush (see p. 86) and makes a nice focal point.

PLANTING REQUIREMENTS
Prefers average to moist, well-drained, slightly acidic to neutral soil but in the wild is found in a wide range of soils from peaty or marshy to dry and sandy. Thrives in part to light shade or full sun. May lose lower leaves as they age and become leggy, so consider planting low-growing shrubs or perennials in front of them. Space 4 feet apart.

PROPAGATION
Ripened seed, division, rooted suckers, cuttings, or layering.

Black Chokeberry (*Aronia melanocarpa*)
Zones 3–7
2–5 feet tall
Native to U.S.

Black Chokeberry is similar to Red, but does not grow as tall, generally maturing at less than 5–6 feet. Its white flowers bloom in late spring, followed by clusters of shining, fat black berries. The smooth, shiny, dark green leaves turn red in the fall. Black Chokeberry is not apt to lose its lower foliage, but the berries shrivel and fall not long after ripening, so this is not a shrub to locate next to a walkway.

The variety 'Elata' can grow as tall as 10 feet and has intense red autumn coloration.

PLANTING REQUIREMENTS

Like Red Chokeberry, Black Chokeberry prefers moist to average, well-drained, slightly acidic soil in light shade to full sun. Other planting requirement comments apply. Space 3–4 feet apart.

PROPAGATION

Ripened or stratified seed, layering, cuttings, or by digging rooted suckers in the spring.

Carolina Allspice (*Calycanthus floridus*)
Zones 4–9
6–9 feet high/wide
Native to U.S.

Unusual deep brownish-red flowers of this native can impart a lovely fragrance to a front entryway, near a walkway, or beside a patio. However, knowledgeable gardeners purchase Carolina Allspice in flower since the fragrance varies widely from plant to plant. If this is not possible, the cultivar 'Edith Wilder' has a pleasant, *reliable* fragrance. A yellow-flowering form named 'Athens' has more heavily textured leaves and its autumn color is generally more gold than yellow.

Carolina Allspice is a good choice for a biohedge or mixed border; it grows well at the edge of a woodland. Its dark green leaves turn a bright clear yellow in the fall. Also known as Sweetshrub, Strawberry Bush, and Hairy Allspice, this is one of the most maintenance free shrubs available.

PLANTING REQUIREMENTS

Prefers average, well-drained soil in part shade or full sun. Flowering tends to be more profuse with more sunlight. Shade seems to produce taller and less compact shrubs.

PROPAGATION

Purchase potted or balled and burlapped plants in flower to guarantee pleasant fragrance. Plant ripened seed immediately as soon as the urn-shaped seed capsules change from green to brown. Branch cuttings taken in midsummer can be rooted in sand, or dig rooted suckers.

Siberian Pea Shrub (*Caragana arborescens*)
Zones 2–6
15–20 feet tall/wide
Siberia, Mongolia

Any plant that originates in Siberia has got to be tough—and cold hardy. And that certainly describes the Siberian Pea Shrub. It tolerates extreme cold, drought, wind, and harsh growing conditions. Although you would probably not plant this as a specimen, if you need a low-maintenance shrub for part of a shelterbelt or a privacy screen, Pea Shrub will fill the bill. The dwarf form 'Nana' is fuller and more floriferous than the species and may be a better choice, even for a shelterbelt. However, individual plants are somewhat inconsistent as to mature height, ranging from to 8 down to 2½ feet, which could be a problem if used for a privacy screen!

There are a few cultivars that actually could be used as specimens, including the very light and ferny 'Lorbergii', which grows 2–8 feet tall and reminds me of a giant asparagus fern. Weeping forms have been hybridized, including 'Walker' and 'Pendula'. When we lived in Minnesota, we had 'Pendula' and I always enjoyed the small yellow pea-like flowers in late spring. It was grafted on a standard and was quite an attractive little weeping tree. I don't think it ever grew taller than 5 feet. The small compound leaves were nice, but had no fall color that I recall. Although Siberian Pea prefers full sun, our tree flourished in morning shade and afternoon sun.

PLANTING REQUIREMENTS

This guy is about as tough as they come. Plant in any kind of soil, in just about any conditions. Does well in part shade or sun. And like other pea species, it will reward you by fixing atmospheric nitrogen. However, too much moisture can cause leaf spot disease, so don't be overly kind to this plant.

PROPAGATION

Seed planted in the fall, softwood cuttings taken in summer, root cuttings, or layering. Weeping forms are generally grafted on standards.

New Jersey Tea (*Ceanothus americanus*)
Zones 4–8
2–3 feet tall/wide
Native to U.S.

Known by early settlers as Red Root, this sturdy native sends its thick, knobby roots deep into the soil. These deep roots make it very drought-resistant. Plume-like cylindrical clusters of small, fragrant white flowers bloom in early to midsummer. New Jersey Tea fixes nitrogen in the soil. It is a larval food source for the Mottled Duskywing Butterfly.

PLANTING REQUIREMENTS
Plant in average, well-drained garden soil in full sun to part shade. Site in its permanent location because once established, the deep roots make it nearly impossible to transplant.

PROPAGATION
Soak fully ripened seed in hot water and plant in the fall. Transplant young seedlings the following spring before the root has a chance to delve too deeply into the soil.

Buttonbush (*Cephalanthus occidentalis*)
Zones 4–9
5–15 feet tall/wide
Native to U.S.
MOIST SOIL REQUIRED

I have always thought this plant looks prehistoric because of the strange "spiked" ball-like white flowers arising above coarse, opposite whorled leaves, giving it one of its common names—Sputnik Plant. These flowers appear in late summer, becoming bright red knobby balls (a little smaller than a boiled egg yolk) in early fall. Buttonbush is a good choice for a difficult wet spot and looks best in a naturalized setting, near a pond, or as part of a wetland planting.

This shrub can be found in the wild growing in standing water, so it definitely loves moisture. I know that it can also survive in regular moist garden soil because one we planted at the foot of a hillside evidently got enough moisture from the runoff and grew there happily. If it becomes rangy, simply cut it back to about 6 inches in fall and it will rejuvenate in spring.

PLANTING REQUIREMENTS
Needs consistently moist, humus-rich soil. Prefers full sun, but will tolerate part to light shade.

PROPAGATION
Plant seeds in fall or take cuttings in late summer.

Summersweet (*Clethra alnifolia*)
Zones 4–9
3–8 feet tall/ 4–6 feet wide
Native to U.S.
MOIST SOIL REQUIRED
Deer Resistant

Gracefulness, intensely fragrant floral spires, rich golden yellow fall leaf color, adaptability—this trouble-free shrub has much to recommend it. It is also known as White Alder and Sweet Pepperbush, perhaps because of its spicy fragrance. As long as the soil is moist and acidic, it is an excellent choice for foundation plantings, groupings in the lawn, mixed shrub or perennial borders, naturalized woodland gardens, near ponds, or as a focal point.

The cultivar 'Hummingbird' is smaller than the species, maturing at 2–4 feet tall. It has pretty, creamy-white flowers and yellow-orange fall foliage. Hardy in zones 3–9, it is resistant to airborne salt damage, suckers readily, and can be utilized as a small, shrubby, slow-spreading ground cover. If the suckering habit is undesirable, simply remove and transplant rooted suckers, or share with neighbors. Or choose 'Compacta' instead. 'Pink Spires', 'Rosea', and 'Ruby Spice' have fluffy racemes of delightfully fragrant pink or rose flowers.

Cinnamon Clethra (*C. acuminata*) is only reliably hardy to Zone 6, marginally hardy in Zone 5. Maturing at 8–15 feet tall, this larger shrub does not flower as profusely as *C. alnifolia*. However, it has attractive, cinnamon-brown exfoliating bark and makes a good privacy screen in damp areas.

PLANTING REQUIREMENTS
For low maintenance, give any Clethra a moist, acidic site. Although it will tolerate dry soil, persistent lack of moisture causes stress, making it susceptible to insect damage, particularly mites. It accepts nearly any light from full shade to full sun, and appears to bloom equally well in either.

PROPAGATION
Transplant rooted suckers. Plant the small seeds in the fall. Michael Dirr reports that cuttings taken in midsummer are "exceedingly easy to root."

Tatarian Dogwood (*Cornus alba*)
Zones 3–7
8–10 feet tall/wide
Siberia, Asia
Deer Resistant

Blood red branches look magnificent against a snowy landscape. In spring, flat clusters of small white flowers glow against the medium green leaves. Small bluish-white berries perch on the ends of bright red stems in late summer, and the autumn leaves turn a rich red. This is truly a shrub for all seasons. Because the youngest stems are the reddest, this shrub requires maintenance pruning at least every other year. Remove ⅓ of the existing growth, particularly the older canes, or cut the entire shrub nearly to the ground in midwinter to force it to resprout. To control the height, canes can be shortened as desired.

There are several cultivars with white-edged leaves including 'Argenteo-marginata', 'Westonbirt', and 'Siberica'. 'Spaethii' has yellow-margined leaves. The variegated forms are not quite as vigorous, but are good for lighting up dark spaces. They also make a good background for similarly variegated hostas. To add that hard-to-get yellow color in the garden, plant 'Aurea'.

Bloodtwig Dogwood (*C. sanguinea*) has similar white flowers in early summer and deep blood-red fall foliage, but is not quite as reliable about producing the colorful winter branches, nor does it have as good a mature shape. 'Wisley Form' has better color. 'Viridissima' has yellow-green stems, while those of 'Winter Flame' are yellow-orange.

PLANTING REQUIREMENTS
Grows in about any situation imaginable and is not fussy about light, moisture, or pH. Takes light to medium shade or full sun and tolerates dry soil.

PROPAGATION
Clean and plant ripened seed immediately or take softwood cuttings in midsummer, or hardwood cuttings in midwinter.

Redosier or Yellow-twig Dogwood (*Cornus sericea*)
Zones 2–7
4–8 feet high/wide
Native to U.S.
MOIST SOIL REQUIRED

A colonizer, this stoloniferous shrub can cover wide areas, creating a good privacy screen or providing erosion control. It has flat clusters of small white flowers in early summer, followed by attractive hanging fruits relished by birds and wildlife. Its bright red winter stems are handsome alone, or combined with contrasting yellow-stemmed dogwoods.

It is susceptible to fungal leaf and twig blights, so the necessity to cut out diseased branches will increase maintenance. However, it thrives on being cut back to within 4–6 inches of ground level in March or early April every 2–3 years. This seemingly drastic measure reduces disease and will also intensify the winter color, since the most brilliant branches are those of the current season. Gardeners unwilling to lop off the entire shrub can try removing about ¼ of the oldest branches each spring.

There are several nice cultivars with a variety of colors, sizes, and growth habits. 'Cardinal' has bright red stems. A drought-tolerant variety called *coloradensis* is hardy to Zone 2. 'Baileyi' does not run like the species and produces larger fruits. Slow-growing 'Isanti' remains relatively short, while 'Kelseyi' is even smaller, seldom growing over 2 feet tall. Be advised that this miniature does not have reliably red winter stems.

'Flaviramea' has yellow winter stems and yellow fall foliage. 'Silver and Gold', also with yellow stems in winter, is the white-edged variegated form.

PLANTING REQUIREMENTS
Plant in consistently moist soil in part shade or sun.

PROPAGATION
Tuck the tips of growing branches into the soil where they will root. Dig rooted suckers, or plant ripened seed immediately. Plant clean, ripened seed in fall, or root cuttings throughout the summer and early fall.

American Hazelnut (*Corylus americanus*)
Zones 4–9
8–16 feet tall/wide
Native to U.S.

Also called Filbert, American Hazelnut is a coarse shrub for natural areas or for use in mixed borders. Its attributes include adaptability and the production of tasty nuts. American Hazelnut is monoecious, with flowers of both sexes appearing on a single plant. Long, drooping tan-brown male catkins and small red female catkins appear together each spring. To prevent it from becoming a dense thicket, you must regularly remove the suckers—definitely a high-maintenance task. There are better low-maintenance shrub choices, but if a privacy screen or naturalized thicket for wildlife is desirable, this plant will do the job.

Beaked Hazelnut (*C. cornuta*), a native hardy in Zones 2–8, is nearly identical.

PLANTING REQUIREMENTS
Both American and Beaked Hazelnut will grow in rocky, gravelly poor soil, average soil, or good loam, and neither is fussy about pH. Given a choice, they prefer a moist or wet planting site, but either will grow well in fairly dry soil. Part shade or full sun. Give Hazelnuts plenty of room to spread, because spread they will.

PROPAGATION
Plant ripened nuts from native trees in fall.

Harry Lauder's Walking Stick (*Corylus avellana* 'Contorta')
Zones 4–8
6–10 feet tall
Europe
MOIST SOIL REQUIRED

Also known as Corkscrew Hazelnut, this is a fascinating European cultivar whose twisted, curly branches are loved by flower arrangers. Even its leaves and catkins are contorted. This conversation piece makes a great accent shrub near a front entry, and seldom gets taller than 7 feet. It is particularly striking in winter when the convolution of the branches is fully evident.

Self-rooted plants are more desirable than grafted specimens because the grafting understock often suckers, causing maintenance problems. Harry Lauder's Walking Stick usually does not produce nuts.

PLANTING REQUIREMENTS
Does best in moist, well-drained soil in part shade to full sun.

PROPAGATION
When you purchase Harry Lauder's Walking Stick, request a specimen growing on its own roots. Root the cuttings of growing branches taken in early summer, or hardwood cuttings in February.

Cotoneaster (*Cotoneaster* spp.)
Zones 5–7
6–36 inches tall
China
Deer Resistant

Slow-growing Creeping Cotoneaster (*Cotoneaster adpressus*) literally lies on the ground and is recommended for rock gardens or as a slow-growing ground cover. This 6–18-inch tall shrub is a good choice for a small space. An even smaller form, 'Little Gem', is grown for its foliage, seldom growing taller than 6 inches.

2–3-foot tall Cranberry Cotoneaster (*C. apiculatus*) is popular because of its colorful fall display. Bright green leaves march on irregular branches, studded with glowing red fruit. In the spring, flowers like tiny roses cover the plant about the same time new foliage begins to emerge. 'Tom Thumb' is a tiny 6-inch cultivar. 'Blackburn' resembles the species, but has even larger, showier bright red fruits.

A similar species, Rockspray Cotoneaster (*C. horizontalis*), has a more symmetrical branching habit. Its cultivar, 'Saxatilis', has creamy white-edged leaves that change to pink-edged leaves in the fall.

Severe cold will kill cotoneasters back to the snowline. However, they will regrow in spring.

PLANTING REQUIREMENTS
Plant in moist, well-drained soil in part shade or full sun. Creeping Cotoneaster will tolerate alkaline soil. Plan to do maintenance pruning from time to time. Stressed plants may be susceptible to leaf diseases and insect damage, particularly in warmer climates.

PROPAGATION
Readily available; or clean and plant ripened seeds, or root softwood cuttings.

Dwarf Honeysuckle (*Diervilla lonicera*)
Zones 2–7

1½–3 feet tall
Native to U.S.

Low maintenance dictates that you "put the right plant in the right place," and Dwarf Honeysuckle is definitely a case in point. This cute little bush honeysuckle spreads vigorously by underground rhizomes, which makes it a bad choice for a small space, but wonderful for a large problem area. It can quickly cover a hillside or streambank, providing good erosion control. Clusters of 5-parted yellow flowers bloom in midsummer. Southern Bush Honeysuckle (*D. sessilifolia*) grows larger, maturing at 3–5 feet. Despite its common name, this cold-tolerant plant is actually hardy in zones 4–9. Its small yellow flowers dangle from the tips of the branches from June to August. The hybrid *D.* × *splendens* matures at 2–4 feet. It is hardy in zones 3–9, has yellow flowers and deep red fall foliage.

Bush honeysuckles profit from severe pruning to keep a nice, dense form. It is advisable to prune in early spring, cutting the branches to within 6 inches of the ground every 2 to 3 years, so this may be a maintenance consideration. However, they can exist without pruning if a little legginess is acceptable. Extremely adaptable, they thrive even in gravel, hence one common name—Gravel Weed!

Serrated leaves distinguish the native bush honeysuckles from the invasive exotic bush honeysuckles (see p. 86), which have smooth-edged leaves.

PLANTING REQUIREMENTS
Plant in moderate shade or full sun. Does well in just about any well-drained soil or pH, and will tolerate drought.

PROPAGATION
Division; dig rooted suckers; root softwood cuttings taken in summer or rhizome cuttings in fall or winter; plant ripened seed in the fall.

Leatherwood (*Dirca palustris*)
Zones 4–9
3–6 feet high/wide
Native to U.S.
Deer Resistant

This native deserves a place on any shade gardener's list. Even though it is termed a shrub, Leatherwood also grows as a unique, small tree, perfect for a limited gardening space or a small lot. It will tolerate light, partial, or even full shade. Its dense branching habit lends an oval to round shape.

Leatherwood is interesting all year. The small yellow flowers, among the first to emerge in early spring, are followed by shimmering oval-shaped light green leaves. The alternate leaves are slightly hairy as they emerge but soon become entirely smooth, and turn a clear yellow in autumn.

As the shrub ages, the smooth grayish-brown juvenile bark becomes exceedingly rough and fibrous and develops fissures, particularly at the base. The branches are so flexible you can tie them in knots! This characteristic earned it its common name. Leatherwood has no serious pests or diseases.

PLANTING REQUIREMENTS
Prefers a shady, moist, slightly acidic location and can be found growing naturally in rich woodland soil. However, it thrives in any type of soil.

PROPAGATION
The small greenish fruit ripens in June and July but is rarely noticed since it falls as soon as it ripens. Cleaned seeds germinate readily. Dirr reports that attempts to propagate this shrub through cuttings have been unsuccessful.

Redvein Enkianthus (*Enkianthus campanulatus*)
Zones 5–8
6–8 feet tall
Japan
MOIST, ACIDIC SOIL REQUIRED
Huge clusters of small urn-shaped, creamy yellow flowers streaked with deep rose dangle from this fascinating shrub in late spring. The striking red-petioled dark green leaves change to brilliant red in the fall. But persnickety? You bet! As long as the moisture and pH needs of Enkianthus are met, it will thrive, requiring minimal maintenance. In less than ideal situations, it will languish and die.

Hybridizing efforts have concentrated on flower color. For white flowers, choose 'Albiflorus'. Deep rose

'Red Velvet' has a more upright growth habit than the species. A later flowering type, var. *palibinii*, has heavier red flower venation and leaves with hairy undersides.

Some gardeners successfully grow Enkianthus in Zone 4. Liberty Hyde Bailey reports it is hardy to Massachusetts. I do not know if this shrub needs a protected place in colder sites, but all other planting requirements must be observed for success and low maintenance. It reportedly can become as tall as 15–30 feet, particularly in the Northeast, but seldom grows very tall in the Midwest.

PLANTING REQUIREMENTS

Combined with other ericaceous shrubs like rhododendrons, laurels, and azaleas, Enkianthus can help create a lovely spring blooming shrub border in a humus-rich, well-drained, moist, acidic site. It prefers sun or part shade.

PROPAGATION

Plant seed in late February or early March. Dirr gives these specific directions: "Sow seed on milled sphagnum in flats, do not cover, place under mist or where high humidity can be maintained." Germination occurs in 6–8 weeks, and by fall the seedlings will be about a foot tall. It can also be propagated by cuttings taken in midsummer or by rooting attached branches by tucking them under moist soil. Dirr reports that rooted cuttings may not be winter-hardy the first season.

Forsythia (*Forsythia ovata*)
Zones 3–8
7–10 feet tall/wide
Korea

Forsythia can be glorious in good years, and nearly barren of flowers in bad. Forsythia's flower buds are susceptible to freezing temperatures. The best spot for it may be in a mixed shrub border, so that other, more cooperative shrubs can camouflage its flowering fickleness.

However, Early Forsythia (*F. ovata* Nakai) appears to be hardy as far north as Zone 3. Leon Snyder reports it blooms annually at the Minnesota Landscape Arboretum. The flower buds of several cultivars of *F. ovata*, including 'Meadowlark', 'Northern Gold', and 'Northern Sun', will reportedly withstand freezing temperatures of down to −36°F.

Weeping Forsythia (*F. suspensa*), hardy in Zones 5–8, tumbles freely over a wall or down a bank, creating a golden curtain in spring.

A few 2–4-foot dwarf forms have been developed as ground covers.

PLANTING REQUIREMENTS

Forsythia prefers full sun but will bloom satisfactorily in part shade. Plant in well-drained, average garden soil. Never prune into a formal hedge shape.

PROPAGATION

Root young branch cuttings taken May–September.

Fothergilla (*Fothergilla gardenii*)
Zones 5–8
2–3 feet tall/wide
Native to U.S.

Bottlebrush flower spikes of white cover this small shrub as new blue-green leaves begin to emerge in midspring. In the fall, the foliage will take on a palette of red, orange, and yellow. Also called Witch Alder, Fothergilla is a good choice for foundation plantings since it does not outgrow its bounds and seldom needs pruning. It can also be effective as a small, natural hedge, in a mixed perennial/shrub border, or as part of a biohedge. It is one of the most trouble-free native shrubs for Zone 5, delightful in any season. Large Fothergilla (*F. major*) is similar in all respects, except that it is larger, maturing at 6–10 feet. The cultivar 'Mr. Airy', perhaps a hybrid of these two, is reportedly hardier and may offer gardeners in Zone 4, or colder spots in Zone 5, a chance to experiment with this delightful little shrub. It gets to be 5–6 feet tall.

PLANTING REQUIREMENTS

For best results, plant in humus-rich, moist, slightly acidic soil in part shade or full sun. However it is quite adaptable, and will tolerate average garden soil amended with peat or rich compost, as long as it has adequate moisture throughout the growing season.

PROPAGATION

Root young branch cuttings taken in June or July. Germinating seed is more difficult. In late August or early September, snugly cover a seed capsule with a nylon stocking, or pick some and enclose in a paper bag to catch the ripened black seeds as the capsules explode. This generally occurs in September. Plant immediately. Unless there is cross-pollination, Fothergillas may not set seed.

Vernal Witch Hazel (*Hamamelis vernalis*)
Zones 4–8
6–10 feet tall
Native to U.S.
Deer Resistant

One of the earliest shrubs to bloom in spring, Vernal Witch Hazel puts on a display of raggedy, twisted confetti-like bright yellow flowers about the time the snowdrops bloom. And what a great combination! Be sure to plant this nifty shrub within easy viewing distance from inside the house. This medium-sized native also rewards with bright yellow fall color, occasionally tinged with oranges and reds.

Another native, Common or Eastern Witch Hazel (*H. virginiana*), hardy in Zones 3–8, is much larger, maturing at 15–20 feet high and wide. Since its spicy flowers emerge in late fall, it may be the *latest* native shrub to bloom. Its bright yellow flowers often persist into December, but are usually obscured by the equally bright yellow autumn leaves.

There are also witch hazels from China and Japan, but most of these are hardy only to Zone 5. Chinese Witch Hazel (*H. mollis*) matures at 10–15 feet. Its fragrant flowers emerge in early January. Japanese Witch Hazel, 10–15 feet, has an extremely wide architectural form that needs a big space. *H. × intermedia*, a hybrid of these two, grows 10–20 feet tall, and is the most commonly planted non-native witch hazel in the U.S. Several cultivars have been hybridized from this exceedingly fragrant witch hazel, including 'Jelena', with "copper-penny" colored flowers; the old, reliable 'Arnold Promise'; and 'Ruby Glow', which has an upright form and red flowers.

PLANTING REQUIREMENTS

Plant native witch hazels in humus-rich, moist, well-drained soil in light or dappled shade or in morning sun. These sturdy shrubs will accept less than ideal planting conditions and can even tolerate dry soil, but suffer if the pH becomes too alkaline. Non-natives like similar planting conditions, but prefer more sunlight.

PROPAGATION

Native witch hazel seeds planted in the fall will germinate the second season. For earlier germination, provide 3 months warm and 3 months cold stratification before planting. It is likely easier and more dependable to just take cuttings of native, exotic, or hybrid witch hazels in early spring. These will root easily in sand or a soilless potting mixture. And of course, vegetative propagation is necessary for hybrids and cultivars anyway.

Rose of Sharon (*Hibiscus syriacus*)
Zones 4–8
6–10 feet tall
Asia

If a shrub that blooms nearly all summer in a wide variety of colors is on your wish list, then Rose of Sharon is the ticket. Often grown as a small, multistemmed tree, it has huge flared flowers that remind me of hollyhocks.

'Blue Bird' and 'Diana' top the long list of available cultivars. 'Diana' is one of the new sterile Egolf cultivars that bloom profusely all season. There are also double-flowered cultivars. 'Blushing Bride' has soft pink flowers; 'Lucy' has double red; and 'Arden', lavender.

Since it blooms on new growth, if any of the branches are winter killed, not to worry! In fact, many gardeners like to prune dormant plants heavily in late February or early March to force new growth and encourage heavier flowering.

PLANTING REQUIREMENTS

Not fussy about soil, moisture, or pH; grows well in sun or part shade. The only things that bother it are extremes—too wet, too dry, too acid, too alkaline—so try to keep growing conditions somewhere "in the middle." Some references list is as hardy only to Zone 5, but my daughter has a beautiful specimen at her home in Minneapolis, while *Hortus Third* reports it is "commonly planted n. to Ontario."

PROPAGATION

Self-sows readily, often to the dismay of neatnik gardeners. Obviously, ripened seeds planted in fall germinate reliably. Root softwood cuttings taken in midsummer, or hardwood cuttings in midwinter. Either will benefit from treatment with a rooting hormone.

Smooth Hydrangea (*Hydrangea arborescens* 'Annabelle')
Zones 3–8
3–5 feet high/wide
Native to U.S.

Spectacular white pompons appear on the cultivar 'Annabelle' in midsummer, lasting through the winter. These hefty beauties change from their summer whites to light green in the fall. As the season ends, huge clusters of elegant light brown blossoms dry and hang on through the winter. These long-time favorites of flower arrangers have graced many a dining room table or sideboard, often displayed in a huge vase or antique soup tureen.

Hydrangeas impart a relatively coarse texture to a mixed shrub border. 'Annabelle' is definitely the best native selection because of its compact growth habit and attractive flowers. Most authorities recommend pruning to the ground in early spring to maintain a compact shape. This shrub blooms on new wood. It will regrow and bloom the same season. However, my daughter reports her 'Annabelle' blooms more profusely when she "forgets" to do the annual pruning. Her shrub still retains its compact shape. Experiment.

Two cultivars can extend the flowering season. 'Praecox' blooms about three weeks earlier than the species, while 'Tardiva', the tardy bloomer, continues into October.

Peegee Hydrangea (*H. paniculata* 'Grandiflora'), native to Japan and hardy in Zones 3–8, is over twice as tall (10–20 feet). When grown as a small tree, it makes a nice accent near an entry, a patio, or even to anchor an island garden. This is another hydrangea to incorporate into a mixed shrub border. It blooms on new wood beginning in late summer and continuing well into autumn. Bigleaf Hydrangea (*H. macrophylla*), reportedly hardy only to Zones 6–8, is also from Japan. Large leaves, large flowers, and a manageable size makes this elegant plant a winner for warmer climates, where its presence is guaranteed to command admiration, blooming profusely on old wood when few other shrubs do. This is the gift plant you see at the florist's.

PLANTING REQUIREMENTS

Hydrangeas prefer moist, well-drained soil with light or part shade. They are not fussy about soil or pH and will survive equally well in loam or clay. Most will tolerate periods of dry soil. Only Bigleaf Hydrangea demands consistent moisture.

PROPAGATION

Plant ripened seeds in the fall or root softwood cuttings in early summer.

Oakleaf Hydrangea (*Hydrangea quercifolia*)

Zones 5–9

4–6 feet high

Native to U.S.

MOIST, ACIDIC SOIL REQUIRED

Few shrubs can rival Oakleaf Hydrangea's impressive floral display. The 12-inch-long pyramidal clusters of bright white flowers change to rosy-pink in late summer, finally becoming a soft brown in fall. Great huge oak-like leaves of deep rich green become glorious shades of red, orange, and yellow in the fall. Smaller cultivars such as 'Snow Queen', 'Sikes Dwarf', and 'Pee Wee' can be used where planting space is limited.

PLANTING REQUIREMENTS

Likes humus-rich, moist, well-drained acidic soil. Prefers a shady location and will even perform well in heavy shade. It also thrives in full sun with adequate moisture. Give this stoloniferous shrub plenty of room to run. It forms large show-stopping colonies, creating a fantastic background for mixed shrub or perennial borders.

PROPAGATION

Easily propagated from seed.

Shrubby St. Johnswort (*Hypericum prolificum*)

Zones 3–8

1–4 feet tall/wide

Native to U.S.

Deer Resistant

This adaptable, trouble-free shrub is an excellent choice for the middle or front of a mixed shrub or shrub/perennial border, or a natural hedge. Masses of 1-inch bright yellow flowers cover the plant, appearing continuously from June to August, accenting the dark green leaves. Kalm's St. Johnswort (*H. kalmianum*) is similar, but not quite as hardy.

PLANTING REQUIREMENTS
Plant Shrubby St. Johnswort in light to part shade or full sun. It is not fussy about soil or pH as long as the planting spot is well drained.

PROPAGATION
Seed germinates readily. Cuttings taken in summer are easy to root.

Virginia Sweetspire (*Itea virginica*)
Zones 5–9
3–5 feet tall
Native to U.S.
Deer Resistant

Fragrant, skinny 4–6 inch long white bottlebrush flowers cover Virginia Sweetspire in late spring and early summer, and it has neat, lustrous dark green leaves in summer, but my favorite season for this small shrub is autumn, when the foliage turns purple-red, burgundy, orangey-red, and crimson. A mass of these at that season is unforgettable.

Virginia Sweetspire may flop a bit, and is a good choice for a mixed shrub border and perennial border or a biohedge. It can also be grown as a specimen, although because of its suckering habit, that specimen may soon become a mass in spite of you. But that is OK.

'Henry's Garnet' has even more intense fall foliage and larger flowers. 'Saturnalia' is a little shorter, and for a teeny-tiny version, look for 'Little Henry'. He only grows 1½ to 2 feet tall and wide and is reported to have even better flowers and fall color than the species.

PLANTING REQUIREMENTS
As undemanding as it is beautiful. Does fine in just about any kind of soil, pH, moisture or light, even full shade. It will tolerate a certain amount of dryness, but why make this wonderful plant suffer? Give it a good long drink if the soil gets too dry.

PROPAGATION
Dig rooted suckers, plant ripened seed in fall, or take softwood cuttings in summer.

Kerria (*Kerria japonica*)
Zones 4–9
3–6 feet tall
China
Deer Resistant

Kerria's pretty, bright yellow flowers burst forth in April and May and then, like Wood Poppy, it will rebloom on and off. Lustrous, dark green leaves generally change to a clear yellow in the fall. Its stems stay bright green all year.

Some authors list this tough plant as hardy only to Zone 5 and winter dieback is occasionally reported in colder zones. However, it can be cut to the ground after flowering if that occurs. A good foundation shrub, Kerria does well in a mixed shrub/perennial border where it may be afforded some winter protection. It generally grows twice as wide as it is tall. It is maintenance free except for needing a bit of shaping every few years.

'Pleniflora', the double-flowered cultivar, has bright yellow to rich golden double chrysanthemum-like flowers. They bloom a little later and last a little longer than the species. 'Variegata' has white-edged leaves. The entire shrub is smaller in all parts. Like the variegated forms of many other plants, this cultivar is not completely stable and may revert to all green. The all-green form is more robust, so be vigilant about removing any parts that lose variegation, or the entire shrub will revert.

PLANTING REQUIREMENTS
Prefers a shady location in average, well-drained garden soil with average moisture. pH can range from neutral to slightly acidic. Kerria sends out

suckers that can eventually create a large mass. If this is not desirable, plant in a large container sunk into the ground, or site it in a confined space where it cannot overrun its boundaries. Since it blooms on last year's wood, prune after flowering to encourage flower production for the following year.

PROPAGATION
Dig rooted suckers in February or March. Take softwood cuttings in summer or hardwood cuttings in winter.

Spicebush (*Lindera benzoin*)
Zones 4–9
6–12 feet tall
Native to U.S.
MOIST SOIL REQUIRED

When I walk the trails at a nearby city park in early spring I am always delighted to come upon Spicebush, its leafless branches laden with clusters of greenish-yellow flowers. Winter-weary gardeners love bringing these spice-scented branches into the house. In autumn, the dark green leaves of this large, upright shrub are transformed to a mass of glowing yellow. Male shrubs of this dioecious species have slightly larger flowers. If a male is nearby, the female shrubs will be adorned with showy, bright red oval berries in the fall, which persist long after they shed their colorful leaves. Birds and small mammals love these fruits.

This hardy native adores a naturalized setting and is a good anchor for a mixed shrub border or biohedge. Its leaves are a larval food source for the Spicebush Swallowtail Butterfly.

PLANTING REQUIREMENTS
Prefers humus-rich, moist, well-drained, slightly acidic to neutral soil in heavy to part shade, or even full sun. Mulch to help retain adequate soil moisture; it will not thrive if the soil becomes too dry.

PROPAGATION
In fall, place ripened berries in a sieve under barely warm running water. Rub gently to remove the pulp and plant the seeds immediately, or cold-stratify 3 months and plant in the spring.

Common Ninebark (*Physocarpus opulifolius*)
Zones 2–7
7–10 feet tall/wide
Native to U.S.

Some people object to the smell of the small white, ball-shaped flowers that bloom in spring, but hummingbirds love the nectar. This arching, spirea-like shrub has curious reddish-brown inflated pod-like fruits, bronzy gold autumn leaves, and exfoliating shaggy reddish-brown bark. Plant Ninebark at the back of a biohedge to encourage wildlife, use it as a hedge, or naturalize it in a woodland setting.

'Nanus' is a dwarf form, seldom exceeding 2–3 feet. Yellow to lime green leaves are the hallmark of 'Luteus' and 'Nugget' as well as the more compact 'Dart's Gold', sometimes sold as 'Gold Dart' and said to be the best yellow-leaf cultivar. The rich purple foliage of 'Diablo' does not fade in the heat of summer. Var. *intermedius*, native to Minnesota and smaller than the species, matures at about 3½ feet. It is a good choice for foundation plantings. A western species, Mountain Ninebark (*P. monogymus*) Zones 4–7, is a tiny, compact shrub, seldom growing taller than 3 feet. It flowers in midsummer.

PLANTING REQUIREMENTS
This indestructible shrub will tolerate full sun to dense shade, moist, average, or even dry soil. Its only requirement is good drainage. If it becomes leggy or unkempt, cut to the ground in the winter when it is dormant and it will rejuvenate in spring.

PROPAGATION
Plant ripened seed in the fall, or root softwood cuttings in moist sand or peat in midsummer.

Pieris (*Pieris* spp.)
Zones (4)5–8
10–12 feet tall
Japan
Deer Resistant

Japanese Pieris (*Pieris japonica*), also known as Andromeda and Lily-of-the-Valley Shrub, is a broad-leaved evergreen. In early spring, it is covered with pendulous racemes of creamy-white flowers.

The deep green leaves of slow-growing 'Variegata' are generously edged with yellowish-white. This striking plant is a favorite for small gardens and can even be grown successfully in a container when it is young. However, don't keep it containerized too long, because it eventually matures at 10–12 feet. There are many cultivars that offer gardeners a wide palette of colors and sizes. 'Pygmaea' is so tiny it can be grown in a trough garden when it is young. It will eventually mature at 1–3 feet. 'Prelude', a semi-dwarf with pink buds and pure white flowers, only grows 12–14 inches tall and is perfect—and perfectly lovely—for the front of a perennial border.

Mountain Pieris, native to the southeastern U.S., is neither as showy nor as readily available as the popular Japanese Pieris. It is slightly more cold tolerant. In the spring, this broad-leaved evergreen is covered with upright racemes of white flowers that show off nicely against dark green leaves. 'Millstream' has large, fragrant flowering panicles that can last up to a month.

Hybrids of *Pieris floribunda* × *japonica* are reputedly more heat tolerant than either parent. 'Brouwer's Beauty' has horizontal panicles of white flowers that arch ever so slightly. Deep purplish-red buds appear in late summer, providing additional interest. It grows 5–6 feet tall and wide.

PLANTING REQUIREMENTS
Plant in moist, humus-rich, acidic soil in a protected spot in part to light dappled shade. Good drainage is critical. It does not appreciate wind. Prune immediately after flowering. The flower buds develop in late summer and if they are cut off, the plant will not flower the following year. Watch for Lacebugs.

PROPAGATION
Plant ripened seed immediately. Take cuttings in the fall.

Fragrant Sumac (*Rhus aromatica* 'Gro-Low')
Zones 3–9
2–4 feet tall
Native to U.S.

Fragrant Sumac can be 2–6 feet tall, but the cultivar 'Gro-Low' rarely gets taller than 2 feet and makes an outstanding ground cover. Or use it as a mass planting on a hillside. Short spikes of yellowish flowers bloom on the ends of the branches in April, just as the new leaves are emerging. Brilliant orangey-red foliage and bright red, fuzzy berries are a knockout in the fall. In addition to being handsome, this sturdy shrub will thrive in a difficult site.

PLANTING REQUIREMENTS
Fragrant Sumac suckers heavily. It is not particular about soil or moisture, but does insist on good drainage. It prefers full sun, but will do fine in part shade.

PROPAGATION
Remove the pulp from the ripe seeds and plant in the fall.

Clove Currant (*Ribes odoratum*)
Zones 3–7
5–7 feet tall
Native to U.S.

Yellow flowers stud the branches of this compact, twiggy shrub in early spring, filling the air with the delicious scent of cloves. Its bluish-green leaves change to shades of red and yellow in autumn. Incorporate in a biohedge or naturalize at the edge of a woodland. It is very similar to Golden Currant (*R. aureum*), a yellow-fruited species that is also hardy in Zone 3. The cultivar 'Crandall' is most widely grown and has large, black, edible fruits that make delicious jelly. Alpine Currant (*R. alpinum*), Zones 3–7, hails from Europe and is slightly smaller, maturing at 3–6 feet tall. Its inconspicuous flowers cannot compete with the native species, nor does it have any fall color. However, this adaptable shrub makes an attractive hedge or foundation planting. The females of this dioecious species produce handsome berries. The males are less susceptible to White Pine Blister Rust than the females, so are often the shrub of choice. The cultivar 'Green Mound' is a dense semi-dwarf that quickly reaches 3–4 feet in height. Slow growing 'Pumilum' pokes along, taking its time to eventually reach a mature height of 3 feet.

PLANTING REQUIREMENTS
Currant bushes are not fussy about pH and will thrive in full sun, part or light shade, in just about any average, well-drained garden soil.

PROPAGATION
Remove the pulp from ripened seed and plant in the fall. Take softwood cuttings in midsummer.

Bridalwreath (*Spiraea prunifolia* 'Plena')
Zones 4–8
3–7 feet tall
China
Deer Resistant

Old homesteads and Bridalwreaths go together "like love and marriage." The best form of this old-fashioned shrub is 'Plena', with double white blossoms that look like miniature roses in midspring. Harrison Flint reports that 'Plena' is "actually the species type since it was the first form given the name *S. prunifolia*, even though it is a horticultural form." The leaves of 'Plena' turn a clear yellow in the fall.

To prune, cut out ⅓ of the oldest branches at ground level after flowering; otherwise, simply leave it alone. This graceful, arching shrub should never be sheared to resemble a formal hedge.

Note: Japanese Spirea is not recommended (see p. 87).

PLANTING REQUIREMENTS
Plant in a protected spot in Zone 4. It prefers full sun or part shade, in slightly acidic, average garden soil that is neither too wet nor too dry.

PROPAGATION
Softwood cuttings root easily in summer. Sow ripened seeds in fall.

Common Snowberry (*Symphoricarpos albus*)
Indian Currant (*Symphoricarpos orbiculatus*)
Zones 3–8
3–5 feet tall
Native to U.S.

These hardy natives, grown primarily for their fall crop of showy round berries, all sucker heavily and provide excellent erosion control. Snowberry (*S. albus*), also called

Waxberry, may be the best species to plant since it seems least susceptible to mildew. Clusters of stark white, rounded fruit hang on in September, persisting until winter. Western Snowberry (var. *laevigatus*) has even larger glowing white fruit.

Indian Currant is also commonly known as Coralberry, Buckbrush, and Turkey Berry. Hardy in Zones 2–7, it grows 2–5 feet tall and 4–8 feet wide. The pinkish white flowers borne in midsummer are relatively insignificant, but its fruit is another story. Large clusters of berries of varying shades of red hang on the branches from midfall to winter, so that mass plantings create a reddish haze. This widely naturalized shrub has a white-fruited cultivar, 'Leucocarpus', and a yellow-edged cultivar, 'Foliis Variegatus'.

A hybrid, Chenault Coralberry (*S.* × *chenaultii*), is hardy in Zones 5–8, or Zone 4 with protection. Its shorter, hardier cultivar 'Hancock' is mildew-resistant and thrives in Zones 4–8. Both have pink flowers that produce two-toned fruits, red on the sunny side and white on the shady side. 'Hancock' only grows 18–24 inches tall but can spread up to 12 feet wide!

PLANTING REQUIREMENTS

These adaptable natives are not fussy about pH, soil type, or even moisture, and tolerate dry soil once they are established. They are a good choice for alkaline, clay soils. Plant in part to light shade, or full sun. Space new ground cover plantings 3–4 feet apart.

PROPAGATION

Remove pulp to exposed ripened seed and sow in the fall. Take softwood cuttings in summer, or dig and transplant rooted suckers.

Lowbush Blueberry (*Vaccinium angustifolium*)
Zones 2–5
6–24 inches tall
Native to U.S.
Good Ground Cover

If there is a spot in your landscape that cries out for a mass planting and the growing requirements can be met, Lowbush Blueberry makes a great low-maintenance ground cover. And wait till those luscious berries ripen! Its only demand is soil with a pH below 5.5. The narrow leaves change to red, scarlet, and crimson in the fall, brightening up the landscape. The cultivar 'Leucocarpum' has white fruits. The most common commercial variety is the heavier fruiting *laevifolium*.

PLANTING REQUIREMENTS
Plant in well-drained, acidic soil in part shade or full sun, and give it plenty of room to run at will. Do not fertilize. It adapts to dry planting sites, although it will also tolerate consistently moist areas. Plant 12–18 inches apart.

PROPAGATION
Dig rooted suckers, divide plants in spring, or take cuttings in early summer.

Highbush Blueberry (*Vaccinium corymbosum*)
Zones 4–8
6–10 feet tall
Native to U.S.
MOIST SOIL REQUIRED

If you possess a partly shaded or sunny spot with naturally *acidic, consistently moist, rich, loamy, well-drained* soil, then Highbush Blueberry should be number one on your low-maintenance wish list. This handsome shrub will delight you with delicate pinkish-white flowers in spring, scrumptious blueberries in midsummer, glossy green leaves that change to brilliant shades of red, yellow, and orange in the fall, and winter stems of yellow-green or red.

But don't despair if your soil is *not* optimal. It is possible to amend existing soil in order to grow it, but low maintenance it will not be. And speaking of maintenance, some gardeners elect to cover bushes with netting if the birds become too greedy. To make fruit gathering easier, others prune their bushes 6–8 feet high. This compact shrub can be planted near the back of a perennial border, incorporated into the vegetable garden, or used as a focal point in the yard. Combine with zone-hardy acid-lovers like Rhododendron, Azaleas, Laurels, Enkianthius, and other ericaceous plants for a great biohedge.

The leaves of Highbush Blueberry are a larval food source for the Spring Azure and Hairstreak butterflies. Over 53 species of wildlife, including birds, butterflies, red fox, and grouse, enjoy the delicious fruits. Plant more than one variety for bigger and better fruit production. Cultivars hardy in Zones 5–8 include 'Atlantic', 'Blue Crop', 'Blue Ray', 'Herbert', 'Ivanhoe', and 'Jersey', each maturing at 6–8 feet. Check with nurseries or the local extension agent to identify varieties that are best for your area.

PLANTING REQUIREMENTS
Demands moist, acidic soil. Amend existing soil with good compost, humus, or peat, test the pH annually to be sure it is (and stays) below 5.2, keep the planting environment moist, and who knows? You may be rewarded with blueberries for your cereal, or maybe even enough for a pie—assuming you can beat the birds to the fruit.

PROPAGATION
Root softwood cuttings taken in May. Purchase balled and burlapped or container-grown specimens from the local nursery.

Cowberry (*Vaccinium vitis-idaea*)
Zones 2–5
6–10 inches tall
Native to US
Good Ground Cover

Cowberry, also known as Foxberry or Lowbush Cranberry, is a neat little evergreen that rewards its owner with pretty pinkish-white flowers, edible dark red fruits that are similar in taste and use to common cranberries, and shiny green leaves that change to burgundy red, brightening the winter landscape.

Mountain Cranberry (subspecies *minus*), also known as Lingonberry, is evergreen and extremely cold hardy. This alpine form hates hot summers, so is a choice for gardeners in cooler climes. It creates a dense mat of lustrous green leaves that set off the pretty pink flowers and edible cranberry red fruits. The best cultivar may be a University of Wisconsin selection named 'Splendor', which has larger fruits and grows about 8–15 inches tall.

PLANTING REQUIREMENTS
Needs humus-rich, acidic, moist soil and will thrive in either partial shade or full sun. It will tolerate consistently moist planting sites, but does not appreciate dry soil.

PROPAGATION
Divide plants in spring. Cuttings taken in early summer will often—but
not always—root.

Mapleleaf Viburnum (*Viburnum acerifolium*)
Zones 3–8
4–6 feet tall
Native to U.S.

Mapleleaf Viburnum is another small but mighty shrub. Maple-like
leaves change to shades of glowing red in the fall on this shade lover.
Flat, fuzzy clusters of yellowish-white flowers appear in early summer,
followed by glistening black berries that hang on until early winter. This
underused native is nice on a hillside or planted ahead of taller viburnums
in a biohedge. It is also known as Maple-leaved Arrowwood.

In the wild, it can be found growing with Wild Geranium, Solomon
Seal, White and Red Oaks, Beech, and Sugar Maples.

PLANTING REQUIREMENTS
Although it prefers moist or average soil, it will thrive even in difficult,
dry planting locations. It does equally well in full shade or full sun.

PROPAGATION
Remove pulp and plant seed in the fall. Root softwood cuttings in
summer.

Hobblebush (*Viburnum alnifolium*)
Zones 2–8
8–10 feet tall
Native to U.S.
MOIST SOIL REQUIRED

Naturalize Hobblebush in moist areas where it will quickly spread,
covering large areas. Its white flowers bloom in June. Reddish fruits hang
on the branches, changing to blue-black in the fall. Downy leaves emerge
in spring, but soon become smooth. They change to shades of bright red
in the fall.

PLANTING REQUIREMENTS
Hobblebush needs moist, humus rich, well-drained soil in part shade.

PROPAGATION
Branches touching the ground will root and can be dug and transplanted.

Burkwood Viburnum (*Viburnum* × *burkwoodii*)
Zones 4–8
8–10 feet tall
Hybrid

In early spring, exceedingly fragrant, creamy white ball-like flower clusters cover Burkwood Viburnum, the "child" of *V. carlesii* and *V. utilis*. As the summer progresses, its red fruits glisten against the rough, dark green leaves. Slowly changing to gleaming black, these small oval berries are loved by wildlife. The burgundy-red fall foliage will enhance any mixed shrub border or biohedge. Plant close to a patio or walkway where the spicy scent can be appreciated.

'Mohawk', a hybrid of *V.* × *burkwoodii* and *V. carlesii*, is reputed to have greater disease resistance and cold hardiness. 'Chesapeake' has shiny green foliage that turns rich red in the fall.

PLANTING REQUIREMENTS
Plant in average, well-drained soil that is neutral to slightly acidic in part shade or full sun. Burkwood is probably a better choice for Zone 4 gardeners than Korean Spice Viburnum because the latter's buds are more often killed by late spring freezes.

PROPAGATION
Cuttings taken in midsummer will root easily.

Korean Spice Viburnum (*Viburnum carlesii*)
Zones 4–7
4–8 feet tall/wide
Korea

In late April or early May, I love to sit on my backyard swing, sipping a cup of coffee and breathing in the wonderful fragrance of a nearby Korean Spice Viburnum. Growing in deep shade, its form is more open and rangy than those grown in more sun, but it still flowers profusely, filling the air with its spicy scent. Our shrub never exhibits more than dull red foliage in fall, perhaps because of the absence of sun. I have seen more brightly colored specimens in sunnier spots. Two cultivars provide smaller versions of the species. 'Aurora' seldom exceeds 5 feet while 'Compactum' only grows 2–4 feet tall. The latter is a good choice for smaller spots, or to for the front of a shrub border.

PLANTING REQUIREMENTS
Plant Korean Spicebush in average, well-drained, neutral to slightly acidic soil in part shade or full sun. Site in a protected spot in Zone 4 (see Burkwood Viburnum above).

PROPAGATION
Root softwood cuttings taken in summer. Remove the pulp from ripened seed and plant in fall. Try to obtain nursery plants growing on their own roots rather than grafted specimens, because cutting out recurring shoots of the more vigorous grafting understock will increase maintenance.

Withe Rod (*Viburnum cassinoides*)
Zones 2–8
5–7 feet tall
Native to U.S.

Shade-loving Withe Rod has soft green foliage, flat white flower clusters, and bunches of blue-black fruits that the birds will fight for. It is an undemanding, adaptable, neat shrub with an upright growth habit, perfect for a biohedge.

PLANTING REQUIREMENTS
Plant in average, well-drained soil in part shade to sun.

PROPAGATION
Softwood cuttings taken in early summer will root easily.

Arrowwood Viburnum (*Viburnum dentatum*)
Zones 3–8
6–10 feet tall
Native to U.S.

We planted a trio of this upright shrub at the top of a hill to give a solid backdrop for the other natives tumbling down the hillside. In May and June fuzzy looking flat-topped flower clusters peep out from new dark green leaves. Huge bunches of bluish-black grape-like fruits ripen in the fall. Birds love them. Autumn leaves become rusty red.

Arrowwood is one of the best viburnums for shady spots. It is adaptable, disease resistant, and maintenance free. 'Autumn Jazz' is a vase-shaped form with beautiful multicolored foliage in shades of red, wine-red, orange, and yellow.

PLANTING REQUIREMENTS
Plant in average, well-drained, neutral to slightly acidic soil in full shade to full sun.

PROPAGATION
Remove pulp and sow ripened seed in fall. Softwood cuttings taken in summer root easily.

Linden Viburnum (*Viburnum dilatatum*)
Zones 5–7
8–10 feet tall
Asia

Birds flock to Linden Viburnum in the fall to gobble its sweet scarlet fruits. The contrast of these brightly colored berries, first against bright green leaves and then against burgundy-red autumn leaves, creates a striking ongoing picture in the fall. This is another great viburnum to create a hedge, add to a mixed shrub border, or mark property boundaries. It needs to be cross-pollinated by other viburnum species or its fruiting will be minimal.

Several cultivars are available, including 'Catskill', a slow-growing compact form whose height seldom exceeds 5 feet, and 'Iroquois', often grown as an 8–10 foot tall privacy screen. Since these two cultivars flower simultaneously, planting both will assure abundant fruit.

PLANTING REQUIREMENTS
Plant in average, well-drained, neutral to slightly acidic soil in part shade or sun.

PROPAGATION
Take cuttings in early summer for best results.

Fragrant Viburnum (*Viburnum farreri*)
Zones 5–8
8–12 feet tall
China

Sweetly fragrant pink and white flowers bloom in early spring before the leaves emerge. Displayed on rosy-red stems (petioles), the coarse, serrated medium green leaves change to a deep red in the fall. For an interesting contrast, add 'Album', the white-flowered form, which has green leaf petioles. 'Nanum' is a slow-growing cultivar that seldom gets taller than 3 feet.

PLANTING REQUIREMENTS
Plant in average, well-drained, slightly acidic to neutral soil in part shade or sun. Harrison Flint recommends planting this near water, if possible, to mitigate fluctuating temperature swings that can kill the flower buds.

PROPAGATION
Softwood cuttings rooted in early summer are more apt to survive the winter.

Judd Viburnum (*Viburnum × juddii*)
Zones 4–7
6–8 feet tall
Korea, Japan
Hybrid

For spicy-sweet–smelling flowers of a delicate pink covering a nicely rounded multistemmed shrub, choose Judd Viburnum. A hybrid of *V. carlesii* and *V. bitchiuense*, it is disease resistant, fragrant, medium sized, and fantastic for shady locations. It appears to be more heat and cold tolerant than either of its parents. The dainty buds emerge rosy red and last quite a while before exploding into open clusters of pink. And the fragrance is heavenly.

PLANTING REQUIREMENTS
Plant in average, well-drained, neutral to slightly acidic soil in part shade or sun.

PROPAGATION
Cut softwood branches in early to midsummer and root.

Wayfaring Tree (*Viburnum lantana*)
Zones 4–8
Europe
10–15 feet

If your soil is alkaline clay, Wayfaring Tree is the viburnum to choose for shady spots. Dependable, adaptable, handsome, wildlife attractant, maintenance free—all accurately describe it. Flat, creamy white flower clusters bedeck this shrub in late spring. In fall, pendulous clumps of individual fruits hang from the branches, changing from yellows and greens to shades of rose, pink, and red, climaxing as shiny black. And how impressive they look against the vivid red foliage!

Plant Wayfaring Tree where you can see it from indoors to enjoy the seasonal changes—and to watch the continual visits by birds seeking out its tasty berries. Use this shrub in a mixed border, as a hedge, privacy screen, or to soften the corners of a building.

For a similar but smaller, more compact shrub, look for 'Mohican'. A yellow-leaf cultivar, 'Aureum', is also available.

PLANTING REQUIREMENTS

Accepts limey soil, clay, average soil, moist loam—you name it. This sturdy fellow is not fussy, and thrives in shade or sun.

PROPAGATION

Sow seed that is not fully ripe in the fall. It will be red, not black. Remove the outer pulp before planting. Dig rooted suckers and transplant.

Prague Viburnum (*Viburnum* × *pragense*)
Zones 5–8
8–10 feet tall
Hybrid

Prague Viburnum, a hybrid of *V. rhytidophyllum* and *V. utile*, has long, narrow, heavily textured leaves of deep gleaming green that may remain evergreen in Zones 6–8. In late spring, large numbers of fragrant white flowers burst forth all over this medium sized shrub. This is another good choice for a mixed shrub border or privacy hedge.

PLANTING REQUIREMENTS

Plant in average, well-drained soil in part shade to sun.

PROPAGATION

Softwood cuttings taken in early summer will root easily.

Doublefile Viburnum (*Viburnum plicatum* var. *tomentosum*)
Zones 5–8
8–12 feet tall
China, Japan
MOIST SOIL REQUIRED

Check out Doublefile Viburnum with its huge flattened balls of bright snowy white flowers that lavishly cover the dark green heavily veined leaves in early summer. This horizontally branched shrub gets the name Doublefile from the flower structure. A cluster of fertile flowers in the center, surrounded by sterile flowers around the outside, creates a flower that resembles a lace cap.

'Shasta' has a more pronounced horizontal growth habit. Although it seldom grows taller than 5–6 feet, can become as wide as 12 feet. Its flowers and fruits are larger and showier than the species. A seedling of 'Shasta' called 'Shoshoni' is its twin except for its shorter 3–4-feet stature. 'Summer Snowflake' and 'Watanabe' both put on a spectacular show of creamy white flowers in spring, and then tease the gardener with additional flower clusters that suddenly appear from midsummer to midautumn, sometimes blooming alongside black fruits and colorful red autumn leaves. Unfortunately, neither is dependably hardy north of Zones 6–8.

PLANTING REQUIREMENTS
Doublefile Viburnum will grow in full shade or full sun as long as the planting site is consistently moist and well drained. This species will languish and sicken if the soil becomes too dry in the heat of summer.

PROPAGATION
Plant ripened seed immediately. Take softwood cuttings and root in early summer.

Downy Arrowwood (*Viburnum rafinesquianum*)
Zones 2–8
5–7 feet tall
Native to U.S.

Dense flat white flower clusters appear in June. In the fall, bluish black berries ripen to tempt local birds. This shrub has a rounded mound-like growth habit and can be used as a hedge, or in a mixed shrub border.

In wild areas, this native is typically found in oak woodlands.

PLANTING REQUIREMENTS

Downy Arrowwood does well in average, well-drained soil, including clay. It thrives in either part shade or full sun.

PROPAGATION

Take softwood cuttings in summer.

American Highbush Cranberry (*Viburnum trilobum*)

Zones 2–8

10–15 feet tall

Native to U.S.

This may be one of the best-known viburnums. Its flat white flower-heads are 2–3 inches across and open in June. Long stamens give them a fuzzy, fluffy appearance. Scarlet fruits beginning in August and persisting until midwinter are tasty fresh and make delicious jams, jellies, and even fruit juice. It has dark green foliage and spectacular autumn color.

For a smaller space, choose 'Compactum'. It only grows 5–6 feet tall and wide. Note: European Cranberry Bush is not recommended (see p. 87). See chapter 3 (small trees) for further viburnum selections.

PLANTING REQUIREMENTS

Plant in average garden soil in light or part shade, or in full sun. It thrives in neutral to acidic pH.

PROPAGATION

Cuttings taken in summer root easily.

Yellowroot (*Xanthorhiza simplicissima*)

Zones 4–8

1–3 feet tall

Native to U.S.

Good Ground Cover

Yellowroot creates a soft reddish purple haze when clusters of small flowers burst into bloom in midspring. This pretty, low-growing shrub has yellow roots and finely toothed dark green leaves arranged in three to five parts, which turn soft shades of yellow and orange in the fall. It will create an effective ground cover in short order.

PLANTING REQUIREMENTS

Yellowroot prefers moist, well-drained soil in shade or part sun, but will tolerate just about any planting environment including wet or dry sites. The more light it receives, the more aggressive it becomes. Its rambunctious spirit can be contained by planting it near concrete driveways or sidewalks, or close to a building.

PROPAGATION

Dig rooted suckers in spring and transplant. Cuttings can be rooted in early summer.

Not Recommended

Japanese Barberry (*Berberis thunbergii*)
Zones 4–8
2–6 feet tall/wide
Asia

The popular Japanese Barberry grows in sun or shade, in just about any type of soil. Promoted worldwide, it is found at all garden centers and is a visible presence in landscapes across the Midwest. Most cultivars have been hybridized from var. *atropurpurea* and include 'Crimson Pygmy', 'Rose Glow', and 'Aurea'. When it escapes to the wild, it spreads uncontrollably.

Russian Olive (*Elaeagnus augustifolia*)
Zones 2–7
10–15 feet tall
Europe, Asia

Widely planted by Midwestern highway departments, Russian Olive's attractive silvery leaves are easily identifiable by passing motorists. Who could have imagined this shrub, touted for erosion control and as a wildlife habitat, could become such a threat to so many areas? Its larger sibling, Autumn Olive (*E. umbellata*), grows equally well in zones 3–8. Control is difficult. Even periodic burning does not eliminate these tenacious shrubs. Definitely not recommended.

Burning Bush (*Euonymus alatus*)
Zones 3–8
8–12 feet tall
Asia

 This has always been one of my favorites because of its intense red fall foliage. It does well in full sun or deep shade, and is not fussy about pH, soil, or moisture. It grows happily in moist or dry spots, so it is truly maintenance free. How unfortunate it has escaped to the wild. This is probably largely due to the abundant berries with seeds that germinate readily. And of course we cannot control where our feathered friends "plant" the seeds they gather. I cannot recommend it. Plant *Aronia arbutifolia* 'Brilliantissima' (Red Chokeberry, see p. 50) instead.

Privet (*Ligustrum* spp.)
Zones 3–8
12–15 feet tall
Europe, China, Japan

 The privet hedge is a familiar sight in cities, towns, and villages across the U.S. Its need for heavy pruning means ongoing maintenance. Allowed to grow naturally, privet produces odiferous white flowers and black berries relished by birds. This heavily suckering plant has spread far and wide, particularly in the eastern U.S. A thicket-maker, Privet displaces desirable native plants as it strides through natural areas. It is a real survivor—nearly impossible to get rid of once established. Don't plant it.

Bush Honeysuckle (*Lonicera* cultivars and species)
Zones 4–9
8–12 feet tall
Asia

 Talk about *invasive exotics!* Amur Honeysuckle (*Lonicera maackii*), Tatarian Honeysuckle (*L. tatarica*), and Morrow Honeysuckle (*L. morrowii*) abound all across the U.S. Masses of them line streets and roadways, invade parks and natural areas. Birds do gobble the berries—and disseminate the seeds widely—but these berries are essentially junk food, providing few nutrients. Exotic honeysuckles create such a dense canopy, virtually nothing grows beneath them. Some emit a substance toxic to other plants nearby. Their foliage begins part way up the stems so that nesting birds become easy prey for feral cats and carnivorous wildlife. Our native honeysuckles can provide much safer nesting sites, and give wildflowers and other native plants the right to exist beneath their branches.

Japanese Spirea (*Spiraea japonica*)
Zones 4-8
3–6 feet tall
Asia

Although they may not know the name, many Americans recognize the shrub with the bright pinkish-lavender, flat-topped flowers that bloom in summer. Numerous cultivars are available. Unfortunately, this popular shrub loves streambanks, roadsides, woodlands, and fields, and has established large colonies in the wild. Because it is more aggressive than native plants, natives are displaced and wildlife habitat suffers. Besides, the pink flowers require constant deadheading so as not to become *brown* flowers.

European Cranberry Viburnum (*Viburnum opulus*)
Zones 3–8
8–10 feet tall
Europe

Viburnums are fantastic for shady spots, and European Cranberry Bush is no exception. Unfortunately, this adaptable exotic displaces the native viburnums, altering the ecosystem and changing the wildlife habitat, so here is one that is not recommended. Our native Highbush Cranberry has better fall color, greater disease resistance, and appears to be more cold tolerant, so it is a better choice anyway.

5.

Good Things in Small Packages

Dwarf Conifers for Shade

'Bright Gold' Yew

Modern gardeners are finally discovering the beauty and diversity of dwarf conifers. Unlike bonsai, these evergreen mutations of familiar full-sized conifers do not need special attention to control their ultimate size. Use as a focal point, to accent shrub or perennial gardens, in rock gardens, or in a conifers-only display bed. The tiniest ones make great additions to trough gardens, and miniature train enthusiasts use them to make their "landscapes" look realistic. Few plants are so versatile! Because of their slow growth habit, many of these little plants may eventually become collector's items, increasing in value. As dwarf conifer expert Robert Obrizok counsels, "The little bun that you plant today may be worth a bundle in the future!"

Although I refer to the plants in this chapter as dwarf conifers, let me add that in the conifer nursery trade, the label "dwarf" is also used in another, more specific way. The *annual rate of growth* determines how a particular plant is listed. Full-sized conifers grow 12 or more inches per year, maturing at over 15 feet in 10 years; intermediate, 6–12 inches with a 10-year size of 6–15 feet; dwarf, 1–6 inches and 1–6 feet at 10 years; and miniature, less than 1 inch per year and less than 1 foot at 10 years. Obviously, growth can be affected by climatic and environmental conditions, so these numbers may vary. The height and width listed for each cultivar is the projected size at 10 years.

Shade has always been a challenge for the conifer aficionado. This chapter lists and briefly describes currently available cultivars that will thrive in shade, chosen primarily from what I call "the shady Ts"—*Taxus, Thuja*, and *Tsuga. Tsuga* has the most offerings, followed by *Thuja* and *Taxus* respectively.

Conifer choices are legion, with enough sizes and shapes to satisfy just about any gardening needs. The number and variety of sizes, shapes, and colors now in the nursery trade are amazing; the list increases annually, and, in fact, has caused some confusion. Whenever possible, gardeners are advised to select individual plants in person. Check in specialty catalogs (see Resources) for many more choices. Or go to the American Conifer Society's website. And if you really get hooked, you may even want to join this venerable organization.

Unless indicated, most of these unique plants are hardy in Zones 4–7. A few are listed as hardy in Zones 2 or 3, and others only to Zone 5, so take note of the hardiness specifications. Yes, it is possible for your little evergreen to don "winter wraps," but that increases maintenance. Besides, winter interest is important. It is a joy to look out the window from November to March and see that welcome touch of color in the winter garden.

Several of these cultivars need some shade in both winter and summer. Winter burn often occurs on evergreens sited in bright sunlight. The snow reflects the sun, intensifying its rays. If your precious dwarf gets a sunburn, lightly shearing off burned tips in the spring can encourage it to grow out of its winter damage.

Sometimes even zone-hardy plants succumb in the winter because of poor pruning practices. Often one finds plants in 1 or 2 gallon pots with no central leader. I am not sure why growers do this: perhaps to create an attractive plant that is both bushy and compact. However, as that little fellow grows, the multiple leaders will each vie for top billing, eventually creating a mature specimen that is much more susceptible to snow and ice damage. Often a beautiful conifer is ruined when one of the leaders breaks from the extra weight, leaving a bare space. Then you may have to remove the plant and begin again. It makes more sense to figure out which is the central leader at planting time. Immediately tip prune the rest back slightly to encourage them to be laterals instead. You will be glad you did.

A few additional notes about pruning. You cannot—*repeat, cannot*—prune an evergreen branch back to bare wood. Be sure to leave at least a few needles on each branch. Unlike deciduous trees, most evergreen branches will not regrow if no green growth is left after the pruning cut. If you take all the needles off, you have killed that branch. Study the shape of the conifer and begin with maintenance pruning, finishing with aesthetic pruning, rather than the reverse. Never prune when the conifer is wet because this encourages disease. Dip your pruning shears into denatured alcohol after each cut, particularly if there is any disease present (a wise practice regardless of what you are pruning, conifer or no).

Dwarf conifers can be expensive, especially the smallest ones—for good reason. Those that are extremely slow growing can take a long time to reach a "sellable" size. However, these tiny gems seldom if ever outgrow their space. The old adage "You get what you pay for" is particularly true with dwarf conifers. Yes, you can find cute little 1-gallon sized plants for $5.97, but beware. Some of these will grow like Topsy, turning into full-sized conifers. Becoming knowledgeable about mature sizes and then shopping correctly may save you the trouble of pulling out an overgrown shrub with your SUV and relocating it. Do some preliminary measuring to match the projected mature size to your planting space and save yourself some backbreaking work. Even if it costs a little more.

That being said, I also encourage you to check local chain or discount nurseries, and even lumber yards and stores such as Target, Wal-Mart, and Kmart when plants are first delivered in the spring. These stores order semi-truckloads of plants and often, when the total order comes up short, special plants are added to "finish the load."

The popularity of dwarf conifers has increased tremendously over the past decade. There is a certain fascination with owning a miniature tree or shrub. And when hostas and daylilies die to the ground and disappear, those little conifers will still be a visual treat even in the snow. No, *especially* in the snow.

PLANTING REQUIREMENTS

Unless indicated, most of the dwarf conifers listed below require moist, humus-rich, well-drained soil in part to medium shade. Many appreciate shelter from the wind to prevent winter burn. Some will benefit by a spray of antidesiccant, and like any full-sized conifer, dwarfs going into the winter season need to be well watered.

PROPAGATION

The best advice for propagation is "Purchase from a reputable nursery." Dwarf conifers do not generally come true from seed, and many seeds are not even viable. Most are nursery-propagated by grafting or by rooted cuttings. Since many dwarf conifers grow only a few inches in 25–30 years, I am certainly not going to suggest "starting" dwarf conifers. Just get out your checkbook!

Dwarf Conifers for Shade
Yew (*Taxus*)

THE PARENT . . .
Japanese Yew (*Taxus cuspidata*)
Zones 3–7
10–40 feet high
10–40 feet wide

Japanese Yew is undoubtedly one of the best *full-sized* evergreen species for shade, although it will also thrive in part to full sun. Buds form on both old and new wood, so heavy shearing does not impair it. Ample foliage grows to the inside, unlike many other evergreens, making for easy, foolproof pruning. The flattened, deep green needles are thick and almost succulent. Rather than cones, yews produce fat, red urn-shaped berries that are poisonous.

Although yews enjoy moist, humus-rich soil, they cannot tolerate deep planting and abhor poor drainage, a fault that will invariably lead to decline and death. These conifers are not troubled by sea salt.

To date there are not large numbers of dwarf Taxus cultivars available commercially. Note: English Yew (*Taxus baccata*) is generally not as hardy as Japanese Yew. 'Corley's Copper Tip', 'Amersfoort', and 'Dovastonii Aurea' are hardy in Zones 5–8.

THE OFFSPRING . . .
'Aurescens'
Zones 4–7
1–6 feet tall
3–6 feet wide

A male cultivar, this is basically a low-growing, compact version of its parent. Rich green foliage is highlighted by golden yellow new growth—its "claim to fame." A conifer friend reports that her specimen thrives in a southern exposure. Even though it gets full sun in both summer and winter, it suffers little to no burning. 'Aurescens' also tolerates part shade, particularly in the afternoon, but with less light the golden foliage may become more chartreuse than deep gold. It grows 1–6 inches per year.

'Bright Gold'
Zones 4–7
6–12 feet tall
6–15 feet wide

Another shade brightener, 'Bright Gold' has a lovely persistent golden yellow color. A broad upright plant with a dense, irregular branching habit, it matures wider than it is tall. Also identified as 'Dwarf Bright Gold', this slow growing, intermediate-sized conifer can increase 6–12 inches per year until maturity.

'Densa'
'Cross Spreading'
Zones 4–7
3–4 feet tall
6–12 feet wide

Wide spreading 'Densa' has short erect branches that can stretch as wide as 8 feet, but will seldom reach higher than 4 feet. In fact, this little cultivar is so slow growing that it will usually remain under 3 feet for years, requiring little or no pruning. Harrison Flint recommends it as "one of the finest low, slow-growing selections." Being a female cultivar, it will produce toxic fruit. When small children are in the household, a male cultivar may be a wiser choice.

Several conifer experts suggest that 'Cross Spreading', from Cross Nurseries in Minnesota, may be even better than 'Densa'. Extremely cold hardy, 'Cross Spreading' is known to withstand winter temperatures to −45°F with no damage.

Note: A popular cultivar with a similar name, 'Densiformis' (*Taxus* × *media*) is a completely different plant. Larger and faster growing, it is not as cold hardy and does not maintain the rich green color of 'Densa', particularly in the winter.

'Nana Aurescens'

Zones 4–7

3–6 feet tall

4–7 feet wide

Densely packed needles cover the upright branches of this handsome spreader. It increases 1–6 inches per year. Its beautiful yellow foliage gleams even more brightly in a little more sunlight.

Plant in part to light shade or in full sun. Like many yellow conifers, 'Nana Aurescens' appreciates a little afternoon shade. The Iseli catalog calls it "a conifer we are proud to offer."

'Silver Queen'

Zones 4–7

4–6 feet tall

5–8 feet wide

'Silver Queen' distinguishes herself with a lovely spring display of emerging silvery white new growth. This semi-dwarf spreads wider than it is tall, adding 6–8 inches each year.

Arborvitae (*Thuja*)

THE PARENT ...

American Arborvitae (*Thuja occidentalis*)

Zones 2–8

30–60 feet tall

10–15 feet wide

Although this familiar evergreen will grow in some shade, it is not as tolerant as either Yew or Hemlock. It dislikes windy locations and being planted on the south side of buildings. American Arborvitae is often used as a windbreak or a privacy hedge. Several dwarf cultivars are listed below. Most prefer part shade or full sun.

THE OFFSPRING . . .

'Danica'
Zones 2–8
3–4 feet tall
8–10 feet wide

If you want a compact, globe-shaped conifer, 'Danica' will fit the bill. Developed in Denmark, it grows into a bright green mound. Since it only grows 1–3 inches annually, young plants will stay 1–2 feet tall and just a tad wider for a long time. In the winter, the foliage of this cold-loving plant deepens to a stunning rich bronze with bluish shadings.

'DeGroot's Spire'
Zones 3–8
4–15 feet tall
1–4 feet wide

'DeGroot's Spire' is the dwarf conifer most likely to earn the title 'The Thin Man'. Ten-year-old specimens have been known to be only 12 inches wide at the base while stretching skyward nearly 8 feet. Now that is thin! Originating as a seedling in Ontario, Canada, 'DeGroot's Spire' can add 6–12 inches per year, but seldom gets taller than 10–15 feet. Its finely textured, dark-green fan-shaped foliage is twisted and somewhat gnarled. In winter it takes on a bronze color.

Use this unique conifer as a sentinel or plant an army of them for an interesting privacy screen.

'Golden Globe'
Zones 3–8
3–6 feet tall
3–6 feet wide

'Golden Globe' is a medium-sized, yellow cultivar that grows 6–12 inches per year. It will seldom exceed 6 feet in a decade, but can ultimately stretch 6–15 feet high. Its natural globe shape seldom needs shearing or pruning. The foliage is resistant to sunburn.

'Hetz Midget'
Zones 2–8
6–18 inches tall
6–18 inches wide

An extremely slow-growing, naturally globe-shaped conifer that needs little pruning or shaping, 'Hetz Midget' is one of the smallest Arborvitae cultivars, normally growing no more than 2 inches per year. Its layered, spray-like branches create a tight, compact ball of scaly medium-green to blue-green leaves, similar to those of the species.

Plant this cute little ball in a rock garden, edge the path, cluster a group together, or use it as a tiny specimen at the base of a boulder. A 12-inch round ball can take 20–30 years to reach its full mature size, ultimately becoming as large as 2–6 feet high and wide. Introduced in 1942, it is similar to 'Danica' and nearly identical to 'Little Gem'.

'Linesville', recently renamed 'Mr. Bowling Ball' in honor of "Chub" Harper, forms an even smaller ball of green, seldom exceeding 20–24 inches in height.

'Rheingold'
Zones 3–8
2–4 feet tall
3–4 feet wide

Seasonal color changes make 'Rheingold' a fantastic landscaping asset. Soft, almost feathery foliage emerges orangey-yellow, then changes to summer yellow followed by shades of gold, copper, and bronze. It maintains the deeper gold coloration throughout the winter.

'Rheingold' is very easy to find in the nursery trade. Its globose shape changes when it becomes a "teenager" to look more like a Hershey's Kiss, broader at the base than at the top. The early, rather fluffy foliage also changes as the plant matures, slowly becoming transformed into the typical flat fans of the species.

It forms a tight mound, a characteristic that can be maintained by annual shearing. Slow-growing 'Rheingold' only adds 1–6 inches annually and does not usually reach its mature height of 10–12 feet until it is at least 20 years old.

'Sherwood Frost'

Zones 3–7
3–6 feet tall
2–4 feet wide

This columnar beauty gets its name from the subtle frost-like, creamy-white variegation on the light green foliage. In the winter, its color changes to olive green with gold-bronze edges.

Best grown in full to part sun, 'Sherwood Frost' will also tolerate part shade. An intermediate grower, it can add as much as 6 inches a year. It is often used as a small tree. Its shape is reminiscent of 'Smaragd'.

'Smaragd'

Zones 3–7

6–15 feet tall
3–5 feet wide

Smaragd, Danish for emerald, aptly describes the bright emerald green foliage of this handsome pyramidal Arborvitae. At the American Conifer Society's website, its form is listed as "narrow upright or fastigiate." According to *Webster's, fastigiate* means "tapering to a narrow point, pyramidal." Also known as 'Emerald' or 'Emerald Green', 'Smaragd' retains its beautiful color in winter. This compact, winter-hardy cultivar is heat tolerant and resistant to spider mites. It increases 6–12 inches per year.

'Smaragd' can be vulnerable to snow and ice loads. To prevent future damage, remove any multiple stems when this cultivar is very young. Pruning to a central leader will encourage strong lateral growth, helping it to tolerate extra weight in the winter.

A relatively new variegated form called 'Emerald Variegated' has foliage liberally splashed with creamy-yellow. This narrow, pyramidal upright has an annual growth rate of 6 inches.

'Techny'

Zones 2–7

5–15 feet tall

6–8 feet wide

Popular with Midwest gardeners, dependable 'Techny' can be counted on for rich, deep green foliage in every season. It is commonly used as a privacy screen because of its tall, broad, pyramidal shape. Slow growing, it is sometimes listed as 'Mission' or 'Techny Mission'.

At a local nursery, a friend found specimens with light green foliage and coarse texture that were labeled 'Techny'. Since 'Techny' is dark green and finely textured, she suspected they were mislabeled. Examine plants closely before you purchase them to be sure that what you want is what you are getting.

'Woodwardii'

Zones 4–7

3–6 feet tall

5–7 feet wide

'Woodwardii' is a well-known, readily available conifer that retains its rounded globe shape with little or no pruning, unlike many of the commonly used foundation shrubs. It usually matures a little wider than it is tall. This popular evergreen is dependable, fast growing, and has pretty, dark-green foliage that changes in the winter to a bronzy-brown.

Its form is similar to 'Globosa' and 'Little Giant'. 'Globosa', more finely textured, is the slowest growing of the three, maturing at 2–3 feet in 20–30 years. Typical of *Thuja* species, these cultivars are apt to have multiple trunks and long vertical branching, making them vulnerable to heavy snow and ice loads. Do not plant where snow will be piled on top of them because they can open up in the middle from the weight. The resulting disfigurement is usually permanent. If snow and ice are "givens" in your area, consider substituting 'Linesville' aka 'Mr. Bowling Ball' or 'Recurva Nana'. These two globe-shaped conifers have a stronger lateral branching habit and as a result can withstand more weight.

Good Things in Small Packages
Hemlock (*Tsuga*)

THE PARENT . . .
Canadian Hemlock (*Tsuga canadensis*)
Zones 3–7
40–80 feet tall
25–35 feet wide
Native to U.S.

Also known as Eastern Hemlock, full-sized Canadian Hemlock is another great choice for those difficult shady spots. In fact, this delicate, flat-needled evergreen actually prefers shade. Its dark green, pendulous branches glow with light green in early summer when the new growth tips emerge. Florists love its small, persistent cones.

Hemlocks grow slowly, but mature, untrimmed specimens can tower 80 feet in the air. Effective as a privacy screen or hedge, this handsome evergreen also looks nice planted as a group, or as a lone specimen. Shallow-rooted, it is easy to transplant when young.

Like full-sized Canadian Hemlocks, dwarf cultivars do not tolerate the higher heat of more southern zones, nor do they appreciate urban pollution or high winds. They need moist, humus-rich, acidic soil and because of their relatively shallow root systems are not particularly drought tolerant. However, like their parent, these little beauties are easy to transplant. Thus, there are tradeoffs.

THE OFFSPRING . . .
'Albospica'
Zones 4–7
6–15 feet tall
3–6 feet wide

Tried and true 'Albospica' was first cultivated in the mid-1800s. Also identified as 'Albo-Spica' and 'Albospicata', this intermediate cultivar sports creamy white tips at the ends of young, arching, dark green branches. What great color contrast! It increases 6–12 inches a year, maintaining a compact, pyramidal form reminiscent of a Christmas tree. Plant in part to light shade to protect the susceptible light-colored tips from the midday sun.

'Beaujean'
Zones 3–7
1–6 feet tall
2–6 feet wide

Smaller 'Beaujean', also known as 'Saratoga Broom', has sturdy branches that fan out, creating a low, spreading nest-like depression in the center of its compact silvery, light green mound. Symmetrical, it only grows 1–6 inches a year and does not reach 6 feet until it is at least 10 years old. It tolerates part or light shade or sun.

'Bennett'
Zones 3–7
2–4 feet tall
3–6 feet wide

Like 'Beaujean', low-growing 'Bennett' forms a small, flat-topped mound that is considerably wider than it is tall. Its ascending branches create a layered appearance. These medium green fan-like branches have tips that droop. It has short, light green needles and only grows 1–6 inches per year. This dwarf spreader usually stays fairly small, taking as long as 15–25 years to reach its mature size of 6 feet. 'Jeddeloh' has a similar growth habit.

'Boulevard'
Zones 4–7
4 feet tall
5 feet wide

Compact 'Boulevard' grows in a handsome pyramidal shape with long needles and branches of varying lengths that curve upward. The dense foliage is a beautiful deep green. It only grows 4–5 inches each year, so even if you start out with a medium-sized plant, it will take at least 30 years for it to reach its fully mature size of 18 feet tall and 12 feet wide.

'Brandley'
Zones 4–7
3 feet tall
2 feet wide

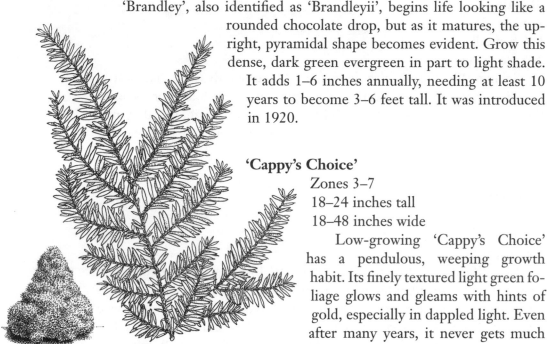

'Brandley'

'Brandley', also identified as 'Brandleyii', begins life looking like a rounded chocolate drop, but as it matures, the upright, pyramidal shape becomes evident. Grow this dense, dark green evergreen in part to light shade. It adds 1–6 inches annually, needing at least 10 years to become 3–6 feet tall. It was introduced in 1920.

'Cappy's Choice'

Zones 3–7
18–24 inches tall
18–48 inches wide

Low-growing 'Cappy's Choice' has a pendulous, weeping growth habit. Its finely textured light green foliage glows and gleams with hints of gold, especially in dappled light. Even after many years, it never gets much taller than 2 feet. Eventually it can spread as wide as 10 feet, but remember—the caveat here is "after many years."

'Cole's Prostrate'

Zones 3–7
10–18 inches tall
2 to 3 feet wide

'Prostrate' is an apt handle for this plant, for it literally lies on the ground. Just like the hair on an old man's head, the centers of maturing branches lose their needles, exposing sections of twisted gray inner branches, so that as 'Cole's Prostrate' ages, it looks even older. Plant this weeping dwarf in a rock garden, site it on a hillside, or locate it where it can flow. It only grows 1–6 inches a year, so after 20–30 years it may be as tall as 3 feet and stretch over 6 feet across. Some gardeners elect to stake this weeper.

It thrives in a part or lightly shaded location as long as the site is shady in the afternoon.

'Cushion'

Zones 4–7

3 feet tall

3 feet wide

Like its cultivar name, this little cultivar is a veritable "Miss Muffet's tuffet." Bun-shaped and finely textured, it has tightly packed short green needles that stand stiffly at attention. New foliage emerges a rusty cinnamon-brown. It grows 1–3 inches a year and will not reach its mature height until it is at least 30 years old.

If you cannot locate 'Cushion', look for 'Palomino', which is similar in growth habit.

'Dawsoniana'

Zones 4–7

6–15 feet tall

3–6 feet wide

Multistemmed, this compact, upright cultivar is generally grown as a small tree. Its arching branches curve downward, emulating a fountain of medium green.

Although 'Dawsoniana' can grow 6–12 inches annually, it is a very slow starter and will take at least 10–15 years to reach its mature size.

'Everitt Golden'

Zones 4–7

3–5 feet tall

2–4 feet wide

True to its name, 'Everitt Golden' has beautiful persistent golden foliage. Also known as 'Aurea', it starts out light yellow-gold, becomes more and more chartreuse as the growing season progresses, and finally ripens to a rich greenish-yellow "old gold" as winter settles in. The intensity of color is determined by available light, so site this plant where it gets at least a few hours of sun each day in the summer. Gentle morning sun is best, and protection from midday sun is advised to prevent foliage burn. Give it more shade in the winter. Some growers recommend a site on the north side of a building or fence.

Layered branches provide interesting architectural texture. This slow-growing evergreen's upright form is more like a tree than a shrub.

It will never be larger than 10 feet tall. A conifer grower in Indianapolis has a beautiful 30-year-old specimen that is still only 5 feet tall.

'Gentsch White'
Zones 3–7
2–5 feet tall
2–5 feet wide

Silvery white foliage appears on the tips of this flattish, bun-shaped cultivar, sometimes referred to as 'Gentsch White Tip'. The Carroll Gardens catalog comments that the dark green needles appear to have been "dusted with snow." Plant in a shady spot, because its pretty white tips will burn in too much sun. It can put on 3–6 inches of growth each year, but can withstand heavy shearing to encourage more compact growth and better color variegation. In Obrizok's *A Garden of Conifers*, a photograph on page 42 shows this plant pruned like a tiny Christmas tree.

'Albospica' and 'Frosty' have similar forms. Both will keep their white tips without shearing.

'Gracilis'
Zones 4–7
1 foot tall
2 feet wide

Sometimes incorrectly called 'Nana Gracilis' or 'Gracilis Nana', little 'Gracilis' forms a dense, nest-like mound that is somewhat flat on top. Its branches spiral out uniformly from the center of the mound, and droop slightly at the ends. Wider than it is tall, it grows 1–6 inches each year, ultimately becoming 3–6 feet tall.

'Henry Hohman'
Zones 4–7
2 feet tall
1 foot wide

'Henry Hohman' has that rugged, manly look, emphasized by the densely needled, slightly arching branches. These appear to march up this upright, cone-shaped evergreen giving rise to the descriptive term "twiggy." Combine all this with crested branch tips and a slightly irregular growth habit, and voila! A handsome gentleman, small though he may be.

'Hussii'

Zones 3–7

2 feet tall

1 foot wide

Picture a tiny, upright evergreen stretching and yawning and you can envision the compact, irregular shape of little 'Hussii'. Some of the branches bend at odd angles and, since there is seldom a central leader, many of the twiggy branches are short and stubby, while others stretch farther out. The dark green needles are packed closely together, creating a dense, congested appearance on each branch.

Plant this interesting little conifer in part shade. A true dwarf, it grows about 1–6 inches a year and may get to be 3–6 feet tall by the time it is 20 years old. And then again . . .

'Jervis' is a little more compact and not quite as open.

'Jacqueline Verkade'

Zones 3–7

18 inches high

14 inches wide

This conifer is truly a *little* miss, with minute stems, tiny green needles, and a pretty conical shape. It has soft, extremely fine, light to medium green foliage. It grows 1–3 inches a year and likes part to light shade. It can eventually become 3–6 feet tall, but not for a long, long time.

'Kelsey's Weeping'

Zones 3–7

2–4 feet high

3–5 feet wide

The common name says it all. Sometimes identified as 'Kelsey's Weeper', this graceful plant has long, pendulous branches that billow like rapids over boulders as they fall, sweeping the ground. It has an asymmetrical growth habit. Plant it in part to light shade in a spot where it can be shown off to best advantage.

Fast-growing, it can add 4–6 inches per year. Some gardeners enjoy seeing it staked, but I think its growth habit, like a rushing river, is too beautiful to try to curb or control. Very similar are 'Sargentii' and 'Pendula'.

'Minima'
Zones 4–7
2–6 feet tall
3–6 feet wide

Delicate, airy fans arch one over another to create a lacy, architectural effect almost like a dainty miniature skirt. Exceedingly resistant to winter sunburn and windburn, the growth habit of this little beauty is reminiscent of the bottom part of a full sized hemlock. 'Minima' grows 4–6 inches per year and will not reach its full 6-foot height until it is nearly 30 years old. It is similar in form to 'Bennett', and the two are often confused in the nursery trade. Both have flat-tops. To confuse the issue even more, a *Taxus* cultivar also bears the name 'Minima', so if this is the dwarf conifer of your dreams, carefully check both scientific and cultivar names to avoid disappointment.

'Minuta'
Zones 4–7
4–8 inches tall
4–8 inches wide

Lilliputian, tiny, minute, itty-bitty—choose any of these adjectives to describe this plant. It is probably the smallest hemlock cultivar available, tiny in all of its parts. It grows 1/4–1 inch per year, so it *may* reach 2 feet after 50 years. This cute little fellow is shaped like a tiny dark green bowling ball. It has a dense, irregular growth habit.

Unlike most dwarf conifers, 'Minuta' actually comes true from seed. It may be fun to experiment—but at ¼ inch a year, who knows how long it will take before you can even *see* the results!

'Rugg's Washington Dwarf'
Zones 4–7
3–6 feet tall
3–6 feet wide

Spring brings bright golden daffodils, yellow tulips and even yellow dandelions. (Horror of horrors, not in *your* yard!) Imagine how these spring flowers would be complemented by the emerging yellow-bronze foliage of 'Rugg's Washington Dwarf'. In addition to striking spring foliage, this little rounded conifer has interesting brown buds and fuzzy stems. It grows 3–4 inches a year, forming an irregular mound. Its needles eventually darken to a deep, rich green.

'Slenderella'
Zones 4–7
6–15 feet tall
2–4 feet wide

I first saw this slender, dainty upright planted on a shady hillside in Jay and Terri Park's Indiana garden, where it rises gracefully, arching slightly at the top. A moderate to fast grower, it has short, medium green, finely textured needles, and when it is young, provides an airy vertical accent in the understory. It reportedly increases 6–12 inches a year and is recommended as a backdrop or screen.

'Stockman's Dwarf'
Zones 4–7
1–2 feet tall
2–4 feet wide

Closely layered branches provide an interesting architectural texture, and eventually form a nest-shaped depression in the center of this small, upright cone-shaped conifer. Its short, medium green needles are densely crowded together. Very slow growing, this miniature conifer only adds 1–2 inches per year, for a total of perhaps 12 inches in 10 years. Its growth habit is reminiscent of 'Gracilis', a much larger evergreen.

'Verkade's Recurved'
Zones 4–7
24–30 inches tall
12–18 inches wide

This upright medium green shrub is similar to 'Curly' but because it is not quite as brittle, 'Verkade's Recurved' may be the better choice. It is also much slower growing, adding 2–3 inches per year. It has an irregular, upright growth habit with twisting needles that curl and curve downward like a cat's claws. Plant it in part to light shade.

'Watnong Star'
Zones 3–8
1–2 feet tall
1–2 feet wide

'Watnong Star' was introduced in 1970. Its common name comes from the starlike appearance of the creamy white new growth. This pretty little soft-looking conifer creates a slow-growing, ball-like mound, increasing 2 inches per year. Eventually it can grow as high as 6–10 feet tall and 6 feet wide. Plant in part to light shade to protect the white growth from burning.

Northern Japanese Hemlock (*Tsuga diversifolia*)
Zones 5–7
4–15 feet tall
2–12 feet wide

This is the only semi-dwarf conifer in this section that is not a mutation of our native. An erratic growth habit distinguishes this bushy, upright dark green evergreen, one of two hemlocks from Japan. Emerging foliage, backed with silvery-white, twists and turns to highlight the color contrast. According to the Iseli catalog, the Japanese call it the "Rice Tree" because of these white undersides. Plant it in part to light shade or in sun. Although most sources list it as hardy only to Zone 5, Iseli rates it as Zone 4, so northern gardeners may want to experiment with this pretty conifer. It can grow 12 inches annually.

Cultivars include 'Gotelli', 'Manifold', and 'Medford Lake'. All are hardy in Zones 5–7.

An "Extra" . . .

Siberian Cypress (*Microbiota decussata*)
Zones 2–8
8–12 inches tall
9–12 feet wide

In addition to "the shady Ts," a few other evergreens have that desirable, easy-care, dwarf growth habit. Siberian Cypress is one. Shade tolerant, this pendulous beauty is extremely low growing, but spreads readily. Plant with upright conifers for interesting contrast. It is effective as a focal point in the landscape, draping down a hillside, or covering the front of the foundation of a home or building.

Cold-hardy Siberian Cypress was first discovered in 1921. Its graceful, soft, lush foliage is so airy that it looks almost feathery. In the fall, the green color changes to a rich bronzy-wine, persisting throughout the winter.

This disease-free evergreen is truly a low-maintenance plant. You can shear it in the spring before new growth begins, or you can elect to let it take its own course and grow as it wishes. It likes part to light shade, but will tolerate full sun and dry soil once established. For easy propagation, root cuttings taken in the fall.

6.

Onward and Upward

Vines for Shade

Dutchman's Pipe

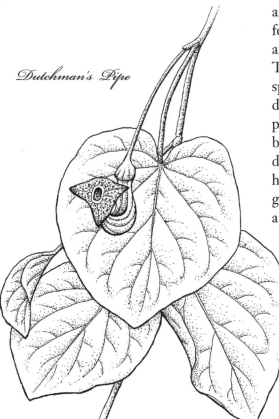

Vines are among the most versatile and useful plants in a gardener's repertoire.

—*Richard Cravens*

Climbing plants have been valued throughout the ages. Vines can camouflage utility areas and trash cans, give shade and privacy, and cover ugly but necessary fences. Most vines are impervious to insect and disease damage and grow quickly. Their roots require very little planting space; planted right next to a sidewalk or driveway, they will never cause heaving problems as trees or shrubs can. They can be sited behind shrubs or a perennial border without infringing. Vines can soften hard architectural edges. Smaller vines will grow happily in a container on the patio, or a planting box set on the ground, given adequate support. In addition to using vines as a vertical accent, some gardeners use vines on a hillside as a ground cover or let them trail over the top of a fence or wall. Vines can scramble over a rock garden, or wind and wend their way through shrubs and small trees. They can provide flowers, changing foliage throughout the seasons, interesting texture, and even food and nesting spots for birds.

Before planting a vine, install a sturdy support to keep it from toppling when it is mature. We used cedar posts sunk in concrete and heavy plastic coated wire to support a Trumpet Creeper, planted to give privacy to a patio. For a rustproof support, choose galvanized materials, plastic coated wire, or aluminum, stainless steel, copper, or plastic tubing. Install a sturdy wood or wire fence or trellis that stands away from the wall to prevent "holdfasts," which act like minute suction cups, from burrowing into crevices on brick or mortar walls. Although this is more work at the outset, it creates less maintenance in the long run (pull a Climbing Hydrangea off a tree trunk or building and you will see parts of the adhesive aerial rootlets left behind).

When it is time to plant the vine, dig a planting hole 18–24 inches deep and twice as wide filled with good loamy, well-drained soil. Spread the roots over a small mound, water thoroughly, and keep moist throughout the first growing season.

Site shade-lovers on the north or northwest side of the house or fence, or beneath a shade tree. Vines planted under trees should have their roots tucked in near the trunk rather than out at the drip line, because a tree's feeder roots do not take kindly to intruders into their territory. Plant a vine at the center of a fence rather than at one end or the other to help distribute the weight as it grows. Keep the roots of a vine planted next to a building away from the corner to prevent wind damage and dry soil. Site early spring–flowering vines in a north, south, or west exposure to give frosted flowers a chance to thaw before being hit by the morning sun. If there is an overhang, locate the roots just outside it so they can get adequate moisture.

Like a child learning to walk, a young vine beginning to climb needs your help. String can keep young vines in place until they learn to grab on alone. If you want the holdfasts on brick or stucco, a chewed piece of gum will anchor the vine.

A vine can be a tremendous asset in the landscape. However, as Richard Cravens warns, "Wrongly employed . . . it can itself turn into a persistent pest." Everyone recognizes Kudzu as the vine that "ate the South." Some vines are called "strangler" for good reason. Although vines are not as much of an investment in time or money as trees and shrubs, it is still important that low-maintenance gardeners choose the right vine for the right site. Vines will create beauty and privacy for humans, even as they provide biodiversity and habitat for wildlife. Every garden should have at least one vine.

Vines for Shade

Hardy Kiwi (*Actinidia kolomikta*)
Zones 4–8
10–20 feet
China, Japan

Downy leaves wildly splashed with pink, white, and green make Hardy Kiwi a popular landscaping choice. It will scramble over arbors or cover fences or trellises. Fragrant greenish-white flowers appear in early summer, but this dioecious vine needs both a male and female to produce the delicious, hairless, grape-sized fruit that ripens in the fall. Plant female 'Krupnopladnaya' (Russian for "large fruit") near male 'Arctic Beauty' to ensure good fruiting. As with birds, the male has more vivid coloring, so if you only want one vine, choose the male.

Planting requirements

Plant in moist, well-drained soil in part shade or in sun. Does not tolerate drought. Needs sturdy support.

Propagation

Sow seeds in spring, take cuttings in midsummer, or layer.

Dutchman's Pipe (*Aristolochia durior* aka *macrophylla*)
Zones 4–8
20–30 feet
Native to U.S.

This sturdy native not only thrives in shade, but will also *provide* dense shade under its canopy of overlapping, heart-shaped leaves, reminiscent of Wild Ginger. The unusual flower appears in late spring looking like a pale purplish Meerschaum pipe veined with mahogany.

A twining, woody climber, Dutchman's Pipe needs a sturdy support. It creates an impenetrable glossy, dark green screen. It will grow over a trellis or arbor, and will happily camouflage an outbuilding. The large leaves, which can be 10–12 inches long and wide, remain green until they fall in late autumn.

Woolly Dutchman's Pipe (*A. tomentosa*) has downy leaves. Both pi-pevines are hardy, seemingly impervious to fungal or insect damage. The larvae of the Pipevine Swallowtail butterfly depend upon *Aristolochia* species for food.

Planting requirements

Plant in humus-rich, well-drained soil in part to light shade or in sun. Dutchman's Pipe is tolerant of urban air pollution. It requires additional moisture until it is established.

Propagation

Dig and transplant rooted suckers, or sow ripened seed immediately. Do not allow seed to dry out.

American Bittersweet (*Celastrus scandens*)
Zones 4–8
20–25 feet
Native to U.S.
Deer Resistant

Native Bittersweet grows wild in the woods in light or part shade, but it needs some light in order to flower and set its distinctive fruit. This dioecious vine needs both a male and female to ensure pollination, so plant them in the same vicinity. In fact, you can even plant them both in one hole, just like hollies. The leaves turn clear yellow in the fall. The colorful fruit hangs after the leaves have fallen and through the winter, or until the birds devour them.

Bittersweet can be vigorous, so is not the best choice for the small garden. I have heard that it can be hard on the trees it decides to climb, but the Sugar Maples in my yard on which Bittersweet has resided for nearly 20 years do not appear to be suffering.

Do not plant the invasive exotic Oriental Bittersweet (described on p. 120).

Planting requirements

Plant in humus-rich, well-drained soil in part to light shade, or in sun. Native Bittersweet is not bothered by wind or cold.

Propagation

Plant seeds in the fall, or take cuttings in midsummer and root.

Clematis (*Clematis* spp.)
Zones 4–9
8–15 feet
Asia, Europe
Deer Resistant

There is disagreement on how to pronounce this word. In their 1999 catalog, Heronswood Nursery assisted with an anonymous poem: "Because it grows upon a lattice / Some people call it clematis / But Mr. Webster won't cease to hiss / Until you call it clematis."

Regardless of how you pronounce it, Clematis will happily cover a trellis or arbor or scramble up trees, peeping out from the deciduous foliage high overhead. The majority of Clematis we buy are hybrids and cultivars. Most of them prefer sun on their heads and shade at their feet, but several tolerate, or even prefer, some degree of shade. My favorite is the old standby 'Nellie Moser', in soft shades of mauve with a handsome rose stripe accenting each petal. There are many other lovely cultivars.

Virgin's Bower (*C. virginiana*) has white flowers that bloom from July to September. This native grows 12–15 feet tall and is very shade tolerant. Hardy in Zones 5–9, the passalong Sweet Autumn Clematis (*C. terniflora* aka *maximowicziana*, sometimes incorrectly called *C. paniculata*) covers itself with fragrant white blossoms in the fall. Give it a little sunlight for the best show. A thug? Yes, but a handsome one.

Clematis can serve as an effective ground cover. Shrub-like perennial forms are also available. Check catalogs and nurseries for myriad selections, but be aware that some are more shade tolerant than others.

Planting requirements

Plant in moist alkaline or limestone soil in part to light shade or in full sun. Protect the base of the vine because it is easily broken. Prune immediately after flowering.

Propagation

Cuttings taken in midsummer will generally root. Plant seed in the fall. A gardening friend may be able to supply you with a self-sown seedling from a plant you admire.

Cinnamon Vine (*Dioscorea batatas*)
Zones 5–9
10–30 feet
Asia

Also known as Chinese Yam or Chinese Potato, Cinnamon Vine grows from huge, long-lived tuberous roots that grow deep in the ground. These tubers can become as long as 2–3 feet. In Eastern Asia and parts of the tropics they are cultivated for food. Creamy white markings splash the leaves of 'Variegata'. Its flowers are green.

Cinnamon Vine twines clockwise. The long, pointed heart-shaped green leaves are glossy and heavily textured with prominent ribs. In the fall, they turn golden yellow, lighting up the shade. White flowers smelling strongly of cinnamon droop from the axils of the leaves, later producing small aerial tubers.

Planting requirements

Plant in rich, well-drained soil in part shade or in sun.

Propagation

Plant the aerial tubers. It takes two years for the vine to mature enough to flower and produce fruit. Or cut pieces from the huge rhizome, as if it were a potato, and plant.

Hops (*Humulus lupulus*)
Zones 3–8
15–20 feet
Native to U.S., Europe

For a vine that rapidly covers an arbor or trellis or creates an effective privacy screen, Hops will give a stellar performance. Because it covers so much territory so quickly, it requires strong support. A friend grows this fast-growing twiner on a white lattice structure behind her extensive perennial bed. By midsummer, the white wood is totally obscured by a wall of heavily lobed, rough green leaves, accented by the interesting straw-colored catkins (hops) that are used for brewing beer. In the winter, the stems die to the ground, only to resprout vigorously the next spring.

Yellow-leaved cultivars will be bright yellow in full sun, chartreuse in part shade. 'Bianca' has golden maple-like leaves. For yellow cone-shaped hops, choose 'Nugget'. Mail-order catalogs list 'Aureus', another gold leaved cultivar, as hardy in Zones 5–8 and claim it can grow 40 feet in a single season. Note: This is another thug.

Variegated Japanese Hops (*H. japonicus* 'Variegatus'), usually grown as an annual, can scramble up 10 feet or more in a single season, creating instant cover for a trellis, arbor, or screen. But it self-sows profusely—creating a maintenance situation you may decide to avoid.

Planting requirements

Plant in humus-rich, well-drained soil in part shade or sun.

Propagation

Take cuttings from shoots at ground level in midsummer.

Climbing Hydrangea (*Hydrangea anomala* spp. *petiolaris*)
Zones 4–7
60–80 feet
Japan, Taiwan

Climbing Hydrangea is an anomaly in the world of hydrangeas; not only does it climb instead of forming the typical shrub, it does so by means of aerial rootlets called holdfasts. It has an architectural quality

Hostas enjoy a dance around the
base of a lacy Japanese Maple.

Many a settler's blushing bride carried a bouquet of
fragrant Allegheny Serviceberry blossoms, one of
the first trees to bloom in the spring.

A young Eastern Redbud heralds spring in front of the Indiana Historical Society, while a severely pruned old Redbud tries valiantly to bloom.

The architectural branching habit of Pagoda Dogwood welcomes nesting birds.

Starry blossoms of Kousa Dogwood shine amid bright green leaves.

A white Flowering Dogwood
beckons through the garden gate.

Soft-pink flowering Crabapple blossoms
bloom gaily along the edge of Fountain Lake
in Albert Lea, Minnesota.

Our nation's capital is graced with the delicate deep red blossoms of Persian Parrotia in early spring.

Flowering Dogwood puts
on a brilliant display in the
fall landscape, attracting
migrating birds to relish
its brightly colored fruits.

After a long winter, homeowners welcome delicate Pink Flowering Dogwood blooms, unique Pawpaw flowers, historic Franklin Tree gems, and soft Magnolia blossoms.

Several *Chamaecyparis thyoides* cultivars, like this little 'Heatherbun', will tolerate partial shade.

Standing like a tall slim sentinel in front of *Taxus* × *media* 'Densiformis', 'DeGroot's Spire' presides over rusty-red mums and the silvery foliage of *Artemisia* 'Powis Castle'.

The vertical growth habit of grasses are a good foil for horizontal ground covers such as this bronzy-red Ajuga.

Variegated Japanese Hakone Grass creates a fountain-like effect, lighting up the front of a shady garden.

In quiet shade, amid Ostrich Ferns, bluebells, and Yellow Archangel, the author's ancient Appalachian chair rests on a patio of historic Marion Pavers.

Foam Flower has delicate white flowers and handsome maple-like leaves, making it a desirable ground cover or accent plant in the shady garden.

Gooseneck Loosestrife
will quickly blanket the
ground, shading out all
comers.

Lavender-pink Cranesbill Geraniums bloom happily above a stone wall.

that is unique among vines. Exfoliating bark on mature vines provides good winter interest.

In midsummer, 8-inch clusters of fertile and sterile flowers bloom over the dark green serrated leaves. The relatively insignificant dull-white fertile flowers, found on the inside of each cluster, are surrounded by brilliant white sterile sepals on the outside, which steal the show. Like the flowers of their shrubby relatives, these clusters persist even after they dry.

Slow to establish, it will not grow much the first 2–3 years. Well-rotted manure worked into the soil over the roots and extra rations of water and fertilizer will help it get off to a faster start. Give this heavy, woody vine sturdy support unless you intend to use it as a ground cover.

The cultivar 'Brookside Littleleaf' has tiny, dainty leaves, which increase in size as the vine matures. 'Skylands' has larger flower clusters than the species.

Planting requirements

Plant in humus-rich, well-drained, neutral to slightly acidic soil in light to medium shade, preferably with an eastern or northern exposure. Consistent moisture is essential for vines planted in full sun. However, plants sited in too much shade will not flower as well. Zone 3 gardeners may need to site this in a protected location.

Propagation

Root stem cuttings in midsummer or purchase started vines.

Honeysuckle (*Lonicera* spp.)
Zones 4–9
8–15 feet
Native to U.S.

The reddish-purple leaves of native Trumpet or Coral Honeysuckle (*Lonicera sempervirens*), among the first to emerge in early spring, change to bluish-green as the season progresses.

Trumpet Honeysuckle has heavy, woody stems and grows by twining around whatever its tendrils can grasp. In late summer or early fall, small red berries appear. It prefers sun, but will grow fine in shade, although it may not flower as freely. Once established, it is quite drought tolerant.

There are many cultivars. Hummingbirds like them all. 'Blanche Sandman', with orangey-red blooms, is reputed to be aphid resistant. It grows 15–20 feet, blooming repeatedly until frost. Brown's Hybrid (*L. × brownii*), a cross of Native Trumpet Honeysuckle and *L. hirsuta*, produced 'Dropmore Scarlet', a cold-hardy cultivar that flowers profusely. Less rambunctious, refined Dutch Woodbine (*L. periclymenum*) has fragrant, flaring flowers in a variety of shades, including pink, rose, yellow or magenta. Consult mail-order catalogs or the local nursery to select the cultivar that offers the desired color, bloom time, and abundance of berries. Avoid planting Hall's Honeysuckle (*L. japonica*), described on p. 121.

Moonseed

Planting requirements

Plant in humus-rich, well-drained soil. Honeysuckle vines thrive in part to medium shade, or in full sun with adequate moisture. Prune after flowering.

Propagation

Sow ripened, cleaned seed in the fall; take cuttings in midsummer for rooting, or layer. Division is also an option if the vine is still young.

Moonseed (*Menispermum canadense*)
Zones 4–8
12–15 feet
Native to U.S., Canada

Moonseed gets its common name from the crescent-shaped seed hidden in its attractive round berries. Also called Vine Maple and Yellow Parilla, it is grown primarily for its handsome lobed "maple" leaves and clusters of black fruit. It also makes a good ground cover. This semi-woody vine is dioecious, requiring both a male and female to produce fruit. But beware! The glossy black berries are poisonous. Moonseed also produces suckers that can be very difficult to eradicate, so if this will create maintenance problems, better choose another vine.

Planting requirements

Plant in any good, well-drained garden soil in part to light shade or in sun.

Propagation

Plant cleaned ripened seed immediately, take cuttings in midsummer, or dig and transplant rooted suckers.

Virginia Creeper (*Parthenocissus quinquefolia*)
Zones 3–9
15–30 feet
Native to U.S.
Deer Resistant

Also called American Ivy, Five-leaf Ivy, and Woodbine, Virginia Creeper can quickly climb the trunks of tall deciduous trees. Small greenish-white flowers bloom in early summer, attracting hummingbirds, butterflies, and bees. This vigorous native vine supplies food and cover for over 35 species of wildlife. In the fall its leaves turn shades of red, yellow, and orange, lighting up the woods. It also makes an effective ground cover.

The cultivar 'Englemannii', with smaller leaves, has a greater propensity to climb and cover brick and masonry walls than the species. Leaves emerge bronzy, change to dark green as they mature, and finally become brilliant scarlet in autumn. It too has the familiar blue-black berries enjoyed by the birds.

Some gardeners swear by this pretty native vine. Others swear *at* it. No doubt about it, it is tenacious. Just remember that natives are survivors, so if its growth habit doesn't suit your property, don't introduce it.

Planting requirements

Plant in humus-rich, well-drained soil in shade or part sun.

Propagation

Sow ripened, cleaned seed in the fall, or dig rooted segments and transplant.

Boston Ivy (*Parthenocissus tricuspidata*)
Zones 4–8
40–60 feet
Japan, China
Deer Resistant

Recommended as a good "city vine," Boston Ivy covers any number of American brick or stone government buildings, historic sites, and institutions of higher learning. Interestingly enough, this familiar clinging vine originated in Japan, not the U.S. Another little known fact: its well-known bright chartreuse-yellow leaved cultivar was originally found at Boston's Red Sox stadium. Arnold Arboretum horticulturists dubbed it 'Fenway Park'.

Boston Ivy loves shady spots. It has no problems clinging to the sides of buildings. Birds gobble the black berries and often nest in its welcoming foliage. Autumnal shades of scarlet, red, orange and yellow make this a popular vine.

A miniature called 'Lowii' has small, delicate leaves. Although it is not as aggressive as the species, it still puts on the same brilliant sunset show in the fall. Another restrained miniature is called 'Beverly Brooks'. Both of these will form a delicate tracery on buildings, rather than covering it as totally as does the species. There is not enough foliage for safe nest construction, but birds still enjoy the tasty blue berries.

Planting requirements

Plant in part to light or medium shade in well-drained garden soil. Do not grow on wooden structures.

Propagation

Sow ripened, cleaned seed in the fall, take cuttings in midsummer, or divide mature plants in spring.

Japanese Hydrangea Vine (*Schizophragma hydrangeoides*)
Zones 5–8
20–30 feet
Japan, Korea

Japanese Hydrangea Vine closely resembles Climbing Hydrangea, with two major exceptions. It clings close to its support, draping down and creating a tracery of branches, unlike the latter plant with its out-reaching architectural growth habit. A little later blooming, Japanese Hydrangea's sterile flowers look slightly different, having only one rather than four sepals. In midsummer, these flowers persist for nearly 6 weeks.

Its dark green heart-shaped leaves are pale green on the underside. In the fall, these become a deep rich gold, effectively lighting up the shade. Using aerial rootlets, this sturdy vine clings tightly to its support and can easily rise high in the air. Although it may take a bit to become established, eventually it will climb on trees, arbors, trellises, or even brick or masonry buildings with aplomb. It is also happy to drape over walls and boulders. It can get as wide as 30 feet, although most do not. Its reddish-brown stems show off nicely in the winter.

'Moonlight' boasts handsome blue green leaves mottled with a silvery overlay, and even larger white flowers than the species.

Planting requirements

Plant in moist, humus-rich, well-drained soil in part to full shade. It will also grow in full sun, if sufficient moisture is present. Space new plantings 12–18 inches apart. Prune in late winter or early spring.

Propagation

Sow seeds in the fall, layer, or take softwood cuttings in midsummer.

Not Recommended

Chocolate Vine (*Akebia quinata*)
Zones 4–8
15–40 feet
China, Japan

Chocolate Vine, originally brought to the U.S. in 1845, has naturalized widely, causing problems in 16 states. Aggressive, it sometimes overtops and smothers shrubs and trees. Shade- and drought-tolerant, it covers the ground so thoroughly that seeds of native plants cannot germinate, and seedlings cannot survive. Insects and disease seldom trouble it.

Each of the dark bluish-green leaves has 5 leaflets, hence another common name—Fiveleaf Akebia. Despite its sweet name, Chocolate Vine is tough to eradicate. The primary offenders for its vicious spread are not birds and wildlife, but gardeners. Don't be tempted.

Porcelain Berry (*Ampelopsis brevipedunculata*)
Zones 4–8
10–30 feet
Asia

It is a shame this stunning vine cannot behave itself. Intriguing clusters of berries in shades of rose, lilac, and blue peep from beneath handsome, dark-green 3-lobed leaves. Its cultivar 'Elegans' has leaves highlighted with white and pinkish variegation. This adaptable invasive exotic festoons trees and creates impenetrable tangles in the wild. Because its seeds germinate so readily, it has spread widely on the East Coast. It is also able to reproduce itself by stem or root segments. Once established, it is extremely difficult to eradicate or even control.

Oriental Bittersweet (*Celastrus orbiculatus*)
Zones 4–8
30–40 feet
Japan, China

This is an aggressive, invasive exotic that displaces native species and is not recommended. Choose native American Bittersweet instead. It is easy to distinguish between the two. The flowers and handsome fruit of the native appear at the ends of the branches, while those of Oriental are in the axils of the leaves, somewhat hidden.

English Ivy (*Hedera helix*)
Zones 4–9
12–15 feet
Europe, Asia

Well-known English Ivy is widely used both as a vine and as a ground cover. Cultivars are legion. According to the Brooklyn Botanic Garden, English Ivy forms "ivy deserts inhibiting the regeneration of wildflowers, trees and shrubs" where little else can grow. Starlings and other nonnative birds relish its blue-black berries, although native wildlife do not. In California, English Ivy grown as a ground cover quickly becomes a haven for rats. Ivy-covered trees are more susceptible to storm damage. The minuses outweigh the pluses for this plant.

Hall's Honeysuckle (*Lonicera japonica*)
Zones 4–8
20–40 feet
Japan, Asia

Warning! Hall's Honeysuckle is causing untold problems, over-topping trees and smothering understory plants. Control is difficult, because common eradication methods simply make it grow even more densely. The only effective control appears to be foliar applications of glyphosate herbicides, like Roundup, KleenUp, or Rodeo. Instead of the joined leaves and red or orange berries common to native honeysuckle vines, Hall's Honeysuckle has distinctly separated leaves and blackish-purple berries. Also known as Japanese Honeysuckle, its common cultivar is 'Hallianan'. It is not quite as bad as Kudzu—but almost.

7·

Nature's Carpet

Ground Covers for Shade

Ajuga 'Burgundy Glow'

When gardeners envision a truly low-maintenance landscape, the two types of plants they immediately think of are shrubs and ground covers. Be aware that ground covers are just that—plants to cover the ground. With enough divisions, all plants have this ability—eventually. There are vines, grasses, perennials, sprawling shrubs—in fact, a veritable army of plants just waiting to do the job.

Think about desirable features for the ground cover. Do you need an aggressive plant, or is the spot small enough for a more restrained choice? Docile, well-behaved ground cover plants will blend and coexist with others, creating interesting patterns in a garden. These can also be used as focal points, or in small spaces. Several natives spread moderately to make satisfactory groundcovers—Wild Ginger, Bloodroot, Wild Geranium, and Celandine Poppy, to name a few. A number of stoloniferous ferns, both native and non-native, can quickly fill in a shady area with their soft, feathery foliage (see chapter 8). Before you choose ferns, remember that nearly all prefer moist soil and will break down or go dormant if conditions become too dry. Most also need slightly acidic soil. Good ground covers include Hay-Scented Fern, Sensitive Fern, New York Fern, Marsh Fern, and Bracken Fern. Many of the Beech Ferns can be used as ground covers.

The most successful ground covers must be classified as aggressors, or even thugs. Aggressive ground covers should never be interplanted, or they will compete for territory resulting in an unkempt mess, and your low-maintenance garden will turn into a maintenance nightmare. Learn how ground covers grow before you choose them, because you can't tame a thug. And thugs will not serve as focal points regardless of how hard you try. But then, the ability to spread rapidly can be a desirable quality. When that aggressive nature is the only solution for a shady problem, aggressive thugs are welcomed and encouraged. Right? OK, so lead on, MacDuff. . .

The majority of the plants in this chapter will happily thrive in average garden soil. Pay careful attention to moisture requirements. pH is another consideration. It is not overly important for some plants, critical for others. Ground covers such as Bunchberry, Partridgeberry, and Wintergreen require moist—and acidic—soil. If your soil is not *consistently* moist and *naturally* acidic, these are not for your garden. Alkaline clay soil can—and probably should—be amended to create a rich, loamy planting bed. But for a low-maintenance garden don't try to force that soil to become acidic. Lowering the pH is an ongoing process and takes a lot of maintenance. However, if you absolutely *must* have an acid-lover or two, it is possible to amend a small planting space by adding aluminum sulfate. Follow the instructions on the package, and realize that soil acidifiers will have to be added annually.

After identifying the type of shade, soil, moisture, and pH that exist in the planting space, decide how much ground you need to cover. There are ways to get enough plants without spending a fortune. Propagation is usually by division in spring or fall, cuttings (taken after flowering), or seed (sown in fall). You might also ask friends for starts. Usually once a ground cover is established it is easy to share, especially if the plant is aggressive. Some ground covers are slower to increase than others, so learn the characteristics of the plants you choose. When you are selecting ground covers, be imaginative. Try to choose interesting and unusual plants that are environmentally user-friendly, whether they are native or exotic. A far wiser choice than those overused invasives listed at the end of the chapter!

And finally . . . plan before you plant. If you "don't fight the site," your ground cover should provide a low-maintenance gardening space that can last for years.

Ground Covers for Shade

Ajuga (*Ajuga reptans*)
Zones 3–9
3–4 inches tall
Europe
AGGRESSIVE
Deer Resistant

In spring, pretty blue flower spires of Ajuga, also called Carpet Bugle and Bugleweed, appear with the daffodils. Bronzy-green leaves arise from a single rosette. These rosettes form mats, which lie close to the ground, so Ajuga is a ground cover in the strictest sense of the word. Many cultivars exist; you only have to search the catalogs to find one that will suit your landscape. For textural interest, you might consider 'Mini-crisp Red' with crinkled bronzy-red leaves, or 'Royalty' with scalloped leaf margins and extremely dark foliage. Both have blue flowers. If you want a large-leafed ground cover with oversized flower spikes, 'Catlin's Giant' might be the choice for you. Its leaves are bronzy-green and the flowers are blue.

Upright Bugleweed (*A. pyramidalis*) does not spread as aggressively. As its name suggests, it is more upright and can be 6–9 inches tall. Geneva Carpet Bugle (*A. genevensis*) is coarsely textured and spreads more slowly than *A. reptans*. Not surprisingly, the variegated form of *A. genevensis* is named 'Variegata'.

PLANTING REQUIREMENTS
Ajugas will grow in nearly any average soil and can tolerate some drought after they are established. However, they will increase more rapidly in well-drained, moist loam, so you may want to consider amending the soil before planting. Space new plantings 8–10 inches apart.

Ajuga loves to take up residence in lawns, causing great frustration to the neatnik who mows that green stuff. It is better not to even *think* about planting Ajuga close to turf grass. It absolutely will not behave!

PROPAGATION
Tease apart the fibrous rooted rosettes and transplant.

Lady's Mantle (*Alchemilla mollis*)
Zones 3–8
8–14 inches tall
Europe

Lady's Mantle is a small plant, usually less than 14 inches tall and half again as wide, with scalloped, gray-green leaves. Unusual yellow-green flowers rise 16–18 inches above the glistening, velvety leaves to lend a soft, almost fluffy appearance. These are favorites of flower arrangers since they last nearly two weeks in a bouquet and can also be dried.

Several cultivars are available including 'Alba', a double-flowered form. *A. vulgaris* is slightly smaller, but otherwise resembles *A. mollis*. A dwarf form, only 6 inches tall, is called 'Erythropoda'.

Well-behaved Lady's Mantle looks nice planted as a small mass or as an edging for a perennial border.

PLANTING REQUIREMENTS
Ordinary garden soil is adequate for this shade-lover, but moisture and good drainage are necessary. It needs little care as long as there is adequate moisture. If the site becomes too dry, the leaves will become brown-edged and tattered, but if clipped or mowed to the ground, the plant will resprout.

PROPAGATION
Propagate by division or seed. Self-sows readily but is not overly aggressive, and unwanted seedlings are easy to remove. Space new plants at least 8–10 inches apart.

Snowdrop Anemone (*Anemone sylvestris*)
Zones 3–9
10–18 inches
Europe, Siberia

Bright white flowers sporting yellow centers open in late spring and early summer. Handsome, downy, compound leaves are deeply incised, with sharply serrated edges. Unlike Japanese Anemone, which grows 2–3 feet tall, Snowdrop Anemone seldom exceeds 18 inches. The cultivars 'Grandiflora' and 'Wienerwald' both have very large white flowers. 'Flore Pleno' has double flowers.

PLANTING REQUIREMENTS
Spreads vigorously by creeping rhizomes. It thrives in light shade and will grow in either acid or alkaline soil as long as the site is moist and well drained. Space new plantings 15–18 inches apart.

PROPAGATION
Propagate by division, root cuttings, or seed.

Rock Cress (*Arabis alpina* 'Snowcap')
Zones 4–8
8–16 inches
Europe

Rock Cress, also known as Mountain or Alpine Cress, is covered with bright white flowers in early spring. The rest of the season, the small, grayish green, oval-shaped, serrated leaves are pleasing. A good choice for rock gardens, it grows 8–16 inches tall, and spreads nearly as wide.

PLANTING REQUIREMENTS
This plant prefers sun, but will grow in a lightly shaded area with average soil. Good drainage is essential. Once established, it is fairly drought tolerant. Space new plantings 8–12 inches apart.

PROPAGATION
Propagate by division, cuttings or seed.

Wild Ginger (*Asarum canadense*)
Zones 3–8
4–9 inches tall

Native to U.S.
Deer Resistant

Wild Ginger probably tops the list of native ground covers. Its beautiful heart-shaped leaves hug the ground. Insignificant brown flowers resembling "little brown jugs" are tucked under the paired leaves. Thin, yellowish, jointed rhizomatous stems grow an inch or two under the soil. Consequently, this ground cover will coexist readily with the fibrous roots of maple or beech trees, colonizing quickly to create a rich green carpet.

Wild Ginger is a larval food source for the Pipevine Swallowtail Butterfly. Whenever I transplant Wild Ginger, my hands smell strongly of this native herb, but I have never tasted it.

I was once the lucky recipient of a start of North Carolina Wild Ginger (*A. shuttleworthii*) and still count it as one of my treasures. Its mottled foliage and wedge-shaped leaves make quite a statement. It has never spread widely enough to be considered a ground cover in my yard, but holds a place of honor near the front entry for all to admire. Two other native gingers on my wish list are Harper's Ginger (*A. shuttleworthii* var. *harperi* 'Velvet Queen') and Virginia Wild Ginger (*A. virginicum* var. *virginicum*).

PLANTING REQUIREMENTS

Wild Ginger tolerates dry shade but, being a woodland plant, it thrives in moist, humus-laden, acidic soil. If it is happy, it will readily carpet the ground. It loves dappled shade, although it will perform well in even deep shade as long as soil conditions are right. Well-drained soil is a critical factor, or the rhizomes may rot. Space new plantings 10–12 inches apart.

PROPAGATION

Division or seed.

European Wild Ginger (*Asarum europaeum*)
Zones 5–9
4–9 inches tall

Europe
Deer Resistant

European Wild Ginger has round, shiny, dark green leaves that shine in dappled sunlight where it will create an ever-increasing clump. Use it to cover small spaces or as a wonderful focal point. It does not cover bare earth nearly as quickly as the native Wild Ginger, but will tolerate more sun.

PLANTING REQUIREMENTS
Flourishes in part sun or dappled shade in moist, humus-rich, well-drained soil. Mulch in colder zones.

PROPAGATION
Divide mature clumps in spring or early fall.

Pumila Astilbe (*Astilbe chinensis* var. *pumila*)
Zones 3–9
8–12 inches
China

Pumila Astilbe is the smallest and undoubtedly the best ground-cover Astilbe. It grows in rapidly increasing mats close to the ground and can quickly fill a small space. This sturdy, dependable little fellow is one of my favorites. The small rosy-lavender flower spikes of Pumila appear in July and August. If you prefer pink flowers, choose 'Vision in Pink' or 'Finale'.

Full-sized Astilbes (see chapter 10) can also be used as ground covers in a moist site. All astilbes bloom best with morning sun.

PLANTING REQUIREMENTS
Likes a moist site, but will tolerate moderate drought better than its bigger siblings. Space new plantings 8–12 inches apart.

PROPAGATION
Dig the plant and gently tease apart the small fibrous-rooted rosettes in spring or fall.

Bergenia (*Bergenia cordifolia*)
Zones 3–8
10–12 inches
Siberia, Mongolia

Bergenia is sometimes called Pigsqueak because rubbing the large, shiny leaves between your thumb and forefinger makes them squeak. This plant is not a rapid spreader, so is often used as a single plant, to highlight a small space, under taller plants, or as a border plant.

Bergenia grows about a foot tall and can be nearly twice as wide. It is semi-evergreen, depending upon the zone. Pretty rose flowers appear in early spring before the new leaves emerge. If there is ample light, the leaves of 'Bressingham Ruby' will become a beautiful reddish green, darkening to burgundy in winter.

PLANTING REQUIREMENTS

Bergenia thrives in average to slightly alkaline soil. It likes a little moisture, but is tolerant of drought. Multiple divisions of this slow grower will be necessary to cover a large area. Space new plants about a foot apart.

PROPAGATION

Propagate by division.

Heartleaf Brunnera (*Brunnera macrophylla*)
Zones 3–8
12–24 inches tall
Siberia
Deer Resistant

Heartleaf Brunnera is another leafy ground cover that will tolerate some drought. Tiny blue forget-me-not flowers float above the large, coarse, heart-shaped leaves in the spring. Also called Siberian Bugloss, Brunnera grows 18 to 24 inches high and wide.

I love the pretty little airy flowers of this plant, but my favorite Brunneras are the variegated-leaf forms. These look elegant in a shady spot and fabulous with hostas. 'Hadspen Cream' and 'Variegata' have wide creamy-white edges and make a striking display either as a ground cover or as a specimen plant. Because of the white edge, they demand a shady spot, and must have adequate, consistent moisture to thrive. 'Langtrees', another interesting cultivar, has irregular, silvery-gray spots near the margins of the leaves and prominent veins. Try at least a couple of these great variegated Brunneras in your perennial garden. They can be ornery about getting established, but once they are happy, they literally glow in the garden.

PLANTING REQUIREMENTS
Brunneras needs moist, average to slightly acidic soil, but will tolerate moderate drought. Space new plants 12–18 inches apart.

PROPAGATION
Propagate by division, root cuttings or seed.

Bellflower (*Campanula* spp.)
Zones 3–8
8–10 inches tall
Europe
  Campanula carpatica 'White Clips' blooms its head off from July to frost. This pretty little plant has dainty scalloped leaves, and bluish-white bell-like flowers. The similar 'Blue Clips' will reward you with violet flowers, while the species has lavender-blue flowers. There are several white cultivars. Some campanulas bloom in the spring, then rest and bloom again sporadically throughout the summer.
  Dalmatian Bellflower (*C. portenschlagiana*) is a rosy-lavender nonstop bloomer that seldom gets over 6–8 inches tall. You can expect bloom from midspring to fall. Hardy in zones 4–8. This great ground cover from Central Europe spreads rapidly in nearly any situation imaginable.

PLANTING REQUIREMENTS
Campanulas like moisture, but must have well-drained soil. Although they prefer a sunny spot, they will perform well in light shade but bloom will be less prolific. However, they don't seem to run quite as freely in the shade either. Space new plants 10–15 inches apart.

PROPAGATION
Propagate by division or purchased seed.

Lily-of-the-Valley (*Convallaria majalis*)
Zones 2–7
6–8 inches tall

Europe, Asia
AGGRESSIVE
Deer Resistant

Lily-of-the-Valley was the only ground cover at my grandmother's house in southern Minnesota. Each spring, a small bouquet of these tiny white bells graced the white metal kitchen table. Whenever I smell these dainty little flowers, I still think of her. Cultivars include the double flowered 'Fore Pleno' and 'Prolificans'. I tried C. 'Rosea', the pink-flowering form, but it did not spread as well and stayed in a small colony. 'Aurea Variegata' has a pretty green and white striped leaf, but is not very vigorous. I use it as an accent plant rather than as a ground cover.

PLANTING REQUIREMENTS
Spreads by rhizomes and can quickly blanket an area if the soil is rich and moist. It can tolerate drought, but the leaves will look tattered with insufficient moisture. Space new plants 6–10 inches apart.

PROPAGATION
Divide in early spring.

Bunchberry (*Cornus canadensis*)
Zones 2–8
4–9 inches tall
Native to U.S., Canada
MOIST ACIDIC SOIL REQUIRED

Bunchberry is a classic, exquisite ground cover. Its whorled, oval leaves have striking parallel veins. The leaves change to a deep red to grace the ground in early fall. If you can supply its cultural needs, it will reward you with brilliant white dogwood-like flowers in the spring and bunches of bright orangey-red berries in the fall. This stunning native hugs the ground and attracts birds.

PLANTING REQUIREMENTS

Moist, humus-rich, well-drained acidic soil is absolutely necessary. Without these required site ingredients, Bunchberry will not survive. Space new plantings 8–12 inches apart.

PROPAGATION

Propagate by cuttings, division or seed.

Epimedium (*Epimedium* spp.)
Zones 3–8
9–15 inches tall
Europe, Asia

Epimedium, also known as Barrenwort, Bishop's Cap, and Bishop's Hat, is a jewel to be cherished in any shade garden. Seldom more than a foot tall, Epimediums are lovely in or out of bloom. Even though these plants can be somewhat slow to increase, the wait is definitely worthwhile.

There are dozens of species including *E. alpinum* (Zone 3); *E.* × *rubrum* (Zone 4); *E. grandiflorum*, *E. versicolor*, and *E. youngianum* (Zone 5). Cultivars have been developed within each species in a variety of flower colors—pink, rose, cream, violet, yellow, and varying shades of white. The leaves can emerge red with green venation, mottled, red-edged, or glossy green. So search the nursery catalogs (Naylor Creek has dozens) and choose your favorites.

The only Epimedium that is reluctant to spread in my garden is dainty *E. youngianum* 'Niveum' with its snow-white flowers. It stays as a neat little clump near a small rock, but it looks happy.

PLANTING REQUIREMENTS

Prefers a moist soil, but when established will tolerate some drought. Space new plants 12–15 inches apart.

PROPAGATION
Divide in spring or fall.

Mrs. Robb's Bonnet (*Euphorbia amygdaloides* var. *robbiae*)
Zones 5–8
14–20 inches
Asia Minor

Mrs. Robb was supposedly an immigrant who smuggled cuttings of her favorite cushion spurge into this country in her bonnet! Perhaps she was intrigued by the unusual chartreuse spring-flowering bracts. This upright pachysandra-like ground cover has beautiful glossy blackish-green foliage. True to its name, the cultivar 'Rubra' has reddish-green leaves that become deep blood-red in fall.

Be aware that the milky latex sap of Euphorbia occasionally causes a rash in sensitive people; take precautions when working with this ground cover.

PLANTING REQUIREMENTS
Euphorbia is quite drought-tolerant and behaves well in dry shade. Some gardeners report aggressive tendencies if the soil is too moist and humus-rich, so don't pamper this plant. Space new plants 12–24 inches apart.

PROPAGATION
Propagate by division or rhizomes. Stem cuttings root easily, similar to sedum.

Cushion Spurge (*Euphorbia polychroma* aka *E. epithymoides*)
Zones 4–8
10–18 inches tall
Europe

This Euphorbia, commonly called Cushion Spurge, forms compact, rounded, half-moon-shaped clumps. Its small oval leaves change from light spring green to rich dark summer green. to autumn burgundy-red. The interesting clusters of spring flowers are actually whorls of colored modified leaves, known as bracts. Colors can range from bright yellow to chartreuse or light green.

E. dulcis 'Chameleon', known as Purple Spurge, has large, almost tropical looking leaves that emerge in spring with reddish hues, then change from dark green to burgundy in fall. The green flower bracts of 'Chameleon' appear in May and June. It is a great foil for gold hostas.

Note: Leafy Spurge (*E. esula*) has become invasive, causing environmental problems. It is not recommended.

PLANTING REQUIREMENTS
Same as for previous species.

PROPAGATION
Propagate by division or rhizomes. Stem cuttings root easily.

Strawberry (*Fragaria* spp.)
Zones 4–9
6–8 inches tall
North America, Europe

Strawberry species can be used as an edible ground cover that can tolerate occasional foot traffic. Beach Strawberry (*F. chiloensis*) (Zones 4–9) has shiny 3-parted evergreen strawberry-type leaves, white flowers, and red fall color. Wild, Scarlet, or Virginian Strawberry (*F. virginiana*) is hardy from Zones 5–9. Native to the U.S., this species yields sweet, small bright red berries. *F. vesca* var. *albocarpa* (Zones 5–10) has unique white strawberries that are quite tasty. I like 'Pink Panda' (Zones 5–8) because of its beautiful clear pink 5-petaled flowers that bloom profusely all summer long. It is a hybrid of *Fragaria* and *Potentilla*.

Fragaria is Latin for fragrance, referring to the smell of the ripening fruit. The practice of using straw under the plants to prevent disease gave rise to the common name of these succulent berries.

PLANTING REQUIREMENTS
Strawberry plants prefer average moist garden soil. They will tolerate light shade, but need at least ½ day of sun for good bloom. In a site with consistent moisture, strawberry species will run and flower freely. My 'Pink Panda' survives in its dry, shady spot, but neither runs nor flowers profusely. Since the dainty bright pink flowers make a nice accent, I put up with the lack of vigor. Space new plants 8–12 inches apart.

PROPAGATION
Propagate by division or by transplanting rooted runners.

Sweet Woodruff (*Galium odoratum* aka *Asperula odorata*)
Zones 4–8
6–10 inches tall
Europe, Asia
Deer Resistant

This exquisite ground cover grows under my towering hemlocks and only fusses if the soil gets too dry. It ignores dense shade and intense root competition that would deter most plants. I also have it in one of my hosta beds. The hostas appear to be floating above a sea of green. It has small, dainty, whorled green leaves. Tiny white flowers appear in profusion in the spring. I occasionally add some to white wine to make May Wine.

Sweet Woodruff only gets 6–10 inches tall. Spring bulbs can be interplanted with it. I prefer using crocus or the minor bulbs because their ripening foliage is less obtrusive.

PLANTING REQUIREMENTS
Sweet Woodruff loves shade, even dense shade. Space new plants 8–10 inches apart.

PROPAGATION
Propagate by division or by cuttings taken in early spring or fall and rooted in sand or a potting medium.

Creeping Snowberry (*Gaultheria hispidula*)
Zones 3–7
2–3 inches tall
Native to U.S.
REQUIRES MOIST ACIDIC SOIL

Creeping Snowberry has tiny, white upside-down bells that bloom in the spring. The shiny dark-green leaves are hairy, which explains the second part of its botanical name. It grows slowly in a tight, ever-increasing leathery mat. Its fall berries are creamy-white.

PLANTING REQUIREMENTS

It requires rich, moist, acidic, well-drained soil. And I do mean *requires*. Space new plants 4–6 inches apart.

PROPAGATION

Propagate by division of the creeping plants, cuttings or seed.

Wintergreen (*Gaultheria procumbens*)
Zones 3–7
3–5 inches tall
Native to U.S.
REQUIRES MOIST ACIDIC SOIL

This "cousin" of Creeping Snowberry has similar flowers but its leaves are smooth. If you are blessed with loamy, moist, acidic soil, plant either or both of these pretty, slow-growing native ground covers beneath acid-loving shrubs to create an easy maintenance site. However, if your soil does not fit the bill, enjoy photographs and spare yourself a lot of frustration. Both of these charmers tolerate moderate foot traffic.

Birds and wildlife relish the bright red fruits that appear in early fall. Wintergreen seldom grows taller than 6 inches.

PLANTING REQUIREMENTS

Give it rich, moist, acidic soil. Space new plants 8–10 inches apart.

PROPAGATION

Propagate by division, cuttings or seed. Before planting, rub the seeds gently in a metal sieve under warm running water until the flesh is removed, let the seeds air dry and plant immediately.

Geranium (*Geranium* spp.)
Zones 3–8
6–24 inches tall
Europe

For those dry shady spots, few plants can surpass perennial Geraniums or Cranesbills. I am always amazed at the adaptability of these sturdy plants, even in extremely difficult sites. (Just for the record, I am not talking about those well-known annuals we all call Geraniums. Covered in chapter 13, those are really Pelargoniums.)

From late spring to midsummer, the long-lasting, hot magenta flowers of Big Root Geranium (*G. macrorrhizum*) are an absolute knockout. It grows 12–18 inches tall from a knobby reddish rhizome that often actually grows above ground. It has a strong herbal scent. Its leaves become rusty red in fall, and remain through the winter in my Zone 5 garden.

The drought-tolerant Bloody Cranesbill (*G. sanguineum*) (Zones 3–8) puts up dark blood-red flowers most of the summer. Its leaves become red in autumn. It is lower growing and more compact than *G. macrorrhizum*.

Geraniums have unique palmate leaves; some are more deeply incised than others, reminiscent of fine fern foliage. Most Cranesbills have an extended bloom season, but there are some cultivars that only bloom in spring and early summer. They come in a wide variety of textures, colors, and sizes. 'Johnson's Blue' has bright blue flowers, while the flowers of Himalayan Cranesbill (*G. himalayense*) are rosy-lavender. *G. wallichianum* 'Buxton's Variety' (Zones 6–8) grows only 4–6 inches tall, but can spread nearly a yard wide. White marbling on soft green leaves is echoed by the bright white centers on dainty lavender-blue flowers. Incidentally, 'Buxton's Variety' survives in our woodland setting with no problems. The native *G. maculatum*, a taller plant, is covered in chapter 11.

PLANTING REQUIREMENTS

Most Cranesbill Geraniums prefer full sun and moist soil for best flower production, but are a great shade-tolerant ground cover as long as they get a few hours of sunlight each day. Once established, they will tolerate moderate drought. Use them under shrubs, along walkways, to edge a perennial border, or as part of a grouping of other similarly restrained ground covers. A number of species are less cold tolerant, so be sure to pay attention to zone hardiness when making your selections. Space new plants 12–18 inches apart.

PROPAGATION

Propagate by division, rhizome or stem cuttings, or seed.

Hellebores (*Helleborus* spp.)
Zones 3–8
8–18 inches tall
Europe
Deer Resistant

Entire books have been written about these elegant shade lovers. Three main species, *Helleborus orientalis* (Lenten Rose), *H. niger* (Christmas Rose), and *H. foetidus* (Stinking Hellebore) are the best known.

Christmas Rose (Zones 4–8) has the greatest cold tolerance of the three. Its huge, beautiful white-cupped flowers often bloom through the snow. The shiny, dark-green, evergreen foliage has sharply cut edges, and is striking against a light colored background. Christmas Rose seldom exceeds 12–18 inches in height. Locate this slow-growing beauty where it can be viewed from within the house on a cold winter's day. Some cultivars, like 'Higham's Variety', actually bloom reliably about Christmas time, but most do not put on their spring show until January or February. A new golden-flowered cultiver, 'Ras Buis', blooms from mid-February through March. Lenten Rose (Zones 5–9), has oval-shaped, serrated leaves and blooms in early spring. Cultivars come in a wide variety of colors, sizes, and shapes. The pale green flowers of the Stinking Hellebore show off to best advantage when placed in front of dark shrubs. It gets its common name from the foul smell of its bruised or broken stems. Taller than most Hellebores, Stinking Hellebore can grow as tall as two feet and spread twice as wide. A grayish-green leafed form with red-tinted stems is 'Wester Flisk'.

Another showy, easy, green-flowered hellebore, *H. odorus*, grows to 20 inches and flowers from December to March. *H. odorus* is not as well known as the "big three," but may be worth searching for.

Lenten Rose

PLANTING REQUIREMENTS
Humus-rich, evenly moist, well-drained soil is the optimum planting medium. Christmas Rose prefers light shade with alkaline soil. It dislikes sun and dryness. Once established, most of the other species will tolerate

some dryness. Space new plantings 12–18 inches apart. Combine with other low-maintenance companions that enjoy similar planting sites. These might include Wild Ginger, Epimedium, Brunnera, hostas, and *Dryopteris* ferns.

PROPAGATION

Propagate by seed or division in early spring or fall. When Hellebores are content, they self-sow abundantly. However, to ensure an identical clone, division is preferred because seedlings produce variations on a theme. Which might not be all bad either!

Coral Bells (*Heuchera sanguinea*)
Zones 3–9
Foliage 6–8 inches tall
Flower stalks to 24 inches
Native to U.S.
Deer Resistant

Coral Bells create tidy little mounds of leaves that are usually evergreen. New cultivars that lend wonderful colors and textures to a garden are introduced on a regular basis. A wide variety of flowers and leaves are available to choose from. Leaves of green, burgundy, chartreuse, silvery, variegated, nearly black, some with pronounced veins, splotched, bronze— you name it and some hybridizer is probably working on it. The flowers are equally varied. Some of the recent cultivars are not quite as cold tolerant, so check recommended planting zones before purchasing. Most are hardy to Zone 4.

Line out these plants as a pretty edging along a garden path, plant one as a focal point near a rock, or mass them as a serviceable ground cover. Removing spent flowers before they have a chance to set seed will lengthen the bloom time—but then that increases maintenance . . .

These dependable plants have been popular since about 1884. They have become a "must-have" companion plant for twenty-first century hosta gardeners.

PLANTING REQUIREMENTS

Heuchera needs moist, well-drained soil and hates to be dry. It prefers light or part shade, but will accept full sun. Space new plantings 10–18 inches apart.

PROPAGATION

Propagate by division in spring or fall, stem cuttings taken in early summer, or seed.

Foamy Bells (*Heucherella*)
Zones 4–9
Foliage 6–8 inches tall
Flower stalks 15–20 inches
HYBRID

Foamy Bells is a hybrid of two natives—*Heuchera* and *Tiarella*. And what a nifty plant it is. The deeply incised leaves are striking and several cultivars have dark venation. If you want spectacular flowers, try 'Dayglow Pink': hot pink clusters rise above clear green leaves with a dark mid-rib. 'Cinnamon Bear' has dark chocolate colored leaves and creamy blossoms. The flowers of 'Cranberry Ice' are bicolored. 'Silver Streak' has delicate pink flowers that bloom above nearly lavender leaves laced with burgundy colored veins. These look—and sound—good enough to eat.

PLANTING REQUIREMENTS

Heucherella prefers moist, well-drained soil like its parents. Mass plants in a small space near a walkway, or as a border so you can easily admire the unique leaves.

PROPAGATION

Space new plants 10–15 inches apart. Propagate by division, stem cuttings, or seed.

Pale St. John's Wort (*Hypericum ellipticum*)
Zones 4–8
To 2½ feet
Native to U.S. and Canada

Our native Pale St. John's Wort is shorter and more cold-hardy than the commonly known St. John's Wort (*H. calycinum*) (Zones 6–10), seldom exceeding 12 inches.

PLANTING REQUIREMENTS
Both species prefer moist, well-drained, slightly acidic soil, but can withstand moderate hot, dry spells. Both have attractive yellow flowers, semi-evergreen foliage, and spread by underground runners. And while both species prefer full sun, they will also thrive in part shade as long as they get a little sunlight each day. Plant Pale St. John's Wort 12–18 inches apart and the larger St. John's Wort 24–36 inches apart.

PROPAGATION
Propagate both species by cuttings or division.

Crested Iris (*Iris cristata*)
Zones 3–9
4–7 inches
Native to U.S.

A friend in Iowa planted a wide swath of Crested Iris, outlining her entire garden. In the spring, they were a striking complement to the multitudes of spring-flowering bulbs. The rest of the season, the small light green sword-like foliage supplied a defining edge to the garden, setting off extensive hosta plantings. Whether asked to serve as an edger, a focal point under a beautiful small tree in blossom, or an extensive ground cover, this hardy little native obliges.

Iris cristata flowers can be white ('Alba'), deep purple ('Abby's Violet'), or bright blue ('Eco Little Bluebird'). 'Shenandoah Sky' has sky-blue flowers splashed with yellow. The oversized flowers of 'Powder Blue Giant' can be as much as a full inch larger than the species, yet this spectacular cultivar seldom exceeds 12 inches tall.

PLANTING REQUIREMENTS
These delicate blue and yellow beauties can carpet an area if the neutral to acid soil is rich, moist, and well drained. Dislikes alkaline soil, but will tolerate dry soil once established.

PROPAGATION
Division of the small, thin creeping rhizomes in late autumn is preferred, although they can also be successfully divided and transplanted in spring

after the spring blooms fade. Transplant like full-sized iris, keeping the rhizomes close to the soil level. Space new plantings 8–12 inches apart.

Yellow Archangel (*Lamiastrum galeobdolon* aka *Lamium galeobdolon*)
Zones 3–9
3–6 inches tall, trailing
Europe, Iran
AGGRESSIVE
Deer Resistant

I have a densely shaded area where, for about ten years, I tried to grow various shade plants. Sugar Maples took the lion's share of the moisture and kept out most of the light, creating a dark, dense shade on the ground, even after limbing up selected trees and thinning upper branches. Worst of all, rainfall had a difficult time reaching and really soaking the ground.

Being aware of the reputation of Yellow Archangel, I reluctantly tried it in a last-ditch effort to establish a successful ground cover. Within a single year, it covered the area and choked out existing weeds. Loose, salvia-like spikes of creamy yellow flowers appear above beautiful silvery marked leaves to carpet the ground in the spring and complement spring bulbs. Bulbs will survive and bloom amidst this ground cover, but after the bulb foliage dies back, little else comes up. My Lamiastrums are contained inside a U-shaped asphalt driveway, so they are not going to "take over the world." However, before you plant it, just remember that it is probably the biggest thug of all. This is *not* something you would ever put where it might spread and cause problems for native plants. Use it only when you can contain its running tendency with some barrier like a sidewalk, driveway, building, or wall. But in the right place, this thug can solve a tough problem.

A less aggressive cultivar called 'Herman's Pride' has the same yellow flowers. Its deeply serrated, heavily variegated leaves are longer and more pointed, and the growth habit is more upright and not quite as sprawling. But compared to the regular Lamiastrum, 'Herman's Pride' is a wimp.

PLANTING REQUIREMENTS
Yellow Archangel will thrive in just about any soil, moisture, or light. Just be sure to plant it where it can't cause problems for other less aggressive plants.

PROPAGATION

Divide established clumps or separate rooted runners and transplant.

Spotted Dead Nettle (*Lamium maculatum*)

Zones 3–9

6–9 inches tall

Europe

Deer Resistant

AGGRESSIVE

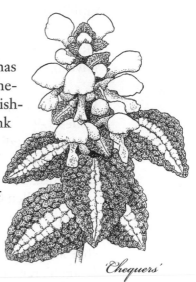

'Chequers'

'White Nancy', a well-known cultivar of *Lamium*, has green-edged white leaves and white flower spires. 'Chequers' boasts marbled green and white foliage and pinkish-purple flowers. Other more recent cultivars include 'Pink Pewter' with silvery-white, green-margined leaves and pink flowers and 'Beedham's White', a white-centered leaf with a more chartreuse edge and white flowers. 'Elizabeth de Haas' has a white diamond in the center of a medium green leaf splashed with cream, yellow, and gold. The flowers are violet. It is exquisite. ('Beacon Silver', similar to 'White Nancy', appears to be more troubled by leaf blight.)

PLANTING REQUIREMENTS

Lamium doesn't compete well with *Vinca minor* or even *Lamiastrum*, but given the right location with high shade it creates a beautiful silvery mass of small leaves. This plant increases quickly in average or moist well drained soil but it does not appreciate wet feet nor prolonged drought.

PROPAGATION

Lamiums spread easily on their own by sending out runners. Propagation is a simple task. Simply cut off some of these runners and plant them where they will fill in another area. Or divide large clumps and replant.

Laurentia (*Laurentia fluviatilis* aka *Isotoma axilaris*)

Zones 5–8

1–2 inches tall

Australia

Minute light blue flowers cover mats of tiny penny-shaped green leaves in spring. Tuck it in between stepping-stones, along a path, or under taller perennials. Small but mighty, this vigorous plant increases quickly, easily spreading 18 inches in a single season. Check for it in the Plant Delights catalog.

PLANTING REQUIREMENTS
Humus-rich, slightly moist, well-drained soil. Space new plants of this rapidly increasing species about 12–18 inches apart.

PROPAGATION
Division or rooted cuttings taken in spring or fall.

Lilyturf (*Liriope spicata*)
Zones 4–9
8–12 inches tall
Japan, China
Deer Resistant
    Also called Creeping Liriope, Lilyturf is a grass-like plant with violet or white flowers spikes that bloom in mid to late summer. These flowers are followed by black berries in the fall. The few cultivars that are available are less hardy than the species and some, like variegated 'Silver Dragon', revert back to the all-green form. Another species, *Liriope muscari*, is not as cold-hardy and will generally survive only to Zone 6.

PLANTING REQUIREMENTS
Lilyturf is drought-resistant and can take a fair amount of sun, although it will also thrive in fairly dense shade. Space new plants 8–12 inches apart.

PROPAGATION
It can be propagated by division or seed.

Gooseneck Loosestrife (*Lysimachia clethroides*)
Zones 3–9
2–3 feet tall
Japan
AGGRESSIVE
    Readers may question why Gooseneck Loosestrife, another Lysimachia species, is in the ground cover rather than the perennial chapter. Well, just consider its aggressive nature. The only way to use this plant

as a focal point is to confine the rhizomatous roots in sturdy containers to curb its rambunctiousness. And don't forget those prolific seedlings. Maintenance will seem less daunting if you just give in and let this guy run! It has beautifully arching, fluffy white "gooseneck-like" flower racemes—hence its name. And think what a vision this tall plant will make as a ground cover.

The European native Yellow Loosestrife (*L. punctata*) is another pretty thug. Some say it is not quite as aggressive, but a friend says that in Germany she has seen entire yards filled with this one plant! You may want to think twice before bringing the Lysimachia clan into your landscape.

Purple Loosestrife (*Lythrum salicaria*) is a totally different genus and species, so even though these fellows are called Loosestrife, they are not even distantly related.

PLANTING REQUIREMENTS
Gooseneck Loosestrife thrives in medium to deep shade, spreads by both seed and rhizomes, and likes just about any type of soil. It prefers moist or even wet soil. Although it will tolerate a limited amount of dryness, prolonged drought makes it very unhappy. Space new plants 12–24 inches apart.

PROPAGATION
Propagate by seed or division in spring or fall, or root cuttings taken during the growing season.

Partridgeberry (*Mitchella repens*)
Zones 5–8
2–4 inches tall
Native to U.S.
MOIST ACIDIC SOIL REQUIRED

Partridgeberry is enjoyed by a wide variety of wildlife including the bird from which it gets its common name. It is also known as Squaw Berry, Teaberry, and Twinberry. Another mat former, this slow-growing, evergreen ground cover has delicate bright white or pink pairs of flowers followed by red berries.

PLANTING REQUIREMENTS

Moist, acidic soil is critical. Accept nothing less for success with Partridgeberry. Space new plantings 6–8 inches apart.

PROPAGATION

Propagate by division, root cuttings, or seed.

Water Forget-Me-Not (*Myosotis scorpioides*)
Zones 5–9
14–18 inches tall
Europe, Asia
Deer Resistant

This plant is commonly called Swamp Forget-me-not or True Forget-me-not. It is a perennial, unlike the biennial variety (*M. sylvatica*) commonly found in seed packets at the supermarket. Shiny bright-green leaves the size of mouse ears complement the clusters of small pink or blue flowers. The scientific name *Myosotis* is Greek for mouse ears.

The centers (or eyes) of the Forget-me-not flowers are generally white, pink or yellow. A long-flowering dwarf variety, *semperflorens*, gets to be only 8 inches tall.

Water Forget-me-not has escaped and naturalized in the eastern U.S., but is not listed as invasive. However, be aware of its "jailbreak" tendencies and site it in a contained spot.

PLANTING REQUIREMENTS

Will not thrive unless the soil is consistently moist or even wet. It is not fussy about pH. It spreads by underground rhizomes. Space new plantings 8–12 inches apart.

PROPAGATION

Root summer cuttings, divide plants in spring or fall, or plant ripened seed immediately.

Allegheny Spurge (*Pachysandra procumbens*)
Zones 4–8
6–12 inches tall
Native to U.S.
Deer Resistant

I think the native Allegheny Spurge is more attractive than its cousin, Japanese Pachysandra (*P. terminalis*). It is slightly taller and slower growing, so more plants may be needed to cover a large area. Its mottled, gray-green leaves are uniquely scalloped. The cultivar 'Forest Green' has no mottling on the leaves and is somewhat easier to propagate. Allegheny Spurge remains evergreen in Zones 6–9. It goes dormant in northern zones, but sends up fresh new foliage in the spring. It may be a challenge to locate, but it is worth searching—and asking—for. I hope that before long our native Pachysandra will become as readily available as its Japanese relative.

PLANTING REQUIREMENTS

Plant in rich, moist, well-drained soil. Allegheny Spurge increases more slowly than Japanese Pachysandra and seems to require more moisture to spread with any speed at all. It likes light or full shade. Space new plants 8–10 inches apart.

PROPAGATION

Divide established clumps when still dormant in spring, or in the fall. Stem cuttings can be propagated in moist sand or water.

Pachysandra (*Pachysandra terminalis*)

Zones 4–8

8–12 inches tall

Japan

Deer Resistant

Japanese Spurge, more often simply called Pachysandra, is a dependable evergreen ground cover. It likes light to fairly heavy shade, but will languish in the sun. In late spring, a white bottle-brush flower appears at the growing tips. It spreads by stoloniferous roots at a moderate rate and is easily propagated by cuttings. A lovely variegated cultivar named 'Silver Edge' is available. Other cultivars have been bred for more glossy foliage ('Green Carpet' and 'Green Sheen'); scalloped leaves ('Cabbage Leaf'); or deeply serrated leaf edges ('Cutleaf', 'Kingwood').

'Silver Edge'

PLANTING REQUIREMENTS

Prefers moist, humus-rich soil in light or full shade, but once established, will tolerate moderate drought. If the soil becomes too dry the plants will lie on the ground until they get water. Space new plants 8–10 inches apart.

PROPAGATION

Root cuttings taken just after blooming in moist sand or water. The roots look like horizontal underground stems and can be cut apart with a leaf at each node and replanted.

Persicaria (*Persicaria filiformis* aka *P. virginianum*)
Zones 3–8
18–30 inches tall
Native to U.S., Japan
AGGRESSIVE

Persicaria has become a favorite of many of my hosta friends. However, this tall, bushy plant with interesting markings on the leaves can be aggressive, even invasive, often popping up unexpectedly in spots near the original planting site. Consequently it may be more desirable to use it as a ground cover, or contain it in a large sturdy pot sunk into the ground.

The cultivar 'Painter's Palette' sports handsome variegated leaves of green and creamy white, accented with a dark chocolate-maroon or pink V-shape. Since the rosy-red flower spikes are long and thin, they put on a better show when planted in a mass. 'Variegata' is green and white. 'Comptons Form' is a dark green leaf with deep chocolate brown markings and red veins.

P. microcephala 'Red Dragon' PPAF brings a deep maroon color to the garden, highlighted by lighter green markings. (Note: 'Red Dragon' should not propagated asexually without permission). *P. amplexicaule* 'Fire Tail' can stretch to 3–5 feet tall. It has green pointed leaves and spikes of dark red flowers. Mass for best effect.

PLANTING REQUIREMENTS

Persicaria prefers moist, well-drained, humus-rich soil, but will grow in any decent garden soil and will tolerate occasional dry spells. Too much drought will cause wilting, and burning of the leaf margins.

PROPAGATION

Divide in spring or fall.

Japanese Butterbur (*Petasites japonicus*)
Sweet Coltsfoot (*P. palmatum*)
Zones 4–9
3–4 feet tall
Japan, Korea, China

Visitors never fail to ask me about the large mass of humongous leaves growing on tall, thickened rhubarb-like stalks. Japanese Butterbur grows beneath tall trees festooned with Virginia Creeper, and hovers behind large hostas and tall, feathery Ostrich Ferns. I introduced this dramatic ground cover into my landscape over 15 years ago. In the spring, strange little flower pyramids shaped like Christmas trees hug the ground. These disappear and soon the kidney-shaped leaves begin to unfold, reaching toward the sky. They become larger and larger as spring progresses, finally reaching sizes of over 3 feet across. One man commented, "Wow! I feel like I'm in the Amazon!"

Although *P. japonicus* does not actually cover the ground, its huge leaves so effectively shade it that nothing else can grow beneath this behemoth. 'Giganteum' has even larger 3–4-foot leaves. *P. hybridus*, a shorter 3-foot form, has smaller heart-shaped leaves. The huge leaves of 'Variegatus' are splashed with creamy white. It also matures at 3 feet, and is not quite as aggressive.

Friends planted the native Sweet Coltsfoot in front of *P. japonicus* at the bottom of their moist ravine, and the combination makes quite a statement. Although it is half the height, it still delivers that same punch. Also called Wild Coltsfoot, Sweet Coltsfoot has huge 12–24-inch, deeply incised, hand-shaped leaves. Its unearthly flower clusters are white. Bright yellow-green leaves of the cultivar 'Golden Palms' gleam and glow in the garden. Other native coltsfoots include Arctic Coltsfoot (*P. trigonophylla*) and Arrowleaf Coltsfoot (*P. sagittata*). Other plants with gargantuan leaves are *Darmera peltata* (aka *Peltiphyllum peltatum*), a West Coast native with early rosy flowers, and Umbrella Leaf (*Diphylla cymosa*), with jagged, split, butterfly-like leaves, white flowers, and blue berries.

PLANTING REQUIREMENTS

Petasites thrives in any kind of shade, including dense shade. It does not enjoy sun unless its roots are constantly moist. In fact, these strange exotic-looking leaves will lie flat on the ground in protest without adequate moisture. However, plants in moist sites can become overly rambunctious, requiring plenty of room to run. In my garden, the soil gets dry in midsummer, but an occasional deep watering quickly brings them back to their upright position. They are not fussy about pH.

PROPAGATION

The rhubarb-like stems rise from thick, heavy underground stems that can be divided and shared with friends. It is possible to move these nearly anytime. Because the leaf and stalk invariably wilt and collapse after transplanting, I just chop them off at ground level. The plant soon sprouts a new leaf and takes off as if nothing happened. Space new plantings 2–4 feet apart.

Greek Jerusalem Sage (*Phlomis russelliana*, aka *P. viscosa*)
Zones 5–9
10–12 inches tall
Asia Minor
Deer Resistant

This looks like a less refined version of Pulmonaria but with larger, pointed, oval-shaped leaves. Its rough, ground-hugging leaves create a dense ground cover. In June, unique clusters of yellow tubular flowers on sturdy stalks rise 18–20 inches above these leaves. This herb-like plant from the Mediterranean readily covers the ground assigned, forming low-growing, coarsely textured clumps of plain gray-green foliage. It lends a sandpaper-like texture, which contrasts with most other plants.

PLANTING REQUIREMENTS

Greek Jerusalem Sage prefers sun, but will tolerate part or light shade. Include this plant in a naturalistic garden, at the edge of the woods, or use it as a small accent in a perennial border. Space new plantings 12–14 inches apart.

PROPAGATION

Seeding is the easiest method of propagation, but this plant can also be increased by taking root cuttings or by division.

Moss Phlox (*Phlox subulata*)
Creeping Phlox (*P. stolonifera*)
Zones 3–9
4–12 inches tall

Native to U.S.
Somewhat Deer Resistant

Whenever I think of Moss Phlox, I picture a high rock wall near our house in Iowa City. The wall was in two parts and one section was partially hidden by small needle-like dark green leaves that were covered by a profusion of bright pinkish violet flowers. There was a small space and then masses of lavender-blue flowers spilled over the rocks. Bright yellow daffodils bloomed gaily above. I always stopped to admire this vision of beauty in the spring. After the flowers faded, the dainty evergreen foliage softened that rock wall. This is the phlox most gardeners refer to as Creeping Phlox. There are many old varieties and even more new cultivars. My favorite is still the old-fashioned 'Atropurpurea' with its rich rosy flowers accented by a crimson inner ring. Hybridizers and Mother Nature have produced multitudes of varieties, including magenta and hot pink, blue with yellow centers, red, white, crimson, purple.

Another low-growing phlox (*P. stolonifera*) that carries the common name Creeping Phlox is not evergreen. It has tiny, oval dark green leaves and spreads by underground runners as well as by "stems" that root when they touch the ground. It detests dry soil; be prepared to add additional water if necessary.

PLANTING REQUIREMENTS

Moss Phlox prefers full sun but will tolerate light shade as well as dry soil. Space new plants 10–12 inches apart. Creeping Phlox prefers light to moderate shade and will even tolerate fairly dense shade. Its one demand is ample moisture, so be sure to provide extra water during drought. Space plants 10–12 inches apart.

PROPAGATION

Propagate by division, cuttings, or seed.

Wineleaf Cinquefoil (*Potentilla tridentata*)
Zones 2–7
2–12 inches tall
Native to U.S.

Wineleaf Cinquefoil is a handsome, low-growing native evergreen ground cover that loves shade. White flowers appear throughout the summer over shiny leathery green leaves. These notched, compound leaves become wine red in fall, hence its common name.

Several other deciduous low-growing cinquefoil cultivars also make useful ground covers, including tiny, 2-inch tall Rusty Cinquefoil (*P. cinerea*), hardy in Zones 3–7, and 3–6-inch shade-loving Spring Cinquefoil (*P. tabernaemontani* aka *P. verna*), hardy in Zones 4–9.

PLANTING REQUIREMENTS
Plant in sandy or average well drained soil, in light or part shade to full sun. Cinquefoil enjoys moisture, but will tolerate dry soil and even periods of drought.

PROPAGATION
Division, cuttings, or seed planted in fall.

Lungwort (*Pulmonaria angustifolia*)
Zones 3–8
10–12 inches tall
Europe
Deer Resistant

A favorite companion for hostas, this speckled, rough-leafed plant lends distinction and charm to any garden. In early spring, small pink and blue bells rise above last year's foliage to greet the daffodils. Hybridizers are churning out cultivars at breakneck speed. The most recent trends seems to be toward heavier silver leaf coloration and longer, thinner leaves.

I have a variety of these plants, the most prolific being *P. saccharata* 'Mrs. Moon', which has spread to fill in a large space under a tall Sugar Maple. 'Sissinghurst White' has pure white flowers and blooms just a little after the pink and blue flowers of 'Mrs. Moon'. Most Pulmonarias will tolerate a limited amount of dryness, except for *P. rubra*, which wilts and lies right down on the ground. Muted silvery spots are just hinted at in the soft green leaves of this early blooming, bright red-flowered variety.

PLANTING REQUIREMENTS
Humus-rich, moist, well-drained soil is preferred, but these plants will tolerate dry soil as long as drought does not continue too long.

PROPAGATION
Pulmonaria self-sows readily or can be divided in early spring or fall. Like self-sown hostas, each seedling is different. My "volunteers" have quite a variety of silvery shading, including a few whose leaves are almost entirely silver.

Lamb's Ears (*Stachys byzantina*)
Zones 4–8
Foliage 4–6 inches tall
Asia
Deer Resistant
Soft, fuzzy Lamb's Ears create a river of silvery gray as an edging. They can also be massed in dappled shade under small-leafed trees. Gardeners either love or hate the jarring magenta flower stalks that rise 12–18 inches above the foliage from midsummer to frost. For those of the latter persuasion, a supposedly nonflowering cultivar named 'Silver Carpet' is available. Its thick leaves are even furrier.

PLANTING REQUIREMENTS
Plant in light shade or full sun. Prefers moist, rich soil, but will tolerate moderate drought. Space 12–16 inches apart.

PROPAGATION
Germinates easily from ripe seed planted immediately. Divide in spring or fall.

Cutleaf Stephanandra (*Stephanandra incisa*)
Zones 5–8
2–4 feet tall
Japan, Korea
Delicate, finely cut leaves cover Stephanandra, a low massing shrub that makes a nice ground cover. Its soft green foliage almost reclines on the ground, yet it has an arching growth habit. I grow the tiny cultivar 'Crispa' in a heavily shaded spot in the woods in front of my home, and

although it has not spread, it leafs out reliably each spring. Although it only gets about 18 inches tall in my garden, it can grow as tall as 3 feet. I have never really noticed the yellow-green flowers or fruit that are supposed to appear on this plant, so they must be insignificant indeed. Or maybe my plant does not flower because of its location. No matter, the lovely leafy form is enough to satisfy.

Although Stephanandra is reportedly hardy only to Zone 5, I got my "start" from a friend in Iowa who grows it in a sheltered, partly shaded spot in her Zone 4 garden, where it still thrives and spreads vigorously.

PLANTING REQUIREMENTS
Plant in acidic to nearly neutral, moist or average well-drained garden soil, in light shade to full sun. It dislikes dry soil and needs deep watering during dry spells. Plants that get more sun will turn more reliably red in the fall.

PROPAGATION
Cuttings taken in summer root easily and reliably.

Ground Cover Comfrey (*Symphytum grandiflorum*)
Zones 4–8
8–12 inches tall
Caucasus, Europe, Asia
Deer Resistant

This rather unexciting plant, also known as Large-flowered Comfrey, is sturdy, dependable, easy to grow, and quickly fills a shady spot. Its natural appearance is particularly nice at the edge of a woodland area or for a border. The plain green, oval-shaped leaves are sandpaper-rough. It has clusters of yellowish-white tubular bell-like flowers in late spring and early summer. Cultivars include *S.* × *rubrum*, which has red flowers, and *S.* × *uplandicum* or Russian Comfrey, with rosy-purple flowers. Lavender-blue flowers grace 'Variegatum', the variegated form. Its leaves have a pretty cream edge, but if the plant is unhappy, the leaves will revert to all green. A taller version (*S. officinale*), known as Healing Herb or Boneset, matures at 3 feet.

PLANTING REQUIREMENTS
Once established, Comfrey tolerates drought. It likes a little more light than some of the other shady ground covers. It is relatively pest-free.

PROPAGATION
Seed or division in spring or fall.

Foam Flower (*Tiarella cordifolia*)
Tiarella (*T. wherryi*)
Zones 3–9
8–10 inches tall
Native to U.S.

Foamy clusters of tiny white flowers are the identifying characteristic of Foam Flower, also called Tiarella. It is another emerging hybridizing favorite and, except for those familiar bottlebrush flower spikes, many cultivars scarcely resemble one another. 'Iron Butterfly' has deeply cut 5-parted leaves with nearly black markings radiating from the center of each leaf. 'Heronswood Mist' has entire leaves that look as if they are sponge painted with shades of chartreuse and yellow. The maple-like leaves of 'Elizabeth Oliver' are marked with chocolate venation. 'Cygnet' has deeply incised leaves accented by tall 19-inch spires of soft pinkish-white flowers, and loves dense shade. Popular 'Running Tapestry' does just that—it runs. Vigorously. Its deeply cut foliage is accented with bright reddish-brown speckles.

Tiarella wherryi has a totally different growth habit. Instead of running, it creates small clumps. These clumps march across moist shady spots with great gusto, creating a lovely mass planting if planting conditions are satisfactory. *T. wherryi* displays a rich red fall leaf color.

A stoloniferous hybrid, *T. × Heucherella tiarelloides*, does well in a woodland setting. Warm pink flowers of the cultivar 'Pink Frost' float above silvery leaves. 'Snow White' and 'White Blush' both have white flowers. This sterile hybrid is hardy in zones 3–8.

PLANTING REQUIREMENTS
Tiarellas need humus-rich, moist, well-drained soil. Space new plants 10–15 inches apart.

PROPAGATION
This plant spreads by short rhizomes that are easily divided in spring or fall. Plant ripened seed immediately for germination the following spring.

Violet (*Viola sororia, V. papilionacea*)
Zones 3–9
8–10 inches tall
Native to U.S.
AGGRESSIVE

Lawn-lovers detest violets. They self-sow and invade lawns nearly as aggressively as dandelions. However, I dig these little beauties and plant them in my woodland garden where they are free to roam and run. I transplanted a huge mass of them under some Sugar Maples in the wild "corridor area" at the side of our house where grass refuses to grow. They made a great ground cover, blended well with accompanying ferns and hostas, spread happily, and cost nothing! If these prolific plants begin to look ratty, I just mow them off and they regrow fresh new leaves in short order.

I incorporate yellow, red, Confederate violets, and even speckled violets into this planting site to protect them from being zapped as weeds in the regular gardens, and they blend well. As a ground cover, Canada Violets are less satisfactory because their growth habit tends to be tall and leggy. Gardeners who are suspicious of the Common Blue Violet should try the better-behaved *Viola cornuta* 'Black Magic'. It looks like a black pansy with a yellow eye and makes a nice ground cover. But you will have to pay money for this one!

PLANTING REQUIREMENTS
Sun or shade, moist soil. But as any gardener knows, this plant will grow just about anywhere—even where it is not welcomed.

PROPAGATION
Violets self-sow readily and don't generally need any help.

Barren Strawberry (*Waldsteinia fragaroides, W. ternata*)
Zones 4–8
4–8 inches tall
Native to U.S. and Canada

Barren Strawberry produces a "mother" crown that sends out runners like a typical strawberry plant. In the spring, clusters of bright yellow flowers cover the plants. These buttercup lookalikes become small, hard, insignificant green strawberry-like fruits. Barren Strawberry, also called Mock Strawberry, creates dark green mats of shiny semi-evergreen leaves that will tolerate moderate foot traffic. Some gardeners use it as a turf substitute in small areas. The light green three-lobed leaves of Siberian Barren Strawberry (*W. ternata*) (Zones 4–7) are more coarsely textured than *W. fragaroides*. Otherwise there is not much difference.

By the way, Indian or Mock Strawberry (*Duchesnea indica*) is an obnoxious weed that is a strawberry lookalike. Gardeners curse while vainly trying to eradicate it by pulling yards and yards of this tenacious, stoloniferous thug. This is a totally different species and I am definitely *not* recommending it!

PLANTING REQUIREMENTS
Both *W. ternata* and *W. fragaroides* prefer sun or light shade and moist soil, but will tolerate some drought. They are not fussy about pH. Space new plants 8–12 inches apart.

PROPAGATION
Propagate by rooted runners, crown division, or stem cuttings.

, Not Recommended

Snow-on-the-Mountain (*Aegopodium podograria* 'Variegatum')
Zones 3–9
10–14 inches tall
Europe

Most gardeners are familiar with Snow-on-the-Mountain, also called Bishop's Weed and Goutweed. This upright plant has green and white leaves and flat umbels of white flowers in early summer that resemble Queen Anne's Lace. If the variegated form reverts to plain green, look out! This tough ground cover is not fussy about sun or shade, does well in average soil, and is relatively drought resistant. It is definitely a plant that you do not want to introduce into your yard—a true thug.

Purple Wintercreeper (*Euonymus fortunei*)
Zones 4–9
12–16 inches tall, trailing
China

Purple Wintercreeper is dependable, undemanding, and easy to grow. Its leaves turn a nice burgundy-red in winter. The cultivar 'Coloratus' is probably the most widely used of all. But since it is so overused, it is also boring. And what is worse than boring, this popular plant invades woodlands, completely displacing native wildflowers, which is why it is not recommended.

Japanese Fleece Flower (*Fallopia japonica* aka *Polygonum cuspidatum compactum*, *P. reynoutria*)
Zones 3–10
1½–3 feet tall
Japan

Japanese Fleece Flower (also called Japanese Knotweed) tolerates sun or shade. It grows rapidly and blooms with pink flowers. However, this plant is tall and somewhat coarse, so it presents a weedy appearance. It is not as attractive as many noninvasive choices, so don't feel disappointed that Fleece Flower is not recommended. *P. perfoliatum* is also not recommended. When you hear it called "Mile-a-minute," you know it is invasive!

Creeping Jenny (*Lysimachia nummularia*)
Zones 3–9
1–2 inches tall
Europe

Creeping Jenny is such an aggressive ground cover that it has naturalized in the U.S. This very low-growing, running plant has tiny, bright-green, penny-sized leaves, which explains another of its common names—Moneywort. Bright yellow flowers in summer are its primary attribute. The golden cultivar *L. nummularia* 'Aurea' is only slightly less aggressive. It will grow in any soil, in sun or shade. A "lawn lover," Jenny practically leaps into turf grass.

Myrtle (*Vinca minor*)
Zones 4–7
4–7 inches tall
Europe, Asia

Myrtle is a favorite of landscapers and home gardeners. It has pretty lavender-blue phlox-like flowers in spring, shiny evergreen leaves, and a neat and tidy growth habit. However, if you have seen this plant growing wild in the woods, you know how it completely covers the ground beneath the woodland trees, displacing all natives. So even though it is well known, attractive, and a tough plant for shade, responsible gardeners seldom include it in their landscapes. Variegated forms of Myrtle are often grown and I do not know if these are also invasive. A larger form, *Vinca major*, also has white and gold edged cultivars.

8.

Softly Elegant

Ferns for Shade

For success with all but the most vigorous [ferns], it is necessary to approximate the conditions under which each thrives in the wild.   —*Edgar Wherry*

Few plants in the garden are more graceful or elegant than ferns. Yet they are also tough. As long as they are planted in loamy, well-drained soil with plenty of moisture, ferns require little or no maintenance. In extreme drought their self-protecting mechanism sends them into dormancy, but come spring, their crosiers coil up out the ground as usual.

Ferns are some of the oldest recorded plants, leaving their remains in fossils. They were once a source of mystery and wonder because they grow so prolifically yet produce no visible seed. Ferns reproduce by means of tiny dust-like spores located on the back of each leaf. Turn over a leaf to discover the small warm brown spots or lines marching along.

Large ferns make a great backdrop to any grouping of perennials, particularly small and medium-sized hostas. Tuck in one or many of the medium ferns just about anywhere for an airy look. Any of the *Dryopteris* species are mid-sized. Even

Maidenhair Fern

Goldie's Fern is usually medium-sized in a garden setting, although it can become a giant in the wild. Miniature ferns seldom grow taller than 10 inches and are incredible accents in rock gardens. Incorporate these minute gems into a trough garden to create a tropical paradise in miniature.

Most ferns are not aggressive, but it is important to know the nature of each individual fern's root system and choose the right type for the right job. Some ferns form larger and larger clumps and will stay just where you put them, never running away. Clump-formers can be exquisite focal points, accent other plants, or serve as part of a well-behaved mass. Clumping ferns can be dug and divided. Be sure to leave a large enough piece for each division. Ferns that are runners have a mind of their own about where they will pop up next. Their aggressiveness will mightily frustrate the keeper of the perennial border. Individuals with small gardens should avoid planting Hay-scented, Ostrich, Broad Beech, and New York Ferns. Instead, use these running or stoloniferous ferns to control erosion or as effective ground covers. Running ferns grow from rhizomes, which can be separated in fall or early spring before the crosiers unfurl.

Ferns require consistently moist soil and thrive on the nutrients provided by crumbled leaves. Since raking in spring can damage the emerging crosiers, either remove excess mulch by hand or just let it lie. No additional fertilizer is necessary. In fact, it can be downright detrimental to the health of the ferns.

Ferns can be transplanted in early spring, but I have found the optimum time to be in the fall, just as they are going dormant. However, ferns are quite adaptable. Anytime I spot a wayward fern in the path or in a spot where it is not supposed to be, I simply dig it up, keeping as much dirt around the roots as possible, transplant it where I want it, and make sure to keep it well watered for at least 3 weeks. I have successfully moved ferns at all times of the growing season. Consistent moisture is the key. To transport ferns safely in the car, roll them in newspaper and stand them up in a bucket with just a little water in the bottom to keep the roots moist until they can be placed back in the ground.

I love ferns, but if I could have only three, I would choose Maidenhair Fern, Japanese Painted Fern, and Autumn Fern. Of course each of the ferns described below is beautiful in its own distinctive way.

Ferns for Shade

Maidenhair Fern (*Adiantum pedatum*)
Zones 3–8
12–24 inches tall
Native to U.S.
Deer Resistant

Maidenhair Fern has finely textured horseshoe-shaped leaves that float atop tall black stems. One could also describe the leaf as an open lady's fan. It is one of the most beautiful ferns in my garden. For contrast, echo a group of delicate Maidenhair Ferns with a backdrop of hefty native Green Dragon, a Jack-in-the-Pulpit relative that has larger horseshoe-shaped leaves. Also known as Northern or American Maidenhair, this fern has thin, wiry-looking black petioles, known as stipes, that rise and then fork into two arching parts. Even the roots of the creeping rhizome look like twisted, thin black wire. Mature plants can fill a 3–5-foot space. Western or Serpentine Maidenhair (*A. aleuticum*), a similar species, is native to the western part of North America as well as to Japan. It is hardy in Zones 3–8. Southern Maidenhair (*A. capillus-veneris*), native to the South and West, is hardy only in Zones 6–9. It is easily distinguished from Northern Maidenhair because its arching stipe does not fork.

PLANTING REQUIREMENTS
Plant in humus-rich, moist, well-drained woodland soil in light to full shade. Prefers consistent moisture. If the soil gets dry in summer they won't grow as large.

PROPAGATION
Divide mature clumps in late winter or very early spring, keeping at least 2 or 3 eyes and several fronds per division.

Ebony Spleenwort (*Asplenium platyneuron*)
Maidenhair Spleenwort (*A. trichomanes*)
Zones 3–8
6–12 inches tall
Native to U.S.

Ebony Spleenwort, which resembles a tiny Christmas Fern, typically grows on the forest floor in the wild. In order to grow either this or its "cousin" Maidenhair Spleenwort successfully it is necessary to duplicate their natural growing environment as closely as possible. Ebony Spleenwort has longer fronds than Maidenhair Spleenwort. The individual leaflets on each frond of Maidenhair Spleenwort are rounded, while Ebony's are longer, narrower, and similar in shape to many other larger fern species. The erect fertile fronds rise above the smaller spreading sterile fronds and are striped with black. Maidenhair Spleenwort has broad strap-shaped fronds with a dark, wiry stem.

These little ferns do well in a rock garden, tucked into a stone wall, or sited with rocks.

PLANTING REQUIREMENTS

Place rocks tightly together and plant the fern in the crevice in loamy, moist, well-drained soil in shade. Once established, both spleenworts can tolerate limited dry periods, but prefer moisture. Both will tolerate a little sunlight.

PROPAGATION

Purchase from a reputable nursery.

Lady Fern (*Athyrium filix-femina*)
Zones 3–8
18–36 inches tall
Native to U.S., Europe

One of the best ferns for moist shade, Lady Fern has delicate, arching 2–3-foot-long fronds. If the soil moisture is adequate, Lady Fern will propagate by spores. Each clump can spread as wide as 2 feet, but it is not invasive. I have this lacy beauty in my woodland garden and consider it slow growing.

It is easy to identify in early spring by its emerging crosier. Most ferns have a flat, coiled crosier. Lady Fern's is dark-brown, scaly, rounded, and somewhat oblong. Sometimes the rising stems have a reddish tint. Northeastern Lady Fern (*A. filix-femina* var. *angustum* f. *rubellum*), the red-stemmed beauty commonly found in the trade, does spread rapidly, so this particular subspecies may not be the best choice for a smaller garden.

Most of the cultivar names apply to altered patterns of leaf division rather than coloration. Cultivars include Tatting Fern 'Frizelliae', whose fronds have rounded leaflets that look like a string of beads. Miss Vernon's Crested Fern ('Vernoniae Cristatum') has forked and crested tips. Easy to grow, it seldom gets taller than 2 feet. Tiny 'Minutissimum' only grows 6–8 inches tall. 'Crispum' has curly fronds, and 'Cristata', frilly ones. Aptly named, 'Ghost' is a silvery sterile hybrid that can reach 3 feet. 'Branford Beauty' has gray-green variegated foliage.

PLANTING REQUIREMENTS
Plant in consistently moist, humus-rich, loamy, well-drained soil in moderate to full shade. Does not appreciate windy or dry locations, although it will tolerate limited amounts of dryness.

PROPAGATION
Divide mature clumps in spring or fall.

Japanese Painted Fern (*Athyrium niponicum* aka *A. goeringianum*)
Zones 4–9
12–18 inches tall
Japan, Asia

Sometimes called Japanese Lady Fern or Silver Painted Fern, this low-growing fern blends with hostas and astilbes in all degrees of shade. 'Pictum' is lovely with its highlights of metallic gray, burgundy, and silver along the burgundy midrib of each graceful frond. 'Ursula's Red' (*A. niponicum* var. *pictum*) has silvery fronds accented by maroon veins, particularly vivid in the spring. Red veins intensify the shades of blue and silver in the cultivar 'Silver Falls'. 'Wildwood Twist' is similar but with green and smoky gray tones. The center of each leaflet of 'Red Select' is a deep maroon.

Japanese Painted Ferns are easy to grow and beautiful in any garden.

PLANTING REQUIREMENTS
Plant in moist, humus-rich soil that is well drained. Can grow in part to full shade.

PROPAGATION
Divide mature clumps in spring or fall.

English Painted Fern (*Athyrium otophorum*)
Zones 4–8
12–24 inches tall
Asia

Despite its name, this rare fern is actually from Asia. It is also known as Eared Lady Fern because the top of each leaflet has a little tab or "ear" near the stem (or rachis). It emerges with violet crosiers and burgundy midribs. The foliage changes colors as it matures, going from shadings of red, yellow, and pale green, and finally finishing as a deep blue-green. The central rib remains burgundy the entire season.

PLANTING REQUIREMENTS
Like Japanese Painted Fern, this Asian native prefers a shady spot in moist, humus-rich, well-drained soil.

PROPAGATION
Divide mature clumps in spring or fall.

Narrow Glade Fern (*Athyrium pycnocarpon* aka *Diplazium pycnocarpon*)
Silvery Glade Fern (*Athyrium thelypteroides* aka *Deparia acrostichoides* and *Diplazium acrostichoides*)
Zones 4–8
12–36 inches tall
Native to U.S.
REQUIRES MOIST SOIL

Easy-to-grow Glade Ferns have an incredible sense of presence. Tall and stately, Narrow Glade Fern gives that desirable vertical accent. This rapid spreader provides good architectural contrast for plants with large, bold leaves. Plant Japanese Butterbur on one side of the path and Narrow Glade Fern on the other. That way they complement rather than compete with each other.

Also called Narrow-leaved Spleenwort, Narrow Glade Fern's deep green fronds seldom get wider than 6 inches. As the season progresses, these change to the russet browns of autumn, adding yet another dimension to the garden. This fern has smooth margins and few to no scales.

The fertile leaves have noticeably narrower leaflets (pinnae) than do the sterile leaves.

Silvery Glade Fern or Silvery Spleenwort has attractive green coloring that fades to straw yellow in the fall. Its fronds are a tad wider than those of Narrow Glade Fern. In the wild it often grows in damp ditches and along old country roads, but in the garden it demonstrates its true handsome character.

PLANTING REQUIREMENTS
Plant in shade in moist, humus-rich, well-drained soil that is neutral to slightly alkaline. Consistent moisture is crucial, or the fronds will become scorched and tattered.

PROPAGATION
Divide the spreading rhizomes of mature clumps in spring or fall.

Deer Fern (*Blechnum spicant*)
Zones 5–8
12–14 inches tall
Native to the U.S.

Small and compact, Deer Fern has leathery, deep green fronds. It can be tucked under tall trees, in a rock garden, or next to a specimen boulder. The sterile fronds of this tiny fern, also known historically as Hard Fern, remain evergreen during the winter in warmer zones.

PLANTING REQUIREMENTS
Plant in moist, humus-rich, slightly acidic soil that is well drained. Prefers a shady spot, and in the wild is found growing among rocks.

PROPAGATION
Divide in early spring or late fall, or purchase from a reputable nursery.

Rattlesnake Fern (*Botrychium virginianum*)
Zones 4–8
6–18 inches
Native to U.S.

This is my grandson's favorite fern because it coils up out of ground just like a snake. When it emerges it resembles a gymnast doing the "arch." Its succulent stalk slowly comes to an upright position and then the leaf, which fully forms underground, mysteriously opens. Although the fertile part withers quickly, the single 3- to 10-inch-long lacy leaf usually remains green all summer as long as there is adequate moisture.

PLANTING REQUIREMENTS

Incorporate into a shady, woodland wildflower garden with moist, humus-rich, loamy soil. Plant two or three just for fun.

PROPAGATION

Purchase from a reputable nursery, or rescue from a construction site. But not from a natural woodland! *Botrychium* species rarely survive more than 3–4 years when transplanted from the wild. Like native orchids, their root systems depend upon a mycorrhizal association with certain soil-borne fungi to provide nutrients and water.

Hairy Lip Fern (*Cheilanthes lanosa*)
Zones 4–8
6–8 inches tall
Native to U.S.

Hairy Lip Fern is easy to grow, tolerating more sunlight than many ferns. The gray-green leaflets are densely covered with minute, downy, rust-colored hairs. It grows 6–8 inches tall.

A similar plant called Lip Fern (*Aleuritopteris argentea*) grows on dry, rocky outcroppings near Beijing, China. Its small green leaflets have a white waxy back that shows off to advantage when this pretty little fern is planted above a path. It is smaller, growing 4–6 inches tall, and is hardy in Zones 5–7. This vigorous species has become a weed on rock walls in portions of the San Francisco Bay area.

Lip Ferns are not fussy about soil as long as there is sufficient moisture and excellent drainage. They will tolerate short periods of dryness, but will become temporarily dormant if moisture is not forthcoming. However, once there is adequate moisture, they will reemerge. When Lip Ferns are happy, their creeping rhizomes form dense mats.

PLANTING REQUIREMENTS

These ferns require protected spots, such as at the base of a tree, next to a boulder, or tucked in a wall in part to full shade. With adequate moisture they will also grow in part sun. Provide sharp drainage, incorporating equal amounts of sand, gravel, and humus.

PROPAGATION
Divide the creeping rhizome in spring or fall and transplant a section. Or order from a reputable nursery.

Bulblet Bladder Fern (*Cystopteris bulbifera*)
Zones 3–8
12–18 inches
Native to U.S.

Soft, lacy, lax fronds tapering to a long narrow point create a very graceful appearance. Bulblet Bladder Fern is especially pretty when it is planted so that the arching triangular fronds can drape downward. Tiny bulblets form on the underside of the frond along the midrib, drop, and create new ferns—hence its common name. Often, a dozen pea-sized bulblets will form on a single frond. Because of the effective germination of these "little green peas," this fern can colonize a planting space quickly, so it needs room to spread.

PLANTING REQUIREMENTS
Plant in neutral to slightly alkaline soil that is well drained in part to full shade. In the wild, it is primarily found in shady, moist sites growing on limestone. It does not appreciate drought.

PROPAGATION
Push bulblets into the ground where they fall, transplant young ferns, or divide mature plants in spring or fall.

Woodland Fragile Fern (*Cystopteris protrusa*)
Zones 2–9
6–10 inches tall
Native to U.S.

Tiny, fresh-green, finely cut ferns emerge all over my woodland garden each spring. Fragile Fern snuggles in with the native wildflowers, creating a delicate carpet. Because the spot where they abound gets dry in the heat of summer, these little creeping ferns disappear like the spring ephemerals. However, they reappear when moisture-bearing cool weather returns.

There are no scales or hairs on its above-ground parts except for a few scales in early spring.

PLANTING REQUIREMENTS
Plant in moist, humus-rich, well-drained woodland soil in part to full shade.

PROPAGATION
Divide mature clumps in early spring or fall.

Hay-Scented Fern (*Dennstaedtia punctilobula*)
Zones 3–8
12–30 inches tall
Native to U.S.
Deer Resistant

Hay-scented Fern is especially fetching in spring when the tall, triangular light green fronds are fresh. These lacy fronds grow 12–30 inches long and are 5–9 inches wide. Autumn brings shades of soft yellow. Crushed and dried fronds exude a pleasant odor, reminiscent of new-mown hay. Few ferns can rival it as a speedy ground cover. Also known as Boulder Fern because of its propensity to scramble among boulders, it can cover whole hillsides. Once established, it tolerates drought. It effectively controls erosion and will keep other plants out of the area, so maintenance becomes minimal. However, do not introduce this aggressive fern unless it is welcome to take up permanent and exclusive residence. It is considered a weed in parts of the northeastern U.S.

PLANTING REQUIREMENTS
Requires adequate moisture until established, then can tolerate moderate drought. Likes a shady location in average to light porous soil, and even thrives in poor soils. However, in sun it requires consistent moisture.

PROPAGATION
Divide mature clumps, separating the slender creeping underground rhizomes in early spring or fall.

Wood Fern (*Dryopteris affinis*)
Zones 4–9
3–4 feet tall
Europe, Africa

There are a multitude of wonderful ferns in the genus *Dryopteris*. In fact, if I could grow only one fern, I would choose a representative of this diverse genus. Generally evergreen or semi-evergreen, these sturdy ferns are almost leathery. They can hybridize, so unique forms can suddenly appear—which is fun. Named cultivars include leathery 'Cambrensis', which has an interesting layered look. 'Cristata the King' is a graceful, arching beauty with tightly crested tips.

A Eurasian form, Golden Scaled Male Fern (*D. affinis* 'Crispa'), gets its common name from the bright golden-russet scales that cover the stalks of its 36-inch fronds. Semi-evergreen, the yellow-green fronds have a wrinkled, rumpled appearance. It grows 24–40 inches tall and is hardy in Zones 4–9. Look down into the center of this fern to appreciate its sturdy, leathery fronds radiating out from the crown. It tends to have a more upright growth habit than Male Fern. A number of cultivars have been introduced, many of which are crested.

The crested form of Golden Scaled Male Fern, called *cristata*, has broad crests that march boldly up and down the outer tips of the frond. Larger than the species, this vigorous fern grows very erect, occasionally topping 4 feet.

PLANTING REQUIREMENTS
Plant in woodland-type, humus-rich, neutral to acidic soil in shade or in part sun with adequate moisture.

PROPAGATION
Divide mature clumps in very early spring, or in late fall.

Toothed Wood Fern (*Dryopteris carthusiana*)
Intermediate Shield Fern (*D. intermedia*)
Zones 2–7
14–30 inches tall
Native to U.S.

These ferns were formerly lumped together as *Dryopteris spinulosa* and are very similar. Because they arise from crowns and do not spread like the rhizomatous ferns, either is a good choice for a limited space and will create an ever-increasing clump.

The lacy texture of Toothed Wood Fern, also called Spinulose Wood Fern or Spinulose Shield Fern, lends a delicate touch in any woodland garden. Finely serrated leaflets march up the deeply divided triangular fronds of this long-lived, undemanding fern and literally glow in the shade. The coverings (indusia) of the sori are shaped like small shields, hence one of its common names. Unlike Leather Wood Fern, these are not near the margins of the leaflets. The stem (stipe or petiole) has pale brown, papery scales, particularly at the base.

Intermediate Shield Fern's evergreen fronds, often 10 inches wide, were once sought by florists.

PLANTING REQUIREMENTS

Site in rich, acidic, woodland-type soil in full or dappled shade. Either is a good choice for a woodland garden, but requires consistent moisture to prevent early dormancy. Semi-evergreen, the fronds collapse and lie on the ground after a hard frost.

PROPAGATION

Neither fern requires dividing, but to increase stock, the scaly rhizomes of mature clumps can be carefully divided in early spring or late fall.

Crested Shield Fern (*Dryopteris cristata*)

Zones 4–8
24–30 inches tall
Native to U.S., Europe

Crested Shield Fern has a distinctive architectural quality. Its fertile fronds emerge in the spring, rising straight and tall. Later, the shorter bluish green sterile fronds begin to unfurl, finally coming to rest at an almost horizontal position around the stately fertile fronds. On fertile fronds, the pinnae tend to twist at the base so as to orient themselves parallel to the ground, creating a "Venetian blind" effect.

Although they are slightly different, both the sterile and fertile fronds are leathery with prominent veins. The fertile frond has a stout stipe (petiole) and much narrower leaflets (pinnae) than the sterile frond. Each part is slightly twisted at angles to the midrib.

Keep this handsome fern out of the wind, but give it a place of honor in the garden.

PLANTING REQUIREMENTS

Plant in humus-rich, woodland-type soil that is well drained. Likes any kind of shade.

PROPAGATION
Divide the short creeping rhizomes of mature clumps in early spring or late fall.

Recurved Broad Buckler (*Dryopteris dilatata* 'Recurvata')
Zones 5–9
18–60 inches tall
Europe, Asia

Recurved Broad Buckler is arguably the patriarch of the fern world. Its formal appearance imparts a grand and stately feeling to the landscape. Also called Broad Wood Fern, it has finely cut, dark-green fronds with impressive crested ends. Although it is usually less than 3 feet tall, with ideal conditions it can rise as high as 5 feet. A beautifully textured lacy fern, it is impressive whether it is planted solo, in groups of 2 or 3, or as a mass. In sheltered spots or in more southern zones, this deciduous fern can remain evergreen during the winter if adequate moisture is available in fall.

'Crispa Whitside' is a lovely vase-shaped cultivar with drooping fronds. 'Jimmy Dyce', much more compact, has stiffly upright, bluish green fronds. Arrowhead Alpines describes this 2-foot-tall cultivar as "one of the best ferns for general landscape use."

PLANTING REQUIREMENTS
Like most ferns, it loves humus-rich, well-drained, woodland soil, located in the shade.

PROPAGATION
Divide in early spring or late fall.

Autumn Fern (*Dryopteris erythrosora*)
Zones 5–9
12–24 inches tall
Asia

Autumn Fern puts on a real show all season long, emerging with coppery hues in early spring. As it matures, the fronds change to bronze, become a luscious deep green, and finally "bring down the curtain" in the fall clad in rich bronze flushed with tones of pink. As if that were not enough, look at the back of the frond to discover beautiful red dots. These are the sori covered by the membrane known as the indusium, and all are dressed in red. What a beautiful performer!

A clump former, it is also known as Japanese Sword Fern and Japanese Red Shield Fern. It has fantastic leathery texture, yet looks as delicate as many of its fern counterparts. Even though fresh, glossy new fronds continue to reappear all season, it is a slow grower. But this gorgeous show-stopper is definitely worth the wait.

PLANTING REQUIREMENTS

Plant in humus-rich, moist woodland soil in the shade. Appreciates a generous covering of mulch, particularly in more northern zones.

PROPAGATION

Divide the slow creeping rhizomes in early spring or late fall, making sure there are some fronds attached to each segment.

Male Fern (*Dryopteris filix-mas*)
Zones 4–8
24–30 inches tall
Native to U.S., Europe

Vase-shaped, upright, sturdy, robust, stately—all amply describe this well-known fern. Our native Male Fern has been collected so heavily that it is considered rare in the wild. However, it is readily available from sources in Europe, where it is also native. 12–40-inch-long fronds are about 8–12 inches wide at the center. Each frond narrows at both the top and the bottom. Early English horticulturists developed a wide variety of cultivars.

Most Male Ferns are deciduous, although a few are semi-evergreen, particularly in warmer zones. They are large and vigorous, spreading 30–36 inches wide, so be sure to leave adequate space for each clump. Another tip—for beautiful textural contrast, plant these near Lady Ferns.

PLANTING REQUIREMENTS

Plant in neutral to acidic humus-rich, woodland soil in the shade, or in part sun. Prefer a moist environment, but will tolerate drier soil than most ferns.

PROPAGATION
Male Ferns form clumps from crowns. Divide in early spring or in the fall.

Goldie's Fern (*Dryopteris goldiana*)
Zones 3–8
3–4 feet tall
Native to U.S.
Deer Resistant

One of the largest wood ferns, Goldie's Fern makes a dramatic statement in any garden. Also known as Giant Wood Fern, it will reward you with a host of massive fronds held erect in a commanding, upright vase shape. These fronds are extremely broad, but taper abruptly at the tip, a distinguishing characteristic. For a tropical look, mass several of these 3–4-foot-tall deciduous beauties, or plant a single clump as a focal point.

In late summer or early fall, new crowns begin to peep through the duff. In the spring, the shaggy fiddleheads emerge like sleeping giants covered with brown and white scales. Like Maidenhair Fern, the stipes are black, but Goldie's fade to pale green near the top of the frond. The fronds change to a pretty, light yellow in the fall. Its rhizomes creep under the ground.

In the wild, Log Fern (*Dryopteris celsa*) is commonly found growing on or next to a rotting log, hence its common name. Its lustrous fronds taper gradually to the tip, unlike those of Goldie's Fern, which taper abruptly. Except for that variation, these two are very similar in appearance, although Log Fern is just a tad smaller. Oversized and semi-evergreen, Log Fern grows from short rhizomes.

PLANTING REQUIREMENTS
Plant in consistently moist, humus-rich, woodsy soil in a cool, shaded spot. It does not appreciate drought and will go dormant if the soil gets too dry.

PROPAGATION
Divide the creeping rhizomes in early spring or late fall. Each plant grows from a hefty rhizome and a raised crown.

Leather Wood Fern (*Dryopteris marginalis*)
Zones 4–8
18–30 inches tall
Native to U.S.

Also known as Marginal Shield Fern or Marginal Wood Fern, Leather Wood Fern is easily identified by the sori (group of spores) located on the margins of the arching fronds. The emerging crown is another easy identification tool in the spring. A ring of "teeth," pointing inward, is surrounded by another ring of last year's stems. The crown's divided globular shape reminds me of those chocolate "oranges" that come wrapped in orange foil. Heavily textured bluish-green fronds rise from the central crown. This vigorous erect fern is probably the most evergreen of the Wood Ferns, peeping through the snow in even in the coldest zones.

A recent hybrid, *D. marginalis* × *australis* has a deep green slender form. It is hardy in Zones 5–9.

PLANTING REQUIREMENTS
Plant in moist, shaded, humus-rich soil. It will tolerate some dryness.

PROPAGATION
Divide in early spring or in fall.

Oak Fern (*Gymnocarpium dryopteris*)
Zones 2–8
4–8 inches
Native to U.S.

Tiny Oak Fern creeps along, covering the forest floor with horizontal mats of green lace, creating a good ground cover in a moist, acidic environment. Each long stipe (petiole) branches evenly near the top into three triangular, finely cut ferny blades.

Northern Oak Fern (*G. robertianum*), also called Limestone Oak Fern, is very similar, but the three ferny blades have a slightly different arrangement with the top blade more prominent than the two lower ones. This species is rare and should be purchased only from a reputable nursery that propagates it. Never dig it from the wild. It prefers limey soil, is also native in Europe and Asia, and is hardy in Zones 2–6.

Hybrid Oak Fern (*G.* × *heterosporum*) is a hybrid of the two previous ferns.

PLANTING REQUIREMENTS
Plant in moist, humus-rich woodland soil in shade.

PROPAGATION
Divide the slender rooted rhizomes carefully to avoid damaging them and transplant in very early spring or fall.

Ostrich Fern (*Matteuccia struthiopteris* aka *M. pensylvanica*, *Pteretis nodulosa*, and *Onoclea struthiopteris*)
Zones 2–8
2–6 feet tall
Native to U.S., Europe, Asia
Deer Resistant

Ostrich Ferns are native to the U.S. and gardeners typically mass them in front of the white, turned wooden pillars on old front porches, march them down the side of aging farmhouses, line them out near a stream, or plant them at the edge of the woods. In my back yard, tall, bold Butterbur grows behind a veil of Ostrich Ferns.

In the fall, plants produce long underground runners that develop new crowns the following year. If these prolific ferns get carried away in your garden, follow my editor's lead and barter them for other plants at the local nursery. Or just cook and eat the tasty fiddleheads in the spring.

When to transplant? The best time is in early spring or late fall, but I move them any time the need arises. Keep the transplant well watered for the rest of the growing season. It requires more maintenance to move them in the height of summer, but I have lost few. These are sturdy, robust ferns.

The English call this Shuttlecock Fern because, like a weaver's shuttlecock, the sterile fronds are broadest above the middle, tapering at both the top and base. The upright fertile fronds are smaller than the sterile fronds. Stiff and woody, they turn cinnamon-brown, persisting through the winter, and are handsome in floral arrangements.

PLANTING REQUIREMENTS
Plant in moist, humus-rich, woodland soil in part to full shade. Fronds will pout and lie on the ground if the soil gets too dry. In drought conditions, they simply go dormant, reemerging when moisture returns.

PROPAGATION
Dig new frond clumps created by the "runners" and transplant.

Sensitive Fern (*Onoclea sensibilis*)
Zones 2–9
12–24 inches tall
Native to U.S.
Deer Resistant

More reminiscent of flowering perennial foliage than of fern, this deeply lobed fellow will go dormant if temperatures dip too sharply. It spreads rapidly, quickly covering the allotted space, so for low maintenance, site it where it can follow its instincts and run. If insects decide to stop for lunch, the broad blades of Sensitive Fern can become raggedy and unkempt, so it may be better to place it farther off in the landscape.

It is also called Bead Fern because of the handsome silvery-black beads clustered at the top third of each rigid fertile stalk. Widely used in floral arrangements, these bead sticks remain handsome throughout most of the winter.

Sensitive Fern will grow in still water and is a good choice for pond or streambanks. It also does well in normal to dry planting environments. Sensitive? Only to frost.

Chain Ferns have coarse foliage that resembles perennial foliage more than ferns. They love moist planting sites. Late to emerge in spring, Virginia Chain Fern (*Woodwardia virginica*) is hardy in Zones 4–10. It is dark green with a greenish-brown stipe (petiole). The unique Netted Chain Fern (*W. areolata*) is hardy in Zones 5–9. Also called Narrow-leaved Chain Fern, it has vegetative fronds that are strikingly similar to those of Sensitive Fern. Strong winds can disfigure the coarse leaves.

PLANTING REQUIREMENTS

Plant in moist, humus-rich, woodland soil that is neutral or slightly acidic. With adequate moisture these shade lovers can also tolerate some sun. Chain Ferns cannot tolerate drought.

PROPAGATION

Divide rooted rhizomes to transplant—and to share with your friends.

Cinnamon Fern (*Osmunda cinnamomea*)
Zones 2–9
24–48 inches tall
Native to U.S., south to South America, West Indies, Asia
REQUIRES MOIST SOIL
Deer Resistant

In early spring, the tightly coiled crosiers sport light woolly hairs. Next, the cinnamon-colored fertile plumes emerge, followed by lustrous deep green sterile fronds, arching from a central clump. These change to a beautiful golden orange in the fall.

Cinnamon Fern is often confused with Ostrich Fern. Not because these two ferns look alike, but because many gardeners assume the persistent, stiff, dark cinnamon-brown fertile frond of Ostrich Fern is the key. Not so. Once Cinnamon Fern's tall upright mahogany fertile fronds drop their spores, they collapse to the ground, becoming small, withered woolly brown tufts. The stems and leaf axils are slightly woolly as well.

Slow to establish, this commanding, upright deciduous fern is very long lived in a consistently moist environment, forming huge clumps. Aficionados of edible wild plants seek out the young crosiers.

PLANTING REQUIREMENTS

Plant in humus-rich, woodsy soil in shade or part sun. Hates drought and will eventually die without adequate moisture.

PROPAGATION
Divide in early spring, or in late fall when the plant is dormant. Mature clumps may be difficult to divide or transplant because the clump-forming rhizomes become so massive.

Interrupted Fern (*Osmunda claytoniana*)
Zones 2–8
3–5 feet tall
Native to U.S., Asia
Deer Resistant
    Interrupted Fern has a spreading, vase-shaped habit. It is easy to grow, and in ideal conditions can become 5 feet tall. Unlike most other ferns, each frond contains both sterile and fertile leaflets (pinnae). The sterile yellow-green leaflets appear at the bottom and top. The ephemeral fertile pinnae, found midway up the frond, wither and fall off in midsummer, leaving behind small woolly tufts and giving rise to the common name "interrupted." In many areas, this species does not produce fertile fronds.

PLANTING REQUIREMENTS
Plant in moist, humus-rich, woodland soil in shade. Can tolerate some dryness.

PROPAGATION
Divide in early spring or in the fall.

Royal Fern (*Osmunda regalis*)
Zones 3–9
24–48 inches tall
Native to U.S., south to South America, West Indies, Europe, Asia, Africa
REQUIRES MOIST SOIL
    Royal Fern is most un-fernlike. As Kay Yatskievych observes, "It would be fun to take a leaf of Royal Fern and one of Yarrow and ask 10 plant novices which one is the fern!" The leaflets resemble those of a locust tree and can be small or huge, depending on soil conditions. With consistent moisture, it becomes bold and almost bush-like. If the soil is too dry, it will remain small and eventually go into early dormancy, or disappear altogether. It is called 'Flowering Fern' because emerging

fronds have clusters of flower-like woolly beads at their tips. In the fall, the pale green leaflets of the sterile fronds are transformed to a vivid yellow. This impressive fern grows from a dark-brown rootstock.

Plant Royal Fern in masses, drifts, or as a focal point. It blends well with moisture-loving perennials and also looks nice combined with more traditional ferns that accent its uniqueness.

Crested Royal Fern (*O. regalis* 'Cristata') has a unique crested form that becomes increasingly striking as the fern matures. It grows 3–4 feet tall. A European cultivar called 'Purpurascens' emerges with purplish foliage, dark stipes, and plume-like "flowers."

PLANTING REQUIREMENTS

Plant in moist, wet, or even boggy acidic soil in shade. It does fine in sun as long as there is consistent moisture.

PROPAGATION

Divide mature clumps in early spring or fall.

Rock Polypody (*Polypodium virginianum*)
Zones 2–8
4–10 inches tall
Native to U.S.
Deer Resistant

Rock Polypody, also known as Common Polypody, Rock Fern, and American Wall Fern, is a favorite of rock gardeners. Coarse, smooth leaflets march up and down the stem with no apparent interruptions, resembling the work of a child with paper and scissors. Each blade is about 10 inches long and 3 inches wide. This unusual evergreen fern grows from mat-forming rhizomes that persist close to the surface. Each fern can become a mass 4–6 feet across!

The Greek word *Polypodium*, meaning "many feet," refers to the stubby base that remains on the rhizome after the leaf breaks off (abscises). Although it may be difficult to establish, once Rock Fern is happy in its environment it will spread quickly, scrambling over rocks and boulders.

Common Polybody (*P. vulgare*) is the European version of Rock Polypody. Also called Adder's Fern and European Wall Fern, it is hardy in Zones 3–8. Larger than our native Polypody, in Europe it is found growing in rocky, acidic soil. It also spreads by rhizomes and serves as a ground cover.

PLANTING REQUIREMENTS

Prefers moist, well-drained, loamy soil that is poor in nutrients. Once established, this fern tolerates drought.

PROPAGATION

Lift and divide rooted rhizomes and transplant.

Christmas Fern (*Polystichum acrostichoides*)
Zones 3–8
15–30 inches tall
Native to U.S.
Deer Resistant

Often called a good "beginner's fern," Christmas Fern is forgiving, adaptable, and easy to grow. Its deep-green, leathery fronds were once used as greenery at Christmastime. Evergreen, it peeps through the snow, assuring winter-weary gardeners that spring will return. In fact, its tightly coiled crosiers covered with silvery-white scales are among the first to emerge in early spring. Lance-shaped fronds, 24 inches long and 4–5 inches wide, taper slightly at the top.

In autumn, a joint at the stipe (petiole) base develops, causing the fronds to fold over and lay flat on the ground. Once the new fronds are developed the following spring, the old ones begin to wither and turn brown.

PLANTING REQUIREMENTS

Prefers acidic to neutral soil that is moist and rich in humus but tolerates clay, sandy soil, and even rocky environments. Once established, will accept drought. Does well in any kind of shade—dense, light, dappled, or partial. Will also thrive in partial sun if there is sufficient moisture.

PROPAGATION
Divide in early spring or fall.

Braun's Holly Fern (*Polystichum braunii*)
Zones 5–8
24–30 inches tall
Native to U.S., Europe, Asia

Picture a beautiful vase full of upright, arching ferns and there is the mature shape of Braun's Holly Fern. Its lustrous fronds are 24–30 inches long and 8 inches wide, remaining green until late autumn frosts turn them brown. Like most Polystichums, all parts of Braun's Holly Fern, from the shaggy silvery fiddlehead to the stems and even the creeping rhizomes, are heavily scaled.

Note: True Holly Ferns are in the genus *Cyrtomium.*

PLANTING REQUIREMENTS
Plant in moist, humus-rich, acidic soil in any kind of shade, including dense shade. Once established, will tolerate dry soil.

PROPAGATION
Divide mature clumps in spring or fall.

Western Sword Fern (*Polystichum munitum*)
Zones 5–8
3–5 feet tall
Native to U.S.

Western Sword Fern seems to grow everywhere in the Pacific Northwest. When I first saw this stiffly upright fern at my sister's home in Tacoma, Washington, I assumed it was an oversized Christmas Fern. I tucked a nice clump into my suitcase, safely rolled in newspaper and wrapped in plastic. Back home in Indiana, it thrives under a deciduous tree outside my office window in a spot that gets little or no sunlight and in midsummer can be quite dry. And it still reminds me of a huge Christmas Fern.

PLANTING REQUIREMENTS
Sword Fern prefers moist, acidic, humus rich soil in any kind of shade.

PROPAGATION
Divide mature clumps in spring or fall.

Japanese Tassel Fern (*Polystichum polyblepharum*)
Zones 5–9
18–24 inches
Japan

Polyblepharum means "many eyelashes." Japanese Tassel Fern, generously endowed with eyelash-like scales, fits the description. Also identified as *Polystichum setosum* or *P.* × *bicknellii,* this dependable, evergreen fern sports shiny, polished looking dark-green fronds that fairly gleam against heavily scaled, dark-brown stems.

In his Munchkin Nursery catalog, Gene Bush writes, "Can only have two ferns in the garden? This is one of them."

PLANTING REQUIREMENTS
Plant in moist, humus-rich soil in shade.

PROPAGATION
Divide mature clumps in spring or fall.

Bracken Fern (*Pteridium aquilinum*)
Zones 1–8
18–60 inches tall
Nearly worldwide
INVASIVE

If you need a solid ground cover of ferns, plant Bracken Fern. If not, don't even *think* about using it! It is much too invasive for normal gardens. In fact, it is considered one of the world's worst weeds. However, in the right location, it can serve a useful purpose. Typically found in open woods or thickets, it can quickly cover hillsides where its deep root system can help to control erosion. This tough, aggressive fern is one of the first plants to reemerge after a forest fire.

Although Bracken Fern is deciduous, leathery new leaves are continuously produced throughout the growing season. The deep green blades branch into 3 parts near the top of the stem. These coarse fronds can become huge, occasionally stretching to 4–5 feet long and 3 feet wide.

Silvery-gray hairs cover the emerging fiddleheads that resemble huge talons. Bracken Fern grows from a cord-like creeping rhizome that branches and runs in every direction. It transplants easily. Both the fiddleheads and the rhizomes are known to be carcinogenic, so should never be eaten. The foliage is poisonous to livestock.

PLANTING REQUIREMENTS
Plant only in environments where its aggressive nature is an asset. It likes any kind of shade, is not fussy about pH, will grow in damp or dry soil, and once planted, is there to stay . . . and spread.

PROPAGATION
Don't worry about propagation. This guy takes care of himself!

Japanese Beech Fern (*Phegopteris decursive-pinnata* aka *Thelypteris decursive-pinnata*)
Zones 4–10
10–24 inches tall
Japan

The narrow fronds of this unusual fern described by We-Du Nursery as "loosely and irregularly cut," have drooping tips and taper at both ends. A clump-former, Japanese Beech Fern spreads slowly by short underground runners, creating a vision of brilliant green in a shaded location. With more sunlight, it becomes bright chartreuse, so gardeners can satisfy individual color preferences by locating this adaptable fern in more or less light. Deciduous, it turns yellow in the fall.

Use this elegant beauty in rock gardens, tuck it into a crevice in a wall, let it shine in a wooded setting, or plant it as a mass in dappled shade with variegated hostas.

PLANTING REQUIREMENTS
Plant in humus-rich, slightly acidic, moist soil in any degree of shade. It thrives in part sun as long as there is adequate moisture.

PROPAGATION
Divide rooted runners and transplant in early spring or fall.

Maiden Ferns (*Phegopteris* spp. aka *Thelypteris* spp.)
Zones 3–9
18–24 inches tall
Native to U.S.

Typically, the triangular fronds of Broad Beech Fern (*Phegopteris hexagonoptera* aka *Thelypteris hexagonoptera*, Zones 4-9) are broader than they are long, with the broadest part of each blade at the base. Also called Southern Beech Fern or Six-Cornered Fern, it turns pale yellow in the fall. This vigorous fern spreads rapidly by shallow, creeping rhizomes. New leaves continually appear during the growing season.

If, as in the song from *Kiss Me Kate*, the nights are "too darn hot," Long Beech Fern (*P. connectilis* aka *T. phegopteris*) will not be on its best behavior and can eventually succumb. However, gardeners in slightly cooler climates will find it easy to grow. This relatively aggressive fern is also known as Northern Beech Fern or Narrow Beech Fern. It is similar to Broad Beech Fern, but the triangular fronds are longer than they are wide, as the common names suggest. The bottom of each frond is reflexed, resembling a blade standing boldly on two outstretched legs.

Another aggressive ground cover, deer resistant **New York Fern** (*Thelypteris noveboracensis*) spreads rapidly by underground rhizomes, forming tight mats. Like many of the Maiden Ferns, it will tolerate moderately dry soil and more sun than most ferns.

As its common name suggests, deciduous Marsh Fern (*Thelypteris palustris*) is a valuable fast-spreading ground cover for those impossible, wet, marshy environments, even growing happily in shallow water.

These deciduous ferns make great compact-looking ground covers, but are much too aggressive for the small landscape.

PLANTING REQUIREMENTS
Plant in humus-rich neutral to slightly acidic soil in the shade. Broad Beech Fern prefers moist soil, but tolerates drier soil than many ferns.

PROPAGATION
Divide creeping rhizomes and transplant rooted sections.

Blunt-Lobed Woodsia (*Woodsia obtusa*)
Zones 4–9
12–18 inches tall
Native to U.S.

Also called Common Woodsia or Cliff Fern, this compact little fern can be found in the wild growing on rocky slopes, in a small crevice in a wall, near boulders, or just growing in the woods. The lacy, dark-green fronds of Common Woodsia are handsome in the rock garden. If it is sited in more light, the fronds will change to a soft gray-green. This is another fern that produces new leaves throughout the entire growing season. It grows from a slowly creeping rhizome and is the easiest to grow of this genus.

Rusty Woodsia (*W. ilvensis*) or Rusty Cliff Fern is a tinier relative, seldom exceeding 3–6 inches. The undersides of its leaves have rusty brown scales. It is hardy in Zones 1–6. It is a good rock garden fern. It likes good drainage, but cannot tolerate drought. Rocky Mountain Woodsia (*W. scopulina*), hardy in Zones 2–9, is smaller still, forming tight clumps only 3–4 inches tall. Fussier and more difficult to grow than the other Woodsia Ferns, it demands its naturally acidic, humus-rich, well-drained soil or it will not survive. An Asian species, *W. polystichoides*, has narrow, silvery fronds. It grows 6–8 inches tall and is hardy in Zones 5–8.

PLANTING REQUIREMENTS
Plant in any type of humus-rich, well-drained soil in part, light or moderate shade. Without good drainage, these ferns may rot into oblivion.

PROPAGATION
Divide in early spring or fall.

9.
Upstanding
Citizens

Grasses and Grasslike Plants for Shade

We owe a lot to grass. Well-known food staples such as barley, corn, millet, oats, rice, rye, sorghum and even sugarcane all belong to the grass family. Grass provides the grain (seedheads) for our flour, gives us sugar and syrup, and feeds the animals that eventually feed us. It keeps hillsides and creek banks from eroding, and provides food, shelter and cover for birds and wildlife both large and small. And as Richard Pohl observes, "In the end, they [grasses] form the sod that covers the sleeping dead."

Nearly every American can walk out of the house and, before taking many steps, find grass. Unfortunately, a large proportion of it is clipped, cut, mowed, watered, fertilized, and pampered, using inordinate resources to keep it looking golf-course green. Not only is growing grass around our homes a real luxury, it is undoubtedly the highest-maintenance "crop" any American grows.

On the other hand, grass allowed to grow naturally is one of the lowest-maintenance plants imaginable. It sends

Gray's Sedge

down extremely deep roots which help it to survive drought, fire, grazing, and yes, even mowing, since the growth tissue originates at the base of the plant. There are over 7,000 species of grass worldwide. Add in over 2,000 species of sedges and over 250 species of rushes and the choices are almost limitless.

Grasses, sedges, and rushes are all monocotyledons and have long, narrow, parallel-veined leaves. They all produce flowers, but most are not overly showy or even very conspicuous.

Grasses

Most grasses prefer full sun, although some will tolerate shade. If your ornamental grass flops, it is likely telling you that it is not getting enough sunlight. You can stake it or move it to a sunnier location.

There are warm-season and cool-season grasses. Warm-season grasses grow best when the weather is at least 80°F. They often have a rich fall color, and bleach in winter. Cool-season grasses prefer temperatures of 60–75°F, so these are the grasses that begin to grow in late fall. They may stay green in winter or go dormant, greening up once again in the spring, depending on the hardiness zone. Cool-season grasses decline in the heat of the summer and revive as autumn temperatures drop.

Grasses grow from a fibrous root and are either runners or clumpers. Clumping grasses, often called bunch grass, stay put, forming larger and larger clumps. Running grasses do just that—they run. Runners are effective ground cover or erosion control and spread over a large area by underground stolons.

Most grasses are wind-pollinated, although a few species are self-pollinated. Grasses seed heavily and some can become weedy. The flower cluster or inflorescence is made up of spikelets which can vary in appearance from one species to another. The flowering stems are round and hollow. The leaf sheaths are usually split. Solid bulging nodes or joints occur only where leaves are attached. Grass literally means "joint," and Lauren Brown suggests that this bit of 1960s slang should help to guarantee recognition of a grass versus a sedge or rush.

It is important to cut grasses to the ground in early spring before the new growth emerges. Some gardeners ask about burning. I burned my small clump of grass early one spring and was thankful I had grabbed my spade and hooked up the garden hose. The flames shot 15–20 feet into the air and ignited the lawn. The experience was terrifying! Now I mow the grass. Mowing is effective and much less hazardous.

Native grasses have every bit as much beauty as exotic ones and are not as likely to cause problems in the environment. Remember *provenance* and choose grasses grown from local seed for best results.

Sedges

Sedges prefer shade. They are most often found in the wild in cool, moist sites, although many are adaptable, accepting both drought and heat. Sedges, like grasses, can be clumpers or runners, so pick the right one for the location. Unlike grasses, sedges seldom become weedy, nor do they migrate far from home. Most sedges found in the wild in the U.S. are native; fewer than 5 percent are exotic.

The flowering stems are solid and have no joints. The majority of sedge stems are triangular, giving rise to the saying, "Sedges have edges." Their leaf sheaths are tubular and are not split. Although many inflorescences are relatively insignificant, there are some that are striking. My favorites are the green, mace-like seedheads of Gray's Sedge (see pp. 187 and 194). Shining Bur Sedge (*C. intumescens*) and Hop Sedge (*C. lupulina*) have similar seedheads. Sedge foliage comes in a variety of green shades and several species don season-long rich, warm autumnal shades of red, orange, copper, and brown.

Sedges are used in meadow restorations and a few (*C. communis*, *C. jamesii*, *C. pensylvanica*) are becoming popular turf-grass substitutes in moist, shady locations. Some will even tolerate periodic submersion.

Rushes

Rushes, true natives of the historic wetlands, also prefer shade. They thrive in ponds and water gardens, but many will also tolerate seasonal drought.

The flowering stems of rushes are round and can be either hollow or solid. Their flowers are quite a bit different than the inflorescences of either grasses or sedges, each resembling a teeny-tiny, rather insignificant lily with three petals and three sepals.

Most of the plants in this chapter are perennial. There are also grasses in the nursery trade that are biennial or annual. One of the handsomest is *Pennisetum setaceum* 'Rubrum', with soft, airy, foxtail-like seedheads of rich purple-red, highlighted by leaves of burgundy and purple-red. It is also marketed as 'Cupreum'. People are always surprised when they learn this is an annual. I have grown it successfully in part shade, as long as it gets either morning or afternoon sun. However, it flops in too much shade and really prefers full sun. Gardeners in Zones 9–10 will likely find it hardy, but it is definitely an annual in the north.

The popularity of ornamental grasses and grasslike plants in the garden has increased steadily over the past two decades. Grasses will provide sound, light, texture, form, and seasonal interest in your garden. And when the wind blows, you can almost imagine you are in a "prairie schooner," buoyed up by a sea of grass.

Grasses, Sedges, Rushes for Shade

Long-Awned Wood Grass (*Brachyelytrum erectum*)
Zones 2–9
1–3 feet tall
Native to U.S.

Generally found in patches in damp woodlands, this handsome grass is recommended for restoring beech-maple forested areas. In the wild, it is often found growing on slopes or hillsides in the company of Sugar Maples, Basswood, Red Oak, and American Beech.

Its wide, light green, downy leaves resemble those of Northern Sea Oats, but the slightly fuzzy flowers that appear from June to August are quite different. These gather into long, slender clusters at the tips of narrow stems, arching gracefully over the broad foliage. Each individual flower has a long awn (bristle) on the end, giving rise to its common name.

PLANTING REQUIREMENTS
Plant in moist, well-drained, humus-rich soil in part to medium shade in naturalized areas.

PROPAGATION
Divide in early spring or fall, or sow ripened seed in the fall.

Woodland Brome (*Bromus pubescens*)
Tall Brome (*B. latiglumis*)
Zones 2–7
3–5 feet tall
Native to U.S.

Brome has over 100 species. Two of our native species have clusters of attractive arching spikelets that appear in the summer. According to Swink and Wilhelm, Woodland Brome is one of our commonest woodland grasses. Primarily used for understory restoration in oak woodlands, it is slightly hairy, and grows 2–3 feet tall. In the wild, it is found in dappled to medium shade near woodland wildflowers like Jack-in-the-Pulpit, Hepatica, and Trillium. In addition to native oaks, it grows near Spicebush and Witch Hazel.

Also known as Ear-Leaved Brome, Tall Brome is a much larger, more robust grass, generally used near ponds, along streambanks, and in moist areas. The showy seedheads of this 3–5-foot-tall grass put on a lovely show in midsummer.

Note: Smooth Brome (*Bromus inermis*), an invasive exotic, is not recommended.

PLANTING REQUIREMENTS
Both recommended native species prefer a damp, well-drained planting site in humus-rich, woodland-type soil. In the wild these grasses grow in dappled to medium shade. Tall Brome will also take full sun.

PROPAGATION
Divide in early spring or fall, or sow ripened seed in the fall.

Feather Reed Grass (*Calamagrostis acutiflora*)
Zones 5–9
3–4 feet tall
Eurasia
Deer Resistant

There is disagreement as to the hardiness of these popular plants. Several sources list Feather Reed Grass as hardy to Zone 4, others only to Zone 5 or even 6. Adventurous gardeners in Zones 3–4 are advised to mulch these plants heavily after the first frost, just as winter begins to get serious about plummeting temperatures.

The green and silvery-white variegated leaves of 'Overdam' emerge very early in the spring and its golden inflorescence rises on rigid stalks in early summer. This dependable grass keeps its good looks even during the hottest days of summer. It likes part to light shade or full sun, and makes a great specimen plant.

'Karl Foerster' (*C. arundinacea*) has a neat compact 2–3-foot growth habit with 5–6-foot-tall panicles of purplish-pink flowers that persist all season, lasting throughout the winter. Hardy in Zones 5–9, it prefers sun but will tolerate part shade. Another cultivar named 'Stricta' is nearly identical, but 'Karl Foerster' blooms 2 to 3 weeks earlier, especially in colder zones.

Korean Feather Reed Grass (*C. arundinacea* var. *brachytricha*) is a moisture lover that does well in part to light shade, or in full sun.

PLANTING REQUIREMENTS
Plant in moist, humus-rich, well-drained soil in part to very light shade or full sun. They also do well in heavy clay or average soil.

PROPAGATION
Divide in early spring; sow ripened seed in the fall.

Brome Hummock Sedge (*Carex bromoides*)
Zones 4–8
1–2 feet tall
Native to U.S.

Similar to native Prairie Dropseed, Brome Hummock Sedge forms dense clumps of finely textured, arching leaves. It blooms in May. Crested Sedge (*C. cristatella*) has finely textured bright green foliage and resembles a medium sized clumping grass. It grows 2–3 feet tall. Delicate and graceful, these beautiful sedges can accent a water garden, grow along the edge of a stream or pond, or be massed in a meadow or moist woodland. Good companions include Soft Rush, Dark Green Bulrush, Cinnamon Fern, and Joe-Pye Weed.

PLANTING REQUIREMENTS
Plant in moist to wet soil in part to light shade or in sun.

PROPAGATION
Divide in spring or early fall.

Common Beech Sedge (*Carex communis*)
Zones 2–7
4–12 inches tall
Native to U.S.

Because of its fine, light-green, grass-like leaves, Common Beech Sedge is sometimes used as an alternative for turf grass in part to moderately shaded environments. It thrives in moist, well-drained woodlands where it is found in close proximity to oak, beech, and maple trees. Also known as Fibrous Rooted Sedge, this hardy little plant grows in tufts or clumps and is suitable for use as a ground cover, a mass planting, or an edging. There are better accent or specimen sedges.

Very similar are Grass Sedge (*C. jamesii*) and Pennsylvania Sedge (*C. pensylvanica*).

PLANTING REQUIREMENTS
Plant in average, well-drained soil in part to moderate shade. Once established, it will tolerate dry soil. It can also be planted in part sun.

PROPAGATION
Divide in spring or late summer.

Black Seeded Sedge (*Carex eburnea*)
Zones 2–8
5–7 inches tall
Native to U.S.

A tiny native, Black Seeded Sedge forms symmetrical 12-inch-wide clumps and looks like stiff green hairs. Tony Avent, who got his original plant from Carex guru Tony Reznicek, describes this diminutive beauty as "absolutely dazzling." Also known as Ivory Sedge, it is typically found growing in the wild on limestone cliffs and outcroppings. It spreads slowly by a rhizomatous rootstock, creating lush, deep-green mounds.

PLANTING REQUIREMENTS
Plant in average, well-drained soil in shade or sun. Black Seeded Sedge is both heat and cold tolerant. In the wild, alkaline soil is its preference, but it is not fussy.

PROPAGATION
Divide mature clumps in spring, or plant ripened seed in fall.

Frank's Sedge (*Carex frankii*)
Zones 4–8
1–2 feet
Native to U.S.

This tough little sedge, used in wetland restoration, is recommended by Spence Restoration Nursery as particularly useful in environments that dry out in the summer. In the wild, it is commonly found in ditches, marshes, creek banks, and damp ravines. It blooms in midsummer.

PLANTING REQUIREMENTS
Plant in full shade to full sun in moist to wet soil. Once established, Frank's Sedge can tolerate summer drought.

PROPAGATION
Divide in spring or early fall.

Gray's Sedge (*Carex grayi*)
Zones 2–8
12–30 inches tall
Native to U.S.

In medieval jousting matches, knights twirled a spiked round mace above their heads before hurling it at their opponents. The unusual yellow-green, 1-inch seedheads of Gray's Sedge resemble these ancient weapons, and persist all summer and into the fall. A clump-forming plant, Gray's Sedge has an upright, arching growth habit. Its foliage remains green until late fall when it finally dries a warm brown. It is frequently identified as Morning Star or Bur Sedge.

In the wild, this native is found in swamps, marshy environments, and moist meadows or in open woodlands. Plant it at the edges of ponds or streams, use it as a conversation piece in the perennial border, and in the fall, incorporate the seedheads into dried floral arrangements.

PLANTING REQUIREMENTS
This moisture lover thrives in humus-rich soil in part to light shade or in full sun, growing from a short, sturdy rootstock. I planted my clump

in average, humus-rich, well-drained soil, but because the site is not consistently moist, it seldom grows taller than 12–15 inches.

PROPAGATION
Divide in spring or early fall, or plant ripened seed in the fall.

Lake Sedge (*Carex lacustris*)
Zones 4–8
3–5 feet tall
Native to U.S.

Aggressive Lake Sedge quickly spreads by scaly, horizontal rhizomes, forming large colonies of tall, arching, bluish-green foliage. On shady wet hillsides, its sturdy mats provide effective erosion control. It will thrive in shallow water, can be used in shoreline installations or to stabilize stream banks, and commonly grows with Sweet Flag, Wild Iris, Pickerel Weed, and Common Arrowhead. Because of its large size, it is an effective accent plant near pools or in water gardens, but must be contained. Planting near a driveway or concrete walk will curb its rambunctious nature.

Sometimes identified as Pond Sedge, Lake Sedge can be used as a ground cover, as a hedge or border, or even as a lawn substitute for difficult shady locations. Because of its imposing size, it would have to be mowed if a more traditional looking lawn is desired.

PLANTING REQUIREMENTS
Prefers moist or saturated soil in shade.

PROPAGATION
Divide mature clumps in spring or plant ripened seed in the fall.

Bottlebrush Sedge (*Carex lurida*)
Zones 4–8
1–3 feet tall
Native to U.S.

Bottlebrush Sedge likes a little more sunlight than some of its sedge relatives. It takes its common name from the distinctive seedheads. Smaller and shorter than Bottlebrush Grass, it has fairly wide, rough leaves. Commonly found in wet environments, it is attractive in a wetland garden or at the edge of a pond. It is recommended for sedge meadow restoration.

The similar Porcupine Sedge (*C. hystericina*) is a bit shorter. This deep green, noninvasive sedge also has spiky, bottlebrush-type seedheads that bloom in May and June. It will tolerate wet soil or even standing water.

PLANTING REQUIREMENTS

Plant in moist, to wet, slightly acidic soil in part shade or in sun.

PROPAGATION

Divide mature clumps in spring or early fall, or plant ripened seed in the fall.

Japanese Sedge (*Carex morrowii*)
Zones 5–9
10–15 inches tall
Japan

Also called Morrow's Sedge, Japanese Sedge has been a popular landscaping plant for many years, with variegated cultivars introduced as early as the mid-1800s. A number of these are readily available from mail-order nurseries as well as from local garden centers. The narrow evergreen foliage of Ohwi Japanese Sedgegrass (*C. morrowii* var. *expallida*) is striped with green and cream. Var. *temnolepis* 'Silk Tassel' is an exciting white-centered sedge. Thin, ⅛-inch, silky leaves create a finely textured mound wider than it is tall. Both are hardy to Zone 5.

The name 'Variegata' encompasses a variety of silvery edged semi-evergreen Japanese sedges.

PLANTING REQUIREMENTS

Plant in moist, slightly acidic, humus-rich, well-drained soil in part shade, or in full sun with adequate moisture. Japanese Sedge is particularly effective planted as a mass, but can also be used in a perennial border, as a specimen, or near a water interest.

PROPAGATION

Divide mature clumps in spring or plant ripened seed in fall.

Palm Sedge (*Carex muskingumensis*)
Zones 3–9
1–3 feet tall
Native to U.S.

Shiny tropical looking, palm-like leaves create an effective ground cover as they sprawl, scramble, and weep over earth, rocks, or fallen logs. Spreading by rhizomes, Palm Sedge forms huge colonies. This unusual winter-hardy sedge can be used as erosion control, a tall lawn substitute, or massed in shady moist planting areas. Its leaves become golden yellow in the fall after the first hard frost.

Several cultivars have been introduced, most hardy to Zones 5–9. 'Wachtposten' creates an upright, almost spiky appearance and will tolerate a drier planting site than the species. 'Little Midge' is a true miniature.

PLANTING REQUIREMENTS
Palm Sedge likes part to full or even dense shade in moist or wet humus-rich soil. It will even thrive in shallow water. Its dark-green foliage tends to bleach in too much light. Space new ground cover plantings 8–10 inches apart.

PROPAGATION
Divide mature clumps in spring or plant ripened seed in fall. Palm Sedge will self-sow.

Black Sedge (*Carex nigra*)
Zones 4–8
6–9 inches tall
Eurasia

Also called Black Flowering Sedge, this tiny plant can serve as a ground cover if you are not in a hurry. Creeping rhizomes eventually create a thick mat. Another moisture-loving sedge, it is often planted near a pond or stream bank. Black Sedge gets its common name from the unusual black scaly inflorescence that blooms just above its pretty bluish-gray leaves. Cut or mow the old foliage back in very early spring before new leaves begin to emerge.

Bright yellow leaf edges and powdery blue-green foliage distinguish the cultivar 'Variegata', which grows 12–14 inches tall. It is hardy to Zone 5.

PLANTING REQUIREMENTS

Plant in moist, wet or even boggy soils in shade or part sun. It will also grow in shallow water.

PROPAGATION

Divide creeping rhizomes in spring and transplant or plant ripened seed in fall. Plants will also self-sow.

Striped Weeping Sedge (*Carex oshimensis* 'Evergold')
Zones 5–9
12–15 inches tall
Japan

Fountains of weeping foliage, striped with deep green and luscious gold, arch from generous 2-foot-wide clumps of 'Evergold' to create a beautiful accent, a stunning mass, or a lovely reflection in a pool. True to its cultivar name, the gold striping persists, becoming richer and creamier as the season progresses. In catalogs, you may find these plants assigned names like 'Old Gold', 'Variegata', and 'Aureo-variegata', but these are just variations on a theme for this single exquisite composition—the cultivar 'Evergold'.

PLANTING REQUIREMENTS

Plant in average, well-drained soil in part sun to full shade. Once established, this sedge tolerates dry soil.

PROPAGATION

Divide in spring and transplant.

Plantain-Leaved Sedge (*Carex plantaginea*)
Zones 4–8
10–15 inches tall
Native to U.S.

The wide, heavily veined leaves of Plantain-Leaved Sedge resemble those of English Plantain, and are often up to 1 inch wide. Also known as Seersucker Sedge, its black 12–24-inch inflorescence emerges before the new foliage in early spring. The sheath at the base of the flowering stem (culm) is marked with accents of purple and burgundy red.

In the wild, this sedge grows with woodland wildflowers typically associated with a beech-maple forest. Although it will tolerate a limited amount of dry soil, too much drought can cause the tips and edges of the shiny, bright green leaves to become crisp and brown. It is easier to provide adequate moisture than try to trim off the browning foliage tips.

An evergreen, it is effective at the margins of ponds, along a stream bank, or at the edge of a water garden. If planted tight, it can make a good ground cover. It naturalizes well, and has been used as a substitute for turf grass. It seems to be slug resistant, unlike other large-leaved species.

'Dr. Richard Lighty' is slightly smaller and its flowering culm seldom exceeds 12 inches in height. Otherwise this cultivar resembles the species.

PLANTING REQUIREMENTS
Plant closely together in moist, humus-rich, well-drained soil in part to full shade.

PROPAGATION
Divide mature clumps in spring or sow ripened seed in the fall.

Tussock Sedge (*Carex stricta*)
Zones 4–8
1–3 feet tall
Native to U.S.

Nurseries often confuse Tussock Sedge with Tufted Sedge (*C. elata*). Native to the U.S., true Tussock Sedge grows like a little mophead. A finely textured, medium-green plant, it dominates North American sedge meadows, forming dense tussocks in marshy and wet environments in the wild. Several butterflies, including Mitchell's Satyr, Little Wood Satyr, Sedge Skipper, and Black Dash, depend on it as a larval food source. Tussock Sedge provides a buff colored architectural accent in the winter landscape and is an excellent choice for ponds, stream banks, or water gardens.

PLANTING REQUIREMENTS

Plant in wet or marshy, neutral to slightly acidic soil, or even in shallow water. Once established, it can tolerate periods of dryness. It will also thrive in average soil with adequate moisture. It prefers part to light shade or full sun. It is slow to get started.

PROPAGATION

Divide in spring or early fall.

Fox Sedge (*Carex vulpinoidea*)
Zones 4–8
2–3 feet tall
Native to U.S.

Fox Sedge has deep-green leaves and forms clumps about as wide as it is tall. This adaptable native is a common resident of moist or wet environments such as ravines, roadside ditches, low open woods, marshes, and swamps. It is highly recommended for sedge meadow installations, and can also prove valuable on stream banks or at the edge of a pond.

PLANTING REQUIREMENTS

Plant in moist or even wet soil in part shade or in full sun. It will survive periodic flooding. Although it prefers moisture, it will tolerate periods of dryness.

PROPAGATION

Divide in the spring or sow ripened seed in the fall.

Northern Sea Oats (*Chasmanthium latifolium* aka *Uniola latifolia*)

Zones 4–9
3–4 feet tall
Native to U.S.
Deer Resistant

A true shade lover, Northern Sea Oats, also called Wild Oats and River Oats, has an upright, gracefully arching growth habit. Check out this robust, warm-season grass just as the setting sun backlights the flat oat-like seedheads and you will know why it is sometimes dubbed Spangle Grass. Its unique inflorescence rises above broad green leaves, and sways in the slightest breeze. A mass of this grass makes a good transition between woodland and lawns. It is pretty hanging over the edge of a stream or pond, does a good job of stabilizing slopes, and makes a handsome statement as a specimen in front of a large tree or boulder. It can be grown in a large container. It even camouflages unsightly ripening bulb foliage.

Like any grass, it will reseed. Those seeds germinate easily and well, so consider cutting them for floral arrangements in the fall before they shatter and hit the dirt. In fact, collect them several times during the growing season, as they change from green to varying shades of rust, copper, and rich browns and finally become light buff after frost. These pretty things retain the color they had when cut.

Young seedlings are easy to weed out, but once they start maturing, their tenacious roots are tough to remove.

PLANTING REQUIREMENTS
Likes shady spots with moist, well-drained, humus-rich soil, but also tolerates average or even poor, dry soil. It will grow in any kind of shade and can even tolerate full sun, given adequate moisture. Cut it to the ground in early spring, before the new leaves begin to poke up. Space new mass plantings 24 inches apart.

PROPAGATION
Plant ripened seed in the fall, divide mature clumps in spring, or let it self-sow, transplanting and even combining clumps of seedlings.

Common Wood Reed (*Cinna arundinacea*)
Zones 2–9
3–5 feet tall
Native to U.S.

Wood Reed Grass or Common Wood Reed has wide leaves 3–4 feet long. Dense panicles of green seedheads point to the sky in late summer, and as the season draws to a close, these become warm, autumnal shades of brown and gold. It is found in woodlands all over the East, South, and Midwest. *C. latifolia* is similar but a bit smaller. Its airy panicles move gently in the breeze, evolving through shades of light green, lavender, and tan. Both species thrive in damp, shady spots and are worthy of inclusion in the shade garden.

PLANTING REQUIREMENTS
Plant in moist, humus-rich, woodland type soil in any kind of shade.

PROPAGATION
Divide in spring or early fall, or plant ripened seed in the fall.

Tufted Hair Grass (*Deschampsia caespitosa*)
Zones 4–9
18–30 inches tall
Native to U.S.

This cool-season native of high mountain meadows greens up early, and is still a major forage grass in the West. Panicles of ethereal silvery-green blooms tinged with purple float above the arching, shining pale-green foliage of the species, blooming throughout the summer. Handsome in mass plantings, this grass is also effective in naturalized gardens as a transition between woods and lawn, or as a companion for bold-foliaged plants like hostas or caladiums. In low-traffic areas, it can substitute for lawn grass. Nurseries carry several beautiful cultivars.

Hair Grass can be evergreen or semi-evergreen, depending upon the hardiness zone.

PLANTING REQUIREMENTS
Plant in light to medium shade in a moist spot with well-drained, humus-rich soil. It is dependent upon consistent moisture and dislikes excessive heat. Space new mass plantings 20–24 inches apart. Cut to the ground in early spring before new leaves emerge.

PROPAGATION
Divide in spring or early fall, plant ripened seed in fall. Hair Grass self-sows; seedlings can be gathered and transplanted in a single spot in the spring.

Crinkled Hair Grass (*Deschampsia flexuosa*)
Zones 2–9
8–12 inches
Native to U.S.

Spikelets of purple to golden bronze light up shady places as they glisten above finely textured, hair-like leaves. The graceful leaves arise from a small basal tuft. But don't be misled by the tiny size and demure countenance of this little miss. Unlike her larger sibling Tufted Hair Grass, this sturdy beauty can stand up to rigorous demands. In fact, in the wild she is generally found gracing dry, rocky spaces in shady woodlands. Crinkled Hair Grass will accept medium to dry planting sites on hillsides, woodlands, in rock gardens or in a perennial border.

PLANTING REQUIREMENTS
Plant in acidic to average well-drained soil in light to medium shade. Very drought resistant once established.

PROPAGATION
Divide in spring or early fall, plant ripened seed in the fall or transplant self-sown seedlings.

Beak Grass (*Diarrhena americana*)
Zones 5–7
12–14 inches tall
Native to U.S.
Small but mighty, Beak Grass can quickly cover a hillside to provide effective erosion control. This child of shady damp woods changes from graceful gleaming green foliage to fall shades of gold that would tempt Midas himself. Long arching seed stalks with unusual beak-like seed grains give this useful grass its common name.

PLANTING REQUIREMENTS
Plant in moist, humus-rich, well-drained soil about 12–15 inches apart. In the wild it can also be found in some very dry rocky sites.

PROPAGATION
Divide in spring or early fall, or plant ripened seed in fall.

Wild Rye (*Elymus* spp.)
Zones 3–8
2–4 feet tall
Native to U.S.

Four mild-mannered native grasses useful for woodland or wetland restoration, erosion control, or perennial gardens and borders are: Slender or Silky Wild Rye (*E. villosus*), which grows 1–2 feet tall and blooms in June. A mass planting makes a lovely meadow. July blooming Virginia Wild Rye (*E. virginicus*), slightly taller, matures at 2–4 feet. It too makes a nice meadow planting, but since it is showier than Silky Wild Rye, it also serves as an ornamental. Riverbank Wild Rye (*E. riparius*) is typically found along the bluffs of streams and rivers and in floodplains. It likes moisture and limey, alkaline soil and is found in the wild with natives such as American Bladdernut, Goldenrod, and False Solomon's Seal.

Noninvasive Blue Wild Rye (*E. glaucus*), commonly found in western North America, is the most useful of the four for garden borders. Hardy in Zones 4–9, it grows 2–4 feet tall and blooms from June to August. A favorite choice for restoration after fire, this non-rhizomatous species creates a huge clump of impressive, broad blue-green leaves, remaining attractive throughout the growing season.

PLANTING REQUIREMENTS
All will grow in part to light shade or in full sun and need moist, well-drained, humus-rich woodland type soil. Virginia Wild Rye is the most shade tolerant of the four.

PROPAGATION
Divide mature clumps in spring or early fall, plant ripened seed in fall, or gather and combine seedlings and transplant.

Scouring Rush (*Equisetum hyemale*)
Zones 4–10
3–4 feet tall
North America, Eurasia
AGGRESSIVE

Native Americans and settlers gathered Scouring Rush or Horsetail from marshy areas, because embedded in its stiff stems are a profusion of silica grains. Try tying these stems together as they did to make an effective pot scrubber. You will be amazed. It can take the finish off Teflon ware and dull your pruning shears! There is no foliage, but the tall jointed stalks are a handsome addition to Japanese-style gardens, wetland sites, ponds, streams and water gardens, and even floral arrangements. Evergreen in most zones.

'Robustum', aka Giant Horsetail or Giant Scouring Rush, grows 4–7 feet tall with a very upright, vertical growth habit.

PLANTING REQUIREMENTS
Plant in part to medium shade or in full sun in moist or even wet environments. Scouring Rush will also grow in standing shallow water. Space new plantings 2–3 feet apart. To contain, plant in a drain tile or other sturdy container, or insert plastic or metal barriers 12 inches deep. Shady Oaks Nursery advises leaving a couple inches of container uncovered with soil so it can't escape over the edge.

PROPAGATION
Spreads vigorously by rhizomes. Divide in spring or fall.

Festuca (*Festuca ovina* var. *glauca*)
Zones 4–9
10–12 inches tall
Europe, Eurasia
Deer Resistant

Finely textured silvery blue spikes characterize this small sun lover. It will tolerate some shade, but may have a more open growth habit with less light. My little clump grows reliably, maintaining its intense color, in a moderately shady spot. Commonly called Sheep Fescue, it occasionally appears in catalogs as *Festuca cinerea*. Several cultivars vary in shades of blue.

PLANTING REQUIREMENTS
Plant in average, well-drained soil in part to light shade or in full sun.

PROPAGATION
Divide mature clumps in spring or fall and transplant to retain the color of that particular clump. Seed will germinate, but the resulting seedlings will not all have the same coloration.

Japanese Hakone Grass (*Hakonechloa macra*)
Zones 4–9
8–12 inches tall
Japan

Whenever I see a mature planting of Japanese Hakone Grass, I imagine some invisible garden giant revealing his presence by huge, drooping, gloved fingers tapping the ground. This tropical looking grass has a pendulous growth habit. In fact, all of its leaves tend to arch to one side—one reason why it reminds me of giant fingers. Also called Japanese Forest Grass, the species has deep green foliage that changes to shades of copper, rosy-red, orange, and bronze in the fall. Although it spreads by creeping roots, it is not aggressive and never invasive. Neither as fast growing nor as robust as some grasses, it often takes a while to become established. *Hakonechloa* is expensive, but its unique beauty motivates many gardeners to pull out their checkbooks anyway.

Cultivars are not as hardy as the species. Most will survive in Zones 5–9, but during harsh winters, extra protection may be needed even in Zone 5. 'Aureola', a stunning variegated form with bright yellow weeping leaves striped with green, has an incredible bronzy red display in the fall. Golden Hakone Grass (*H. macra* 'Urahajusa Zuku') is another grass that Midas touched. The golden leaves glitter and glimmer in the shade, and when fall rolls around, tones of pinkish copper are added, eventually changing to rose and bronze.

PLANTING REQUIREMENTS
Plant in moist, humus-rich, well-drained soil in light shade. Yellow forms may need more light to maintain intense coloration. Dislikes dry soil and needs additional water during drought. Space new plantings 12–15 inches apart. Provide cultivars with a generous winter blanket of mulch.

PROPAGATION
Divide in spring or early fall.

Blue Oat Grass (*Helictotrichon sempervirens*)
Zones 4–8
12–36 inches tall
Europe, Eurasia
Deer Resistant

For intense silvery blue color, few grasses can beat well-mannered Blue Oat Grass. Like grapes or many of the blue hostas, the smooth leaves of this coarsely textured grass boast a "bloom" that is one of its selling points. Emerging stiff and erect, these long slender leaves arch ever more gracefully as the season progresses. It does flower, but sparsely.

Panicles of pale blue spikelets rise above the foliage from June to August, nodding on tall arching stems. These change to a pale whitish beige as they ripen.

Blue Oat Grass makes a beautiful focal point. It can be massed, incorporated into foundation plantings, or tucked into the ground at the point where two stone walls meet. Plant it near other blue-leaved plants or conifers, and provide striking contrasts with bright yellow hostas. A bluish-gray cultivar named 'Saphirsprundel' ('Sapphire Fountain' aka 'Sapphire') is hardy in Zones 4–9. It is more heat tolerant than the species.

PLANTING REQUIREMENTS

Plant in moist, humus-rich, well-drained soil in full sun or in part shade. Needs at least 4 hours of sunlight each day. It will flop in too much shade and may develop rust or other fungal diseases. Once established, it flourishes in hot, dry sites. Cut to the ground in early spring before new growth arises. Remove any unsightly leaves during the growing season.

PROPAGATION

Divide in spring or early fall, or plant ripened seed in the fall. Space new plantings 24 inches apart.

Bottlebrush Grass (*Hystrix patula*)
Zones 4–8
3–5 feet tall
Native to U.S.

This native is a true shade-lover, often found in moist woodlands. The pale greenish seedheads bloom from June to late August and look like those round brushes used to scrub the insides of bottles, hence its common name. Its genus name, *Hystrix*, is from the Greek, meaning porcupine. These spiky inflorescences stand 18–24 inches above broad, dark-green foliage, and catch any dappled light that flits across shaded spaces, lending an ethereal look to the shadows. A mass of this unique grass is effective in a naturalized garden or a shady perennial border. However, the show is over in the fall when the seedheads shatter and the leaves turn brown.

PLANTING REQUIREMENTS

Prefers moist, humus-rich, well-drained soil in light to moderate shade, but will accept nearly any growing conditions except a site that is too dry and sunny. This shade lover can tolerate full sun only in a consistently moist site with excellent drainage. Space new plantings 24–36 inches apart.

PROPAGATION

Divide in spring or early fall, or plant ripened seed in the fall.

Soft Rush (*Juncus effusus*)
Zones 4–8
1–4 feet tall
Native to U.S., worldwide

These leafless plants grow in wet, marshy environments, providing food and shelter for wildlife, controlling erosion, and spreading about as wide as they are tall. Naturalize Soft Rush along ponds or streams, or plant directly in shallow water for vertical interest. They also give good height to floral arrangements. These vigorous plants need room to spread and can form large colonies when conditions are favorable.

Also called Common Rush, Soft Rush has a golden brown or rust colored inflorescence that juts out about ⅓ of the way from the top of the tall straight leafless stalk (culm). These yellow-green culms become yellow-brown in fall, and tan in winter, providing consistent seasonal interest. Variegated forms have even more interesting coloration, putting on a good show in fall. Generally smaller than the species, they are useful as a group or mass, or planted as a specimen in a container.

PLANTING REQUIREMENTS

Plant in moist, boggy or even wet soil or in shallow standing water in part to light shade or in full sun. Cut to the ground in early spring. Space new plantings 18–24 inches apart. Will shrivel if conditions become too dry.

PROPAGATION

Divide creeping roots in spring or very early fall. May self-sow, but the minute seeds are difficult to collect. Seedlings of cultivars will not come true.

Snowy Woodrush (*Luzula nivea*)
Zones 4–9
8–24 inches tall
Europe

Glistening dewdrops sparkle on the downy white hairs that line the dark-green leaves of Snowy Woodrush. This striking rush is another native of the forest. Large clusters of creamy white flowers hover above the slender gray leaves, becoming the palest of porcelain beige as they age. Florists use these flowers in both fresh and dried arrangements. Underground rhizomes spread slowly into a solid mat, creating an effective ground cover, particularly under shrubs where little else will grow. It will also serve as a control for erosion. Note: It is much too aggressive for rock gardens or perennial borders.

'Marginata' has creamy-edged variegated foliage that lights up the forest floor, and tolerates more shade than the species. It is hardy in Zones 4–8. 'Snow Bird' only grows 8–12 inches high and wide. It has whiter flowers, narrower grayish-green leaves, and is smaller in all of its parts.

PLANTING REQUIREMENTS

Plant in moist humus-rich, slightly acidic soil in part to light shade. Once established, will tolerate dry shade. Space new plantings 18–24 inches apart.

PROPAGATION

Divide in spring or early fall. Seed will germinate but seedlings may not be true to type.

Purple Siberian Melic (*Melica altissima*)
Zones 4–8
6–12 inches tall
Eurasia
MOIST SOIL REQUIRED

Another cool-season grass, Purple Siberian Melic has dainty panicles in shades of purple and soft buff on 2–3-foot stems. It is effective in the middle of the shady perennial border as a "see-through" plant, provided other perennials or summer annuals are planted in front of it to take its place in midsummer in case it goes dormant. It is sometimes planted as a mass, combined with other grasses in a naturalized meadow, or used as a lawn substitute in a spot where drifts of its purple flowers can be enjoyed.

PLANTING REQUIREMENTS

Purple Siberian Melic enjoys consistently moist, humus-rich, well-drained soil in part to moderate shade. It abhors hot sunny planting sites or dry soil and will quickly go into early dormancy in such conditions. For dry planting sites, look for the native *Melica mutica* as an alternative.

Remove spent seedheads if self-sowing is undesirable. Cut dormant plants to the ground and they will resprout when temperatures cool.

PROPAGATION

Divide mature clumps in spring or early fall.

Purple Moor Grass (*Molinia caerulea*)

Zones 4–9

1–3 feet tall

Eurasia

In midsummer, thousands of tiny purple flowers appear, dancing 6–7 feet above the tufted, arching foliage of this bold, warm-season grass, and soon change to shades of gold, orange, and brown. This noninvasive grass is gathered for fresh or dried floral arrangements, planted in shady gardens or perennial borders, and massed as a transition between lawn and woodland. The long, narrow leaves take on autumnal shades in the fall. With the advent of the first hard frost, it completely breaks off at ground level and goes dormant, reappearing the following spring. This low-maintenance plant is on a par with a self-cleaning oven!

Most gardeners are familiar with the popular Maiden Grass (*Miscanthus* spp.), but I think Purple Moor Grass and its unique cultivars beat it "leaves down." Look for 'Strahlenquelle', 'Heidebraut', 'Moorflamme', and 'Rotschopf'. 'Skyracer' (*M. caerulea* subsp. *arundinacea*) is one of the tallest cultivars, reaching 7–8 feet tall. These are all hardy in Zones 4–8. Little 'Variegata', seldom exceeding 12–18 inches tall, has beautiful leaves with creamy yellowish-white striping. Purple flowers stand about a foot above the variegated foliage, blooming in late June. Hardy in Zones 5–9, it flourishes in light shade.

PLANTING REQUIREMENTS

Grows best in part to light dappled shade or in full sun. Plant in moist, acidic, well-drained soil, rich in humus. It will tolerate some dryness. It is slow to get established or for an individual clump to reach any appreciable size, so purchase the largest clump you can afford. Space new plantings 15–24 inches apart.

PROPAGATION

Divide mature clumps in spring or early fall. May self-sow.

Deer Tongue Grass (*Panicum clandestinum*)
Zones 4–9
1–4 feet tall
Native to U.S.

Imagine a warm-season native grass that looks like bamboo and acts like a ground cover. This is the perfect plant for those wild spaces where something interesting is allowed to just "do its own thing." And interesting it is, with its short, wide, tongue-like leaves that jut out at angles from hairy rust-colored stems. Deer Tongue Grass emerges deep green in early spring, but by autumn it lights up the shadows with its bright yellow leaves. Its inflorescence resembles that of our native Switch Grass (see below), lasting for nearly the entire growing season. It dies to the ground in late fall, reappearing the following spring.

It can be used in a naturalized area, along a path, on a hillside, near a pond or stream, or at the edge of the woods as a transition between the wild and civilized areas. Just don't plant it in your shady garden because it is far too rambunctious.

PLANTING REQUIREMENTS

Plant in moist, humus-rich, well-drained soil in part to moderate shade. The deep-green leaves will become yellow-green in more light.

PROPAGATION

Divide in spring or early fall, or plant ripened seed in fall.

Switch Grass (*Panicum virgatum*)
Zones 4–9
3–5 feet tall

Native to U.S.
Deer Resistant

A deep-rooted denizen of the prairies, this sturdy, warm-season grass stands straight and tall in my moderately shaded garden, blooming heartily every year. Switch Grass has always been one of my favorites because it has light airy panicles, described by some as "sprangled," a graceful, upright arching growth habit, and rich, warm, yellow autumn hues.

A versatile clumping grass, it sends down deep fibrous roots to hold the soil, which makes it an excellent choice for stabilization and erosion control on banks and hillsides, particularly along highways and roadsides. It provides food and cover for wildlife, looks nice near water, can be used as a ground cover or a transition between lawn and natural areas, and occasionally graces floral arrangements on my dining room table. What more can one ask of a native grass?

'Heavy Metal' has glorious metallic powdery blue leaves that are often a bit broader than those of the species. It has an upright form and grows 3–4 feet tall, turning bright yellow in the fall. 'Cloud Nine', another blue cultivar, has darker gold fall leaves. 'Dallas Blue' has handsome wide blue leaves and pale mauve flowers in late summer. For leaves with an intensely red fall color, choose 'Haense Herms' which boasts bright reddish-orange fall color. The dark green foliage of 'Shenandoah' ripens to red in July, then deepens to burgundy wine in the fall. 'Rotstrahlbusch', a 4-foot-tall beauty, also has striking red fall foliage.

PLANTING REQUIREMENTS

Prefers moist, humus-rich soil in part to light shade or in full sun. More adaptable than either Big Bluestem or Indian Grass, Switch Grass is tolerant of extremes, thriving in either dry or heavy, wet soil and even in boggy areas. Since it can quickly dominate new prairie plantings, gardeners are advised to use lower concentrations of this seed.

PROPAGATION

Divide in spring or plant ripened seed in the fall. Named cultivars do not come true from seed.

Bluegrass (*Poa* spp.)
Zones 4–7
12–24 inches tall
Native to U.S., Europe

Most Americans are familiar with Kentucky Bluegrass (*P. pratensis*), since homeowners all across North America spend so much time watering, fertilizing, spraying and mowing it. However, did you know there is a native bluegrass available as an alternative for lawns? Spence Restoration Nursery offers Woodland Bluegrass (*P. sylvestris*), a species of damp woodland that loves the shade. It blooms in April and May. Although it prefers consistent moisture, it can also be found in dry sites in the wild. Use it as a continuation of your formal lawn, extending that wonderful swath of green up into the woods.

Wood Bluegrass (*P. nemoralis*), also known as Wood Meadow Grass, is a European version. It grows 12–24 inches tall and is hardy in Zones 3–9. It has finely textured, medium green foliage, a pretty inflorescence from June through August, and best of all, it loves shade. Unlike sod-forming Kentucky Bluegrass, Wood Bluegrass does not increase by creeping rootstocks. Naturalized in the U.S., it grows in meadows and open woodlands in the wild. Hardy in Zones 4–7, Forest Bluegrass (*P. chaixii*) is less dependent upon consistent moisture, but is the least heat tolerant of these lawn substitutes. This shade lover really suffers in hot climates.

Other Poa species are available as alternatives for traditional lawn grass. Consider planting one of these shade-lovers for a natural looking, no-maintenance lawn for less formal areas or stretching up into a woodland. Of course if you start watering, fertilizing, spraying and mowing it, then you may as well stick with good old Kentucky Bluegrass (which is not even native to Kentucky, but, like so many of our ancestors, came here from Europe).

PLANTING REQUIREMENTS
These species are tolerant of a wide variety of soils, but given a choice, prefer growing in moist, slightly acidic soil in light shade.

PROPAGATION
Seed in fall or early spring. Once established, these grasses effectively reseed.

Dark Green Bulrush (*Scirpus atrovirens*)
Wool Grass (*Scirpus cyperinus*)
Zones 4–8
2–5 feet tall
Native to U.S.

Long before Pharaoh's daughter found baby Moses hidden in the bulrushes in his little "boat," people have admired these plants as ornamentals for wet places. Dark Green Bulrush, also called Willdenow, grows in wet ditches. It sends up a 3–5-foot stalk (culm) in June with several small ball-like clusters of spikelets at the top. These change from green to cinnamon-brown. This bulrush provides a nice vertical accent and is easy to grow in wet environments.

For the star of the show, look for Wool Grass. This unique bulrush produces a seedhead in late summer that will elicit rave reviews—guaranteed. Plant this pretty thing near a pond or in a wet, boggy area, but try to site where you can appreciate its beauty from inside the house.

PLANTING REQUIREMENTS
Plant in moist or wet soil. Both species prefer full sun but will tolerate light shade.

PROPAGATION
Propagate by division in spring or early fall, or plant ripened seed in the fall. Self-sows.

Prairie Cord Grass (*Spartina pectinata*)
Zones 4–7
4–7 feet tall
Native to U.S.
AGGRESSIVE
Deer Resistant

This warm-season native forms a solid, impenetrable mass of rhizomes within two years, which explains why Neil Diboll calls it the "grand master grass of wet prairies and sloughs." One of the principal grasses of the tall-grass prairie, it can send its roots 10 feet into the earth. Try weeding that out! This is definitely not for the traditional perennial border. But what a winner when it is asked to hold slippery wet hillsides or crumbling edges of ponds or streams, or to bring beauty to a marshy environment.

Prairie Cord Grass emerges in early April, growing quickly. In late summer, 8–9-foot-tall stalks soar up into the bright blue skies, creating a haze of dainty purplish-brown spikelets. Brilliant golden yellow leaves create a shimmering fountain in the fall. In winter, this gracefully arching grass stands up to snow and rain, creating good winter interest. Once established, it will tolerate extremes, surviving in wet or dry situations.

Variegated 'Aureomarginata', also known as Golden-edged Prairie Cord Grass, has green leaves narrowly edged with soft yellow. The entire clump becomes a clear yellow in the fall. Like the species, it is an aggressive colonizer.

PLANTING REQUIREMENTS
Plant in moist soil where it is allowed to run and spread. It prefers full sun but will thrive in part or very light shade. Too much shade will cause it to flop.

PROPAGATION
Plant seed in the fall in moist soil. Divide rhizomes in spring or fall.

Frost Grass (*Spodiopogon sibericus*)
Zones 5–8
2–3 feet tall
Asia, Siberia

Frost Grass forms a neat upright clump of bamboo-like leaves that appear to be gathered together in a compact, tightly rounded shape. Non-invasive, it is perfect for a small space. Its downy inflorescence sparkles and glistens in the shade, especially when backlit by the sun. Often in late fall, the rich medium green leaves are transformed into glowing tones of burgundy wine and red. However, fall color is not always predictable on this tropical looking, warm-season grass since it is susceptible to early frosts.

Use as a transition between woods and lawn, in a mass or undulating swath, in a mixed shrub border, as a specimen or focal point, or even as a hedge. Some sources list it as hardy in Zones 4–8.

PLANTING REQUIREMENTS
Plant in part to light or moderate shade or in full sun in moist, humus-rich, well-drained soil. More shade will produce a looser form and it may flop. It will not tolerate drought.

PROPAGATION
Divide in the spring or plant ripened seed in the fall.

Not Recommended

Reed Canary Grass (*Phalaris arundinacea*)
Zones 4–9
2–5 feet tall
Eurasia

Highly touted as a good erosion control and source of forage for animals, rhizomatous Reed Canary Grass has spread so aggressively that it is now on the invasive exotic list. Although there may be a North American genotype, strains of European seed, imported into the U.S., have proved more vigorous. Since it is impossible to distinguish the invasive exotic from the native, neither is recommended for planting.

Ribbon Grass (*Phalaris arundinacea* var. *picta*)
Zones 4–9
18–36 inches tall
Eurasia

Ribbon Grass has been a favorite since Victorian times. This cool-season grass has creamy-yellow or white striped variegation. It tolerates just about any kind of growing conditions from wet to dry, sun to shade, poor to rich soil. However, like its big brother, Canary Reed Grass, it is overly aggressive, crowding out native species and causing untold problems for wildlife and conservation managers. Commonly available cultivars include 'Dwarf Garters', 'Feesey's Form' (aka 'Strawberries and Cream'), 'Luteopicta', 'Picta', 'Tricolor', 'Woods Dwarf', 'Gardener's Garters'. None are recommended.

Common Reed (*Phragmites australis*)
Zones 4–10
8–18 feet tall
Eurasia

Common Reed is a veritable giant, sometimes stretching over 15 feet tall. Huge, dark plumes rise above the wide, stiff, hollow-stemmed leaves. Often used as a focal point, it does not remain a specimen for long. Soon it multiplies and divides, popping up in one unexpected spot after another and defying anyone to stop it. It fills up ponds and standing water, crowds out native plants, and creates a monoculture that is unfriendly to wildlife populations. Cutting or burning simply invigorates it. Like Houdini, it can escape nearly any attempt at confinement. Don't plant this alien invader! There is also a native genotype, but it is best to avoid planting that as well.

Bamboo (*Pleioblastus* spp. aka *Arundinaria* spp.)
(*Phyllostachys* spp. in Zones 5–10)
Zones 4–9
2–15 feet tall
Asia

Many gardeners appreciate the interesting foliage and texture of bamboos, as well as their unfailing ability to increase rapidly, but when you read grass books that include "eradication" as a major part of the plant description, you *know* trouble is lurking. In Japan, I once saw a bamboo forest that appeared to go on forever. Nothing else grew in this massive site. Beautiful in the slanting rays of the afternoon sunlight, it was nevertheless a warning that this plant is not to be trusted. I know that many authors insist some species are not aggressive, but as far as I am concerned, Bamboo spells t.r.o.u.b.l.e. My personal advice is to look at photographs, read about it in books, or visit Japan, but never, never invite it into your yard.

Other invasive grasses that I don't recommend are Giant Reed (*Arundo donax*), Asiatic Sand Sedge (*Carex kobomugi*), Fountain Grass (*Pennisetum setaceum*), Stilt Grass (*Microstegium vimineum*), and Burma Reed (*Neyraudia reynaudiana*).

10.

Indispensable Allies

Perennials for Shade

Columbine

Perennials reduce maintenance while giving stability, continuity, color, texture, and fragrance to your shade garden. They are truly your allies. In this chapter, I have chosen herbaceous plants that every gardener or nursery owner recognizes as "perennials." (Many perennials listed in chapter 7 such as Lady's Mantle, Brunnera, Epimedium, and Euphorbia are also suitable for the perennial garden or border.) All will tolerate at least some degree of shade; whether or not they are truly low maintenance largely depends on where they are sited. As Bonnie Lee Appleton says, "Growing conditions determine which plants will thrive in your landscape."

Some perennials may go dormant in too much drought, or die back to the ground when the temperatures drop too low. Once, after returning from vacation during an exceptionally hot, dry summer, I found my beautiful stand of Astilbe dried up and looking *very* dead. It was fortunate that I did not pull them out of the garden that fall, because the following spring they leafed out and bloomed as usual.

As I stated in chapter 2, there is no such thing as a no-maintenance garden. To achieve genuine low maintenance, combine plants that are equally hardy and enjoy similar planting requirements. Experiment and be creative. Make a photographic record of the garden's progress throughout the season, and if the results do not please, do a little rearranging in the fall.

Some perennials rarely need dividing. Others should be lifted and divided every 3–4 years. If you have to divide a plant more often than that, it ceases to be a low-maintenance choice, but there will be times when you may decide that growing it is worth the extra labor.

Alternating 2–3 species of a similar plant can extend the bloom season. Some friends plant mixed masses of early, mid-season, and late-blooming yellow daylilies. Using 3 varieties, they plant "early, mid, late; early, mid, late" to create a continuous swath of yellow that lasts and lasts.

To prevent tall perennials from flopping, consider pinching out the terminal growth or even cutting the plant back about ⅓ early in the season. This results in a sturdier, bushier plant that can stand on its own. Often it encourages heavier flowering as well, but the flowering may be later in the season. If you want the full-sized perennial rather than a shortened version, plant several varieties close together to support each other. In Britain, they stake with sticks and branches, which look more natural and are less obtrusive than the green wire things Americans purchase. In lieu of staking, elect to ignore the flopping tendency, or omit the floppers altogether.

Most perennials bloom for 1–3 weeks. We gardeners assume the purpose of flowers is to provide beauty, color, and fragrance in the garden. However, plants *know* that the purpose of each flower is to attract pollinators. After pollination, the flower withers and dies. Removing spent flowers, called deadheading, tricks the plant into producing new flowers, but what an arduous task! I rarely deadhead unless I am trying to curb volunteers that result from fallen seed (a very effective practice, by the way). If I think that rebloom is desirable on a particular plant, I wait until it has bloomed about ½ to ⅔ of its normal blooming time, then deadhead the whole plant at once. After a short lull, the plant puts forth a fresh show of flowers. This method is probably not as effective as daily deadheading, but is surely a lot less work.

Nursery owners use liquid fertilizer regularly, which is why their potted specimens look so large and healthy. And of course the extra ration of water does no harm either. In fact, adding additional water may be the most important way to encourage vigorous plant growth on many perennials.

Most of the perennials in this chapter are not overly susceptible to heavy insect damage or other diseases. Often, disease is the direct result of poor gardening practices. Plants prone to mildew attacks are telling you they need extra space for good air circulation. Those exhibiting symptoms of rust should be removed and not composted. Use sulfur if you need a fungicide. Insecticidal soap or even a strong stream of water will take care of most insects. I sometimes resort to chemical fungicides, but seldom use potent insecticides because I know those broad-spectrum chemicals dispatch the good guys as well as the bad guys. Besides, I love butterflies and know that to have those fluttering beauties you must put up with the voracious eating machines called larvae, so I consider a few munching-holes acceptable. I dispatch Japanese Beetles by knocking them into a pailful of soapy water.

Our climate has changed in the past few years, and drought now seems the norm. As you read this chapter, realize that plants that need a moist site should be planted only there—in a site that is *naturally* moist, not one made moist by the garden hose or a sprinkler system. If your site often dries out, choose other plants.

I rarely water my perennials. They send their roots deep into the soil to survive. In summers with intense drought some plants will go dormant, but I lose few. My soil is loamy and I keep a 2–3-inch mulch over the roots (but not next to the crown). Granted, my gardens look more lush and beautiful in spring and early summer when there is adequate natural rainfall. If they begin to look a little ratty by the end of the summer, that is part of my contribution to the environment. Besides, I have always hated dragging hoses!

I make two exceptions to this no-additional-water rule. I keep newly installed plants thoroughly and consistently watered for at least 3 weeks after planting and then water periodically throughout the first growing season. I also water those special plants that I do not want to risk losing through my tough love. When I do water, I water long and deeply, often pouring a whole bucket of water over a special plant, especially trees and shrubs. The worst kind of watering practice is sprinkling. If a plant only gets sprinkled, its roots will fan out over the surface and then when more moisture is not forthcoming, those roots will dry out and die. If you water deeply and less often, the roots delve deep into the soil, making stronger, healthier plants.

Many gardeners keep plant diaries. I use my wall calendar to record the day a particular perennial begins to bloom. Occasionally I remember to record when they quit blooming as well. Such a record is helpful in planting or redoing a perennial garden, especially for flowering plants.

It is also helpful to tag plants to identify flower color. I like to mass yellow daylilies and invariably get an apricot one stuck in where it does not belong. Sometimes I write the color on a daylily leaf. However, the writing disappears when the leaves turn brown, so be sure to transplant before that happens.

In my back yard, the turf grass follows the shade line. In this way I got rid of the spindly grass that was not getting enough sun. The rich carpet of green sets off the perennial beds. I have paths winding through the gardens, and have put a bench, swing, or chair so I can sit *in* my garden to enjoy it. The soil in my gardens is covered with plants most of the season and few weeds dare creep in. Any that do are yanked out on my weekly rounds. For a successful low-maintenance perennial garden, study your particular site and plant accordingly. With careful planning and planting, your shade garden will not only be the coolest place in the heat of the summer, it will also be "cool," as my grandchildren say. Just remember to take time to enjoy your "indispensable allies."

Perennials for Shade

Monkshood (*Aconitum* spp.)
Zones 3–7
3–5 feet tall
Europe, Asia, U.S.
REQUIRES MOIST SOIL
Deer Resistant

This striking plant boasts flowers that resemble a monk's hood or a soldier's helmet, hence two common names—Monkshood and Helmet Flower. Aconitum species and cultivars come in a variety of colors, including pink and white. Alternate plantings of Common Monkshood

(*A. napellus*) with Azure Monkshood (*A. carmichaelii* aka *A. fischeri*) to extend the bloom season. The first has dark blue flowers in early to mid-summer. The latter's light blue flowers will continue the show into the fall. The dark green cut leaves of both are handsome all season. The tuberous roots are poisonous; there are conflicting reports on the toxicity of other parts of the plant.

These tall, clump-forming plants, somewhat resembling delphiniums, look good toward the back of the garden. If they flop, encourage them to stand upright by planting small shrubs or mid-sized perennials in front, or choose shorter selections with sturdy stalks like Azure Monkshood, 'Blue Sceptre', or 'Bressingham Spire'. And of course staking is an option, but *you* know about maintenance!

PLANTING REQUIREMENTS

Grows well in partial shade or full sun. Set the crown 1 to 1–1/2 inches under the soil, and plant in humus-rich, well drained, neutral to slightly acidic soil that is consistently moist. Dislikes alkaline soil or drought. Space 12–18 inches apart. Mulch in more northern zones. Once established, just leave alone.

PROPAGATION

Divide plants in spring or fall or plant seed as soon as it ripens.

Striped Sweet Flag (*Acorus calamus* 'Variegatus')
Zones 4–9
24–36 inches tall
Europe, U.S.
REQUIRES MOIST SOIL

Most gardeners seek vertical accents; when variegation is part of the package, how can anyone resist? Striped Sweet Flag has narrow iris-like leaves of soft green and creamy white. What a beauty for a troublesome wet spot! And of course the all-green form (*A. calamus*) is tough as nails. An iris lookalike, it is no relation.

Zone 5 gardeners might check the Plant Delights catalog for selections such as 'Licorice Sweet Flag'; *A. gramineus* 'Minimus Aureus', with a tiny golden narrow leaf; and a dwarf Striped Sweet Flag (*A. gramineus* 'Variegatus') which gets to be only 6–12 inches tall and can be used as a ground cover in a damp spot.

PLANTING REQUIREMENTS

Prefers very moist, even boggy, soil, but will grow in any loamy, well-drained garden soil with consistent moisture. Plant in light shade, part shade, or full sun. Space 8–15 inches apart.

PROPAGATION

Divide in early spring, or in August.

Bluestar (*Amsonia tabernaemontana*)
Zones 3–9
18–36 inches tall
Native to U.S.
Deer Resistant

    Mass this maintenance-free plant at the edge of the woods, near a walkway, or in a perennial border. In the spring or early summer, tiny light-blue stars will cover the ever-increasing clumps of narrow dark-green leaves, creating a heavenly scene for several weeks. The seedpods are reminiscent of milkweed pods. In the fall, the willow-like leaves change to a clear yellow. For a shorter version, try *A. montana*, which seldom gets much taller than 12–15 inches.

    Bluestar will grow in light shade, but appreciates a little sunlight each day or it can become leggy. If that happens, cut it back hard after flowering and it will resprout. Other options include letting it lean against other perennials or installing a support ring early in the season for the leaves to grow through.

PLANTING REQUIREMENTS

Thrives in just about any soil in light shade, part shade or full sun. Space new plantings 12–18 inches apart.

PROPAGATION

Sow seed immediately after ripening. Although you may divide this plant in spring or fall, it is best to leave it alone once established.

Japanese Anemone (*Anemone japonica*)
Zones 4–8
30–48 inches tall
Japan, Asia
Deer Resistant

Japanese Anemones with their shades of pink, rose, and white rise above gleaming dark green foliage and live up to their other common name—windflower—as they dance and sway in the autumn breezes. 'Honorine Jobert' (*A.* × *hybrida* var. *alba*) has striking white 2–3-inch flowers with golden centers that light up dark spaces until a hard frost nips their beauty. 'Whirlwind' has white double flowers with bright yellow centers. Other good cultivars include 'Queen Charlotte', semi-double soft pink flowers; 'Pamina', deep rose-red; 'Max Vogel', pink; and 'Richard Arends', silvery lavender-pink. For a lovely dark-pink double, look for 'Serenade'. 'September Sprite' is a tiny one, seldom exceeding 15 inches tall.

Another late-season bloomer is Grapeleaf Anemone (*A. tomentosa* aka *A. vitifolia* 'Robustissima'), more compact than *A.* × *hybrida*. Its silvery-rose and bright-pink flowers float 24–36 inches above rich green lobed and scalloped leaves. Fluffy white seedheads provide winter interest. 'Robustissima' withstands drought, seldom needs help standing proud, increases readily, and will survive to Zone 3. 'September Charm' (*A. hupehensis*), hardy in zones 5–8, has flowers in shades of silver, rose, pink and purple. False Anemone (*Anemonopsis macrophylla*) demands consistent moisture and will not survive in a dry site. (See chapter 12 for more anemones.)

PLANTING REQUIREMENTS

Anemones prefer moist soil, but will flourish in any good garden soil as long as it is well drained. They are happiest in bright dappled shade, or sited where they get 3–4 hours of sunlight each day. Space new plantings 18–24 inches apart. Zone 4 gardeners may want to add additional mulch for added winter protection.

PROPAGATION

Plant ripened seed in the fall, or divide and transplant mature clumps in the spring. These are pass-alongs; you should be able to beg a start from a gardening friend.

Columbine (*Aquilegia canadensis*)
Zones 3–8
12–30 inches tall
Native to U.S.

Hybrids
Deer Resistant

Columbine is a workhorse of the shade garden. It blooms in the wild, can be easily naturalized in woodlands, and reproduces happily in perennial borders. The native species has delicate reddish-orange and yellow flowers. A multitude of hybrids and cultivars offer a wide array of flower colors, sizes, and shapes, including double flowers. Most do not bloom as long as the native, however. Dwarf columbines are particularly effective at the front of a border.

I usually cut my columbines to the ground after they flower to force new leaves to grow. The resulting mound of foliage stays neat and tidy all season. If leaf miners start making their winding white trails, cut and discard affected leaves. These little insects are not lethal, just a cosmetic nuisance.

Columbine is one of the larval food sources for the Columbine Duskywing butterfly, and the nectar-rich flowers are a favorite of hummingbirds.

PLANTING REQUIREMENTS
Likes good, rich well-drained garden soil in any kind of shade or in sun.

PROPAGATION
Seeding is the best method because established plants resent being tampered with. Once the seedpods are dry, shake the small black seeds like pepper on unmulched ground in the fall. They germinate well. In the spring, I often carefully dig and transplant tiny seedlings that gather around the base of the mother. Some seedlings survive; others do not. Consistent moisture is the key to success.

Arum (*Arum italicum*)
Zones 5–9
12 inches
Asia
Deer Resistant

Dark green arrow-shaped leaves mottled with silvery white veins appear unexpectedly in late fall and remain evergreen for months. I have a mass of Arum outside my kitchen window and as I look out at the wintry world, it is nice to see this little touch of green. Then in early summer, a white flower resembling a Calla Lily suddenly shoots up and the leaves disappear until autumn. I usually plant white impatiens to fill in the blank spot. A relative of Jack-in-the-Pulpit, Arum next produces a huge dense cluster of berries. These come in a multitude of sunset colors that shimmer in the shade.

Arum is handsome as a focal point near the base of a mature tree or a large boulder. It is a good no-maintenance companion for ferns, hostas, and astilbe.

PLANTING REQUIREMENTS
Plant the fat tubers 8–10 inches deep in a moist, well-drained spot in part shade in either spring or fall.

PROPAGATION
In the fall, place the ripened berries in a sieve under barely warm running water and rub gently to remove the pulp. Plant immediately and do not allow to dry out. Remove offsets from the tubers and transplant.

Goatsbeard (*Aruncus dioicus*)
Zones 3–8
3–4 feet tall
Native to U.S., Europe, Asia
Deer Resistant

Goatsbeard's feathery upright plumes of creamy white gleam above beautifully cut dark-green leaves and light up the shade. This perennial makes a dramatic statement at the back of any border, especially when sited in front of tall evergreens. If your gardening space is not large enough to accommodate the hefty native species, the European cultivar 'Kneiffii', with its heavily cut ferny foliage and smaller size, may be a better choice. However, it is not as hardy.

Colston Burrell also recommends Korean Goatsbeard (*A. aethusifolius*), 'Child of Two Worlds', a 2–3-foot-tall cross of native and European Goatsbeard, and *A. dioicus* × *aethusifolius*, a shorter 1–2-foot-tall hybrid with a very compact growth habit.

PLANTING REQUIREMENTS
Shade to part shade in humus-rich, moist, well-drained soil. They will also grow in somewhat dry sites. Allow lots of room for this large plant

to spread and show off. Korean Goatsbeard needs a little more sun to bloom profusely.

PROPAGATION
Divide in spring or fall or plant ripened seeds in fall.

Aster (*Aster* spp.)
Zones 3–8
12–36 inches tall
Native to U.S.
Deer Resistant

Blues and purples are coveted colors in gardens, and with asters you can have them. Although most asters prefer full sun, there are a few that do well in varying degrees of shade. 'Purple Dome', a more compact cultivar of New England Aster (*A. novae-angliae*) covers itself with rich, deep-purple flowers with golden centers. We planted it on a partly shaded hillside. 'Purple Dome' tolerates our average to dry planting site, blooms well, and does not flop.

The lavender-blue ray flowers of Blue Wood Aster (*A. cordifolius*) begin blooming in September and continue into October. It grows 12–36 inches tall, looking like a little bush covered with tiny blue stars. White Wood Aster (*A. divaricatus*) is similar, but with white ray flowers in the fall. Both do well in average to dry soil in part to full shade. However, they will flop a bit in deep shade. The lavender-flowering Short's Aster (*A. shortii*) is another that puts on its lovely display in September and early October and does well in shade. Side-Flowering Aster (*A. lateriflorus*) has prolific white flowers in September and October. Mass at the edge of the woodlands for a spectacular effect. It gets about 2 feet tall and loves a partly shaded spot. Foliage of dark-purple hues complement bright white, daisy-like flowers surrounding raspberry-red centers on the 36-inch-tall *A. lateriflorus* 'Prince'. Zone 5 gardeners may enjoy the mum-like *A. dumosius* 'Wood's Pink'. It has handsome lavender-pink ray flowers with bright golden centers. This compact, disease-resistant plant gets to be 16 inches tall.

Butterflies and hummingbirds delight in the nectar of asters.

PLANTING REQUIREMENTS

Asters thrive in average well-drained soil and tolerate limited dryness. Note light requirements for individual species listed above. Mass them for the most impressive effect.

PROPAGATION

Seed in the fall, or division in spring or fall. Cultivars must be divided, since they will not come true to type from seed.

Astilbe (*Astilbe* spp.)

Zones 4–8

6–30 inches tall

Asia, U.S.

PREFERS MOIST SOIL

Deer Resistant

Airy spires of tightly packed flowers rise above the finely cut green leaves of Astilbe, one of the most beloved plants for the shade garden.

Astilbes can be very effective en masse as either a single hue or as a kaleidoscope of color. The divided leaves have toothed edges. Beautiful all summer, they complement virtually any shade plant. Cultivars are too numerous to catalog here. The stoloniferous *chinensis* Astilbes tolerate more dryness and make good ground covers (see chapter 7).

Did you know that there is even a native Astilbe (*A. biternata*)? It is also known as False Goatsbeard because of its strong resemblance to that perennial (*Aruncus dioicus*), although it is less tolerant of full sun. At 3–5 feet tall, it is a "back of the border" plant.

PLANTING REQUIREMENTS

Astilbes need a moist, well-drained, neutral to slightly acidic soil. They can tolerate sun if the soil is kept consistently moist. In fact, they flower better with a little more light, so you may want to put them near the edge of your shady garden.

PROPAGATION

Divide and transplant in early spring or late fall.

Roger's Flower (*Astilboides tabularis*)
Rodgersia (*Rodgersia* spp.)
Zones 4–7
3–5 feet tall
China, Korea
REQUIRES MOIST SOIL

Picture a child sneaking off to the garden with a scissors in hand, using it to make little snips all around each large rounded leaf of *Astilboides*. Handsome in their own right, these interesting leaves are topped by tall white panicles of bright white flowers in early summer.

Astilboides tabularis is often listed in reference books as *Rodgersia tabularis*. The primary difference in the two species is in the huge leaves. *Rodgersia's* big, bold leaves are compound or palmate, while *Astilboides* has simple rounded ones.

Also called Roger's Flower, Rodgersia demands moist, well-drained soil but cannot tolerate wet feet, so good drainage is as essential as consistent moisture. I planted my first Rodgersia in our woodland garden, but the soil was not consistently moist, so the plant never bloomed and eventually disappeared altogether.

Rodgersia's huge astilbe-like plumes of summer blooming flowers are spectacular. There are several species, each with distinctive characteristics. Creamy pink flowers rise like a vision on hairy stalks over the bronzy, heavily textured foliage of *R. aesculifolia*. Rich dark-green "hands" and rosy-pink summer flowers characterize *R. pinnata henrici*. 'Hercules' has color-crayon pink flowers above leaves with red stems. The 5-fingered leaves of *R. podophylla* emerge bronzy green, turn deep green and then change to autumnal tones of rich bronzy reds. Yellowish-white flowers are the hallmark of this plant. Neat *R. sambucifolia* has a tidy growth habit with huge, flattened, creamy white flower sprays.

PLANTING REQUIREMENTS
Plant in moist, shady spots in humus-rich, well-drained soil. These perennials will tolerate some sun if the soil is consistently moist.

PROPAGATION
Divide in spring or fall, or sow seeds in fall.

Masterwort (*Astrantia major*)
Zones 4–8
12–24 inches tall
Europe
REQUIRES MOIST SOIL

Pincushion-like flowers on dark wiry stems float above Masterwort in May and June and then rebloom throughout the summer. Masterwort appreciates having its spent flower stalks cut to the ground as an alternative to deadheading.

A. major 'Rubra' has bright red flowers with an interesting greenish circle surrounding a star-like red center. 'Sunningdale Variegated' sports rich green foliage with a creamy yellow edge which reverts to all green as the summer progresses. Its pale creamy-pink flowers bloom on and off all summer. 'Shaggy' is just that—shaggy! But interesting. It has larger flowers than the species.

PLANTING REQUIREMENTS

Average to moist garden soil in partial to medium shade. Does well when planted near a stream. Will languish and die in dry soil.

PROPAGATION

Divide in spring or fall, or sow seeds in the fall. Cultivars will not come true from seed, so need to be divided.

False Indigo (*Baptisia* spp.)
Zones 3–9
18–48 inches tall
Native to U.S.

Also known as Wild Indigo, these tall perennials are wonderful at the back of the border. Baptisias have grayish-green foliage and large, heavy black seedpods that rattle in the breeze in the fall. The flower spikes of the tallest, Blue False Indigo (*B. australis*), can stretch up to 6 feet. White False Indigo (*B. leucantha*) and Cream False Indigo (*B. bracteata* aka *B. leucophaea*) both mature at about 3-4 feet.

30-inch *B. pendula* 'Alba', another white flowering form, has a weeping growth habit rather than the typical upright form.

PLANTING REQUIREMENTS

Baptisia loves average well-drained garden soil and will do fine in dry sites. Although this prairie plant loves full sun best, it also thrives in part or light shade as long as it gets some sun or bright light each day.

PROPAGATION

In the fall soak ripened seeds overnight and plant the next day. Baptisia is a prairie plant with a deep, hefty rootstock, so it does not like to be transplanted once it is established, but very young plants can be divided and transplanted in spring or fall.

Hardy Begonia (*Begonia grandis* aka *B. evansiana*)
Zones 5–9
14–16 inches tall
Asia

Hardy Begonia is a late riser, coming up well after most perennials in the spring. Plant this where the slanting rays of the early morning or late afternoon sun can shine through the heavily red-veined leaves. Since the tops of the leaves are green and the undersides a rich reddish color, the angular light creates an almost transparent rosy glow. Long racemes of rich pink flowers dangle like fancy earrings from its arching stems. This one is definitely worth including in the landscape.

PLANTING REQUIREMENTS

Try to get a start from a friend rather than purchasing from a nursery. Pass-alongs seem to get established more quickly. Hardy Begonias prefer moist, well-drained, humus-rich soil in partial to medium shade. Even though the loamy soil in my yard occasionally gets a little dry in mid-summer, my begonias do not appear to suffer. They do not like full sun. They appreciate extra mulch in colder zones.

PROPAGATION

Self-sows readily. Sow seeds in fall, or carefully divide in the fall.

Blackberry Lily (*Belamcanda chinensis*)
Zone 5
24–30 inches tall
Japan
Deer Resistant

Red-speckled, soft orange flowers bloom above fans of iris-like foliage in midsummer. Each one lasts only a day, but bloom continues for an extended period. Then clusters of black berries, nice in dried flower arrangements, rise above the foliage.

A dwarf form called 'Hello Yellow' (*B. flabellata* aka *B. flava*) has clear butter-colored blossoms and dark-brown anthers. This 12- to 20-inch-tall lily looks nice planted near the front of a perennial border.

PLANTING REQUIREMENTS
Like average, well-drained soil and will thrive in partial or medium shade or in full sun.

PROPAGATION
Gently remove the pulp from the berries and plant in the fall, or just let the berries drop and self-sow. Divide established plants in early spring or fall.

Blue Cohosh (*Caulophyllum thalictroides*)
Zones 3–8
1–3 feet tall
Native to U.S.

The dainty notched and divided foliage of Blue Cohosh, reminiscent of Meadow Rue, lends a delicate texture to a wild garden. Yellowish-green insignificant flowers bloom in May, followed by handsome deep blue berries that give this plant its common name. After spring ephemerals have gone dormant, the soft green foliage of Blue Cohosh persists in a naturalized area.

PLANTING REQUIREMENTS
Plant in humus-rich, well-drained soil in shade or part shade. Flourishes in a moist site, but can withstand dry spells with heavy mulch.

PROPAGATION
Divide in spring or fall, making sure that each section has 2–3 eyes. Space new plantings 18–24 inches apart. Will self-sow under favorable conditions, but the seeds can take up to 3 years to germinate!

Pale Indian Plantain (*Arnoglossum atriplicifolium* aka *Cacalia atriplicifolia*)
Zones 4–8
2–3 feet

Native to U.S.
REQUIRES MOIST SOIL

Neil Diboll of Prairie Nursery calls Pale Indian Plantain "the closest thing to a 'native hosta' that we know of." Huge, deep blue-green cut and ruffled leaves thrive in moist sites. In mid to late summer, commanding 6-foot-tall stalks rise from these leaves, topped with upright vase-shaped clusters of creamy white flowers. Plant one or several in a mass. What a show.

PLANTING REQUIREMENTS

Grows in moist, well-drained sites in the wild in either part shade or sun. Can be found in the wild growing near Spiderwort, Virginia Creeper, and Chokecherry.

PROPAGATION

Divide in early spring or fall, or seed in the fall.

Turtlehead (*Chelone* spp.)
Zones 3–9
2–3 feet tall
Native to U.S.
REQUIRES MOIST SOIL

This plant will fascinate children who remember the Dr. Seuss story of *Yertle the Turtle*. Squint just a bit to visualize rows of turtle heads marching up the stiff stalks. There are four native Turtlehead species. Turtleheads and White Snakeroot bloom about the same time, and are handsome planted together in a naturalistic garden.

Beautiful soft rosy pink flowers and dark green leaves enhance Pink Turtlehead (*Chelone lyonii*), hardy to −40°F. It naturalizes well, but is also a nice addition to any perennial garden. It grows 3–4 feet tall, but if shorter, bushier plants are desired, simply pinch out the growth tips in early spring before the plants grow more than a hand high. White Turtlehead (*C. glabra*) likes consistent moisture since it is native to wet areas. White flowers, often tinged with pink or mauve, appear in August and September when other perennials are winding down. It grows 2–3 feet tall. Deep rosy-pink flowers bloom on Red Turtlehead

(*C. obliqua*), the tallest of the Turtleheads. It grows 2–4 feet tall and makes a nice show when massed in a perennial border, or planted with its siblings. It is reportedly hardy to Zone 5, but does fine in Zone 4 with extra mulch. The fourth species, *C. nemorosa*, is native to California and the West.

PLANTING REQUIREMENTS

Turtlehead needs moist, humus-rich, well-drained soil and prefers part to medium shade. With adequate moisture, it can also be grown in sun. Mulch the roots heavily with 4–6 inches of old manure. Space new plantings 15–18 inches apart.

PROPAGATION

Sow seeds in the fall, divide plants in early spring or fall, or take cuttings and root them in sand in the summer.

Black Cohosh (*Actaea simplex* aka *Cimicifuga racemosa*)
Zones 3–8
4–6 feet tall
Native to U.S.

I wish scientific names did not get changed so often. I have always identified Black Cohosh as *Cimicifuga racemosa*, but now it has undergone a name change to *Actaea simplex*, putting it with the Baneberries. To add to the confusion, it is also commonly known as Black Snakeroot and Bugbane. Call it what you will, Black Cohosh is well suited to shade. The tall, thin, candelabra-like spires appear to float above a mass of cut green leaves. There are several cultivars available.

American Bugbane (*Cimicifuga americana*) blooms in early fall, later than Black Cohosh. I don't know if it got its scientific name changed or not. Two other natives, Kearney's Bugbane (*Actaea rubifolia* aka *Cimicifuga racemosa* var. *cordifolia*) and Komorov's Bugbane (*A. heracleifolia*), are both worth searching out in the nursery trade. *If* you can figure out what to ask for!

PLANTING REQUIREMENTS

This great plant needs a moist, humus-rich, well-drained planting site in shade.

PROPAGATION
Divide in early spring or fall, or sow ripened seeds in the fall.

Yellow Corydalis (*Corydalis lutea*)
Zones 4–9
8–12 inches tall
Europe

I love Yellow Corydalis with its soft grayish-green foliage. It blooms constantly from early summer until frost. When it is happy, it will self-sow and spread moderately. Often called False Bleeding Heart, it can go dormant if it gets too stressed in the heat of summer. To stave off dormancy, I simply give it a good long soak. *C. elata*, hardy to Zone 5, is a blue-flowering form that seems to tolerate heat quite well.

There are numerous cultivars to experiment with, although these are often less hardy. 'Blue Panda' is pretty but temperamental. One friend calls it a $10 annual! The green leaves of 'Golden Panda' become more golden as the season progresses, while *C. flexuosa* 'Purple Leaf' has deep purplish leaves and blue flowers. Heat and drought may cause this one to go dormant early. Given consistent moisture, it is actually somewhat aggressive and will readily fill in a blank spot in the shady garden.

The larger White Corydalis (*C. ochroleuca*) is hardy to Zone 5, or Zone 4 with additional winter protection. It grows 18–20 inches tall with ivory flowers and blue-green foliage. *C. ophiocarpa*, originating in the Himalayas, is even larger. Hardy to Zone 3, it can grow 18–30 inches tall, with creamy white flowers and gray-green leaves. Both are nice choices for naturalizing in shady spots.

Purple Corydalis (*C. bulbosa*), also known as Fumewort, is a 4–6-inch-tall spring ephemeral. Rosy-purple flowers nod over delicate foliage in April and May. I have it in my woods planted among yellow and white wildflowers and spring bulbs, and, although it self-sows, it is neither aggressive nor invasive. *C. solida* is similar, but hardy only to Zone 5.

PLANTING REQUIREMENTS

Plant in humus-rich, well-drained soil with adequate moisture in dappled or part shade.

PROPAGATION

Yellow Corydalis self-sows readily when it is happy, but is difficult to transplant. It has a small thickened taproot and seems to resent being moved, particularly the larger specimens.

Purple Corydalis springs from a small brown-black bulb that can be dug after flowering just before the plant becomes dormant. Or mark the spot and dig and transplant in the fall.

Hardy Cyclamen (*Cyclamen* spp.)

Zones 5–9

2–6 inches tall

Europe

Hardy Cyclamen looks just like the familiar houseplant, only smaller. Cyclamens are particularly handsome tucked under a large tree or next to a boulder to accent their unique flowers and pretty leaves. Either white or pink reflexed petals are "swept upwards" to rise above dark green and silvery-white marbled foliage. It is possible to march through most of the growing season with Hardy Cyclamen blooms.

Look for *Cyclamen coum* flowers about the time Lenten Roses, early daffodils, and crocus are in bloom. Late-season Cyclamens are dormant in spring and midsummer, arising to bloom and put out new leaves at the end of the growing season. *C. purpurascens* blooms in August followed by *C. cilicium* in the fall. However, these two often do not survive extreme cold temperatures in Zone 5, so mulch heavily or site in a protected spot. *C. hederifolium*, hardy to Zone 6, can be experimented with in Zone 5 with winter protection. It blooms in the fall.

PLANTING REQUIREMENTS

Hardy Cyclamen likes moist, humus-rich, well-drained soil in dappled or part shade. Mulch for winter protection in the more northern zones.

PROPAGATION

Sow seed in fall, or purchase tubers.

Bleeding Heart (*Dicentra* spp.)
Zones 3–9
12–14 inches tall
Native to U.S.
Deer Resistant

Fringed Bleeding Heart (*Dicentra eximia*), one of my favorite natives, resides in many places of honor in my shade gardens. This miniature relative of Old-fashioned Bleeding Heart produces pink or hot pink heart-like flowers from mid-spring to frost. Its delicate, ferny foliage stays neat all summer long. It is an excellent companion for hostas. The cultivar 'Alba' is pure white.

Western Fringed Bleeding Heart (*D. formosa*) is native to the western U.S. Exquisite 'King of Hearts' has soft gray-blue foliage and a tiny white heart in the center of each hot pink heart. Pacific Bleeding Heart (*D. formosa* 'Alba') has pure white flowers, while 'Langtrees' is a soft creamy-pink. For a genuine conversation piece, plant Yellow Bleeding Heart (*D. macrantha*). Yes, the little hearts are really yellow! Hardy in Zones 5–8, it can be grown in Zone 4 with winter protection.

PLANTING REQUIREMENTS
Plant in loamy, well-drained soil with adequate moisture in shade or part shade.

PROPAGATION
Fringed Bleeding Heart self-sows readily and young seedlings can be transplanted as long as the soil is kept consistently moist. Larger specimens resent being moved unless a large enough soil ball comes along.

Old-fashioned Bleeding Heart (*Dicentra spectabilis*)
Zones 3–8
2–3 feet tall
Japan
Deer Resistant

This plant was a mainstay of my grandmother's Minnesota flower garden; as a child, I remember picking the arching stems of dangling, rich pink hearts for her special cut glass vase. Old-fashioned Bleeding Heart is taller and much larger in all parts than Fringed Bleeding Heart. Its leaves turn yellow as the plant goes dormant in midsummer. In my garden, it grows between large clumps of hostas where a blank space is acceptable later in the season. My grandmother always grew annuals from seed, and some years I follow her lead and tuck in a few annual seedlings after my large Bleeding Heart plants have gone dormant.

Many gardeners prefer the white-flowered forms. For vibrant yellow leaves try 'Gold Heart'. It lights up dark spaces with its glowing golden leaves and looks spectacular near red or burgundy foliage plants. The flowers are deep pink.

PLANTING REQUIREMENTS
Plant in loamy, well-drained soil with adequate moisture in shade or part shade.

PROPAGATION
Divide the rootstock in early spring, or sow seed in fall.

Gas Plant (*Dictamnus albus*)
Zones 3–7
3–4 feet tall
Europe, Asia
Deer Resistant

I planted Gas Plant at our home in Minnesota because I was intrigued by the notion that its fumes could be ignited by a match. It never worked. Regardless of the plant's lack of pyromaniac tendencies, it is nonetheless admirable. Hardy to −40°F, it has fragrant spires of white flowers in late spring or early summer. After the flowers fade, interesting star-shaped seedpods form. Gas Plant grows into a compact, almost shrub-like clump with shiny green compound leaves.

PLANTING REQUIREMENTS
Dislikes being moved; site it where it can stay. Prefers well-drained, humus-rich soil, and does equally well in sun or partial shade. Once established, it can tolerate drier soil, but will die in a poorly drained site.

PROPAGATION
Purchase plants in 1–2 gallon containers for best results, or sow seeds in the fall. Gas Plant moderately self-sows and the resulting seedlings can be transplanted in early spring. Established clumps can be divided, but be advised that both parts may die; this plant resents being disturbed.

Fairy Bells (*Disporum* spp.)
Zones 4–8
24–30 inches tall
Native to U.S.

Fairy Bells (*Disporum flavens*) remind me of native Bellwort with drooping yellow flowers and lance-shaped leaves, or of a smaller version of Solomon's Seal. The straight stem of this native woodland plant branches near the top and the yellow bells hang from these branches. Fairy Bells can coexist with tree roots. Yellow Mandarin (*D. lanuginosum*) is a little shorter at 18–24 inches. It has drooping, lime-yellow, bell-like flowers in early spring and handsome red fruit in the fall. Nodding Yellow Mandarin (*D. maculatum*) has white flowers spotted with purple, and yellow hairy fruits. *D. hookerii* has greenish-white bells and orangey-red fruits.

Variegated Fairy Bells (*D. sessile* 'Variegated') is my favorite because its creamy variegated leaves and white bells make such a nice foil for similarly variegated hostas. It grows 1–2 feet tall and originates in Japan.

PLANTING REQUIREMENTS
Plant in humus-rich, well-drained woodland soil in part to full shade.

PROPAGATION
Divide creeping rootstocks in early spring or fall and transplant. Remove pulp from berries and plant seed in fall.

Purple Coneflower (*Echinacea purpurea*)
Zones 3–8
18–30 inches tall
Native to U.S.
Deer Resistant

Purple Coneflower is usually considered a sun-lover, but it blooms well at the edges of my woodland garden. Too much shade will cause it to flop, so I try to site it where it can get a few hours of sunlight each day. Like many prairie plants, Purple Coneflower performs better in lean soil, so I do not fertilize. *Echinacea* means hedgehog or sea urchin, which aptly describes the bristly high-domed center of the Purple Coneflower. This center is surrounded by rich rosy ray flowers. The long-lasting flowers bloom in July and August, attracting butterflies and hummingbirds. Chickadees and goldfinches love to peck out the ripened seed in fall. 'Kim's Knee High' is a special dwarf selection offered by Plant Delights.

There are two other native *Echinacea* species. Pale Purple Coneflower (*E. pallida*) has narrow pale-lavender ray flowers and blooms a little earlier. It is about 3 feet tall. Narrowleaf Coneflower (*E. angustifolia*) is about a foot shorter with similar lavender flowers. Planting these three together in a mass can extend the bloom season.

Yellow Coneflower (*Ratibida pinnata*), no relation, will also grow and bloom in part shade. (By the way, this dependable native is one of the best flowering perennials to incorporate into a new sunny prairie garden). Deer reportedly do not bother Coneflowers, but burrowing animals such as groundhogs and woodchucks may eat the roots. Space plantings farther apart if these fat little dudes come for lunch.

PLANTING REQUIREMENTS

Plant in average, well-drained garden soil in part shade or full sun. Coneflowers like adequate moisture, but these prairie plants will tolerate dry soil.

PROPAGATION

Self-sows. Plant ripened seed in fall or divide in early spring or fall. Cultivars need to be divided because they will not come true to form from seed.

Rattlesnake Master (*Eryngium yuccifolium*)
Zones 4–8
3–5 feet tall
Native to U.S.

Picture a small yucca plant with tall stalks rising above. At the ends of the stalks are clusters of spiky, creamy white balls. That is Rattlesnake Master. This dramatic native was commonly found on the Great Prairie, so it obviously prefers full sun, but it will grow and bloom in part shade as long as it has sunlight part of the day.

PLANTING REQUIREMENTS

Plant Rattlesnake Master in rich, moist, well-drained soil in full sun or part shade. Once established, it tolerates drought well because of its deep roots.

PROPAGATION

The thick rootstock plunges deep into the ground, so mature plants are literally impossible to move. It moderately self-sows, and young seedlings can be transplanted where they are to stay. Sow ripe seed in the fall.

Joe-Pye Weed (*Eupatorium* spp.)
Zones 3–9
6–10 feet tall
Native to U.S.

Native Sweet Joe-Pye Weed (*Eupatorium purpureum*) has a commanding presence in my woodland garden, attracting myriads of butterflies. Its huge, pale mauve-pink, dome-shaped flower clusters tower over nearby plants. Whorls of 5–6 leaves march up the solid stalks, sometimes rising 7–9 feet in the air. Four leaves generally comprise each whorl. Spotted Joe-Pye Weed (*E. maculatum*) grows to 3–6 feet tall with flat lavender flower clusters. Its stems are purple or spotted with purple. Hollow Joe-Pye Weed (*E. fistulosum*) ascends nearly 8 feet into the air. I occasionally pinch out the central leader when the plant is about ⅓ grown to encourage bushiness. Instead of one large cluster of flowers, this produces several smaller clusters. The cultivar 'Gateway' is "short" at 5–6 feet, and has deep reddish-purple blooms in late summer.

Boneset (*E. perfoliatum*) has large flat clusters of creamy white flowers in the fall and leaves pierced by the hairy stems. It grows 3–5 feet tall. White Snakeroot (*E. rugosum*) creates a haze of delicate beauty in the fall when not much else is in bloom. Until it blooms, this 2–3-foot-tall shade lover looks more like a weed than a perennial, so it is a plant for the wild garden. Mistflower (*E. coelestinum*), often called Perennial Ageratum, has lavender-blue flowers on 18–24 inch stems. It spreads aggressively in part shade or sun, so this is another that works well in a wild garden, but not in the traditional perennial border. A tall cultivar with chocolate colored leaves, appropriately dubbed 'Chocolate', has bright white flowers that light up shady spots. It grows 3–4 feet tall.

PLANTING REQUIREMENTS

Eupatoriums like moist, well-drained, woodland soil, but will do fine in average garden soil as long as there is adequate moisture. They tolerate a certain amount of dryness and do not need fertilizer. Eupatoriums thrive in part shade or full sun.

PROPAGATION

Eupatoriums self-seed readily and the seedlings can be transplanted in early spring. Or divide mature plants in early spring or fall.

Queen of the Prairie (*Filipendula rubra*)

Zones 3–9
4–6 feet tall
Native to U.S.
REQUIRES MOIST SOIL

Also known as Meadowsweet, Queen of the Prairie has airy, loose clusters of rich soft pink flowers in the summer. I try to site my plants between other perennials because if the flower heads get too heavy, they tend to flop. 'Kakome', a miniature cultivar only 8–12 inches tall, blooms in early to midsummer. The dark green leaves of Queen of the Meadow (*F. ulmaria* 'Variegated') look like some mad painter splashed lines through their centers. Creamy white flowers echo the variegation.

A double white flowering cultivar of native Dropwort (*F. vulgaris* 'Plena', also known as 'Flore Plena'), is 12–24 inches tall. It blooms in mid to late summer. Dropwort has finer, more ferny foliage.

There are two exotic species available that are similar to the native. Siberian Meadowsweet (*F. palmata*) has short-lived baby pink flowers that fade to a creamy white. Bright hot pink flowers of Japanese Meadowsweet (*F. purpurea*) emerge above handsome, serrated, deeply incised blue green leaves. As the flowers mature, they become a rich deep purple.

A veritable collage of Wild Columbine, Shooting Stars, False Solomon's Seal, and Trillium leaves.

Native spring ephemerals bloom on the "front lawn" of the author's shaded suburban garden only seven miles from downtown Indianapolis.

The Mayapple lives up to its name by producing small, pale-green edible "apples" in late summer.

Few perennials can rival the native Wild Geranium for season-long beauty in the shade.

(opposite) Oak-like leaves and recurring bright yellow flowers make Celandine Poppy a stunning native shade plant.

Resembling a seat for visiting Druids, this weathered stump is surrounded by spring Bluebells, Mayapples, and Wild Ginger.

(opposite) Squirrel Corn corms are bright "corn" yellow, as opposed to the pinkish-beige corms of Dutchman's Breeches. Bluebells grow from unusual, crisp, dark molar-like rhizomes.

An unusually shaped pink Flowering Dogwood is complemented by a gently curving bed of matching pink tulips.

Masses of white daffodils spill down a hillside.

Three porcelain yellow tulips float above a sea of blue forget-me-nots.

Blue Wood Hyacinths provide
interest in a shaded spot.

The dangling "earrings" of exquisite Hardy Begonia grace red-veined leaves that glow when backlit by the afternoon rays of the sun.

Sparkling in an unexpected sunbeam, Pink Turtlehead stands straight and tall in the warmth of summer.

A single spray of Bleeding Heart's delicate pink and white flowers lights up the shade.

This massive rock surrounded by bright daylilies creates a sense of presence in a shaded corner.

The deep purple flowers of Spiderwort last only a day, but a multitude of buds make this a long-blooming perennial for shady spots.

(opposite) A magnificent specimen of H. 'Sagae' is complemented by pots of huge, brightly colored Caladium, variegated Solomon's Seal, and Sweet Woodruff (bottom right).

H. 'Gold Standard' turns parchment gold with extra light at the edge of an undulating garden of impatiens and hostas.

Raindrops glisten on H. 'Sun Power' surrounded by spring ephemerals.

Bold Ostrich Ferns rise above a blooming H. 'Gold Edger'.

(opposite) H. Antioch sets the point for a collection of hostas.

Variegated hostas, ferns, conifers, and yellow flowering Epimedium surround a birdbath, creating a welcoming spot for feathered garden visitors.

Tiny yellow H. 'Feather Boa', H. 'Gold Standard', and H. 'Lancifolia' bloom in tandem with white impatiens in the author's shady garden.

Interesting paths are
important components of
the shady landscape.

A stone cherub, lost in thought, ponders salmon geraniums.

A Victorian porch is graced by containers and hanging baskets filled with brightly colored annuals.

(opposite) Every shady garden needs a place to sit and relax.

Multiple containers of early season annuals bloom amid tulips and conifers in the Indianapolis White River Garden.

An imaginative homeowner hung this elegant "annual chandelier" at the edge of his garden path to prove that creativity counts!

By placing a raised pot in the center of an urn, this gardener produced a lovely mounded effect.

A striking red and green Caladium in the author's front entryway.

Four seasons in the author's Indianapolis garden.

PLANTING REQUIREMENTS

Since it likes moist, humus-rich soil, it is a good choice for a bog garden or for planting near a stream or pond. However, my plants flourish in ordinary garden soil in a spot that gets morning sun and afternoon shade. The native Dropwort will tolerate a dry planting site.

PROPAGATION

Divide in early spring or fall, or sow ripened seed in the fall. Seed planted in spring should be cold stratified.

Gentian (*Gentiana* spp.)

Zones 3–8

12–18 inches tall

Native to U.S.

REQUIRES MOIST SOIL

Electric blue clusters of unusual bottle-shaped blooms appear above the shiny green leaves of Bottle Gentian (*Gentiana andrewsii*) in September and October. I grow this wildflower in two locations. The first gets about half a day of sun; the other is in light shade all day. Both bloom well, but the latter plant flops. Long-lived perennials, Gentians thrive in the same moist, loamy soil enjoyed by Cardinal Flower and Blue Lobelia. Overzealous gardeners may unwittingly weed them out in the spring, so learn to identify this plant in its infancy—or use a plant marker. Closed Gentian (*G. clausa*) is very similar. *G. calycosa* has upright, open cobalt blue flowers in late summer. Earlier blooming Soapwort Gentian (*G. saponaria*) is similar to Bottle Gentian, but the tips of its lighter blue bottle-like flowers are slightly open. *G. septemfida* var. *lagodechiana*) has deep blue, upright bells on plants 6–15 inches tall. *G. septemfida* is similar, but only 4 inches tall. It is good for border edging, rock gardens, or naturalized at the edge of the woods. Willow Gentian (*G. asclepiadea*), hardy to Zone 5, is a taller plant with long, tubular bell-like flowers set between lance-shaped leaves. *G. dahurica* forms a 12 inch mound of dark bluish-purple flowers accented with white at the base. Fringed Gentian (*G. crinita*) is a biennial and difficult to establish except in ideal locations.

Gentians are available through many wildflower or specialty nursery catalogs.

PLANTING REQUIREMENTS
Gentians prefer humus-rich, moist, well-drained soil in part or light shade, but I have found them blooming in sun along railroad rights-of-way in poor gravelly soil. Set the crown at least one inch deep.

PROPAGATION
Divide in spring or fall, or sow seed in fall. Gentians generally prefer fall transplanting just before dormancy. Otherwise, consistent watering is crucial to their survival.

Bowman's Root (*Gillenia trifoliata* aka *Porteranthus trifoliatus*)
Zones 4–8
2–3 feet tall
Native to U.S.

For a summer-blooming perennial that really takes center stage, try planting several clumps of airy, shrub-like Bowman's Root. Clouds of pinkish-white, star-shaped flowers hover above dainty three-parted dark-green leaves. In the fall, these nearly sessile leaves turn shades of yellow and red. Also known as Indian Physic because of its medicinal qualities, it has red stems and persistent red sepals (calyces) around the base of the flowers.

The related American Ipecac (*G. stipulata* aka *Porteranthus stipulatus*), a similar native that may be a little easier to get established, has green stems. However, its white flowers are smaller and the overall form is more open. Once established, it can tolerate drier soil.

PLANTING REQUIREMENTS
Bowman's Root likes humus-rich, well-drained, average soil in part or light shade, or in sun. It sometimes flops, so installing a support ring early in the growing season may reduce maintenance.

PROPAGATION
Divide in early spring or fall. Sow ripened seed in fall.

Woodland Sunflower (*Helianthus strumosus*)
Zones 4–8
3–5 feet tall
Native to U.S.

Bright yellow daisy-like flowers of Woodland Sunflower light up a woodland in late summer and early fall. This is not a plant for the perennial border because it aggressively colonizes, spreading by underground runners. However, it is great in a naturalized shady setting, blooming where few other yellow flowering plants will perform. I have a large colony of Woodland Sunflowers in my woods and the birds love to peck out ripened seed in the fall.

PLANTING REQUIREMENTS
Plant in light or part shade in moist, well-drained soil. It will also grow happily in average garden soil or even in sand.

PROPAGATION
Divide in spring or fall, or sow seed.

False Sunflower (*Heliopsis helianthoides*)
Zones 4–8
3–5 feet tall
Native to U.S.
Deer Resistant
False Sunflower has golden ray flowers with deeper gold centers. The brown anthers stick up like stray hairs around a bald pate. Also known as Ox-Eye, False Sunflower has a lengthy bloom period—from July to September. It is a clumper, so it stays where you put it. It self-sows.

PLANTING REQUIREMENTS
Plant in light or part shade. It can also be grown in full sun. It prefers moist, well-drained soil, but will grow in average garden soil or even sand. It is also a good choice for clay soil.

PROPAGATION
Divide in spring or fall, or sow seed.

Daylily (*Hemerocallis* spp.)
Zones 2–9
18–36 inches tall
Asia
Hemerocallis fulva, the invasive orange ditch lily, is impossible to get rid of once you have it. Offers of free plants should be firmly refused.

People often call it Tiger Lily and believe it is a native wildflower. The approximately 45,000 cultivars of *Hemerocallis*, on the other hand, are worthwhile and among the most low-maintenance plants in existence. While most will not bloom profusely without ample light, they will provide color in part or very light shade. Daylilies come in all sizes from miniatures to giants. There are single and double flowers, ruffled or smooth edges, and myriad color choices. A number will rebloom.

Mass for a spectacular effect or tuck them into a perennial border for neat green foliage and colorful flowers that open for a day. Combine 2 or 3 of the same color that bloom at different times to extend the flowering season. I like to plant my daffodil bulbs with daylilies to disguise the ripening daffodil foliage.

Cultivars are too numerous to list, but some of my favorites include 'Lemon Custard', a lemony yellow; 'Orange Slush', like cooling orange sherbet; the deep yellow-gold 'Mary Todd', and 'Classic Delight', a ruffled soft pink beauty. 'Hawaiian Party Dress' looks like yummy ripe watermelon, and 'Karen Sue' reminds me of strawberries and cream. I also love the rich, true red of 'Palace Guard'.

However daylilies happen to arrive in your garden, be assured they will give years of dependable beauty as long as they are treated to enough light and moisture to suit their needs.

PLANTING REQUIREMENTS
Plant in average, well-drained soil in part to light shade, or in humus-rich, moist soil in full sun. In too much shade, flowering will be minimal. Space miniatures 12–18 inches apart, full sized daylilies 18–30 inches apart. Mulch to retain moisture.

PROPAGATION
Divide in early spring or fall, or sow ripened seeds. Hybrid daylilies, like hostas, will not come true from seed, but this is how hybridizers encourage new varieties.

Alum Root (*Heuchera richardsonii*)
Zones 3–9
6–8 inches tall
Native to U.S.
Deer Resistant

Our native Heuchera resembles familiar Coral Bells, treated with other Heucheras in chapter 7. Its rather insignificant yellow-green flowers bloom on 20-inch stems above scalloped dark green leaves in late spring. My Alum Root plants grow near Celandine Poppy, Wild Geranium, and a few ferns, and the flowers actually look interesting there. Poker Alumroot (*H. cylindrica*), a similar species, has silvery mottled leaves and pale yellowish-green or cream flowers. Another native, later-blooming Alum Root (*H. villosa*) sends up tall puffs of white to pinkish-white flowers in mid summer. The leaves turn wine red in the fall except in warmer zones where they remaining evergreen through the winter. Hardy to Zone 5, *H. villosa* 'Autumn Bride' is an improved form with profuse creamy white bells in September and October. This is a good choice for difficult dry locations.

PLANTING REQUIREMENTS
Alum Root does well in average garden soil with adequate moisture in part to medium shade. Space plants 10–12 inches apart.

PROPAGATION
Sow ripened seed, or divide plants in early spring or fall.

Hosta (*Hosta* spp.)
Zones 3–9
6–48 inches tall
Japan

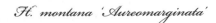

H. montana 'Aureomarginata'

Aside from wildflowers, of all shade-loving plants my favorite is the indomitable hosta. This popular perennial is probably the first that comes to mind when a new homeowner confronts a shady yard, at least in the East and Midwest. In the Chicago suburbs so many front walkways are edged with long rows of identical hostas that the plant has earned the nickname "Weed of Winnetka." This is a neat and tidy look, but you can do so much more.

Just a few ideas: Mass the upright 'Royal Standard' near the entry or patio so the perfume of its white flowers can be inhaled on a hot August evening. Create a composition of green and white or blue and gold or chartreuse—or all of the above—under a shade tree. Mix in complementary companion plants if you wish. Tuck a huge 'Sum and Substance' in a corner, surround with medium-sized 'Gold Standard', then edge with a small, rapid increaser like 'Lemon Lime' or 'Golden Tiara'. Decorate the edge of a pond with hostas, or sprinkle them among wildflowers in a woodland. Mix sizes, colors, and shapes to your heart's content. The permutations are endless. On a budget? You can still enjoy the subtle beauty of passalongs like 'Lancifolia' or white-edged *undulata* 'Albomarginata'. Or plant a swath of *H. ventricosa* on the shady side of the house and admire its deep violet blooms in June.

Hosta plantaginea

Bright yellow 'Sun Power' gleams in the morning sun outside our bedroom window. Its offspring, 'Paradise Power', has those same yellow leaves edged with an irregular band of green. I had to have one and planted it with 'Sun Power', 'Hadspen Blue', and a huge 'Blue Angel'. Little 'Geisha' is the first hosta up in the spring and the last to go to bed in the fall, and its narrow, gold-centered, dark green-edged leaves stay handsome all summer. Some hostas are teeny (*H. venusta*, 'Popo', 'Tiny Tears', 'Thumbnail'). Some are humongous, like 'Sum and Substance' and *H. nigrescens* 'Elatior'. New cultivars are constantly being registered and introduced. There are now literally thousands.

With all of this variety, there is a real danger of addiction, adding up to very high-maintenance gardening indeed. But if you can limit your collection to no more than fifteen cultivars (the Top Ten plus five more), you should be okay. At least that's what hosta collector Glen Williams says, and he should know, as he has upwards of 1,000!

These lovely foliage plants rank among the easiest shade perennials to grow. Do a few things to make their lives better and they will be even lovelier. First and foremost, give them plenty of moisture. Dry soil causes stress, which can contribute to diseases. Make sure they get at least 1 inch of water per week, and 3 inches is even better. Second, fertilize if and when you have the time. Third, if slugs are a problem, beer in styrofoam cups or tuna cans sunk to ground level works best. Deer unfortunately love hostas and can be very determined when a tasty snack is in store. In my yard, they are not a problem. Those who have suffered deer invasions are legion and so are their defenses: human hair, bars of soap, electric fences, Milorganite, and countless other remedies abound. Hinder and Plantskydd are effective repellants.

PLANTING REQUIREMENTS
Hostas do best in moist, well-drained, loamy garden soil in all degrees of shade. Some varieties, such as the green-leaved ones, will tolerate full sun if there is adequate moisture. Mulch conserves moisture and cuts down on weeding, but gives a hiding place for slugs and may encourage fungal attacks, so there are tradeoffs. The large leaves of hostas themselves will discourage weed growth in the bed.

PROPAGATION
Divide in spring or in late September, or any time as long as the soil is kept moist while the transplants get established. If the leaves flop and refuse to perk up, just chop them off at ground level and force the plant to resprout. You may feel squeamish, but never fear: they will send up new leaves.

Cultivars will not come true from seed; every hosta seed will produce its own unique plant, most of which, but not all, are green. If you want to try hybridizing your own hostas, it is a fun and exciting hobby that I highly recommend.

Iris (*Iris* spp.)
Zones 3–8
16–18 inch foliage
Japan, U.S.
Deer Resistant

Stiff, sword-like leaves, especially variegated forms, are valuable additions to the mixed perennial border. Although Bearded Iris need full sun to bloom well, a few other species will accept part or light shade. Siberian Iris (*I. siberica*) forms graceful clumps. It loves moisture, but once established will tolerate dry soil in light shade. 'Caesar's Brother' is an old reliable with deep velvety purple flowers.

Native *Iris missouriensis* will grow in either dry or wet environments. For variegated leaves, try Variegated Sweet Iris (*I. pallida* 'Albo-variegata'), with blue-green foliage striped with white, or Zebra Iris (*I. pallida* 'Aureo-variegata'), with yellow striping. Either will grow in shade.

Japanese Iris (*I. ensata*) will also tolerate quite a bit of shade. 'Waka Murasaki' is particularly handsome with its silver-edged velvety purple flowers.

In addition to the little native *Iris cristata* (see chapter 7) there are other dwarf iris including native *I. lacustris* and 'Nana' (*I. setosa*), which resembles a miniature Siberian; Dwarf Japanese Woodland Iris (*I. gracilipes* 'Alba'), 8 inches tall; Plum Iris (*I. graminae*), a fragrant 10–15-inch, plum-colored beauty; and another native, *I. verna*.

Yellow Flag (*I. pseudacorus*), a tall wetland iris, will bloom its head off in part shade with golden yellow flowers in early to midsummer. This stately exotic has been known to escape and naturalize. Any *pseudacorus* is best placed in a contained site and not near a stream or waterway where it may cause problems in the future. 'Variegata' is the form with green and yellow striped leaves.

PLANTING REQUIREMENTS
Plant in average to moist soil in part to light shade or in full sun. Do not bury the rhizomes deeply. Several of the above selections can take dry soil; others tolerate wet sites or even standing water.

PROPAGATION
Dig and divide immediately after blooming, or in the fall.

Waxbells (*Kirengeshoma koreana*)
Zones 4–7
3–5 feet tall
Asia
REQUIRES MOIST SOIL

About the time the Japanese Anemones begin blooming, another little-known plant also bursts forth: tall, multiple-stemmed Waxbells

(*K. koreana*). Delicate spires of airy yellow bells float on tall dark stems arching above handsome maple-like leaves. Waxbells can bloom for a month or more. Flowers give way to three-horned, brownish-green seed capsules. Yellow Waxbells (*K. palmata*) blooms a little later and is slightly shorter at 3 feet tall. Hardy to Zone 5, it also has drooping light yellow bells and maple-like foliage. The foliage of both Waxbells turns yellow in the fall.

PLANTING REQUIREMENTS
Requires consistently moist, humus-rich soil. Prefers shade or part shade.

PROPAGATION
Divide in late fall or very early spring. Sow seed in fall.

Ligularia (*Ligularia* spp.)
Zones 3–9
3–4 feet tall
Japan
REQUIRES MOIST SOIL

The large, colorful leaves of Ligularia are a great foil for hostas and other shade lovers, although I cannot say much for the orangey-yellow daisy-like flowers. Bigleaf Ligularia (*Ligularia dentata*) emerges in early spring with huge reddish purple, leathery, heart-shaped leaves. As the season progresses, the tops become a rich bronzy-green, but the backs and stems remain reddish-purple.

Gray-green leaves backed with brownish-purple are the trademark of 48-inch 'Desdemona'. 'Othello' is more compact, growing only 36 inches tall.

'The Rocket' (*L. stenocephala*) is my favorite, but it really fusses if the soil is not consistently moist, so I have had a harder time keeping this Ligularia alive. Commanding bright yellow flowers zoom like tall, thin rockets to the tops of nearly black stems, and bloom above beautifully cut and serrated green leaves.

That impossible-to-pronounce Ligularia called *L. przewalskii* is also called 'The Rocket'. It has unusual, heavily toothed triangular leaves and yellow flower spires. The leaves are huge, sometime as large as 7–9 inches across, creating a bold accent for any shady spot. This 4-foot tall beauty sends up 6-foot flower stalks in June.

PLANTING REQUIREMENTS

Ligularias demand humus-rich, consistently moist soil in shade. They look good at the back of the moist perennial border, or near water. Give them plenty of space, with at least 2–3 feet between similar plants.

PROPAGATION

Divide in early spring or fall. Sow seed in the fall.

Lily (*Lilium* spp.)
Zones 3–7
3–4 feet tall
Asia

Shade gardeners often bemoan the fact that most lilies will not thrive for them. Behold the hardy Martagon, with multiple little turban-like flowers marching up and down its tall, sturdy stems. It loves the shade. Think of a color—any color. 'Mahogany Bells', 'Orange Marmalade', and 'Port Wine' all reflect their given names. There are countless more.

A few native Turk's Caps like shade. Yellow Meadow Lily (*L. canadense*) has purple-spotted yellow flowers on 3–5 foot stems. The flowers of *L. superbum* can be either yellow or yellow-orange. This native can grow 5–8 feet tall, and hummingbirds love it.

Plant Delight's Variegated Bamboo Lily (*L. japonicum forma albomarginatum*) is hardy in Zones 5–9 and it has green and white variegated leaves and pale pink trumpet flowers. It requires moist, well-drained soil in shade or part sun.

PLANTING REQUIREMENTS

Lilies should be planted at least 8–10 inches deep in well-drained, humus-rich soil. Those listed all enjoy a cooling, shady planting site.

PROPAGATION

Purchase field grown bulbs. It is possible to start lilies from some of the "scales" on the onion-like bulb, but the wait for blooms is long.

Great Blue Lobelia (*Lobelia siphilitica*)
Cardinal Flower (*L. cardinalis*)
Zones 4–9
2–3 feet tall

Native to U.S.
Deer Resistant

 The bright blue flowers of Great Blue Lobelia electrify the shaded garden. Unlike its relative, Cardinal Flower, Great Blue Lobelia will tolerate average soil and even occasional dryness. It blooms in late summer. 'Blue Peter' is an improved cultivar. Cardinal Flower demands moist to wet soil. I have this planted outside my kitchen window, and hummingbirds and butterflies love the 2–5-foot stalks loaded with brilliant red flowers. The soil is merely average amended garden soil, so to ensure adequate moisture, I give it a drink each time I water my nearby container plants. Available cultivars have flowers in shades of shrimp, pink, rose, deep purple, and pure white, but, while I freely admit that all are desirable additions to the moist perennial border, my little kitchen garden has room for only one Cardinal Flower, and for that view from the window, my prejudice runs in favor of the species.

 Not surprisingly, hybridizers have cross-pollinated Cardinal Flower with Great Blue Lobelia, resulting in more delicious cultivars.

Great Blue Lobelia

PLANTING REQUIREMENTS
Provide moist, humus-rich, loamy, well-drained garden soil in part to light shade or full sun. Moisture is key, particularly with the shorter-lived Cardinal Flower. Cardinal Flower grows from ground-hugging rosettes that like to be mulched, but not smothered. Excessive mulch will rot the rosettes.

PROPAGATION
Divide and transplant rosettes in the spring, being careful not to plant them too deeply. For successful seed germination, let the seed lie on top of the ground and do not cover. If the ground near the mother plant is kept clear of mulch, Lobelias will self-sow.

Maltese Cross (*Lychnis chalcedonica*)
Zones 4–8
24–36 inches tall
Russia

For brilliant orange-red flowers, Maltese Cross is hard to beat. Although this long-lived perennial prefers full sun, it will tolerate part to light shade as long at it gets several hours of either direct sunlight or bright light each day. Its handsome flowers resemble the Maltese cross, hence its common name. This is another perennial guaranteed to bring hummingbirds and butterflies to the garden.

The biennial Rose Campion (*L. coronaria*) aka Mullein Pink (small pink flowers and woolly leaves), is reported to be deer resistant, but I have no information on *L. chalcedonica*. Experiment.

PLANTING REQUIREMENTS
Plant in average, well drained garden soil in light to part shade or in full sun.

PROPAGATION
Sow seed in the fall, or divide plants in spring or fall.

Yellow Loosestrife (*Lysimachia punctata*)
Zones 4–9
18–24 inches tall
Europe

Bright lemon yellow flowers grow in dense whorls around stiff stalks, opening their faces upwards. What a happy sight! Rest assured that Yellow Loosestrife, also known as Circle Flower, is no relation to the infamous Purple Loosestrife (*Lythrum salicaria*) outlawed in many states because of its threat to wetland environments. It is, however, assertive, to say the least. The soft green leaves of the variegated cultivar 'Alexander' emerge in spring with unusual coral-pink and gold edges. As the summer progresses, these change to a beautiful creamy white. In midsummer, the flower stalks are heavily laden with dense whorls of golden blooms. 'Beaujolais' (*L. atropurpurea*) has long-blooming deep burgundy-rose flower spikes.

Fringed Loosestrife (*L. ciliata* 'Atropurpureum') grows about 40 inches tall with yellow flowers above dark reddish-purple leaves.

PLANTING REQUIREMENTS
Plant Yellow Loosestrife in average, well-drained garden soil in part or light shade, or in full sun. Plants grown in light shade will tolerate moderately dry soil. This plant, like its relatives Gooseneck Loosestrife

(*L. clethroides*) and Creeping Jenny (*L. nummularia*), can also be aggressive, so give it space to "do its thing," or it will not be a low-maintenance addition to the garden. Alternatively, plant in an oversized container sunk into the ground.

PROPAGATION
Divide in spring. Sow seed in fall.

Plume Poppy (*Macleaya cordata*)
Zones 3–9
6–8 feet tall
China, Japan
Deer Resistant

I have included this sun-lover because it creates such a spectacular focal point in a garden. It towers over other perennials and has beautifully sculpted, heavily lobed leaves of soft, silvery grayish-green. Soft airy panicles of pinkish-cream flowers "float" nearly 8 feet in the air. These are followed by interesting clusters of seedpods.

Plume Poppy is stoloniferous and aggressive, particularly in moist sites, so locate in a spot where it cannot escape—in a small, contained planting space, or near the sidewalk or driveway. It will tolerate some shade, but tends to lean. In my lightly shaded garden, I plunk a tomato cage over the emerging leaves in early spring to support the tall stiff stalks. It can be used at the back of a mixed perennial border, but I like it best planted in its own space with a few ground-hugging plants at its feet.

PLANTING REQUIREMENTS
Plume Poppy likes any average, well-drained soil with adequate moisture, although it will tolerate some dryness once established. It performs best in part to bright shade, or in full sun.

PROPAGATION
Dig and transplant rooted runners in early spring or fall. Self-sows readily.

Monarda (*Monarda didyma*)
Zones 3–9
1–4 feet tall

Native to U.S.

Deer Resistant

Another aggressive perennial, Monarda, also called Oswego Tea, Bee Balm, and Bergamot, can be planted in an oversized container to curb its rambunctious nature. Even though this square-stemmed member of the Mint Family can get carried away with itself, it is a valuable addition to the perennial or naturalized garden, providing bright color in the shade and delighting hummingbirds, bees, and butterflies. Several cultivars resist mildew. Consider 'Jacob Cline', with oversized red flowers; raspberry flowering 'Raspberry Wine'; bright red 'Panorama Red Shades', or rosy-pink 'Marshalls Delight'. For white flowers, emulate Prince Charming and choose 'Snow White'. 'Blue Stocking' has purple flowers.

M. fistulosa, often found in the wild, may be the most drought-tolerant. Although the pale lilac flowers on this 4-foot native are not particularly showy, a mass of it is lovely in a perennial border or naturalized garden. 'Prairie Knight' is a good cultivar.

The common white native often called Basil Balm (*M. clinopodia*) also grows to 4 feet tall.

PLANTING REQUIREMENTS

Monarda thrives in average, well-drained garden soil with adequate moisture in part to light shade or full sun. Be sure to leave adequate air space around these plants to prevent mildew. If plants get too dry, they become stressed, contributing to mildew problems.

PROPAGATION

Dig and transplant rooted runners in early spring or fall. Divide mature plants in spring or fall, or sow ripened seed in the fall.

Japanese Peony (*Paeonia japonica*)

Zones 4–8

18–24 inches tall

Japan

Deer Resistant

Imagine a peony that prefers shade. Well, this is it! Japanese Peony has beautiful single 3-inch white flowers with a confetti-like cluster of bright yellow stamens in the center. Add soft gray-green foliage, a tidy mounding growth habit, and even some outstanding "color crayon" red and blue fruits in the fall, and how can anyone resist? This is a shady treasure.

Woodland Peony (*P. obovata*) resembles Japanese Peony but may be more cold tolerant. It has single deep rose flowers.

PLANTING REQUIREMENTS
Japanese Peonies prefer light to medium shade in humus-rich, well-drained soil with consistent moisture.

PROPAGATION
Mature plants can be divided in late fall. However, it is easier to purchase potted plants.

Beardtongue (*Penstemon digitalis*)
Zones 4–8
2–4 feet tall
Native to U.S.

Native Beardtongue, usually referred to as just plain 'Penstemon', is an upright clumping plant with nodding clusters of small tubular flowers.

The University of Nebraska introduction 'Husker Red' has deep maroon leaves and flower stalks, with pinkish-white flowers in early summer. 'Sour Grapes' (*Penstemon ovatus*), with larger rosy-purple flowers, blooms most of the summer. Check mail order catalogs and local nurseries for a wide variety of cultivars.

Small's Penstemon (*P. smallii*) can be short-lived, but flowers prolifically, self-sowing when it is content. Shorter than *P. digitalis*, it only grows 18–24 inches tall. The long pinkish-purple flowers have throats striped with white.

PLANTING REQUIREMENTS
Penstemon likes any average, well-drained spot and, once established, actually prefers a hot, dry environment. Grow in part shade or full sun.

PROPAGATION
Divide in spring or fall, sow seed in fall.

Phlox (*Phlox arendsii* × *P. paniculata* 'Spring Pearl')
Zones 4–8
16–20 inches tall
Hybrid

Most Phlox prefer sunny locations, but this pretty hybrid would rather have a little shade. Shorter in stature than common garden phlox, it blooms earlier. If deadheaded it will bloom nearly all summer long. 'Miss Jill' has soft white flowers with a small bright pink eye, 'Miss Karen' blooms in a dark rose with a darker red eye, and 'Miss Mary' has red flowers. 'Miss Jo Ellen', very fragrant, has pinkish-white flowers with a larger red center. Others in this "clique" include the short 'Miss Margie', a perfumed lavender-blue, and 'Miss Jessica' aka 'Miss Wilma' with pale pinkish-lilac white-eyed flowers. Some catalogs list 'Spring Pearl' as 'Summer Pearl'.

PLANTING REQUIREMENTS
Plant in average well-drained humus-rich garden soil with adequate moisture in part shade or sun.

PROPAGATION
Divide in early spring or fall.

Obedient Plant (*Physostegia virginiana*)
Zones 3–9
18–30 inches tall
Native to U.S.

Move the flowers of Obedient Plant to the right or left and they remain where you put them. However, it is not so obedient when it comes to running, and may have to be contained to reduce maintenance. Also known as False Dragonhead, this tall perennial "spikes" into tubular lavender-purple "dragon's head" flowers.

As one would expect, bright white 'Miss Manners' is the best-behaved cultivar. She stays where you plant her, and seldom requires staking. Smaller 'Vivid' has vivid deep rose flowers and grows about 24 inches tall. And of course there is a variegated form. Three-foot-tall 'Variegata' has deep-green leaves with a wide creamy yellowish-white border. Combine that with bright pink flowers and here is a real winner.

PLANTING REQUIREMENTS
Obedient Plant will grow in average, well-drained garden soil in light shade or sun. Dividing every 3 years keeps the plants more vigorous.

PROPAGATION
Divide in early spring or fall, or sow seeds in fall.

Balloon Flower (*Platycodon grandiflorus*)
Zones 3–9
8–24 inches tall
China

Little balloons pop open to create small star-shaped bells. Usually found in pastel shades, Balloon Flower comes with color-descriptive names such as 'Sentimental Blue', 'Shell Pink', 'Misato Purple', 'White', 'Fairy Snow', and 'Alba'. 'Misato Purple' and 'Fairy Snow' are 8–10 inch dwarfs. 'Double Blue' and 'Hakone Double White' are—you guessed it—double. The inflated purplish-blue buds of long-blooming 'Komachi' never lose their distinctive balloon shape.

PLANTING REQUIREMENTS
Plant in average to slightly acidic well-drained garden soil in part to light shade or full sun.

PROPAGATION
Divide mature clumps in spring or fall, or plant seeds in the fall.

Pasque Flower (*Pulsatilla vulgaris*)
Zones 4–9
8–15 inches tall
Native to U.S., Europe

Hairy stems protect little Pasque Flower from the chilling winds in early spring. This wonderful rock garden plant also looks nice massed in the mixed perennial border. Opposites on the color wheel always create a striking picture, and the anemone-like flowers of 'Purple' are enhanced by the bright yellow centers. Pasque Flower also comes in shades of ruby red, lavender, or white. Add to that feathery, ferny foliage and this is a real eyecatcher in the spring garden.

PLANTING REQUIREMENTS
Pasque Flower will grow in any average garden soil with good drainage. It prefers more sun than less, but will bloom and grow well in part to light shade. Cutting back the foliage after flowering will create a tidy mound of foliage for the rest of the summer.

PROPAGATION

Divide immediately after flowering or in the fall. Sow seeds in the fall.

Black-Eyed Susan (*Rudbeckia fulgida*)
Zones 3–8
20–30 inches tall
Native to U.S.
Deer Resistant

Although these bright yellow daisy-like flowers are touted as sun perennials, I grow them successfully in light or part shade, where they light up many of my shady spots from late summer until frost. They invariably flop forward, reaching for the light, but I plant them in the middle of the border and don't mind having them peek out at the front. In nearby Holliday Park, these perennials grow in at least half day of sun and stand straight and tall, so I assume my floppers simply crave more light. But I like them all the same.

The popular cultivar 'Goldsturm' covers itself with yellow-orange daisies and makes a much more upright, sturdy clump. However, it seems to need a few more hours of sunlight each day to bloom as profusely as the species in my garden.

PLANTING REQUIREMENTS

Plant in any good well drained garden soil in full sun or part to light shade.

PROPAGATION

This pass-along self-sows readily. Transplant young seedlings, divide mature clumps in early spring or late fall, or sow ripened seed in the fall.

Rue (*Ruta graveolens*)
Zones 4–9
15–24 inches tall
Europe

Rue's softly divided, ferny blue foliage enhances any shady spot, complementing plants with large or roughly textured leaves. For the bluest foliage, look for 'Blue Mound', 'Jackman's Blue', or 'Blue Beauty', all beautiful cultivars with small bright yellow flowers. The leaves of 'Variegata' are splashed with creamy yellow.

When working near Rue, be aware that some individuals have a poison ivy–like reaction to the juice produced by broken stems.

PLANTING REQUIREMENTS
This low-maintenance plant likes warm, dry, well-drained soil and can be grown in part or light shade or full sun. Once established, it is quite drought-tolerant.

PROPAGATION
Rue will self-sow and seedlings can be dug and transplanted. Divide in early spring or fall, root softwood cuttings in summer, or sow seed in the fall.

Japanese Burnet (*Sanguisorba obtusa*)
Zones 4–8
3–5 feet tall
Japan, Asia, U.S.

Japanese Burnet does well in light to part shade, but needs sun for at least a few hours each day to perform well. Tall spiky flowers, resembling bottlebrushes, rise high above long, basal gray-green leaves. These rich rosy-pink flower spikes begin blooming in late summer, becoming lighter pink as they age. A neat cultivar called 'Lemon Splash' is available.

Narrow-leaf Burnet (*S. tenuifolia*) has exotic, fat burgundy catkin-like flowers that hang on tall stems high above narrow, finely cut serrated leaves. For brighter, more attractive flowers, choose its white cultivar 'Alba' or pink-flowering 'Rosea'. Chocolate-maroon flowers nod on the tall arching stems of 'Atropurpurea'.

The shaggy white bottlebrush flowers of the native Canadian Burnet (*S. canadensis*) can ascend as high as 5 feet. Hardy to Zone 3, it is commonly found in bogs and moist sites in the wild. Then there are *S. minor* and *S. officinalis*, which are reportedly edible.

PLANTING REQUIREMENTS
Burnet can grow in any decent garden soil that is moist but well drained. It prefers part shade and part sun.

PROPAGATION
Divide in early spring or fall, or sow seed in fall.

Pincushion Flower (*Scabiosa columbaria*)
Zones 4 –9
12–15 inches tall
Deer Resistant

Picture a perennial border edged with these spiky little flowers. Even the soft, ferny foliage is neat and tidy. Pincushion Flower likes alkaline soil and is usually considered a sun perennial, but a few cultivars have been hybridized that perform well in shade. Butterflies love the lilac flowers of 'Butterfly Blue' and the clear pink blooms of 'Pink Mist'. Both cultivars have the typical porcupine-quilled flower heads, but the flowers of the latter are slightly larger. These two bloom heavily from early summer to frost. Deadheading encourages rebloom, but of course "deadheading equals maintenance."

PLANTING REQUIREMENTS
Plant as a border or mass in any average, well-drained garden soil in partial shade or full sun. Deadheading notwithstanding, this is a good low-maintenance choice for alkaline soils.

PROPAGATION
Divide these cultivars in early spring or fall. Seed will not come true to type.

Blue-Eyed Grass (*Sisyrinchium angustifolium*)
Zones 4–8
4–10 inches tall
Native to U.S.

A clump of ordinary looking grass is transformed in late spring when small blue starry flowers with yellow eyes suddenly emerge. Plant this pretty little native under a tree near a path to enjoy it when it is in bloom. It is a member of the Iris Family. Other native species of Blue-eyed Grass include *S. mucronatum*, with dainty thin leaves, and *S. atlanticum*, a shorter form that frequents moist areas. Summer-blooming *S. montanum* has wider leaves and the flower stalks can ascend as high as 2 feet.

Bright yellow stars gleam atop the 4–10-inch hairy, grass-like stems of Yellow Star Grass (*Hypoxis hirsuta*), a small native similar in growth to Blue-eyed Grass. Mark it well or undoubtedly it will get yanked out as "grass out of place." It is a member of the Narcissus Family.

PLANTING REQUIREMENTS

Plant in part to light shade in a border, rock garden or natural area. Most species like average loamy soil, but *S. atlanticum* needs a moist planting site.

PROPAGATION

Divide in early spring or fall.

Meadow Rue (*Thalictrum* spp.)
Zones 4–9
16–20 inches tall
Europe, Asia, U.S.
Deer Resistant

"Soft" describes the Thalictrums. Delicate clouds of fluffy flowers, in soft shades of purples, pinks, yellows, and whites, hover over finely cut foliage. Even the foliage comes in shades of soft grays and blues. There are a number of species, each handsome in its own right.

Our native Early Meadow Rue (*T. dioicum*) has delicate sprays of greenish yellow flowers in early spring. This species grows in my woodland garden. Another native, Purple Meadow Rue (*T. dasycarpum*) has sturdy purplish stems topped by airy purple-lavender flowers.

One of the earliest summer bloomers, Columbine Meadow Rue (*T. aquilegifolium*), also called Feathered Columbine, sends up its flowering clouds of pink, purple or white over a low growing mound of columbine-like foliage in May and early June. In midsummer, Yellow Meadow Rue (*T. flavuum speciosissimum glaucum*) delights with clusters of yellow balls rising above blue-green leaves. The airy flowers of *T. rochebrunianum* 'Lavender Mist' often float 5–6 feet in the air. This sturdy-stemmed species blooms from midsummer to early fall. Double lavender flowers grace the elegant 'Hewitt's Double', a 4–5-foot cultivar of *T. delavayi* that blooms most of the summer.

Japanese Meadow Rue (*T. kiusianum*), the smallest of the lot, only grows 3 inches tall. Creating mats of purple-green foliage covered with persistent lavender flowers, it makes a nice ground cover or addition to a shady rock wall.

PLANTING REQUIREMENTS

Thalictrum likes moist, humus-rich, well-drained soil in part or light shade or sun.

PROPAGATION

Divide mature clumps in early spring or fall. Sow seed as soon as it ripens or cold stratify and plant in the fall or spring.

Spiderwort (*Tradescantia* spp.)

Zones 4–9

15–24 inches tall

Native to U.S.

Hybrids

Spiderwort has 3-petaled flowers that open in the morning and close in the late afternoon. Each lasts only a day, but there are so many that the bloom cycle seems never-ending. Most *Tradescantia* species go dormant after setting seed. I love the hot rose flowers of my Spiderwort, which I assume is *T. bracteata*. I plant it among clumps of variegated grasses or daylily foliage to make it stand up better, but once it sets seed in midsummer, it disappears.

The new improved cultivars will stick around much longer. These can be cut to the ground after blooming, causing new leaves to emerge and a second flush of blooms in late summer. Choices come in shades of blue, rose, purple, pink, and white. 'Double Trouble' has flowers with extra petals; 'Little Doll' is a 10-inch plant good for edging. 'Sweet Kate', a hybrid from England, is a beauty with golden foliage and blue flowers. The more light it gets, the brighter gold it becomes. The white flowers of 'Osprey' are accented with a center of dainty soft lavender blue filaments tipped with bright golden anthers. 'Snowcap' is pure white. 'Bilberry Ice' has purple flowers edged with icy white.

PLANTING REQUIREMENTS

Spiderwort like humus-rich, moist, well-drained soil in light shade, but will grow in any average garden soil. It does not bloom well in heavy shade.

PROPAGATION

Divide in spring or fall.

Toad Lily (*Tricyrtis hirta*)
Zones 4–8
2–3 feet tall
Japan

What unusual perennial blooms in shade in the fall? Toad Lily is the answer. Plant these near a walkway or close to an entrance so the small lily-like flowers can be appreciated close up. Several species exist in the nursery trade, most of which produce speckled flowers in shades of lavender, purple, white, or even yellow. The hardiest cultivars are related to *T. hirta*. I have *T. hirta* 'Albo-marginata', a pretty, 3-foot-tall clumper with thin white edging on its narrow leaves. I also grow 'Miyazaki', whose lilac-spotted white flowers parade on long graceful stems. For golden-edged leaves, try 'Miyazaki Gold'.

Although *T. stolonifera* (aka *T. formosana*) spreads by underground runners to make large clumps, this disease-resistant species is neither invasive nor hard to find. Heavily spotted with brownish-purple, *T. macropoda*'s yellow flowers bloom in June, rising on tall stems above very broad dark green leaves. 'Kohaku' has a pendulous growth habit, which makes it a good choice for cascading down over a wall or boulder.

Cultivars with unusual leaves, like 'Lightning Strike' with two-toned leaves of light and darker green or white-edged 'Variegata', are particularly welcome in the perennial border. The former has unspotted flowers, unusual for toad lilies.

PLANTING REQUIREMENTS

Toad Lilies like moist, humus-rich, well-drained soil but will grow in average soil as long as it is well-drained. Plant in light to part shade, or in full sun.

PROPAGATION

Divide in early spring or fall.

Globeflower (*Trollius* spp.)
Zones 4–7
2–3 feet tall
Europe, China
REQUIRES MOIST SOIL

Bright yellow globe-shaped flowers spring forth in May, brightening stream banks, edges of ponds, and moist perennial borders. If dead-headed, Globeflower will rebloom in mid to late summer. The handsome foliage remains neat and tidy all season long.

With its bright yellow globes and striking leaves, early spring blooming *Trollius europaeus* 'Superbus' is truly magnificent. The flowers keep their round globe shape until the petals fall off. *T. chinensis*, sometimes identified as *T. ledebourii*, blooms in midsummer. This species has spiky upright centers surrounded by cupped petals. Its cultivar 'Golden Queen' with large yellow-orange flowers can be propagated reliably from seed.

PLANTING REQUIREMENTS
Mass several for the best effect and plant in humus-rich, moist, well-drained soil in light shade or full sun. Do not allow to dry out.

PROPAGATION
Divide in the spring or fall.

Speedwell (*Veronica* spp.)
Zones 4–9
15–18 inches tall
Asia, Europe

Speedwell is another of those sturdy, dependable border perennials. Many species, cultivars, and hybrids are available, with sizes, colors, and growth habits to suit any garden. A few suggestions include 18-inch 'Sunny Border Blue'—a Veronica that blooms . . . and blooms . . . and blooms. *Veronica spicata* 'Royal Candles', with "candles" of royal purple, forms a neat, compact 15–18 inch clump. Clear pink spikes bloom above the dark green lance-shaped leaves of 'Giles Van Hees', only 6 inches tall. Exceptionally large flowers of the palest blue characterize *V. gentianoides* 'Pallida', an 18-inch knockout with glossy green foliage.

Veronica provides vertical interest, long lasting color, persistently good-looking foliage, and easy care. What more can any gardener ask?

PLANTING REQUIREMENTS
Veronica will grow in average garden soil that is well drained. It prefers full sun but will also do fine in part to light shade, although it may not bloom as profusely.

PROPAGATION
Divide in early spring or fall, or sow seeds immediately.

Culver's Root (*Veronicastrum virginicum*)
Zones 3–9
3–6 feet tall
Native to U.S.

Culver's Root is another prairie plant that loves sun but will tolerate light to part shade. Tall, commanding spires of creamy white flowers stand high above the deep green whorled leaves. Blooming in midsummer, it rivals Delphinium for vertical interest without the need for staking. These low-maintenance natives know how to behave! Cultivars 'Album' and 'Spring Dew' are improved creamy-white forms. 'Rosea' and 'Apollo' both have light pink spires.

PLANTING REQUIREMENTS
Plant in average garden soil in sun or part to light shade. Mass for best effect. It prefers moist soil, but will tolerate dry soil once it is established.

PROPAGATION
Divide in early spring or fall. Sow ripened seeds in the fall or cold stratified seeds in the spring. It can also be propagated by cuttings.

Golden Alexanders (*Zizia aurea*)
Zones 3–8
12–20 inches tall
Native to U.S.

In early spring, this plant really zings in a naturalized woodland. Large clusters of bright yellow flowers bloom on stiff medium green stalks and divided leaflets. I like it because it attracts any butterfly larva that uses plants from the Parsley Family as a larval food source, encouraging the resulting beauties, especially Swallowtails, to take up residence.

Heartleaf Golden Alexanders (*Z. aptera*) is similar with thick, undivided leaves.

PLANTING REQUIREMENTS
These early spring natives grow in moist meadows in the wild, and prefer a similar moist planting environment in civilized society. Either light shade or full sun is acceptable.

PROPAGATION
Divide in spring or fall. Sow ripened seed in the fall or cold stratified seeds in the spring.

Not Recommended

Foxglove (*Digitalis purpurea*)
Zones 4–8
3–4 feet tall
Europe

Foxglove, a well-known resident of shady perennial borders, has escaped to the wild, naturalizing in disturbed soil and causing problems for native plants. Cultivars include 'Foxy', which blooms the first year from seed, 'Apricot Beauty', *D. ambigua* (aka *D. grandiflora*), yellow-flowering *D. lutea*, and salmon-rose *D. mertonensis*. Dwarf forms like *D. carillon*, a 16-inch yellow flowering plant, and tiny 12-inch *D. thapsii* 'Spanish Peaks' with raspberry flowers in early spring are also offered. I am not sure if these cultivars will create the problems caused by the species, but to protect our environment, it is probably wise to choose other, less invasive plants.

Dame's Rocket (*Hesperis matronalis*)
Zones 3–8
18–24 inches tall
Europe

Dame's Rocket blooms just as the spring ephemerals go dormant, in shades of pink, lavender, and white, when little else in bloom. Each flower has 4 petals, unlike common garden phlox, which has 5. A member of the Mustard Family, it self-sows readily, creating a rosette the first year and blooming the second. It also acts as a perennial, blooming from the base of last year's rosette. Unfortunately this phlox-like pass-along is another exotic escapee that can be seen in parks, along roadsides, in natural woods, and along streams all across the Midwest. Although I love this plant, I cannot recommend it.

Purple Loosestrife (*Lythrum salicaria*)
Zones 3–9
4–10 feet tall
Eurasia

If there were a Public Enemy #1 of the plant world, Purple Loosestrife would be it. It colonizes wetlands, crowding out native plants and creating a desert for wildlife who can neither get adequate nutrition from its prolific seeds nor find suitable sites to raise young. Although illegal in many Midwestern states, it is still offered by unscrupulous nurseries, usually under a different name. Whether it is called Lythrum, Purple Rocket, Purple Spikes, Rosy Spires, 'Atropurpureum', 'Roseum Superbum', or 'Robert', it causes untold headaches and expense for our country. *Lythrum virgatum*, a slightly smaller species with narrower leaves, is equally invasive. Cultivars of *L. virgatum* include 'Morden Pink', 'Morden Gleam', 'Morden Rose', and 'Dropmore Purple'. Claims that these are sterile have proven false. Unfortunately, gardeners have no control where the seeds that birds gobble will eventually be deposited, so it is to be hoped that they will not plant Purple Loosestrife—regardless of its beauty.

11.

Natural Beauty

Woodland Wildflowers for Shade

White Baneberry

Nature is a good teacher. We can learn many valuable lessons about gardening by observing plants growing in the wild.   —*Colston Burrell*

Spring is a special time of year, especially in the Midwest. Bulbs and spring ephemerals put on their show before the weeds even think about germinating, so the spring garden is as close to no-maintenance as you can get. And don't believe it if someone tells you that wildflowers are fragile. Once established, they are tough as nails and can deal with just about any kind of weather imaginable. These natives are the survivors. Trust me.

As you know, ephemeral means "fleeting." Spring ephemerals are just that. They appear before the tree leaves emerge, bloom, set seed, and go dormant until the following year. In early spring, my gardens are filled with blooms of Dutchman's Breeches, Squirrel Corn, Trillium, Spring Beauty, Shooting Star, True and False Rue Anemone, and Toothwort. This ethereal vision is enhanced by a sea of yellow and white daffodils.

To have a successful wildflower garden, you must anticipate doing some hard work at the outset. If wildflowers like the spot you prepare for them, they will flourish and spread with abandon. If not, they will simply vanish. So it is crucial to duplicate the soil that wildflowers naturally grow in. Well-drained woodland loam is the optimum planting bed for both wildflowers and spring bulbs (see chapters 1-2).

As you begin, mulch winding paths through the proposed garden so you and your friends can stroll together to appreciate these little natives. Next get the planting bed ready. Plant wildflowers in drifts or colonies as they grow in nature. Plan to intersperse ephemerals with non-ephemerals such as Celandine Poppy, Wild Geranium, Jack-in-the-Pulpit, and of course ferns. That way you won't be tempted to plant something else in that "blank" space. And although there will not be an overabundance of colorful flowers once the spring ephemerals have gone to sleep, you can count on the woodland garden to be calm, lovely, and green from spring until fall.

When you are growing wildflowers, you need to look carefully at nature. Whoever heard of an army of neatniks marching into the woods armed with rakes? Instead, when fall arrives, use a mulching mower rather than a rake, allowing the chopped leaves to lie where they fall to disintegrate over the wildflower bed. The resulting duff will keep that loamy soil loose and friable and full of nutrients. Besides, think how much less maintenance that plan requires than the raking, bagging, and burning ritual we have been programmed to perform.

Gardeners frequently ask where they can get wildflowers. Because of the recent interest in native plants, even local garden centers are stocking them, and it is possible to order many species from specialty nurseries. (Inquire to be sure the nursery is not collecting from the wild. If the prices seem too low, be suspicious.)

Another source of wildflowers are those ever-present construction sites. These sites have provided the bulk of native wildflowers growing and thriving in my yard. They have increased mightily in the past 20 years, making my investment in time and energy definitely worthwhile. For tips on collecting from a construction site, see *Go Native!* chapter 11, pp. 177-79. It is also possible to grow your own wildflowers from seed. Once again, look to nature for your guide—and see *Go Native!* chapter 11, pp. 175-76.

Finally, don't worry about creating a high-maintenance garden when you plant wildflowers. Once wildflowers become established, they will take care of themselves and in severe drought will simply go dormant.

Given the proper conditions, these exquisite little natives are literally carefree.

Woodland Wildflowers for Shade

White Baneberry (*Actaea pachypoda*)
Red Baneberry (*A. rubra*)
Zones 3–8
12–24 inches tall
Native to U.S.
REQUIRES MOIST SOIL

Dense clusters of white bottlebrush flowers appear above the beautiful astilbe-like leaves of *A. pachypoda* in the spring. In late summer, round white berries with a single dark spot appear, giving rise to the common name Doll's Eyes. Red Baneberry (*A. rubra*) is nearly identical except the leaves are not cut quite so deeply, and the shiny, fleshy berries are red. It likes a little more light than White Baneberry. A mass of either makes a handsome display in the fall as long as the plant sets berries. If not, it will go dormant in midsummer. My baneberries are in heavy shade, and some years I have a good crop of berries, while in other years they "disappear." But of course they return the following spring.

PLANTING REQUIREMENTS
Being woodland plants, baneberries thrive in humus rich, moist, loamy soil in shade or part shade. Red Baneberry needs slightly acidic soil. Space new plantings 12–18 inches apart.

PROPAGATION
Divide the coarse rootstocks in spring, making sure each division has at least 1–3 eyes (like a peony). Or remove the pulp and plant freshly ripened seeds in the fall. Please don't eat the berries; they are poisonous.

Nodding Wild Onion (*Allium cernuum*)
Zones 4–9
8–20 inches tall
Native to U.S.

Dainty, umbrella-like clusters of soft pink or white flowers nod above strappy foliage in midsummer. After the flowers bloom, pompons of small round seeds persist until late fall. Nodding Wild Onion's clumps get larger and larger each year. If happy, the plants will also self-sow, but seedlings are not difficult to weed out. Better yet, site it where it can increase at will.

This Allium's companions in the wild include Heath Aster, Shooting Star, Black-eyed Susan, Pale Purple Coneflower, and Spiderwort.

PLANTING REQUIREMENTS

Plant in average, well-drained garden soil in nearly any light exposure from full sun to deep shade. This prairie remnant survivor also does fine in dry sites. Plants will bloom more profusely with more light. I have a mass of these near the edge of a woodland planting. They also blend into a perennial border.

PROPAGATION

Separate the large clumps of reddish onion-like bulbs in spring or fall, or plant ripened seed in fall.

Wild Leek (*Allium tricoccum*)
Zones 4–8
6–12 inches tall
Native to U.S.

In early spring, Wild Leek's broad, strappy daffodil-like leaves emerge. Just after the surrounding deciduous trees fully leaf out, these leaves wither and go dormant. In late spring or early summer, umbels of white to greenish-white Allium flowers rise on rigid, naked green stalks. In late summer, interesting seeds appear in place of the flowers. This plant moderately self-sows and large colonies are often found in the wild. However, my plants have remained as single clumps for years, so it is not aggressive or invasive.

Also called Ramp or Ramps, Wild Leek is edible and was used by Native Americans and early settlers. Foragers continue to seek out this plant, and upscale big-city restaurants are featuring it on their menus.

PLANTING REQUIREMENTS

Wild Leek likes moist soil in spring and early summer when the leaves and flowers are being produced, but later becomes drought tolerant. The soil can be neutral to slightly acidic. These onion-like plants enjoy the sun of early spring before the leaf canopy emerges, but then grow well in part, light, or full shade.

PROPAGATION
Dig and divide the bulbs just after flowering. I have also lifted and transplanted entire clumps in early spring with no apparent ill effects.

Rue Anemone (*Anemonella thalictroides*)
Zones 3–8
4–6 inches tall
Native to U.S.
REQUIRES MOIST SOIL

Delicate pink flowers resembling a fairy's bridal bouquet open in early spring, hovering above tiny green paw-shaped leaves. Rue Anemone usually blooms from mid-March to mid-April in my Indiana garden. This dainty native forms small clumps rather than colonizing like False Rue Anemone. In the wild it is generally found as a solitary specimen, although a number of these clumps bloom in the immediate vicinity.

PLANTING REQUIREMENTS
Plant 1 inch deep in moist, humus-rich, woodland soil under deciduous trees. Space new plantings about 4–5 inches apart.

PROPAGATION
Grows from tiny dahlia-like tubers. A good-sized clump can be lifted and divided. Make sure there are adequate "eyes" in each clump. When grown in ideal woodland conditions, it moderately self-sows.

Jack-in-the-Pulpit (*Arisaema triphyllum*)
Zones 3–8
12–30 inches tall
Native to U.S.
REQUIRES MOIST SOIL

A native that fascinates children is Jack-in-the-Pulpit, with its bloom resembling a pulpit in an old European church. Jack (the spadix) "preaches" under his own special hooded canopy (the spathe). This canopy can be green, burgundy-brown, or striped. To make Jack preach (he really squeaks!), gently rub the stem just below his pulpit with thumb and forefinger.

After the flower withers and dies, handsome, densely packed clusters of bright green berries form, slowly changing to bright red. A mass planting is quite a sight in late summer and early fall. Weather and environmental conditions determine whether this will be a Jack or a Jill. Adequate moisture is critical to ensure female fruit production and delay early dormancy. Compost around the base of the plant helps keep the soil moist.

A sibling, Green Dragon (*A. dracontium*), has a horseshoe-shaped leaf, reminiscent of Maidenhair Fern. In fact these two natives complement each other nicely. It grows a little taller than Jack-in-the-Pulpit, often maturing as high as 36–48 inches. Green Dragon's orangey-red fruits turn deep red in late fall. It is hardy in Zones 4–9.

PLANTING REQUIREMENTS
Provide moist, humus-rich woodland soil in any kind of shade, including full shade, for both Jack-in-the-Pulpit and Green Dragon. Plants in too much sun will be stunted.

PROPAGATION
Sowing seed is the easiest and most reliable way to propagate. Place ripened berries in a sieve under tepid running water and gently rub to remove the pulp, which actually retards germination, and expose the small seed. Gently push the cleaned seed into the ground near the mother plant or sow where more Jacks are desired. Do not allow the seed to dry out. The tiny seedling will appear in the spring. It is easily identified because its 3 leaves are arranged like an upside-down T, unlike evenly spaced Trillium leaves. It takes at least 3 years for these seedlings to flower.

It is also possible to remove cormlets from mature corms. Wear gloves because some individuals develop a poison ivy–like rash from handling the corms. Plants started from cormlets generally flower sooner than those started from seed.

Spring Cress (*Cardamine bulbosa*)
Purple Cress (*C. douglassii*)
Zones 3–8
4–20 inches tall
Native to U.S.

Members of the Mustard Family are called crucifers because their four flower petals are arranged in the shape of a cross. Spring Cress demonstrates this heritage with its spring-blooming, 4-petaled flowers in shades of pink, lavender, or white. Unlike many mustard species, it is not invasive and goes dormant after setting seeds. Spring Cress is the taller of the two species, occasionally maturing at 20 inches tall. Purple Cress grows only 4–12 inches tall. Snip the young foliage of both cresses for soups and salads. Early settlers used the tiny tuberous root as a substitute for horseradish.

PLANTING REQUIREMENTS
Will grow in any woodland or well-drained regular garden soil in part to medium shade.

PROPAGATION
Dig and transplant the small tubers 2–3 inches deep immediately after blooming in the spring, or sow seeds.

Spring Beauty (*Claytonia virginica*)
Zones 3–9
4–6 inches tall
Native to U.S.

In early spring, woodlands and dappled meadows are filled with a soft haze of white. Spring Beauty lives up to its name, for it is truly a beauty. Its long, thin leaves resemble succulent grass. The white to pinkish-white flowers have dark pink veins leading to the center—perhaps to lead insects to the spot that needs pollinating. It self-sows readily but is not invasive.

Called "Fairy Spuds" by early settlers, the round, button-like, dark brown tubers were prized as a crunchy delicacy.

PLANTING REQUIREMENTS
Plant tubers 2–3 inches deep in humus-rich, well-drained woodland or loamy garden soil in part to high medium shade or full sun. Plants can

be safely transplanted as soon as they emerge until they go dormant in late spring.

PROPAGATION

Dig and divide mature clumps, or transplant young seedlings. The seeds are tiny and difficult to collect, so it is fortunate that this little ephemeral obligingly self-sows.

Dwarf Spring Larkspur (*Delphinium tricorne*)
Zones 4–7
12–18 inches tall
Native to U.S.

Bright purple-blue spurred flowers nod and dance on graceful stems above finely cut buttercup-like foliage in late spring. Occasionally flowers will be highlighted with white. If Spring Larkspur is happy it will seed itself and spread moderately. If conditions are not up to par, it will simply disappear.

PLANTING REQUIREMENTS

Dwarf Larkspur is another ephemeral that likes the early spring sunlight, followed by dappled to high medium shade later in the season. Plant in moist, humus-rich, well-drained woodland soil in a spot where the delicate flowers and leaves can be appreciated close up.

PROPAGATION

This plant grows from small tubers, but is difficult to propagate, so the best bet is to transplant young seedlings into your woodland setting.

Cut-leaved Toothwort (*Cardamine concatenata* aka *Dentaria laciniata*)
Zones 3–9
4–10 inches tall
Native to U.S.

Our woodland has masses of these 4-petaled white flowers in early spring, blooming gaily with Spring Beauty, Bluebells, Dutchman's Breeches, and Squirrel Corn. A few have escaped to the lawn, but cause no problems since the leaves yellow and go dormant before the grass needs mowing. It was believed that Toothwort alleviated toothache; hence both its common name and its former scientific name, *Dentaria*. Other native Toothworts include Crinkleroot (*C. diphylla*), which has more leaves than flowers, and Slender Toothwort (*C. heterophylla*) with narrow lance-shaped leaves. Both are hardy in Zones 4–8.

Showy Toothwort (*C. pentaphyllos*) also makes a nice addition to the natural garden. This 6–8-inch European beauty has ruffled lavender-pink 4-petaled flowers.

PLANTING REQUIREMENTS
Plant the small rhizomes 2–3 inches deep in moist, humus-rich, well-drained soil.

PROPAGATION
Dig the rhizomes and transplant. Toothwort self-sows moderately.

Dutchman's Breeches (*Dicentra cucullaria*)
Squirrel Corn (*D. canadensis*)
Zones 3–7
8–12 inches tall
Native to U.S.

Bright yellow spurs accent the inflated white flowers waving above the soft, ferny blue-green foliage of Dutchman's Breeches. If happy it self-sows. It grows from a pinkish-tan tuber about the size of a marble, formed of multiple tiny bulblets. It is very fragile and easily broken apart. Each tiny bulblet will eventually form a new plant, but takes several years to reach blooming size, so be gentle when transplanting. The tiny white or lavender-pink hearts dangle from Squirrel Corn's dainty stems over bluish-green foliage nearly identical to Dutchman's Breeches. Squirrel Corn gets its name from the bright yellow corn-kernel bulblets that comprise its marble-sized tuber. Each of these kernels is many times larger than the bulblets of Dutchman's Breeches. These small ephemerals both appear in early to midspring, bloom, set seed, and then disappear until the following spring.

Fringed Bleeding Heart, which is not ephemeral, is discussed in chapter 10.

PLANTING REQUIREMENTS
Plant 2–3 inches deep in humus-rich, well-drained woodland soil in dappled shade. The tubers will eventually seek their own level. Space 3–4 inches apart.

PROPAGATION

The tubers are easily located just under the duff and can be transplanted, or even broken apart. It is possible to sow seed, but the opportunity is fleeting, so it generally easier to let the plant self-sow and transplant seedlings the following spring.

Shooting Star (*Dodecatheon meadia*)
Zones 4–8
12–18 inches tall
Native to U.S.

Swept-back petals, resembling a shooting star, nod from a tall stem above a rosette of lance-shaped leaves. Also known as Prairie Pointers, American Cowslip, Rooster Heads, and Cranesbill, Shooting Star is a plant of the prairies. It is particularly effective when planted en masse as a drift. Its flowers come in shades of pink, rose, lavender and white with bright yellow markings surrounding the pointed "beaks."

PLANTING REQUIREMENTS

Shooting Stars thrive in moist, humus-rich, well-drained soil in light to medium shade, or in full sun.

PROPAGATION

Divide fibrous rootstock just as the plant goes dormant, or in the fall if the dormant plants can be located. Several wildflower nurseries list this lovely native in their catalog.

Yellow Trout Lily (*Erythronium americanum*)
White Trout Lily (*E. albidum*)
Zones 3–9
4–8 inches tall
Native to U.S.

If you are rescuing Trout Lilies from a construction site, be sure to bring a spade; the small bulbs reside deep in the soil. Each plant has two medium green leaves mottled with silvery gray. Part of the Lily Family, Trout Lily is also called Dogtooth Violet, Adder's Tongue, and Fawn Lily. It often carpets large sections of the woodland, producing many more leaves than flowering plants. Leaves and flowers all disappear after these ephemerals bloom and set seed.

Yellow Trout Lily grows in the eastern part of the U.S. to Indiana. Its sibling, White Trout Lily, begins in woodlands of Indiana, spreading westward. I have both in my woodland garden.

PLANTING REQUIREMENTS

Plant in part to full shade in moist, well-drained, humus-rich woodland soil. Cover the small bulbs with 3–5 inches of soil. Bulbs delve deeper as they mature. If planted over a buried rock slab to halt this descent, bulbs expend less energy and bloom sooner and more reliably.

PROPAGATION

Rescue mature plants from construction sites and transplant into loamy woodland soil, or order from a specialty nursery that grows them. It takes 7 years for a seed to become a blooming plant.

Wild Geranium (*Geranium maculatum*)
Zones 3–8
15–24 inches tall
Native to U.S.

This useful, clump-former has lavender-pink flowers in April and early May, but its best attribute is its leaves. Deeply divided but not cut to the center, they look good all summer, easily filling in spaces left bare by the dormancy of spring ephemerals.

Mass this peony-sized plant, plant it as a specimen, or intersperse with other shade lovers. It is beautiful in any setting.

PLANTING REQUIREMENTS

Humus-rich, well-drained, woodland soil in part or light shade. Blooms better with some light, but will make a nice leafy clump in full shade. If conditions become too dry, it will simply go dormant until next year.

PROPAGATION
Self-sows moderately, is easy to grow from seed, or divide the coarse brittle rhizome mass in early spring or fall, keeping at least two buds or more on each division.

Sharp-Lobed Hepatica (*Hepatica acutiloba*)
Zones 3–7
4–6 inches tall
Native to U.S.

Emerging deep reddish-brown, the tri-lobed leaves soon change to green. Occasionally the green is mottled with silver. This is one of the earliest wildflowers to bloom. Pink, blue, lavender, rose, or white flowers with prominent anthers bloom on cold-protecting hairy stems above last year's leaves. Compact clumps of new leaves unfurl as the flowers fade, remaining pretty all summer long.

Round-leaved Hepatica (*H. americana*) is basically the same with rounded rather than pointed leaves. Growing requirements are identical and the two species can be found growing together in the woods. Hybridized hepaticas include 'Eco Blue Harlequin' (silvery mottled leaves); 'Eco Indigo' (deep blue flowers); and 'Eco White Fluff' (shaggy double white flowers).

PLANTING REQUIREMENTS
Plant in moist, humus-rich, woodland soil, preferably on a well-drained east-facing slope to catch the morning sun.

PROPAGATION
Division in late spring or early fall is generally recommended, but I have not had good luck and usually lose both pieces. It will self-sow if the ground around the mother plant is kept clear and moist as the seeds fall. Seedlings take 3–4 years to flower.

Swamp Rose Mallow (*Hibiscus moscheutos*)
Zones (4)5–10
3–7 feet tall
Native to U.S.

Humongous flowers open daily in midsummer on this shrub-like native perennial. It makes quite a statement in the garden. Flowers, resembling huge hollyhocks, easily measure 4–8 inches across in shades of white, pink, or red. Protruding from the dark center of each flower is a tall pistil, its lower half surrounded by bright yellow stamens. Mark the spot where it resides, because it is a late riser, often "sleeping in" until June.

Cultivars include 'Anna Arundel' with 9-inch pink blooms, ruffled 'Sweet Caroline', and 10-inch clear-white 'Blue River II'. 'Fireball' is burgundy-red. A deep red eye accents the pure white 12-inch flowers of 'Kopper King', with coppery-red foliage.

PLANTING REQUIREMENTS

A plant of wet spaces in the wild, it will grow in the home garden in loamy, humus-rich soil in light shade or full sun. Once established, it can tolerate average soil.

PROPAGATION

The roots of established plants are too deep and tough to easily transplant or divide. Take tip cuttings in early summer, plant seeds in the fall, or purchase started plants from reputable nurseries.

Goldenseal (*Hydrastis canadensis*)

Zones 3–8

6–12 inches tall

Native to U.S.

Overcollected, this native is not often found in the wild, but is easy to grow in a naturalized woodland setting with moist, loamy soil. A single spiky white flower blooms on each crinkled, deep green maple-like leaf in early spring. In midsummer gardeners have to look twice because there, in place of the flower, is a single deep red, nonedible, raspberry.

I rescued my Goldenseal from a centuries-old woodland that has been transformed into lawn with "velcro bushes" complementing brick, glass, and cement. They now thrive in my woods. Specialty mail-order nurseries, such as Munchkin Nursery, offer this plant.

PLANTING REQUIREMENTS

Plant in humus-rich, moist woodland soil in part to full shade. Mass as many plants as possible for the best display, or plant near a rock or large tree as a focal point.

PROPAGATION

It is possible to propagate Goldenseal by dividing its rhizomes, or by separating the small seeds from the pulp and sowing them outdoors in the fall. I have not had much success with either method and find that plant rescue or purchase is easier.

Virginia Waterleaf (*Hydrophyllum virginianum*)
Zones 3–8
14–24 inches tall
Native to U.S.

Once established, Virginia Waterleaf takes care of itself, blooming reliably each spring. Long stamens protrude from the lavender-blue, bell-like flowers that hover in clusters over finely cut leaves. When the leaves emerge, they are marked with silvery-white spots. Virginia Waterleaf grows from a scaly rootstock and is often confused with Fern-leaved Phacelia (see p. 288). Appendaged Waterleaf (*H. appendiculatum*), probably a biennial, has coarser maple-like leaves and lavender-blue flowers. The stamens do not protrude as far, which helps distinguish it from Virginia Waterleaf. Broad-leaved Waterleaf (*H. canadense*) makes a handsome 6–20-inch-tall ground cover that stays green all summer long. It grows from a reddish-brown rhizome that resembles the scales of a pine cone. It lies horizontally under the ground.

PLANTING REQUIREMENTS

Plant in humus-rich woodland soil or in average well-drained, loamy garden soil in part to medium shade.

PROPAGATION

Sow ripened seeds immediately. Divide rhizomes of Broad-leaved Waterleaf.

Blue Flag Iris (*Iris virginica* var. *shrevei*)
Larger Blue Flag (*I. versicolor*)
Zones 2–8
18–36 inches tall
Native to U.S.
REQUIRES MOIST SOIL

Blue Flag Iris is a genuine moisture-lover, often found standing in water in the wild. However, it can also grow in normal garden soil with sufficient moisture. Its lavender-blue flowers, marked with yellow and white, bloom in May and early June. White flowers are the hallmark of 'Alba'.

Also called Wild Iris, Larger Blue Flag (*I. versicolor*) is a little taller. Blooming in June and July, its flowers rise above the sword-like foliage. An even larger cultivar, 'Contraband Girl', can reach 6 feet. Its oversized flowers are a luscious bluish-purple. 24-inch 'Kermesina' has magenta blooms, 'Rosea' has pink flowers.

PLANTING REQUIREMENTS
Plant in moist or wet site, in dappled or part shade or in full sun.

PROPAGATION
Divide rhizomes after flowering, as with Bearded Iris, leaving a fan of leaves attached to each division. Set each rhizome horizontally barely below the soil. Sow seeds in the fall. These take 3 years to mature enough to bloom.

False Rue Anemone (*Isopyrum biternatum*)
Zones 3–8
3–7 inches tall
Native to U.S.

A colonizer, False Rue Anemone can carpet a woodland floor or dappled meadow with its sweet 5-petaled white flowers that bloom with bluebells and daffodils. Its medium green columbine-like foliage is finely cut and airy looking. After the seeds ripen, the leaves of this semi-ephemeral turn yellow and die back, but reappear late in the summer.

The roots form thick mats. When I dig them for transplanting, it is like pulling up a rug of anemones.

PLANTING REQUIREMENTS
Plant in humus-rich, moist soil in light to full shade.

PROPAGATION
Divide mats after the plants set seed and transplant.

Twinleaf (*Jeffersonia diphylla*)
Zones 4–8
8–15 inches tall
Native to U.S.

Near my front door, a large, upright, vase-shaped clump of Twinleaf thrives under a small Tricolored Beech. It gets several hours of dappled morning sunlight and is in shade for the rest of the day. The twin butterfly-like leaves of this vigorous specimen are a rich green—and huge. The bright white flowers resemble those of Bloodroot, but do not last as long. Twinleaf is not ephemeral; the fascinating leaves remain beautiful all summer. It can function as a mass, or as a focal point.

PLANTING REQUIREMENTS
Plant in humus-rich, moist, well-drained soil in part, light or full shade.

PROPAGATION
Divide in early spring or fall. After ripening, sow seeds near the mother plant. They will self-stratify and germinate the following spring. Transplant young seedlings where they are to grow.

Wild Lily-of-the-Valley (*Maianthemum canadense*)
Zones 2–7
3–6 inches tall
Native to U.S.

Also known as Canada Mayflower and Bead-Ruby, Wild Lily-of-the-Valley looks like a miniature False Solomon's Seal, fluffy flower spike and all. It flowers in late spring or early summer, then produces small clusters of red berries in fall. It spreads by thin rhizomes that creep under the ground. It spreads readily below shrubs and trees where little else will grow, especially if well mulched.

Var. *interius* has downy leaves and stems (petioles). Slightly different in all parts, it flowers about 2 weeks later. A Eurasian form (*M. bifolium*) is a little taller, maturing at 9 inches.

PLANTING REQUIREMENTS
Plant in humus-rich, slightly acidic to neutral soil that is well drained in part to full shade. Mulch thoroughly to preserve moisture.

PROPAGATION
Order from specialty wildflower nurseries. Or dig and separate the thin, white rhizomes, making sure each division has two or three "eyes." Sow cleaned seed in the fall. Seedlings must mature at least three years before they will bloom.

Virginia Bluebells (*Mertensia virginica*)
Zones 3–9
  12–20 inches tall
  Native to U.S.
Bluebells self-sow readily, filling moist woods with their spatulate leaves and arching stems, heavy with dangling bells. The tightly closed flower buds emerge pink, but change to the familiar sky-blue as they open. Plant with daffodils, Celandine Poppy, and False Rue Anemone for a spectacular spring display. Since Bluebells are ephemeral, intersperse with ferns or non-ephemeral wildflowers.

PLANTING REQUIREMENTS
Plant in humus-rich, loamy, well-drained soil that is neutral to slightly acidic. Cover the white "eyes" with 2–3 inches of soil. Plants will seek their own level. When I dig them, I often find them 5–7 inches deep. Bluebells love the warm spring sunlight that filters through naked

deciduous trees. They flower, set seed, and finally go dormant as the tree leaves emerge.

PROPAGATION

Transplant just after the foliage yellows. The decaying leaves fan out over the ground, making it easy to locate the large, black, molar-like rootstock. The inside of the brittle rootstock is coconut-white. There are 4 nut-like seeds in each flower. Let them sow where they fall, or gather and either plant immediately or put them in a film canister in the refrigerator to plant in the fall. Do not let the seeds dry out. They will germinate readily the following spring.

Bishop's-Cap (*Mitella diphylla*)
Zones 3–8
8–10 inches tall
Native to U.S.

Also known as Mitrewort, Fringe Cap, and Fairy Cup, Bishop's Cap gets its common names from the shape of its flowers—tiny, white fringed cups that march up either side of the arching stem rising above a cluster of heart-shaped, maple-like leaves. Later, shiny black seeds take their place on the flower stalk.

This well-behaved plant forms an ever-increasing clump. Mass for an effective ground cover, or combine it with other spring wildflowers like Wild Geranium, Spring Beauty, or Hepatica.

PLANTING REQUIREMENTS

Plant in humus-rich, moist, well-drained woodlands in shade.

PROPAGATION

Locate and divide rooted rhizomes in early spring or fall. Sow ripened seeds immediately, pushing them into the soil near the mother plant. Young seedlings can be transplanted the following spring.

Ginseng (*Panex quinquefolius*)
Zones 4–9
10–15 inches tall
Native to U.S.

Ginseng has been collected in the wild almost to the point of extinction, but in typical woodland soil that is naturally loamy and rich with leaf mold it grows easily, reappearing reliably year after year. Small white insignificant flowers bloom in July, but are easily missed. The real show comes in the fall when the fat clusters of deep red berries peep over deep-green, heavily-veined leaves. Each leaf has 5 leaflets spread out like a palm. There are 3 of these leaves in a whorl on each plant.

A grouping is handsome in the natural garden. But you had probably better not crow too loudly, or your Ginseng may come up missing.

PLANTING REQUIREMENTS
Dig a hole deep enough to plant the tapering carrot-like rootstock straight into the ground without bending it and cover the eye with 2–3 inches of soil. Plant in part to medium shade. Mulch.

PROPAGATION
Clean the red pulp from the seeds and plant near the mother plant immediately. Seeds take up to 2 seasons to germinate. Next, wait 3–5 years for the seedling to mature. Or just purchase from a reputable wildflower nursery that does not practice wild-collection.

Fern-leaved Phacelia (*Phacelia bipinnatifida*)
Zones 4–9
12–24 inches tall
Native to U.S.

A haze of pale lavender-blue appears in my woods each spring. Phacelia is a delicate plant with finely cut ferny light green leaves. Once established, this biennial will reappear annually. For a striking picture, intersperse Phacelia with bright yellow flowering plants like Celandine Poppy and Buttercups. In the wild, it is found growing with Wild Ginger, Baneberry, and Blue Cohosh. It goes dormant in midsummer.

Miami Mist (*P. purshii*) and Fringed Phacelia (*P. fimbriata*) are annuals, but will generally reseed themselves, reappearing the following season.

PLANTING REQUIREMENTS
Plant in humus-rich, well-drained, woodland soil in part to full shade.

PROPAGATION
Self-sows readily, but is not invasive. Transplant first-year seedlings.

Wild Blue Phlox (*Phlox divaricata*)
Zones 3–9
12–18 inches tall
Native to U.S.

Few sights are prettier than a woodland or dappled meadow covered with Wild Blue Phlox, particularly when it is joined by masses of white False Rue Anemone. This little native has 5 petals on each flower and looks just like a garden phlox in miniature. It is can occasionally be found in the wild in pink, lavender, or white, but typical flowers are true blue.

'Clouds of Perfume', 'White Perfume', and 'Blue Perfume' are cultivars bred for fragrance. Plant these near the patio or a low window and inhale their sweetness on a pleasant spring evening. Another white form, 'Fuller's White', has notched petals.

PLANTING REQUIREMENTS
Plant Wild Blue Phlox, also known as Sweet William, in moist, humus-rich, well-drained, woodland soil in part to medium shade.

PROPAGATION
Lift established clumps and divide in early spring, or immediately after flowering. Sow seed or root stem cuttings in the fall.

Mayapple (*Podophyllum peltatum*)
Zones 3–9
12–18 inches tall
Native to U.S.

A vigorous colonizer, Mayapple refuses to be a focal point, so be aware of that trait when choosing a site to plant it. Poking up through the newly warmed soil in early spring, they look like neatly closed umbrellas. Flowering plants have a large round bud on top of the folded umbrella, resembling an oversized green pea. If the top is flat, the emerging plant has only a single leaf and is not mature enough to bloom. Large, deeply divided green leaves stand on either tall straight stalks or Y-shaped stalks. The flower blooms in the axil of this Y. Later, the edible fruit, resembling a small green lemon, hangs on a short stalk from this Y.

Mayapples occasionally get rust, a fungal disease that produces yellow pustules on the top of the leaf and bright orange spots on the underside.

Dig and destroy infected plants, or spray with a fungicide in early spring in any areas where it occurred the previous season.

Leaves and roots are poisonous.

PLANTING REQUIREMENTS

Give this native plenty of room to run and spread in humus-rich, well-drained soil in part to full shade.

PROPAGATION

Mayapple spreads by horizontal creeping roots that resemble tan branches about the size of a pencil. Dig and snip sections of the root apart, making sure each section has at least 1–2 eyes. Also self-sows, or plant seeds in the fall.

Jacob's Ladder (*Polemonium reptans*)
Zones 3–8
8–12 inches tall
Native to U.S.

Also called Greek Valerian, this native has loose clusters of pretty blue bell-like flowers in midspring. Ladder-like leaves form a neat clump in the garden, remaining for the entire season. For a tidier look, remove spent flower stalks. Use it as a ground cover, along a garden path, or as a focal point.

P. caeruleum, a little taller, matures at 14–24 inches. The leaves of 'Brise d'Anjou' are edged in creamy white and persist all season long. A European Jacob's Ladder dubbed 'Heavenly Habit' (*P. boreale*) has larger blue flowers and shinier leaves than the native species. It forms a compact 12-inch clump.

PLANTING REQUIREMENTS

Plant in moist, humus-rich, well-drained woodland soil in part to medium shade. It will also tolerate full sun in more northern zones. Space 12–15 inches apart.

PROPAGATION

Lift and divide mature clumps in early spring or fall, cutting through the fibrous roots. Self-sows readily, or seeds can be planted immediately after ripening to germinate the following spring.

Giant Solomon's Seal (*Polygonatum giganteum*)
Zones 2–8
4–6 feet tall
Native to U.S.
Deer Resistant

Here is the ultimate vertical accent for the woodland garden—at least 4, sometimes as much as 6 feet tall! White bells hang from the arching stems in early spring, changing to dark blue berries in early to mid-summer. These berries are relished by wildlife, and self-sow. *P. giganteum* is sometimes identified in plant catalogs as *P. commutatum* or *P. canaliculatum*. Solomon's Seal (*P. biflorum*) is smaller and shorter.

European Solomon Seal (*P. multiflorum*) flowers more heavily than the native. A beautiful 30-inch variegated Solomon Seal called simply 'Variegatum', with creamy white edged leaves, comes from this species. Japanese Solomon's Seal (*P. humile* aka *P. falcatum*), hardy in Zones 4–8, is a tiny 6-inch dwarf with glossy green foliage. It makes a nice ground cover and tolerates dry soil in midsummer. Variegated Japanese Solomon's Seal (*P. odoratum*) is another white-edged form. It grows to 36 inches and tolerates dry shade.

PLANTING REQUIREMENTS
Plant in moist to average garden soil in part to full shade. Mass for best effect.

PROPAGATION
Plant ripened seed in the fall to germinate the following spring, or dig and divide the rhizome, leaving at least one eye per piece.

Bloodroot (*Sanguinaria canadensis*)
Zones 3–8
6–12 inches tall
Native to U.S.

Early in the spring, brilliant-white poppy-like flowers with 8–12 shiny white petals and bright yellow stamens venture forth. Each single flower is clasped tightly against the cold by a convoluted leaf that reminds me of a large paw. Bloodroot grows from a thickened pencil-like reddish-brown rhizome. If broken or wounded, this exudes a reddish liquid.

Not a true ephemeral, Bloodroot usually graces the garden until temperatures soar and the ground becomes dry. Then it goes dormant until the following spring. If woodland gardeners can identify native wildflowers by their leaves, when there is an opportunity for a plant rescue on a construction site, more desirable plants can be saved. Thanks to its distinctive leaves, Bloodroot is one of the easiest to learn, along with Wild Geranium and Celandine Poppy.

A beautiful double-flowered form, *S. canadensis* 'Multiplex', can be found in the nursery trade. It is sometimes identified as 'Flore Pleno'.

PLANTING REQUIREMENTS

Bloodroot enjoys dappled shade, although it will perform well in even deep woodland shade. It requires moist, humus-rich soil that is well drained, so the rhizomes do not rot. Mass for a ground cover, or plant a group at the base of a tree or near a boulder.

PROPAGATION

After the flower petals fall, a long thin, pale-green capsule is revealed, containing light green seeds. These ripen to dark brown in about four weeks. If the soil at the base of the plant emulates woodland soil—rich, and moist with plenty of humus—these seeds will drop and self-sow. It is possible to collect fully ripened seed, but it must be planted immediately and not allowed to dry out. Transplant tiny seedlings the following spring. Or lift and divide the rhizomes. Cut the 1-inch thick pencil-like rhizome, leaving at least 1 eye per division, and replant 2 inches deep. Space new plants 6–8 inches apart.

False Solomon's Seal (*Smilacina racemosa*)
Zones 2–8
2–3 feet tall
Native to U.S.

More appropriately called Solomon's Plume, False Solomon's Seal is not quite as upright as Solomon's Seal (*Polygonatum* spp.). Mass this plant and in late spring a multitude of 3–5 inch white bottlebrush flowers will light up the edge of the woods. In mid to late summer, clusters of shiny, rust-colored berries hang from the arching stems. Like true Solomon's Seal, it grows from a fat white rhizome that grows horizontally about 2–3 inches under the soil.

PLANTING REQUIREMENTS

Solomon's Plume likes bright light, dappled shade, or even full shade, but will be stunted in too much sun. Plant it in average soil that is well drained.

PROPAGATION

Dig and cut apart long rhizomes, keeping at least 1 eye per division. Remove pulp and plant seeds near the mother plant, or just let this native self-sow. It will.

Skullcap (*Scutellaria* spp.)
Zones 4–8
12–16 inches tall
Native to U.S.
REQUIRES MOIST SOIL

Delicate, airy, dainty—these adjectives amply describe the tiny lavender-blue flowers of Showy Skullcap (*S. serrata*). Heavily textured, dark-green serrated leaves form a tidy clump. It blooms in May and June. Alpine Skullcap (*S. alpina*) has purple flowers tipped with yellow. Mulch these two in northern zones for adequate winter protection. Next to bloom, in midsummer, is Downy Skullcap (*S. incana*), which grows 2–4 feet tall. It also has lavender-blue flowers, and is striking planted near red Bee Balm, mauve Joe Pye Weed, and white Boneset. Pink Skullcap (*S. integrifolia*) is one of the naturally occurring forms of Hyssop Skullcap, a blue-flowering skullcap. And talk about mad! Mad-Dog Skullcap (*S. lateriflora*) has small bluish-purple flowers that spout out of the axils of the serrated leaves. Each arching stalk has small flowers that hang on one side. It is commonly found in marshy areas, but grows nicely in the average garden. Early Blue Skullcap (*S. ovata*), found in sunny spots in the wild, blooms in June. It will tolerate part or light shade. All of these are members of the Mint Family and have square stems.

PLANTING REQUIREMENTS

Plant in any fertile garden soil with adequate moisture in part to light shade. Skullcaps dislike dry soil. Mark the planting site because they are "late risers" in the spring.

PROPAGATION

Divide mature clumps in early spring or fall, keeping 2–3 eyes per division. Sow ripened seed immediately, or take cuttings in midsummer.

Zigzag Goldenrod (*Solidago flexicaulis*)
Zones 3–8
1–3 feet tall
Native to U.S.

Bright yellow flowers zig and zag up the stems of Zigzag Goldenrod, so this plant is well named. Most goldenrods prefer full sun, but Zigzag likes a shady spot. It spreads by underground runners to form a nice 2–3 foot tall dark green ground cover. In the wild, it is found in limey soils. This is definitely a plant for the wild garden because until it blooms it looks more like a weed than a wildflower. I like it because it provides that last bit of color in the fall just before the shady garden goes to bed for the winter. But be advised: Zigzag Goldenrod will spread aggressively in moist woodlands, happily covering the ground—definitely low-maintenance, but don't plant it if you can't allow it to roam at will.

Rough-leaved or Swamp Goldenrod (*S. patula*) will also tolerate part shade. It grows 4–6 feet with a cone-shaped spike of yellow flowers in the fall. It likes clay soil and is not aggressive.

PLANTING REQUIREMENTS

Plant Zigzag Goldenrod in well-drained soil in shade. Swamp Goldenrod needs moist soil and part shade to full sun.

PROPAGATION

Dig and transplant rooted runners of Zigzag Goldenrod. Divide mature clumps of Swamp Goldenrod. Plant seeds of either species in the fall.

Indian Pink (*Spigelia marilandica*)
Zones 4–9
12–20 inches tall
Native to U.S.

Few plants in my garden attract as much attention as Indian Pink, a medium-sized summer spectacular. Bright red tubular flowers are tipped with yellow. This long-blooming native will grow in moist or dry soil in sun or shade. If deadheaded, it will rebloom. It is one of my favorite natives because it is so reliable, easy to grow, and beautiful. It has a tidy clumping habit and grows equally well in the wild garden or in a perennial border. Slow growing, it is seldom invasive or aggressive. Indian Pink is worthy of inclusion in any garden.

PLANTING REQUIREMENTS
Plant in moist or average well-drained garden soil in part to medium shade or in full sun.

PROPAGATION
Divide mature clumps in early spring or fall. Take tip cuttings in mid-summer and root. Sow ripened seed immediately. It self-seeds readily.

Starry Chickweed (*Stellaria pubera*)
Zones 3–8
6–12 inches tall
Native to U.S.

Starry white flowers bloom with early spring ephemerals. Also known as Giant Chickweed, this native does not cause the problems of some of its cousins and is not invasive. Opposite leaves appear to be attached directly to the stem. This plant forms a small clump, so that when it is in bloom it resembles a petite bouquet.

PLANTING REQUIREMENTS
Plant in humus-rich, well-drained, woodland soil in part to full shade.

PROPAGATION
Divide in early spring. Keep the ground around the plant clear of mulch and it will self-sow moderately.

Celandine Poppy (*Stylophorum diphyllum*)
Zones 4–8
18–24 inches tall
Native to U.S.

Bright yellow poppy-like flowers bloom lustily in the spring and then on and off all summer. Readily identifiable in the wild, Celandine Poppy has deeply divided oak-like leaves. Its fuzzy seedpods fill with viable seed, so this delightful fellow happily sows new plants in the garden. However, unwanted seedlings are easy to weed out and there are always willing hands to take them. Or just leave them to create a mass of beautiful plants.

Too much sun or dry soil will cause the leaves to yellow. If this happens, just cut the plant to the ground and it will resprout.

PLANTING REQUIREMENTS

Celandine Poppy prefers moist, humus-rich woodland soil, but will thrive in average, well-drained garden soil with adequate moisture. Plant it in any degree of shade.

PROPAGATION

Easily grown from seed. Transplant young seedlings in early spring.

Drooping Trillium

Trillium (*Trillium* spp.)
Zones 2–8
6–18 inches tall
Native to U.S.

Trillium is so named because all parts of this beautiful native are produced in threes—3 leaves, 3 petals, 3 sepals. Most trilliums are easier to grow than gardeners realize. Once established, they reappear faithfully year after year.

First to appear in March is the tiny Snow Trillium (*T. nivale*). This one can be difficult and demands well-drained soil or it will just disappear. Nodding (*T. cernuum*) and Drooping or Bent Trillium (*T. flexipes*) both have white flowers on short stems. The flower hangs down between the three huge leaves, giving rise to its common names. Wake-robin, also known as Stinking Benjamin (*T. erectum*), has a deep maroon flower in the spring. It grows 6–18 inches tall.

The leaves of both Prairie and Sessile Trillium are heavily mottled with silvery white blotches, but Prairie Trillium (*T. recurvatum*) has little short stems (petioles) on the leaves, while those of Sessile Trillium or Toadshade (*T. sessile*) attach directly to the tall stem. Both have a single deep red flower that perches atop the three leaves. Yellow Trillium (*T. luteum*) has similar leaves but a pale yellow flower. Plant singly or in a mass. Showy or Great White Trillium (*T. grandiflorum*) produces a large up-facing white flower that turns to shades of pink as it ages.

Great White Trillium

There are many other native trilliums, some of which have specific soil requirements that are difficult to create and maintain.

PLANTING REQUIREMENTS

Plant the stout rhizomes 4–6 inches deep in moist, humus-rich, woodland soil or in loamy garden soil in light to full shade. It is important that the soil be well drained, or the rhizome will rot.

PROPAGATION

Trillium seeds take two years to germinate and 3–5 years to reach blooming size. If you are not blessed with the virtue of patience, purchase plants from a specialist nursery.

Bellwort (*Uvularia perfoliata*)
Zones 3–8
12–18 inches tall
Native to U.S.

Prairie Trillium

A plant fairy must flit through the woods, stopping now and then to stitch stems through leaves. Bellwort has to be one of her favorites. Its vertical growth habit is similar to Solomon's Seal, but the perfoliate leaves are a dead giveaway, making identification foolproof. In early spring, elongated bright yellow bells droop from the arching stems.

Great Merrybells or Large-flowered Bellwort (*U. grandiflora*) is also perfoliate, but this species is larger in all parts. Wild Oats (*U. sessilifolia*) is the smallest of this crew, maturing at only 6–10 inches. Consider planting all three together for interesting contrast, mass individual species, or plant as a focal point.

PLANTING REQUIREMENTS
Plant in light or dappled shade in moist, humus-rich woodland soil, or in any good garden soil with good drainage.

PROPAGATION
Carefully separate clumps in early spring or fall. Sow seeds next to the mother plant immediately after ripening. Keep the surrounding soil free of mulch and Bellwort will self-sow. Transplant young seedlings in spring.

Not Recommended

Lesser Celandine (*Ranunculus ficaria*)
Zones 4–8
2–3 inches tall
Eurasia

I first saw this little plant blooming gaily in a neighbor's yard 20 years ago. It is pretty in the spring with its bright, shiny buttercup-like flowers, but I rue the day I introduced it. Over the years, my small piece of Lesser Celandine has exploded into every nook and cranny of our property. Its roots have nutlets, similar to a violet's, and it seeds heavily. It is ephemeral, going dormant after blooming and setting seed. However, the debris creates an impenetrable mass, so to keep other plants from being suffocated I must rake it up with a vengeance. It is awful stuff. One year a friend begged for some. I warned against it, to no avail. She dug every plant from a large section. The following spring that section was as filled with the pest as before, so digging it out is not the answer. I may have to resort to Roundup.

Bulbs . . . self-sufficient, self-contained, self-sustaining.
—*John Bryan*

12.

Incredible

Packaging

Bulbs for Shade

Bulbs are amazing. They get tucked into the ground, where they wait through rain, sleet, snow, freezing and thawing until the weather begins to warm. Then up come their familiar leaves followed by colorful flowers. And what joy they bring to winter-weary gardeners!

Like wildflowers, bulbs prefer loamy soil, but will grow happily in average garden soil as long as it is well drained. They like to be watered at planting time and appreciate adequate moisture just before they are to bloom, but once dormant will do fine in dry soil. I generally broadcast 12-12-12 fertilizer just as they are emerging and again right after flowering, but bulbs will perform with or without it.

For best results, purchase top-quality bulbs that are large, firm, and feel somewhat heavy. Bargain bulbs are often undersized and are usually not the bargain they claim to be. Bulbs are relatively inexpensive, very low maintenance,

Glory of the Snow

and last for years. After going to all the trouble of digging the holes and planting multiple bulbs, you may as well spend a little more money and enjoy the best-looking flowers possible. If you really want a show, order in bulk from some of the reputable bulb catalogs. You will have to spend several hours planting, but oh, what a thrill for many springs to come.

Plant spring-flowering bulbs in fall, and fall-blooming bulbs in spring. Even though bulbs planted "any which way" may eventually come up, give the poor things a fighting chance by making sure they are planted right side up. Plant in multiples for the greatest effect. Some gardeners just toss bulbs and plant wherever they land. I tried this, but invariably lost some in the existing foliage so now I just set my bulbs in what seems to me to be a reasonably sized grouping and chunk them into the ground. Most bulb experts recommend digging the planting holes 2 to 3 times as deep as the diameter of the bulb or corm. The usual planting depth ranges from 2–10 inches depending on the size of the bulb, but check individual species for specific recommendations. Deeper planting can help keep bulbs from dividing too quickly.

To plant a mass of bulbs, remove the dirt from a large area, place the bulbs, and replace the dirt. Dig one hole at a time for individual bulbs. You can use a spade, a dibbler, or a bulb planter. Or purchase a "planting drill." These fit on any electric power drill.

Do not cut the foliage too early, and do not braid it. Instead, when the flower begins to bloom, go to your calendar and mark the day that occurs exactly 6 weeks later. The bulb needs to keep its foliage a minimum of 6 weeks to store adequate food and nutrients for proper bloom the following year. Allowing it to ripen is essential. Consider planting bulbs with daylilies or other perennials with strappy foliage to disguise the ripening leaves.

To rejuvenate clumps that no longer bloom profusely, or to increase your stock, dig these "incredible packages" after the blooms have faded. I either heel them in or replant immediately, keeping the newly transplanted bulbs well watered until the foliage finishes ripening. Many experts recommend digging after the bulbs are dormant, but I can never find them and end up chopping too many in half. However, cut bulbs will produce bulblets that often flower the following season, so sometimes chopping is not all bad. If you do not transplant immediately, then dry, separate, and store the lifted bulbs in mesh bags until fall.

Some of the minor bulbs, such as Siberian Squills, Striped Squills, or even species Crocus, can be naturalized under the lawn sod. Early spring ephemerals such as Toothwort and Spring Beauty also do well when planted in a lawn. But then don't get carried away and mow too soon. Give the foliage a chance to ripen 6 weeks if possible.

Spring Bulbs for Shade

Flowering Onion (*Allium* spp.)
Zones 4–9
2–3 feet tall
Europe
Deer Resistant

Alliums are readily available in the nursery trade. Most prefer full sun, but will also thrive in part to light shade. I have a white Allium (*A. nigrum* aka *A. multibulbosum*) that faithfully reappears each spring in a moderately shady spot. The leaves appear in April. Domed umbels of white flowers, veined with green, begin opening in late May and last until at least late June. Each flower center resembles a small green pea. Naked flower stalks, rising 24–30 inches above wide strappy foliage, add a tall vertical accent behind the hostas, pulmonarias, and bleeding hearts.

The larger globe like Alliums seem to need at least 4–5 hours of sunlight to survive from one season to the next.

PLANTING REQUIREMENTS
Plant 4–8 inches deep in fall in well-drained, humus-rich garden soil in part to light shade or in full sun. Large bulbs should be planted deeper than smaller bulbs. Space large bulbs 8–10 apart; small bulbs 4–6 inches apart.

PROPAGATION
Remove offsets from the mother bulb and transplant.

European Wood Anemone (*Anemone nemorosa*)
Grecian Windflower (*A. blanda*)
Zones 4–8
3–8 inches tall
Europe, Asia

Often called Windflower, this beautiful woodland ground cover closes its blossoms when the weather turns cloudy or rainy. These are ephemerals, and disappear after setting seed. Varieties include Double Wood Anemone (*A. nemorosa* var. Vestal) with large double white flowers; lavender-blue *A. nemorosa* var. Robinsoniana; and Yellow Windflower (*A. ranunculoides* var. Superba) also called Buttercup Anemone. Windflowers are so called because they tremble in the slightest breeze.

Grecian Windflower (*A. blanda*), hardy in Zones 5–8, has daisy-like flowers in a variety of colors. Only about 4 inches tall, windflowers grow from tiny bulbs, sold with daffodils and tulips in the fall. The ones I plant in the fall in my front woodland garden bloom the following spring. In time, these brightly colored flowers will form larger and larger colonies.

PLANTING REQUIREMENTS
Plant 4 inches deep and 3–4 inches apart in the fall in average, well-drained garden soil. All anemones like light shade and will naturalize.

PROPAGATION
Grecian Windflower is readily available from garden centers in the fall. It may be necessary to order European Wood Anemone from specialty nurseries, like Munchkin or Arrowhead Alpines, but ask.

Wild Hyacinth (*Camassia scilloides*)
Zones 4–8
20–30 inches tall
Native to U.S.

Starry blue flowers float high above the steadily warming spring soil. The wide strappy leaves resemble those of common Wild Leek arising from a central point. Occasionally flowers found in the wild will be white, cream, or even purple. Also known as Eastern Camas, Wild Hyacinth bulbs can be ordered from bulb mail-order catalogs. Mark the planting spot, since these go dormant shortly after the seeds ripen. There are several other native species, including *C. leichtlinii*, *C. quamash*, *C. cusickii*, all of which have been hybridized freely, producing cultivars with names like 'Blue Danube', 'Blue Melody', and 'Orion'.

PLANTING REQUIREMENTS
Plant 4–6 inches deep in late summer or early fall in loamy garden soil that is well drained. Space bulbs 6–8 inches apart. Like daffodils, Wild Hyacinth soon forms clumps. Blooms in all types of shade.

PROPAGATION
Dig mature clumps and separate bulbs, or take offsets. The seeds readily sprout, but it takes several years for seedlings to attain blooming size.

Glory of the Snow (*Chionodoxa forbesii* aka *luciliae*)
Zones 3–8
5–6 inches tall
Turkey
Deer Resistant

In early spring, tiny green stems with eight to ten starry lavender-blue flowers appear. Each tiny flower has a bright white eye. Chionodoxa, a favorite of gardeners since the late 1800s, naturalizes readily, forming large colonies.

Hybrids, such as 'Pink Giant', var. *gigantea* aka *luciliae*, and 'Alba' produce larger flowers in shade of pink, bright blue, or white.

PLANTING REQUIREMENTS
Plant bulbs 3–4 inches deep and 4 inches apart in humus rich, well-drained soil in part to light shade in the fall. Naturalize in woodland gardens or in the lawn.

PROPAGATION
Self-sows readily. Purchase and plant bulbs in the fall.

Crocus (*Crocus* spp.)
Zones 3–8
1–3 inches tall
Mediterranean
Deer Resistant

Crocus will grow in part shade but need at least ½ day of sun to persist and multiply. Squirrels and chipmunks love them, making replanting necessary more often then most low-maintenance gardeners like.

However, the cheerful little flowers shout, "Spring is here!" so effectively the effort seems worth it.

Species Crocus naturalize readily, often spreading through large spaces. Look for species names like *biflorus*, *chrysanthus*, *sieberi*, and *tommasinianus*. These are smaller than the named hybrids of Large Flowering Crocus (*C. vernus*) and bloom earlier.

Autumn Crocus (*Colchicum autumnale*), also called Meadow Saffron, is a lookalike, resembling an oversized crocus. It sends up leaves in the spring, and then in the fall, like Surprise Lily, blooms on naked stems in shades of purples, blues, and whites. It is deadly poisonous.

PLANTING REQUIREMENTS

Plant species crocus 4 inches deep and 3–4 inches apart in humus-rich, well-drained soil. Large Flowering Crocus and Autumn Crocus have larger corms and need to be set a little deeper in the earth. Usually 5–6 inches is adequate. Prefer sun but bloom fine in part or light shade.

PROPAGATION

Divide established colonies, transplant cormlets, or purchase new corms in the fall.

Winter Aconite (*Eranthis hyemalis*)
Zones 4–8
3–6 inches tall
Europe
Deer Resistant

About the time the Snowdrops are in their full glory, Winter Aconites pop out of the ground. These little yellow flowers have bright green centers surrounded by yellow stamens. The green is echoed in the divided leaves and the recurving sepals that form a ruff under each 6-petaled flower. After the flowers fade, the foliage continues to grow taller, then yellows and goes dormant until next spring.

I bought and planted many bags of Winter Aconite with little success. Finally a friend shared some of her colony, and now I have colonies of my own. She said it transplants best when the leaves are still green.

The similar *E. cilicica*, from Greece, has slightly larger flowers that open later. Its heavily divided foliage emerges bronze and changes to green as it ages. However, *Hortus Third* reports this species is "not quite as robust."

PLANTING REQUIREMENTS
Plant 3–4 inches deep and 3–4 inches apart in early fall in humus-rich, well-drained garden soil in part to light shade or full sun.

PROPAGATION
Divide after blooming when the plant is about to go dormant, or mark the spot and dig in the fall. This plant self-sows and colonizes. Young seedlings can be transplanted.

Snowdrops (*Galanthus nivalis*)
Zones 2–9
5–10 inches tall
Europe, Asia
Deer Resistant

I am always delighted when I spot the first tightly closed buds of Snowdrops in late January. The buds quickly open, and voila! There are the classic, hanging white flowers marked with spring green. These persist for weeks, merrily blooming through cold, rain, and snow.

In late spring the narrow foliage yellows, lies on the ground, and disappears. If you have any thoughts of transplanting or sharing this little plant, mark it well because once it starts to go dormant, it is "here today and gone tomorrow."

Giant Snowdrop (*G. elwesii*) has larger flowers and blooms a tad earlier. Double Snowdrop (*G. nivalis* var. Flore Pleno) has delicate double hanging flowers.

PLANTING REQUIREMENTS
Plant 4 inches deep and 2–4 inches apart in humus-rich, well-drained soil in shade or sun.

PROPAGATION
Divide mature clumps and transplant. Self-sows readily. Or purchase bulbs in the fall. As with Winter Aconites, the success rate is highest if dug while in active growth.

Hyacinth (*Hyacinthus* spp.)
Zones 4–8
6–12 inches tall
Spain
Deer Resistant

Delicate, airy, pale blue bells hang from either side of the arching stems of Alpine Hyacinth (*H. amethystinus*), a wild form of the common hybrid hyacinth. A good plant for naturalizing, it colonizes vigorously, carpeting the woodland garden with flowers in spring. It grows from a cluster of basal leaves. This is also sometimes listed as *Scilla amethystinus* or *Brimeura amethystinus*.

Sacks of large Common or Dutch Hyacinth (*H. orientalis*) bulbs can be found just about everywhere in fall. The densely packed flower stalks are exceptionally fragrant and come in a variety of colors. Although hyacinths prefer full sun, they bloom reliably in part to light shade in my garden.

PLANTING REQUIREMENTS
Plant Alpine Hyacinths 4–6 inches deep and 4–6 inches apart. Common Hyacinths should be set 5–6 inches deep and 5–6 inches apart. Both enjoy humus-rich, well-drained soil in part shade or sun.

PROPAGATION
Separate bulbs in mature clumps and transplant, take offsets in the fall, or purchase from a mail-order catalog.

Spanish Bluebells (*Hyacinthoides hispanica*)
English Bluebells (*H. non-scripta*)
Zones 3–9
8–14 inches tall
Spain, Portugal

After the early spring ephemerals have put on their show, tall spikes of soft blue, pink, or white bells light up the woodland garden. Spanish Bluebells were formerly known as *Scilla campanulata*, and English Bluebells as *Scilla nutans. Hortus Third* identifies them as *Endymion hispanicus* and *Endymion non-scriptus* respectively. Fortunately, the bulb catalogs have kept up with these revisions. And the flowers haven't changed! The two species are nearly identical, although English Bluebells are fragrant. They are listed in some catalogs as hardy only in Zones 5–8.

PLANTING REQUIREMENTS
Plant bluebells 3–4 inches deep, 4–6 inches apart in moist, humus-rich, well-drained soil. Like most bulbs, these will tolerate dryness in summer.

PROPAGATION
Divide and separate the bulbs in mature clumps or take offsets in fall. These will also self-sow and naturalize readily.

Dwarf Rockgarden Iris (*Iris reticulata*)
Zones 4–9
4–6 inches tall
Caucasus

These tiny spring bloomers are miniature counterparts of their later blooming big brothers, and, like them, come in a wide variety of colors. 'Natascha' is the palest blue, highlighted with bright yellow and white. Deep purple 'Harmony' looks lovely planted near 'Ida', with its lavender and purple flowers, while the purplish-red flowers of 'J. S. Dyt' complement the bright yellow flowers of 'Danfordiae'.

Obviously Dwarf Iris looks good in a rock garden setting, but a mass of it also makes a nice display near the front entry.

PLANTING REQUIREMENTS
In the fall, plant bulbs 4 inches deep and 4–6 inches apart in humus-rich, well-drained garden soil in part to light shade or in full sun.

PROPAGATION
Divide clumps after blooming and separate bulbs to transplant, or purchase bulbs in the fall.

Spring Snowflake (*Leucojum vernum*)
Zones 4–9
6–12 inches tall
Europe

In early spring, shortly after the Snowdrops fade, Spring Snowflakes take over. Both have bright white flowers, but Snowflakes are taller, and the bell-like flowers, marked with yellowish-green, are larger and more flared. If undisturbed, these long-blooming beauties will reward you with ever-increasing clusters of flowers each spring.

Very similar in appearance, Giant or Summer Snowflake (*L. aestivum*) grows 12–15 inches tall and blooms in late spring and early summer. The flowers of this species are bright white marked with bright green. They will last for several weeks if the weather does not get too hot too quickly.

PLANTING REQUIREMENTS

Plant 4–6 inches deep and 4–6 inches apart in humus-rich, well-drained soil in part to light shade. They like damp places, but tolerate dry soil in midsummer.

PROPAGATION

Dig and separate mature clumps and transplant individual bulbs, plant offsets or purchase from mail-order catalogs.

Surprise Lily (*Lycoris squamigera*)

Zones 4–9

24–30 inches tall

Japan

Deer Resistant

It is fun to plant Surprise Lilies among large hostas. The lilies put up strappy 12-inch leaves in early spring. As this foliage yellows and dies back, the emerging hosta foliage camouflages it. The surprise comes in midsummer when each lily bulb sends up a single naked stem with a cluster of lavender-pink blooms at the top. Garden visitors are always amazed at these "hosta" flowers. There are also red, yellow, and white-flowering cultivars, but these are less hardy than the species.

Surprise Lily, also known as Autumn Lycoris, Resurrection Lily, Magic Lily, Naked Ladies, and Hurricane Lady, can be camouflaged with daylily foliage as well. (The many common names are an indication of the popularity of this indestructible plant.)

PLANTING REQUIREMENTS

Plant the bulbs 5–7 inches deep in humus-rich, well-drained soil in late summer or early fall. I often transplant Surprise Lily in the spring when the yellowing leaves are easily located. My lilies thrive in moderate to heavy shade. They will also do well in part to light shade or in full sun. They like moisture in the spring, but do not mind being a bit dry in midsummer.

PROPAGATION
Separate bulbs or offsets and transplant. Or purchase bulbs in the fall.

Grape Hyacinth (*Muscari armeniacum*)
Zones 4–9
5–6 inches tall
Asia Minor
Deer Resistant

Short spikes of tightly clustered grape-colored flowers clutch the tops of short green stems, nodding above thin, grass-like leaves. Bend down to inhale the sweet fragrance of these tiny urns. Grape Hyacinths will quickly colonize a natural area, but are neither invasive nor obnoxious. They bloom, set their seeds, and go happily off to sleep until the next spring, when they arise ready to do it all again.

There are many *Muscari* species, including a deep blackish-purple flowering form called *M. neglectum* that has been grown in gardens since the late 1500s. It is artistically touched with pale blue and white. This little beauty blooms in early April and grows 8–10 inches tall. The delicate silvery-blue flowers of 'Valerie Finnis' are worth a second look. Or how about *M. botryoides* var. Superstar? This one resembles those 3-toned frozen delights from the musical ice-cream truck. Its flowers start out light blue at the top, deepen to dark blue in the middle and then finish the mini rocket-like spike with light blue. Wild!

PLANTING REQUIREMENTS
Plant 2–4 inches deep, 4–6 inches apart in humus-rich, well-drained soil in shade or sun.

PROPAGATION
Dig large clumps, then separate and transplant the small bulbs. Grape Hyacinths self-sow, naturalize readily, and are maintenance-free.

Daffodil (*Narcissus* spp.)

Zones 3–8

6–18 inches tall

Europe, North Africa

Deer Resistant

'Ice Follies'

Daffodils prefer sun—no doubt about it. However, I have hundreds in the woodland garden that constitutes our front yard, tucked in with Virginia Bluebells, Wild Blue Phlox, False Rue Anemone, Mayapples, and ferns. The clumps increase annually, and although they are neither as large nor as floriferous as daffodils grown in full sun, they bloom reliably each spring.

I sprinkle 12-12-12 granular fertilizer around the clumps after blooming ceases. Foliage is allowed to ripen for at least 6 weeks after the flowers fade. The narrow, yellowing foliage blends into the wild garden and eventually lies unobtrusively on the ground and disappears.

There are 13 daffodil divisions. Hybridizers continue to develop new and exciting flowers of different sizes, shapes, and colors. Prices for a new introduction can easily be in the double digits for a single bulb. But the old standbys are beautiful, and inexpensive, too. In general, early bloomers tolerate shade best. 'Ice Follies', 'Carlton', and 'Jetfire' will all do well for you in shade. Incidentally, bulb experts tell me that the famous yellow trumpet known as 'King Alfred' has disappeared from the trade—current yellow trumpets sold by that name are all imposters. If you buy 'King Alfred', who knows what you'll get?

PLANTING REQUIREMENTS

In mid-fall, plant bulbs 6–8 inches deep, 4–6 inches apart in well-drained, humus-rich loamy or sandy garden soil in part to light shade or full sun.

PROPAGATION

Dig and separate bulb clumps and transplant, or purchase bulbs in the fall.

'Pipit'

Striped Squill (*Puschkinia scilloides*)
Zones 3–8
4–6 inches tall
Turkey, Iraq, Iran, Lebanon
Deer Resistant

A pale porcelain blue star-like bell with darker greenish striping blooms over the dark green basal rosette in early spring. Striped Squill naturalizes easily and self-sows.

'Alba' is the pure white version of this pretty little squill. Lebanon Squill (*P. scilloides* var. *libanotica*) is a variety of Striped Squill with slightly smaller flowers.

PLANTING REQUIREMENTS
In the fall, plant Striped Squills 2–4 inches deep, 4–6 inches apart in humus-rich, well-drained soil in part to light shade, or in sun.

PROPAGATION
Striped Squills can be increased by offsets, seed, or by dividing and separating established clumps. Or purchase bulbs.

Siberian Squill (*Scilla siberica*)
Zones 3–8
4–5 inches tall
Siberia
Deer Resistant

As I walked through a nearby neighborhood in early spring, I admired a haze of bright electric-blue, stretching solidly across 4 large front lawns. I returned several times, curious about this incredible mass of Siberian Squills. One day, the elderly occupant of one of these houses was outside. He told me that when he was about 12, he took the train to visit his grandmother, and brought back a shoebox of squill bulbs from her yard. He dug a hole and deposited the entire boxful in it. Now, probably 70 years later, those squills have spread to cover nearly an acre. while I stood marveling at this beautiful sight, the kind gentleman found a spade and a shoebox and dug some up for me.

The soft blue flowers of *S. bifolia*, occasionally listed as Twin Leaf Squill, bloom above a single pair of leaves. Its delicate pink form is known as 'Rosea'. For white-flowering Squills, purchase 'Alba'. *S. tubergeniana*, a bluish-white form with darker midribs, is also available.

PLANTING REQUIREMENTS

Plant 4–5 inches deep, 4–6 inches apart in humus-rich, well-drained soil in part to light shade or sun. Squills come up through lawn grass, bloom, and begin to go dormant before the lawn needs mowing.

PROPAGATION

Dig and separate bulbs after blooming and transplant, push the fat green seed-ball into the ground, or purchase bulbs. Squills self-sow, colonizing widely when they are happy.

The glory of annuals is that they are temporary.
—*Marjorie Mason Hogue*

13.
... And the Last shall Be First

Annuals for Shade

Wax Begonia

Annuals are usually the first things a novice gardener thinks of to plunk into his yard. Experienced gardeners know better. Granted, annuals provide constant color throughout the growing season, but to achieve genuine low maintenance, it is wiser to make use of all the other kinds of plant material presented in this book before ever touching that six-pack of impatiens!

However, although annuals may not be the first or the only plants recommended for an ongoing low-maintenance shade garden, nothing surpasses them for constant and consistent color. Besides, as every child knows, annuals are genuinely fun to grow.

Shade gardeners generally think first of impatiens, wax begonias, and coleus. Tried and true, these three never disappoint. But there are a host of other shade-tolerant annuals to choose from, including some real beauties that will make your gardens a joy to behold.

It is possible to grow annuals from

seed, but, especially in the more northern zones, sowing those seeds outdoors in May will not reliably produce flowering plants until late summer. Instead, sow seeds indoors at least 4–6 weeks prior to the last freeze. Warm-season bedding plants also prefer being transplanted into warmer soil, so don't be too hasty to set them out. Many annuals do their own reseeding, dropping seeds on the ground in the fall that will be ready to germinate as soon as the temperatures are favorable. One year I neglected to clean up all my impatiens plants and was surprised the following year when familiar leaves suddenly appeared in early summer. These volunteers bloomed in a wide variety of colors, later than my purchased bedding plants, and stayed smaller and closer to the ground, which I liked. Be advised that named varieties are hybrids. They do not generally come true from seed, and often produce muddy, off-colored flowers.

Most shady annuals prefer moist, loamy soil and appreciate being mulched to conserve water and keep down weeds. Annuals that receive plenty of water for the first three weeks after planting seem to grow sturdier and get bigger more quickly than those left to fend for themselves. Some gardeners put a half dose of liquid fertilizer in the watering can as a little extra boost, but I believe the additional water is the key. Pinching out the growth tips can produce a bushier plant. For larger flowers, remove side buds. But if you think that is too much maintenance, just enjoy them.

In addition to designing flowerbeds and borders with annuals, consider using them under shrubs, in front of vines or ferns, or here and there in the perennial bed. I leave a vacant arc at the front of a perennial bed or a large undulating space within, knowing I will fill it with a mass of annuals in the spring. I like to edge my hosta beds with a wide border of white impatiens or plant bright red low-growing annuals under a deciduous holly.

I am loath to remove very many flowers from the perennial border, so I march my cutting-garden annuals in straight rows in the vegetable garden. There the soil is loose and friable. When my husband waters his vegetables, my flowers get a welcome drink. And the more you cut, the more they bloom.

Annuals are ready-made for containers. My only suggestion is to water thoroughly and often. Or if you know you are lax, as I am, and forget that regular task too often for the good of the annuals, fill your own pots with good potting soil, mix in some water-retaining crystals, purchase small potted plants, and design your own container. Put some mulch on the top and water thoroughly. Place containers near a source of water to make life easier.

In addition to flowering annuals, try thinking outside the box for a minute. In early spring, haunt lumberyards, hardware stores, and variety stores just as seeds and bedding plants come to the fore. Business owners, anxious to make room for these special displays, drastically reduce the prices of huge tropical houseplants. Snap up as many as your car will hold and plant them directly into the ground outdoors. A few houseplants added to your outdoor landscape can help create your own little tropical paradise. Mass them in the back of perennial beds, plant 2–3 in a group near the patio, or install a single one as a focal point by the front door. These tropical beauties bring a totally new dimension to the garden. And if you want to overwinter them in the house, there is nothing to stop you from repotting them and doing just that.

When it is time to bring plants indoors after a summer outside, I do not flinch at using chemicals. An ounce of precaution saves a pound of maintenance misery later. If you have ever battled whitefly or spider mites on houseplants, you know what I mean. Before bringing any outdoor plants into the house, spray thoroughly with a liquid insecticide like Malathion or Orthene, drenching both top and bottom of the leaves as well as the soil. Do this on day one, and repeat the process three days later and one week later to cover the life cycle of most insects.

One of the most enjoyable things about annuals is the ability to create a palette of colors to your liking. Choosing appropriate colors in your annuals can actually affect how comfortable you feel on a hot patio or in a cool, damp part of the yard. A *monochromatic* scheme uses flowers of the same hue. I once saw a planting of petunias in red and pink. What a vibrant and exciting combination! My friend Jan has a white garden, a yellow garden, an orange garden, a purple garden, and a blue garden. By using lighter tints and deeper shades of a single hue, Jan "paints" with flowers, making each garden a work of art. *Analogous* color schemes use the three colors that reside next to each other on the wheel. Hostas lend themselves well to this with varying tints and shades of blue-green, green, and yellow-green. *Complementary* colors, those that are opposite each other on the color wheel such as purple and yellow, red and green, or orange and blue, are exciting and dramatic. *Polychromatic*—every color of the rainbow—is my daughter's favorite. An artist, she works with this riot of color skillfully and effectively, so that rather than being a cacophony,

Karen's patio flower beds reflect her joie-de-vivre and elicit rave reviews from garden visitors.

Wayne Winterrowd describes annuals as "carpe diem plants, prepared to seize and make the most of their short day." They bring a special excitement to the garden, provide unexpected combinations of color, texture, and scent, and make you smile, so they are worth any extra maintenance. And if you don't like the effect you created this year, there is always next year. Annuals may be temporary, but that is their glory.

Annuals for Shade

Chenille Plant (*Acalypha hispida*)
1–6 feet tall
Malaya, New Guinea
Good in Containers

Whenever I see Chenille Plant, also known as Philippine Medusa, I imagine Cheshire cats meeting for a tête-à-tête in a leafy bower. But, instead of the inscrutable smile of Alice's cat, they show only their bright red tails, which can be 18–20 inches long! This shrubby annual is great in a container, but abhors dry soil. Pinch growing tips to encourage bushy, compact growth. Overwintered containerized plants can tolerate hard pruning in the spring.

A. repens lies on the ground. Also sold as var. *pendula*, it has 2-inch fuzzy red tails.

PLANTING REQUIREMENTS
Plant in humus-rich, moist, well-drained soil in part to light or dappled shade or in sun. Keep soil consistently moist. Feed every 3–4 weeks throughout the growing season.

PROPAGATION
Take cuttings in late summer or early fall, or overwinter containerized plants indoors.

'Golden Jubilee' (*Agastache foeniculum* 'Golden Jubilee')
18–20 inches tall
North America

A 2003 All America Selection, 'Golden Jubilee' commemorates the 50-year reign of Queen Elizabeth II. Bold spikes of lavender flowers bloom above light green serrated leaves. A member of the mint family, this annual is a good choice for the fragrance garden. Bees collect its nectar for honey.

'Golden Jubilee' is an annual cultivar of the native perennial herb Anise Hyssop (*A. foeniculum*). The species prefers full sun and can be propagated by seed.

PLANTING REQUIREMENTS
Plant in average, well-drained garden soil in part shade or in full sun. Space new plantings 12 inches apart.

PROPAGATION
Divide the mother plant in early spring or late fall. Cuttings taken in mid to late summer can be rooted to overwinter indoors. The perennial species will self-sow.

Floss Flower (*Ageratum houstonianum*)
6–12 inches tall
Mexico, Central, South America
Deer Resistant

Ageratum, from the Greek, means "not growing old" or everlasting. This common bedding plant blooms lustily all summer unless the weather becomes extremely hot and humid. It forms compact mounds of tightly clustered lavender-blue flowers. Its distinctive leaves are heart shaped at the base.

Cultivars are also available in pink, lavender, and white. A few, such as heat-tolerant 'Capri', are bicolored. There is not much question about the flower colors of 'Pacific Rose', 'Pinky Improved', 'Fields White', 'Summer Snow' or 'Red Sea'. For blue flowers, look for names like 'Blue Horizon', 'Blue Danube', or 'Blue Blazer'.

PLANTING REQUIREMENTS
Plant 6–12 inches apart in humus rich, moist, well-drained garden soil in part or light shade or in full sun. Too much shade will produce leggy plants. Adequate moisture is important, but too much can promote rot and susceptibility to fungus disease.

PROPAGATION
Sow purchased seed 8–10 weeks before the last frost date. Set the seedlings outside to harden off for at least 48 hours before planting in the ground.

Giant Caladium (*Alocasia cuprea*)
2–4 feet tall
Borneo, Eastern Asia

This plant didn't get its common name by mistake. Its heavily textured leaves, in shades of iridescent purple and metallic green, are accented by a prominent blackened midrib. The undersides are a rich rosy-purple. These colorful leaves, which grow at the end of 18–24 inch stalks, can be 18 inches long and up to a foot wide. Also identified as Copper Alocasia or Elephant Ear, it makes quite a statement in the shade or at the edge of a water garden. It has been a greenhouse favorite for decades.

There are several other species known as Elephant Ear, most of which can be found under the genus names of *Alocasia* or *Colocasia*. Some may be listed as *Caladium esculentum*. Nearly all Elephant Ears require full sun or they will flop. However, a new cultivar of Taro (*Colocasia esculenta* 'Black Magic') can tolerate part shade. It grows 20 inches tall and 3–4 feet wide.

PLANTING REQUIREMENTS
Plant in moist, humus-rich, well-drained soil in part to dappled shade. Giant Caladiums appreciate consistent moisture as well as an occasional drink of liquid fertilizer or manure tea. Good drainage is essential.

PROPAGATION
Plant seed in March in 4-inch pots filled with soilless potting mixture or take root cuttings. Overwinter plants indoors and divide tubers in spring.

Love-Lies-Bleeding (*Amaranthus caudatus*)
3–5 feet tall
Africa, India, Peru
Good in Containers

This heat-loving plant, also known as Tassel Flower, has 2-foot long panicles of twisted, ropey, chenille-like red flowers that poke out from leaf axils and droop from the ends of tall, upright stalks. For brilliant color in your garden, this coarse fellow will do the job. The large, edible, alternate leaves are long ovals and protrude almost at right angles from the stem. The genus name, *Amaranthus*, from the Greek, means "unfading."

Love-lies-bleeding has several cultivars including two green-flowered forms: 'Green Thumb', a bright green that fades to cream, and 'Viridis', with chartreuse flowers.

PLANTING REQUIREMENTS
Plant 1–2 feet apart in half-day shade or in full sun in moist, average, well-drained soil. It will also tolerate dry conditions. *Amaranthus* species can be grown in containers.

PROPAGATION
Sow seeds indoors in a soilless potting mix 6–8 weeks before the last frost. If you barely cover the seeds and keep the planting medium slightly warm (68–70°F) and evenly moist, germination should occur in 7–21 days. Plants will self-sow. Or take cuttings in late summer to overwinter indoors.

Maurandia Vine (*Asarina barclaiana*)
6–10 feet tall
Mexico

Sometimes annual vines are just the ticket for a particular location. Also identified as *Maurandya barclaiana*, Maurandia Vine twines and scrambles up chain-link or bamboo fences, as long as there is some support it can twist around. Hummingbirds love the deep pinkish-purple trumpet flowers that appear in profusion in late summer, continuing until frost.

Downy hairs cover all parts of Creeping Gloxinia (*A. erubescens* aka *Maurandya erubescens*), so this vine literally sparkles with the morning dew. It has large, soft rose-pink flowers.

PLANTING REQUIREMENTS
Plant in moist, humus-rich, well-drained soil in part to light shade or in full sun.

PROPAGATION

Sow ripened seed in the fall or clean and refrigerate it in a film canister, then plant in soilless potting mix 6–8 weeks before the last frost date. May self-sow.

Begonia (*Begonia* spp.)
6–24 inches
South America, Tropics
Good in Containers
Deer Resistant

Fibrous or Wax Begonias (*Begonia semperflorens-cultorum*) are "major players" in the world of bedding plants. Adaptable and undemanding, these popular annuals grow from fibrous roots, thriving in part, light, or moderate shade or even in full sun as long as the soil is moisture-retentive. Varieties with bronzy-red leaves need more light than green-leaved forms.

Tuberous Begonias (*B. tuberhybrida-cultorum*) require a shady spot and are generally grown in containers. They form tubers rather than fibrous roots, as the common name indicates. Compact bedding types, called Non-stop Begonias, grow 12–24 inches tall, with beautiful blooms all summer. However, they are not as easy to grow as Wax Begonias and may rot in poorly drained sites.

Any of the many begonias grown as houseplants can be used as container plants or planted directly into the garden for the summer. Hardy Begonia (*B. grandis*) is described in chapter 10.

PLANTING REQUIREMENTS

Moisture and loamy soil are more important than specific light conditions for Fibrous Begonias. Space 6–12 inches apart. Tuberous Begonias need well-drained soil and shade. They will bleach and burn in too much light. Place tuber, concave side up, in a container half filled with soil. Fill the container with soil and water well.

PROPAGATION

Root cuttings from containerized plants brought in for the winter. Sow the dust-like seeds of Fibrous Begonia indoors in January or February by sprinkling them on top of moistened planting medium. Cover with plastic wrap or a pane of glass and do not allow to dry out. Germination takes 14–21 days.

Non-Stop Begonia seed can be germinated in humus-rich, well-drained soil in midwinter, but it is easier and not much more expensive to purchase and plant the tubers.

Swiss Chard (*Beta vulgaris*)
9–14 inches
Eurasia

We have grown Swiss Chard in our vegetable garden for years, so I never thought of it as an ornamental. A few years ago, I saw it planted as a mass near the edge of a perennial border in a public garden and it was impressive.

You can buy seeds for Swiss Chard with bright yellow stalks and chartreuse-green leaves, deep green leaves with crimson-red veins and stalks, as well as stalks and veins in shades of gold, pink, yellow, or white, all accenting wavy green leaves. Check out cultivars with names like 'Bright Lights' or 'Rhubarb'.

And if you get tired of looking at this leafy plant in the perennial border, just chop it off and cook it for supper. The plants will soon send up new leaves.

PLANTING REQUIREMENTS
Plant in average, moist, well-drained soil in part shade or in sun. Provide adequate moisture throughout the growing season.

PROPAGATION
Sow seed directly into the ground in spring, a week or two before the last frost date. It takes 7–10 days to germinate. Keep soil consistently moist until plants are well established. Or start seed in pots indoors 6–8 weeks before the last frost date.

Browallia (*Browallia speciosa*)
8–24 inches tall
South America
Good in Containers

Hummingbirds love Browallia. Also called Bush Violet, Sapphire Flower, and Amethyst Flower, it has 5-petaled, saucer-like flowers that flare outwards in shades of lavender, purple, and blue. These are about 2 inches wide with white "eyes," and appear toward the top of the stalk in the axils of the leaves. Bring a potful of this heavy bloomer indoors for the winter.

B. americana aka *B. elata* is a smaller species, seldom growing taller than 18–24 inches. For an even tinier plant, look for its cultivar 'Nana', only 10–12 inches tall. *B. americana* has notched blue-violet flowers, as does its sibling, *B. viscosa*.

PLANTING REQUIREMENTS

Plant in average, well-drained garden soil in part or light shade on in morning sun. Browallia abhors hot, afternoon sun. Fertilizing produces more leaves than flowers on this tomato relative.

PROPAGATION

Sow seed, barely covered, indoors 8–10 weeks before the last frost date. Germination requires light and can take up to 3 weeks. Pinch young seedlings to encourage branching. Flowering should begin 2½–3 months after germination and continue all summer. Root cuttings and transplant after danger of frost has passed.

Caladium (*Caladium bicolor* aka *Caladium × hortulanum*)
20–30 inches tall
South America

Every spring, my friend Norma Jean orders Caladium tubers by the dozens. She plants Caladiums in the perennial border, tucks them in here and there in the hosta garden, and grows them in pots and hanging baskets. Although the flowers are insignificant, the beautiful leaves come in a multitude of colors, leaf patterns, sizes, and shapes. Although it is possible to dig and store the tubers in the fall, she finds it easier simply to order new ones.

Growers frequently remove a small core from the tuber. Wounding stimulates bud growth and helps boost the number of leaves.

PLANTING REQUIREMENTS

Start tuber in moistened soil 8–10 weeks before the last frost. Cover with 3–4 inches of soil and keep the planting medium moist but not wet. Be sure the pot is well-drained.

When danger of frost is past, transplant outdoors in moist, humus-rich, well-drained soil in part, light, or medium shade. Caladium leaves will scorch and burn in sun. Tubers may rot if the soil has not warmed sufficiently. I plant my specimen outdoors in mid to late spring when soil is warm enough to plant green beans.

PROPAGATION
Dig and clean tubers in the fall and store in a cool place in slightly moistened sphagnum peat moss for the winter. Or order new ones.

Coleus (*Coleus* × *hybridus*)
1–3 feet tall
Africa, Asia
Good in Containers
Deer Resistant

Coleus, an old shade-garden favorite, is another annual grown primarily for its foliage. You can find these frilly leaves in a rainbow of colors. Massing one variety is always effective, or choose a mixed flat with leaves arrayed in unimaginable color combinations of red, cream, green, chartreuse, maroon, deep purple, or pink. Allan Armitage reports that the newer vegetative cultivars prosper in more light, while the older seed-grown plants, generally sold as bedding plants, still prefer shade.

In addition to the traditional upright forms, check out the Ducksfoot series, useful as a colorful, low mounding ground cover. Sun-loving trailing forms make nice additions to hanging baskets.

PLANTING REQUIREMENTS
Plant 10–12 inches apart in moist, humus-rich, well-drained soil in part to full shade or in morning sun. Coleus appreciates afternoon shade when temperatures soar. Provide consistent moisture or the leaves will wilt.

PROPAGATION
Sow seed indoors 10–12 weeks before the last frost date. Germination takes 14–21 days. Set young seedlings outdoors to harden off before transplanting. Root cuttings in fall to winter over indoors, or in the spring

from plants brought in for the winter. Coleus roots easily in sand, perlite, or even water.

Dragonhead (*Dracocephalum moldavicum*)
12–24 inches tall
Eurasia

Dragonhead, a member of the mint family, is easily identified by its square stems and the herbal aroma of its crushed leaves. Racemes of rosy-lavender or white flowers, resembling snapdragons, grow in whorls near the top of the stem, like those of perennial False Dragonhead (*Physostegia*). Incorporate into a moist shady perennial border, or naturalize at the edge of a woodland.

PLANTING REQUIREMENTS
Plant in moist, well-drained, average to rich garden soil in part to light shade. Dragonhead does not flower as reliably in sun, and plants particularly appreciate shade in the heat of the afternoon. Pinch seedlings to encourage bushiness.

PROPAGATION
Sow seed 6–8 weeks before the last frost date, or plant directly into the ground after frost danger has passed.

Mole Plant (*Euphorbia lathyris*)
2–3 feet tall
Europe

Also called Gopher Purge, Myrtle Spurge, and Caper Spurge, Mole Plant reputedly contains chemicals that repel burrowing animals. Effective or not, it is tall and handsome. Ranks of leathery, lance-shaped, 4–5 inch-long leaves march, one set above another, providing an effective vertical, architectural accent. In the fall these bluish-green leaves put on a striking display of rich red and burnished copper. It can be grown as an annual or a biennial.

PLANTING REQUIREMENTS
Plant in average, well-drained soil in part shade or in full sun singly or combine to create clumps.

PROPAGATION
Sow seed 8–10 weeks before the last frost date, or let second-year plants self-sow in place.

German Violet (*Exacum affine*)
8–24 inches tall
Socotra, Ceylon
Good in Containers

Also called Persian Violet, this pretty little annual boasts delicate, fragrant 5-petaled flowers all summer. Bright yellow stamens protrude from these lavender-blue, purple, or white blooms, usually only ½–¾ inches across. Its shiny oval leaves gleam in the shade. 'Blue Midget' and 'White Midget' only grow 5–6 inches tall. German Violet makes a good edger, can be massed near the patio, or planted in a container.

E. macranthum, a biennial, grows to 2 feet with large, rich purplish-blue flowers.

PLANTING REQUIREMENTS
Plant in moist, well-drained soil in part to light shade or in morning sun 8–15 inches apart.

PROPAGATION
Sow seed indoors 10–14 weeks before the last frost date.

Fuchsia (*Fuchsia* × *hybrida*)
12–24 inches tall
Central and South America
Good in Containers

I have a love-hate relationship with Fuchsias. These temptresses are luscious in hanging baskets, but when hot weather hits, my poor under-watered Fuchsia simply lies over the edge of the basket, shrivels, and dies. Fuchsias are beautiful, but low maintenance they are not.

There is one Fuchsia, however, that I have had success with. The tiny tubular flowers of 'Gartenmeister' resemble little dark orangey-red firecrackers. It is also identified as 'Gartenmeister Bonstedt'. At 20–24 inches tall, this bronzy-green leafed beauty is much more bushy and upright than its sensitive siblings. Perhaps growing directly in the garden in loamy, well-drained garden soil helps it survive. It continues blooming indoors during the winter and goes back outside the following spring. 'Koralle', a similar Triphylla Hybrid from Germany, has lighter foliage and coral firecrackers.

PLANTING REQUIREMENTS
Fuchsias demand consistently moist, humus-rich soil and prefer shade, although they can tolerate morning sun as long as they have adequate moisture.

PROPAGATION
Take cuttings in late fall and overwinter plants indoors. Cultivars do not come true from seed.

Heliotrope (*Heliotropium arborescens*)
12–30 inches tall
Peru
Good in Containers

I always enjoyed sitting on my mother-in-law's porch because she made sure her old wicker planters included Heliotrope, sometimes called Cherry Pie. Whenever I smell its delicious fragrance, it stirs memories of glasses of lemony iced tea and a plate heaped with *Kringla*, her pretzel-shaped Norwegian cookies. Heliotrope means "turning to the sun," which is just what the flowers do. Butterflies and hummingbirds love Heliotrope. And so do I. Even the spent flowers are attractive as they change to dark purple and black. It is not a good cut flower, but then who cares when potted specimens smell so heavenly?

PLANTING REQUIREMENTS
Plant 10–12 inches apart in humus-rich, well-drained soil in part to light shade or in morning sun. Pinch to encourage bushiness.

PROPAGATION
Take cuttings in late summer or from overwintered plants in March. Sow seed indoors 10–12 weeks before the last frost date. Seeds take 4–6 weeks to germinate.

Polka Dot Plant (*Hypoestes phyllostachya*)
10–24 inches tall
Africa, Southeast Asia, Madagascar

This blends well with other foliage plants like coleus, caladiums, or hostas, makes a nice filler in a perennial border, and can even be used as an edger. A specimen planted against the base of a clematis does double duty by serving as an accent while it protects the fragile base of the clematis from clumsy feet.

The dark green leaves of Polka Dot Plant are splashed and spotted with pink and white, giving rise to other common names like Freckle Face, Measles Plant, and Pink Dot. Look for new cultivars containing the word 'Splash' or 'Confetti Mix'.

PLANTING REQUIREMENTS
Plant 6–10 inches apart in moist, humus-rich, well-drained soil in part to light shade.

PROPAGATION
Take cuttings from indoor plants, or sow seed indoors 10–12 weeks before the last frost date. Although it is easy to start from seed, Polka Dot Plant is inexpensive and readily available, so I purchase it at the local garden center.

Garden Impatiens (*Impatiens walleriana*)
New Guinea Impatiens (*Impatiens hawkeri*)
6–24 inches tall
Africa, New Guinea
Good in Containers

Ask gardeners to choose a foolproof flowering annual for those impossible shady spots and Garden Impatiens (*I. walleriana*) will win hands down. Also known as Busy Lizzie, Patient Lucy, Sultana, and Patience Plant, it blooms in nearly every color of the rainbow except yellow. Contrasting centers or "eyes" bring a new dimension to this old favorite. There are even impatiens with variegated leaves and double camellia-like flowers. Even though this low-maintenance plant blooms nonstop all summer, it never needs deadheading. It has two idiosyncrasies: it dislikes afternoon sun, and it cannot tolerate dry soil.

New Guinea Impatiens offer larger flowers and more colorful leaves, but this plant also abhors dry soil and will dry crisp as you please if you forget moisture for even a moment. Consequently, I don't grow these beauties any more, but I appreciate their presence in a moist, well-watered garden. Sun is acceptable for part of the day as long as there is afternoon shade. Many New Guinea Impatiens must be vegetatively reproduced from cuttings, but 'Tango', a 1988 All America Selection, breeds true from seed.

PLANTING REQUIREMENTS
Plant 10–12 inches apart in moist, humus-rich, well-drained soil in part to full shade.

PROPAGATION
Plant seed indoors 8–10 weeks before the last frost date. Germination takes 10–14 days. If you don't clean up spent impatiens plants in the fall, they will lightly self-sow. These seedlings will begin to bloom in late June. It is also possible to overwinter plants or to root cuttings, but I find it easiest to just purchase new plants.

Garden Balsam (*Impatiens balsamina*)
12–30 inches tall
Asia

My Aunt Ruth loved to augment her perennial border with Garden Balsam each spring. She told me this was also called Rose Balsam because "They look just like little roses." A very erect plant, Garden Balsam is covered with tiny single or double flowers that come in nearly every color of the rainbow.

Now, a new, low-growing series called 'Ice' has been developed, offering cultivars with variegated foliage and two-toned double flowers. 'Tom Thumb Mix' only grows 8–12 inches tall. Aunt Ruth would have loved them.

Jewelweed (*I. capensis*), the native woodlander, is Balsam's wild sibling.

PLANTING REQUIREMENTS
Plant in moist, humus-rich, well-drained garden soil in part to moderate shade.

PROPAGATION
Sow seed indoors 8–10 weeks before the last frost date, or take cuttings in late spring from plants overwintered indoors.

Peacock Ginger (*Kaempferia atrovirens*)
6–12 inches tall
Borneo, Southeast Asia

Hosta lovers will adore these heat-loving annuals. Imagine leaves that are 6–12 inches long and nearly as wide in deep, rich shades of burgundy, chocolate-brown, purple, bronze, and silver. Then to complete the picture, position blue or white phlox-like flowers that hover just above the incredible leaves. Unfortunately, these tropical beauties, often called 'Southern Hosta', need temperatures in excess of 75°F to do well so we can only grow them as annuals.

There are over 50 known species with a wide variety of leaf colors: check out *K. gilbertii*, *K. pulchra*, *K. rotunda*, *Cornukaempferia aurantiaca*, or species preceded by the genus name *Siphonochilus*.

PLANTING REQUIREMENTS
Plant in moist, humus-rich, well-drained soil in deep shade. Leaves will bleach out in sunlight.

PROPAGATION
For availability, contact specialty mail-order nurseries. It is unlikely this plant will be a common commodity at local garden centers until garden nuts "squeak" loudly enough.

Venus' Looking Glass (*Legousia speculum-veneris*)
8–18 inches tall
Europe

Plant Venus' Looking Glass at the edge of a perennial border and soon you will be rewarded by masses of pretty little violet-blue flowers clustered in the upper leaf axils. Slightly less than 1 inch wide, they will open 6–8 weeks after germination. This cool-season plant may stop blooming in the heat of summer, but will begin again once temperatures go back down. There are white-flowering forms, but most are in shades of blues and violets.

Venus' Looking Glass is related to campanulas, as indicated by another scientific name, *Campanula speculum-veneris*. It is occasionally identified as *Specularia speculum*.

PLANTING REQUIREMENTS
Plant in moist, humus-rich, well-drained soil in part to light shade.

PROPAGATION
Plant the shiny, mirror-like, reddish-brown seeds indoors 6–8 weeks before the last frost date, or plant directly outdoors once further frost damage is unlikely. A second planting in mid-June will increase fall flowering. Germination takes 7–10 days.

Lobelia (*Lobelia erinus*)
4–9 inches tall
South Africa
Good in Containers
Deer Resistant

Most gardeners envision bright blue when they think of Lobelia, a favorite for patriotic floral plantings. When I first started gardening, 'Crystal Palace' was the norm. Now local garden centers carry a multitude of choices with names like 'Compact Royal Jewels' and 'Emperor William'. Seed packets labeled 'String of Pearls' will produce a variety of flower colors. Most cultivars have small green, bronze, or bronzy-green leaves. Compact, bushier plants are becoming increasingly popular.

After the first flush of blooms, shear plants back to 2 inches to encourage reblooming. If the foliage looks distressed, cut it back halfway, keep the plants well watered, and new foliage should sprout after 2–3 weeks. Lobelia thrives in spring and early summer, but will lag and sag when the temperatures soar. In cooler weather, the prolific flowering resumes.

Vegetatively propagated lobelia (*L. ricardii*) comes in two shades of blue and is touted as longer blooming and more reliable in the heat of summer than seed-grown *L. erinus*. 'Kathleen Mallard' has double blue flowers.

PLANTING REQUIREMENTS
Plant 6–10 inches apart in humus-rich, well-drained garden soil in light shade or in morning sun and afternoon shade. Adequate moisture is important.

PROPAGATION
Sow seeds indoors 8–12 weeks before the last frost date. Seeds take 14–21 days to germinate. Or purchase plants in early spring.

Sweet Alyssum (*Lobularia maritima* aka *L. maritimum*)
3–10 inches tall
Mediterranean
Good in Containers
Sweet Alyssum, another patriotic favorite, has a growth habit similar to Lobelia, so the two are often used together to edge a border. Sweet Alyssum tolerates drought better than Lobelia, but its flower production also declines in the heat of summer. The Wonderland series exhibits better heat tolerance.

An improved version of the old standby 'Carpet of Snow' is called 'New Carpet of Snow'. Hummingbirds and butterflies love Sweet Alyssum.

PLANTING REQUIREMENTS
Plant it near the walk or patio to enjoy its fragrance. Space new plantings 6 inches apart in average, well-drained garden soil in part shade or light shade, in morning sun and afternoon shade, or in full sun. Cut back these cool-season annuals in the hottest part of the summer to encourage re-blooming when temperatures moderate.

PROPAGATION
Sow barely covered seed indoors 8–10 weeks before the last frost date. Light is necessary for germination, which takes 7–14 days. Plants often self-sow.

Money Plant (*Lunaria annua*)
24–30 inches tall
Europe
Money Plant produces masses of rosy-purple, 4-petaled flowers in

mid to late spring, complementing late-blooming daffodils and wildflowers. The flat dark brown seeds lie between translucent greenish coverings. These change to grayish-white when the seed is ripe, and can be peeled off to reveal the oval, parchment-like "silver dollars" prized for floral arrangements.

Also called Honesty, Moonwort, and Satin Flower, it is a biennial that self-sows moderately, sometimes far from the original planting. If seedlings appear where they don't belong, transplant, give away, or weed out. It is important to be able to identify the broad, coarsely toothed first-year leaves or you will invariably yank them out as weeds. First-year seedlings can survive winter's chill through Zone 4.

The leaves of 'Variegata' are edged in creamy-white. There are also pink- or white-flowering forms.

PLANTING REQUIREMENTS
Plant 8–12 inches apart in average, well-drained garden soil. Money Plant tolerates wet or dry conditions and will flower in any degree of shade.

PROPAGATION
Sprinkle the ripened seeds outdoors in midsummer or early fall.

Monkey Flower (*Mimulus* spp.)
18–24 inches tall
Native to U.S.

Monkey Flower prefers consistent moisture and thrives in poorly drained or even wet sites. Most species transplant easily at any stage of their development as long as the roots are kept consistently moist. They often self-sow. The flowers indeed resemble a grinning monkey's face.

Large Monkey Flower (*M. guttatus*) prefers standing water, making it a good choice for wet or boggy environments. It blooms profusely in early summer when temperatures are cooler, covering itself with brassy yellow flowers spotted with reddish brown freckles. Cutting plants back as temperatures rise encourages better late-summer flowering.

Readily available seeds of *M.* × *hybridus* produce a wide variety of jewel-toned flowering plants. Bush Monkey Flower (*M. aurantiacus*), usually reproduced from cuttings, has slender dark green leaves and lovely apricot-orange flowers. Award-winning 'Calypso', a compact cultivar, comes in a variety of colors. These tender perennials are often hardy from Zone 7 south. In colder zones, dig a few to bring indoors for the winter.

The native Monkey Flower (*M. ringens*), a hardy perennial, can be counted on to return year after year.

PLANTING REQUIREMENTS

Prefers moist planting sites in part to medium shade or in morning sun and afternoon shade. If it begins to look straggly, pinch it back, make sure it is well watered, and it should soon start blooming again. Space new plantings 6 inches apart.

PROPAGATION

Refrigerate seed in a film canister until planting time. Press the dust-like seeds into the top of moistened planting medium 3–4 months before the last frost date and cover with glass or plastic wrap. Germination occurs in 7–21 days. Pick out seedlings after they have at least 3 sets of true leaves and transplant into larger containers. Pinch out terminal growth to encourage branching. Never allow to dry out.

Annual Forget-Me-Not (*Myosotis sylvatica*)
5–12 inches tall
Europe

Masses of blue forget-me-nots carpet my friend Helen's award-winning garden each spring. Bright yellow daffodils and pink bleeding hearts rise from this vision of blue, creating an unforgettable picture. A wonderful pass-along plant, Annual Forget-me-not self-sows with abandon, always returning to bloom the following spring.

PLANTING REQUIREMENTS

Plant 6–12 inches apart in moist, well-drained, humus-rich or average garden soil in part to light shade or in morning sun.

PROPAGATION

Sow seeds indoors 8–10 weeks before the last frost date, or plant them outdoors early fall or in April. Seeds will germinate in 7–28 days. After existing plants have bloomed, allow the seeds to ripen and self-sow before removing the plants, or sprinkle ripened seed where you want plants.

Flowering Tobacco (*Nicotiana* spp.)
2–5 feet tall
South America

Flowering Tobacco is a "see-through" plant. Even though it is tall, it can be planted at the middle or even the front of the perennial border. Stalks of airy, tubular flowers, popular with hummingbirds, seem to float above the coarse leaves. Some are late afternoon or night bloomers, others bloom during the day.

Winged Tobacco (*N. alata*), so called because the stems of the basal leaves have flattened "wings," has stark white flowers with lavender throats that sweeten the night air. Site between other perennials or stake to keep it from flopping. It needs at least half a day of good strong sunlight for optimum performance and is quite drought tolerant. 'Sensations' has pink-red flowers. For shorter plants, check out the Nikki series, which seldom get taller than 16–18 inches. In 1979, 'Nikki Red' was an All America Selection. These compact versions are not as fragrant as the species.

Chartreuse bells dangle gracefully from wiry stems above pale green leaves on *N. langsdorfii*, which grows 3–4 feet tall. This species will not look its best in the high heat and humidity of midsummer but perks up when cooler weather returns.

Hybrid Flowering Tobacco (*N.* × *sanderae*), generally shorter and more compact than parent species *N. alata* and *N. forgetiana*, is available in a variety of colors. 'Avalon Bright Pink', only 15 inches tall, was an All America Selection in 2001. Domino Series plants, reputed to be heat resistant, grow 12–18 inches tall and flower in shades of pink, purple, apricot, white, and even lime green. The 18-inch-tall Heaven Scent Series produces colorful flowers with better fragrance than most.

Clusters of impressive long white trumpets dangle from arching stems above the extra-large leaves of Woodland Tobacco, also called White Shooting Stars (*N. sylvestris*). Butterflies, moths, and hummingbirds go crazy over its beautiful, fragrant flowers.

PLANTING REQUIREMENTS
Plant 12 inches apart in moist, humus-rich, well-drained soil in part to light shade, morning sun, or in full sun.

PROPAGATION

Sow seed indoors 8–10 weeks before the last frost date, or outdoors after all danger of frost is past. Do not cover. Germination usually takes 12–21 days. Prick out indoor-grown seedlings after they form the third set of leaves and transplant into individual pots, giving them at least half day of strong "window-light." Water with half-strength liquid fertilizer once a week. Plants will also self-sow, but those seedlings will bloom later in the summer.

Love-in-a-Mist (*Nigella damascena*)
12–24 inches tall
Southern Europe, Africa

I first saw this delicate blue flower in a friend's cottage garden, hovering above thread-like, misty green leaves and weaving in and out of a mass of bright pink poppies. I was enchanted. This cool-season annual only blooms 4–7 weeks, but successive seeding every 2–3 weeks until late June can prolong the bloom period.

Love-in-a-Mist is also called Devil-in-the-Bush because its seedpods resemble a pale green head wearing a horned crown. These unusual seedpods eventually dry to a warm buff and make nice additions to dried floral arrangements. Break open the ripened seedheads and sprinkle the seeds wherever you want more plants to grow.

PLANTING REQUIREMENTS

Plant 12 inches apart in drifts in moist, well-drained garden soil in part to light shade or in full sun. Weekly watering with half-strength liquid fertilizer will produce heftier plants.

PROPAGATION

Sow seed outside in the fall, or in early spring. Thin seedlings to 6–8 inches apart. Established plants have a long taproot and seldom transplant successfully. Self-sows.

Geranium (*Pelargonium* spp.)
12–18 inches tall
South Africa
Good in Containers
Deer Resistant

Most Pelargoniums, whose *common* name is Geranium, tolerate part shade nicely. In fact, Martha Washington (*Pelargonium* × *domesticum*), primarily grown as a houseplant, prefers it. The common bedding geraniums (*P. hortorum*) are called Zonal Geraniums because of the brownish-maroon ring (zone) that appears on many of the scalloped leaves. Although Zonal Geraniums are profuse bloomers, you must dead-head or else blooming will slow or even cease. A definite maintenance chore. Zonal Geraniums are tolerant of dry conditions.

Scented geraniums (*P.* × *fragrans, crispum, odoratissimum, tomentosum, graveolens*, etc.) are favorites in gardens for the senses. Plant a variety of these near the patio, where it is easy to grab a leaf or two, and sniff familiar fragrances like apple, lime, rose, peppermint, and even nutmeg. Scented geraniums do not flower heavily. Scented leaves are their claim to fame. They grow fine in the shade.

Ivy Geranium (*P. peltatum*) is popular in hanging baskets and window boxes. It likes afternoon shade, but flowering will peter out without ample light.

In the nursery trade, vegetatively propagated geraniums produce larger flowers with more petals, while those grown from seed usually have smaller, single flowers. However, the latter are often more reasonably priced, so "you pays your money and you takes your choice."

PLANTING REQUIREMENTS
Plant 8–15 inches apart in average, well-drained garden soil in part to light shade or in full sun. More light increases flower production. Too much nitrogen fertilizer will produce more leaves than flowers.

PROPAGATION
Take 4-inch cuttings either in the fall or from plants overwintered in-doors. Or sow seed indoors 3–4 months before the last frost. Germination takes 7–21 days.

Chinese Basil (*Perilla frutescens* 'Atropurpurea')
18–36 inches tall
Asia

After growing it for several years, I have mixed emotions about rec-ommending this annual because it self-sows so heavily, cropping up all over the place. However, the intense deep wine-red color looks fantastic with yellow- or chartreuse-foliage plants, and even the spikes of pinkish-white flowers are attractive. Because it is so distinctive, it is easy to spot and even easier to yank out. In early spring, I pull out all stray seedlings, gather them together into "bouquets," and stick them in the ground. Each bouquet produces a large instant clump. Without consistent moisture, newly transplanted seedlings will wilt. Established plants, on the other hand, thumb their noses at heat and drought.

Chinese Basil (no relation to Sweet Basil, *Ocimum basilicum*) is also called False Coleus, Beefsteak Plant, and Purple Shiso. The species has purple spotted green leaves. Striking *Perilla frutescens* var. *crispens* aka *P. nankinensis* has heavily toothed purple-bronze leaves with frilly margins.

PLANTING REQUIREMENTS
This adaptable plant prefers a site in part to light shade or in morning sun in average, well-drained soil, but will grow just about anywhere. Space new plantings 15–18 inches apart.

PROPAGATION
Propagates itself, but for those who want more control, remove the flowers before they seed. Sow seeds outdoors just before the last frost date, or indoors 6–8 weeks earlier. Light is required for germination.

Mexican Mint (*Plectranthus amboinicus*)
12–16 inches tall
Africa
Good in Containers

Mexican Mint, reminiscent of Coleus, is grown primarily for its handsome, dark green scalloped leaves. Also called Cuban Oregano, it has square stems and definitely smells herbal. In spicy tomato-based recipes, Mexican Mint offers a unique flavor all its own.

The toothed leaves of 'Athens Gem' are a luscious lemony-chartreuse, edged with dark green. It grows 12–18 inches tall. 20–24-inch 'Variegatus' has green leaves with white margins. Both are Athens Select plants. 'Marginatus' (*P. forsteri*), a spreader, will create a good-looking annual ground cover, or trail out of a hanging basket. Its rich green, hairy leaves are edged with dainty white scallops. It is sometimes offered as 'Iboza'.

PLANTING REQUIREMENTS

Plant in average, well-drained soil in part, light, or dappled shade, or in full sun. Pinch to encourage bushiness.

PROPAGATION

Take cuttings any time, dig rooted runners, or sow seed indoors 8–10 weeks before the final frost date.

Polyanthus Primrose (*Primula* × *polyanthus*)

5–7 inches tall

China

Hybrid

Primula means "the first in spring." As soon as temperatures even hint at rising, hundreds of 4–6 inch pots of blooming primroses are snapped up by winter-weary gardeners. Brightly colored Polyanthus Primroses, also called Florist's or Garden Primrose, are often marked with yellow centers. These cheery little plants grow from a ground-hugging rosette of long, spatulate, crinkly green leaves. True cool-season annuals, they will bloom only until the temperatures starts to heat up. But that is OK, because by then, other annuals and perennials are in bloom.

There are many other choices. Whorls of pink, violet, or white flowers float 6–8 inches above Fairy Primrose (*P. malacoides*). German Primrose (*P. obonica*) is also called Poison Primrose because some people develop a rash after touching the hairy leaves. It grows 8–15 inches tall with tiers of whorled flowers. My favorite primrose was given to me by my friend Jan when we were neighbors in southern Minnesota. This sturdy little bright yellow plant returns faithfully each spring. I suspect it may be *P. veris*, commonly called Cowslip, but I am not sure. It is hardier than most Polyanthus Primroses, although some of those surprise me and come up again in my Zone 5 garden. Most primroses are tender perennials in warmer zones.

PLANTING REQUIREMENTS

Harden off purchased plants before transplanting outdoors. Plant in moist, humus-rich, well-drained soil in part shade.

PROPAGATION

It is possible to grow primroses from chilled seed by sowing it 10–12 weeks before the last frost date. But for instant gratification, just grab one or two of those blooming potsful of primroses and plant them where you can look outside and reassure yourself that spring *is* on the way.

Salvia (*Salvia* spp.)
8–30 inches tall
Mexico, South America, Europe
Good for Containers
Deer Resistant

Hundreds of *Salvia* species exist, most of which require full sun. The following will tolerate part to light shade. Compare the bright red flowering racemes of late-blooming Bloody Sage (*S. coccinea*) with those of Scarlet Sage (*S. splendens*), the popular bedding plant. Bloody Sage, also called Texas Sage, is more open and airy. It grows 2–3 feet tall, with cultivars named 'Lady in Red', 'Nymph', and 'Cherry Blossom'. Consider planting a mass of Scarlet Sage in front of an all-green shrub border. Cool down the intensity by adding a few white flowers. Growers have developed cultivars of all shapes and sizes.

Gentian Salvia (*S. patens*) has large, rich violet-blue flowers. Mealy-Cup Sage (*S. farinacea*), another blue-flowering salvia, produced such cultivars as electric blue 'Victoria' and blue and white 'Strata', a 1996 All America Selection. Mealy-Cup Sage is very cold-tolerant, often overwintering in Zone 5 as a small cluster of leaves. It is great for attracting hummingbirds and finches.

The totally different looking Clary Sage (*S. viridis*) has large pink, purple, or white bracts atop 12–20 inch stems. It appreciates shade, particularly in hot weather. Clary Sage looks lovely combined with gray- or silver-leaved plants. It is often used in fresh or dried arrangements.

Roseleaf Sage (*S. involucrata*) blooms happily with a half day of sun. From Mexico, it has showy bracts and striking dark magenta-pink flowers. It can grow 3–5 feet tall.

PLANTING REQUIREMENTS

Mass plants 10–18 inches apart in drifts in moist, humus-rich, well-drained soil. Salvias bloom best in morning sun/afternoon shade or in full sun. Occasional deadheading will keep the plants shapely and encourage consistent bloom. Most salvias are drought tolerant.

PROPAGATION
Soak seed overnight. Barely press into moistened soiless potting mix 7–10 weeks before the last frost. Keep the medium consistently moist. Seeds should germinate in 12–14 days. Or purchase plants from the local garden center and transplant outdoors after all danger of frost has passed.

Fairy Fan Flower (*Scaevola aemula*)
4–10 inches tall
Australia

If you are a lefty, you definitely need this plant! The name *Scaevola* means "left-handed." Also called Blue Fan Flower, the five petals spread outward from a single point, like a small fan or hand. Most cultivars, such as 'New Wonder', 'Blue Shamrock', 'Sapphire Blue', and 'Purple Fan' are in shades of blues and purples. 'White Charm' is the current white-flowering form.

PLANTING REQUIREMENTS
Plant in well-drained soil in dappled shade, morning sun, or in full sun. Like Goldilocks, Fan Flower likes soil that is "just right," neither too wet nor too dry.

PROPAGATION
Sow seed indoors 6–8 weeks before last frost date or take cuttings in late summer to overwinter indoors.

Dusty Miller (*Senecio cineraria*)
8–20 inches tall
Mediterranean
Good in Containers
Deer Resistant

Dusty Miller, a popular bedding plant, lights up borders with its heavily cut silvery-gray foliage. *Senecio*, from the Latin, means "old man." It is still occasionally identified by its older name, *Cineraria maritima*. Stroll through public parks or wander past downtown buildings and you will invariably find this furry fellow in front of some kind of red flower—red salvias, short, fat red begonias, or tall red cannas.

Dusty Miller is very cold tolerant, frequently wintering over and flowering the second season. Although it is a maintenance task, I recommend removing the creamy-yellow flowers. They always look out of place and detract from the total picture.

For shorter plants, look for cultivars with names like 'Cirrus' or 'Silver Queen'. I have seen other species with gray foliage identified as Dusty Miller, so check botanical names to get the one you want.

PLANTING REQUIREMENTS
Plant 10–12 inches apart in average, well-drained garden soil in part to light shade or in full sun.

PROPAGATION
Sow seed indoors 8–10 weeks before the last frost date. Or plant seeds outdoors in mid April. Do not cover the seed.

Persian Shield (*Strobilanthes dyerianus*)
3–5 feet tall
Burma
Good in Containers

Wow! Talk about an impressive foliage plant. A mass of these is guaranteed to stop garden visitors in their tracks. The deep green 6–8-inch-long lanceolate leaves appear to be infused with a rich burgundy-purple, highlighted with darker green veins. An overall silvery sheen makes these iridescent leaves glow in the garden. Then peek under one of these 3–4-inch-wide beauties to discover an underside of dark purple. Like I said—Wow!

PLANTING REQUIREMENTS
Plant in consistently moist, humus-rich, well-drained soil in part or afternoon shade or in full sun. Pinch to encourage bushiness.

PROPAGATION
Take cuttings in mid to late summer to overwinter indoors. Grow indoors as a houseplant in as much light as possible.

Bacopa (*Sutera grandiflora*)
24–48 inches long
Africa
Best in Containers

Early in spring, I bought a hanging basket containing one huge double impatiens. Spectacular in its own right, it was made even more lovely because of the addition of 'Giant Snowflake' Bacopa. Long leafy green stems covered with white flowers hung like long tresses around the entire planter. Even though its fragrance is not particularly appealing, Bacopa is glorious. 'Snowstorm' is supposedly more heat resistant than 'Snowflake'.

PLANTING REQUIREMENTS
Bacopa requires moist, humus-rich, well-drained soil in part to light or filtered shade. Consistent moisture is essential.

PROPAGATION
Root cuttings taken in early spring or summer, or purchase plants. Containers brought in for the winter will perform admirably outdoors the following year.

Black-Eyed Susan Vine (*Thunbergia alata*)
5–8 feet tall
Africa
Good in Containers

Picture bright golden Black-eyed Susan climbing up a post, hanging from a basket or planter, twisting around shrubs, or scrambling through a perennial bed. Some varieties have creamy white, yellow, or bright orange flowers. This self-twining annual vine has square, slightly hairy stems and opposite leaves. These heavily notched, wedge-shaped, dark green leaves are attached to unique winged petioles.

There are over 100 species. Bush Thunbergia (*T. battiscombei*) is a scrambler with violet blue flowers that grow in the axils of its glossy dark green leaves. It can stretch 2–3 feet tall. Kings' Mantle (*T. erecta*) has an erect, 3–4 foot tall form, with yellow-throated flowers in shades of purple and blue. Orange Clock Vine (*T. gregorii*), similar to Black-eyed Susan Vine, is not quite as floriferous. Its rich dark orange flowers do not have contrasting eyes.

PLANTING REQUIREMENTS
Plant 12 inches apart in moist, well-drained garden soil in morning sun/afternoon shade. Provide additional water during hot spells.

PROPAGATION
Soak the hard-coated, dark brown seeds overnight and plant them indoors 6–8 weeks before the last frost date, or outdoors when freezing temperatures are no longer a threat. The former will bloom earlier. Germination takes 14–21 days. Or take cuttings from new growth and overwinter indoors for next season's vine.

Glory Bush (*Tibouchina urvilleana*)
3–5 feet tall
Brazil
Good in Containers

Luscious rosy-violet to purple flowers with deep purple anthers bloom a day at a time over the leathery, deep green leaves of this striking tropical shrub. Glory Bush is also known as Brazilian Spider Flower, Purple Glory Tree, and Princess Flower. It may be listed in catalogs under a number of scientific names including *T. grandiflora*, *T. semidecandra*, *T. urvilleana*, and *Pleroma macrantha*.

PLANTING REQUIREMENTS
Plant in moist, humus-rich, well-drained soil in part to dappled shade, in morning sun/afternoon shade, or in full sun. Treat as an annual or containerize for overwintering indoors.

PROPAGATION
Propagate from cuttings taken in early to midsummer or sow seed 8–10 weeks before the last frost date.

Wishbone Flower (*Torenia fournieri*)
Yellow Wishbone Flower (*Torenia flava*)
8–12 inches tall
Tropical Asia, Africa
Good in Containers

Wishbone Flowers, reminiscent of foxglove or snapdragon, come in a variety of velvety blues and purples as well as in pastel colors. Most have yellow throats. Look for offerings in the Clown Series, Duchess Mix, or Panda Mix. 'Summer Wave Blue' has oversized blue flowers accented with white. *T. hybrida* is a great vining, trailing plant that is perfect for containers. Plant in borders, containers, or mass in a shady spot.

Yellow Wishbone Flower is just that—yellow. It has a purple-red throat. It slightly resembles a Monkey Flower, but is not as upright, often trailing and creeping along the ground. The pretty, yellow-orange flowers of 'Suzie Wong' are distinguished by a dark, nearly black throat.

PLANTING REQUIREMENTS
Plant 6–8 inches apart in moist, humus-rich, well-drained soil in part to dappled shade. A shady location produces larger flowers, but sun encourages a greater abundance of them. Morning sun/afternoon shade is always a good combination.

PROPAGATION
Sow seed indoors 10–12 weeks before the last frost date, or plant outdoors in late April or early May. Do not cover the seed. Germination occurs in 7–21 days. Blooming occurs about 3–4 months after germination. Pinch to encourage branching. Wishbone Flower may self-sow.

Blue Throatwort (*Trachelium caeruleum*)
2–4 feet tall
Mediterranean

This beautiful annual boasts lightly fragrant clusters of tiny starry blue or rosy-lavender flowers attractive to butterflies and hummingbirds. The dense, dome-shaped flower clusters measure 2–4 inches across.

It is widely grown commercially for the cut-flower trade. Cultivars such as 'Blue Umbrella' and 'White Veil' have a compact growth habit.

PLANTING REQUIREMENTS
Plant in moist, humus-rich, well-drained soil in part to light shade or in morning sun/afternoon shade.

PROPAGATION
Sow seed indoors 8–10 weeks before the last frost date. Germination can take up to a month. Take cuttings in summer to overwinter indoors. Can

be grown as a biennial by sowing seed in late summer in pots and over-wintering the seedlings indoors.

Pansy (*Viola* spp.)
4–12 inches tall
Europe, Asia
Good in Containers

After a tiresome winter, gardeners long for any flower that even hints at balmy breezes. Pansy hybrids (*Viola* × *wittrockiana*), like spring bulbs and primroses, deftly do that job, so plant them en masse in early spring. Unfortunately, blooming stops as soon as temperatures rise. However, these colorful, cool-season annuals can withstand relapses into wintry weather, so they have also become popular bedding plants for fall. As trees begin to shed their autumn leaves, look in public gardens across the U.S., and you will find thousands of happy-faced pansies ringing masses of Ornamental Cabbages and Flowering Kale.

Cute little Johnny Jump-up (*V. tricolor*) has always been a favorite. Who could resist those whimsical, velvety purple and bright yellow flowers that bloom unceasingly? Also known as Heartsease, Johnny Jump-up occasionally reseeds in my garden, and I am always happy to find those volunteers.

Ivy-Leaved Violet, also called Tasmanian or Australian Violet (*V. hederacea*) creeps by stolons, forming dense mats. Hardy from Zone 8 south, it has small flowers of either white or blue.

PLANTING REQUIREMENTS
Plant 4–6 inches apart in moist, humus-rich, well-drained soil in morning sun and afternoon shade or in full sun.

PROPAGATION
Pansies can be difficult to raise from seed, so after several unsuccessful tries I gave up and now I purchase plants. However, if you enjoy a challenge, refrigerate seed for 7–10 days and sow indoors in late winter. Cover sown flats with dark plastic because darkness is necessary for effective germination. Germination takes 14–21 days.

Not Recommended

Bachelor's Button (*Centaurea cyanus*)
12–24 inches tall
Europe, Asia

This old garden favorite is so vigorous and reseeds so prolifically that it can quickly crowd out native species, especially in the grasslands and rare prairie remnants of the American Northwest. Sometimes called Cornflower, Bachelor's Button produces bright blue, white, or pink flowers. Mistakenly believed to be a native wildflower, it is often found in wildflower seed packet mixes, joining such other recognized invasives as Dame's Rocket. Please think twice before planting this invasive fellow.

The most important maintenance task is to sustain
the health of the earth.
                                    —*Ken Druse*

14.
Final
Thoughts—
Not Just for
Shade

In an article entitled "When Good Plants
Go Bad," Carole Ottesen writes about
plants that have a tendency to become too
aggressive, eventually causing maintenance problems as well as potential environmental concerns. Whether a particular plant becomes a "bad plant" often
depends on the particular region or area
of the country where it is growing, or
even the idiosyncrasies of the specific site
in which it is nurtured. *Helleborus foetidus* is not a problem in the Midwest,
but may be in California. Some
drought-tolerant plants go crazy
when supplied with increased
moisture or if the soil is amended
beyond "normal" requirements.
Chameleon Plant or *Houttuynia* spreads
rapidly by means of underground rhizomes. Pronounced *How-toe-in-e-ah*, this
ground cover has wildly splashed, tricolored, heart-shaped leaves on an upright
stem. It will quickly cover an area if the
soil is consistently moist and loose, but
a dry planting site can help to curb its
overly aggressive nature.

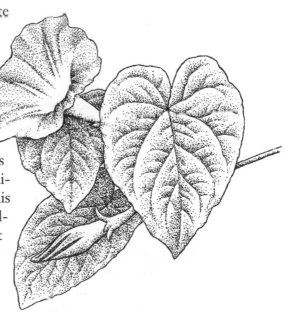

Even natives can behave differently depending upon the locale. An article in *Wildflower* magazine discussed vanishing Celandine Poppy populations in Canada. This wildflower is alive and well in the Midwest, and can even be overly zealous in the Southeast. Many gardeners love the tenacity of Virginia Creeper, while others rip it out. Some of the native grasses such as Little Bluestem, Northern Sea Oats, Switch Grass, and Sideoats Grama can become invasive if their normally lean growing conditions are radically altered. Otteson writes, "Once an aggressive plant gets a roothold in the garden, it can become an ongoing maintenance problem," requiring relentless weeding. If you decide to use an overly aggressive plant, be sure it can be confined within your allotted space and will not cause a threat to the wild: sandwiched in between concrete driveways and walkways, for example! And of course if the plants have tasty seeds to attract birds or small mammals, then all your boundary precautions become moot.

Exotic plants that escape to the wild, spreading and displacing existing native plants, are considered invasive. Many of these will be found at the ends of chapters under the subtitle "Not Recommended." These are not simply personal prejudices. The Brooklyn Botanic Garden's Winter 1996 booklet, entitled *Invasive Plants: Weeds of the Global Garden*, describes some of these problem plants. Several websites list a number of well-known nonnative garden plants that now pose a threat to the natural environment. Native plant societies nationwide regularly distribute information warning of the dangers of invasive exotic plants in their particular region.

And why should we care? Because when non-natives displace native species, essential food and nesting sites for wildlife are destroyed, drastically reducing their populations. Rare and endangered wildflowers and animals are threatened with extinction. And our important almighty tax dollars are spent over and over in futile attempts to curb and control these rampant exotics that even threaten agricultural interests. Costs for invasive control and agricultural losses are estimated at more than $15 billion per year in the United States alone.

My reason for identifying these common garden plants as *Invasive, Not Recommended* is neither to frustrate gardeners nor to antagonize plant propagators and nursery owners, but to make them aware of plants that have become unexpectedly troublesome. I have included a number of thugs in this book and sincerely hope none will be transformed into the

Purple Loosestrife or Kudzu of the future. As you plan your garden, read the caveats carefully and determine whether incorporating a particular plant into your planting site might adversely impact nearby wild areas. At a recent conference on invasive species, Cliff Chapman emphasized that some of the worst exotic pests of today, such as Multiflora Rose and Garlic Mustard, lived as "good citizens" for decades before they exploded out of control.

Promoting healthy ecosystems and native habitats are the ultimate responsibility of every caring American. All that is asked of any citizen of the world is to "be responsible." We each need to do our part to maintain the health of our fragile environment.

Indeed, it is the only one we have.

Gardening adds years to your life and life to your
years.   *—Anonymous*

Resources

I contacted most of the nurseries listed below and would like to report that nursery owners are very genial folks. Not surprising. Most are mail-order nurseries; a few are walk-in only. Nurseries listed as "Wholesale only" are just that. Please do not contact them for retail sales. Instead, give their address to your local garden center.

Because telephone numbers, email, and website addresses change frequently, only the postal address is listed here. Some nurseries charge for their catalogs, an amount generally deducted with the first order. Many are established businesses, others are just starting. A stamped, self-addressed envelope is appreciated when you write for information. Nurseries with websites generally include the name of the nursery in the address. Using www. followed by the name of the particular nursery and then adding .com will usually get you connected with the site.

Ambergate Gardens
8730 County Road 43
Chaska, MN 55318
Unusual plants, Martagon Lilies

Andre Viette Farm & Nursery
Route 1, P.O. Box 16
Fishersville, VA 11929
Perennials for shade and sun

Arbor Village
P.O. Box 227
Holt, MO 64048
Conifers, shrubs

Arrowhead Alpines
P.O. Box 857
Fowlerville, MI 48836
Wildflowers, perennials, rock plants, conifers,
shrubs; delightful catalog

Bachman's Nursery
6010 Lyndale Avenue South
Minneapolis, MN 55419
Trees, shrubs, perennials, annuals

Blue Sterling Nursery
372 Seeley Cohansey Road
Bridgeton, NJ 08302
Conifers, Japanese Maples

Bluestem Prairie Nursery
Route 2, P.O. Box 92
Hillsboro, IL 62049
Illinois native plants and seeds

Bluestone Perennials
7211 Middle Ridge Road
Madison, OH 44057
Seedlings in flats, 400 varieties

Breck's
P.O. Box 65
Guilford, IN 47022
Bulbs

Brent and Becky's Bulbs
7463 Heath Trail
Gloucester, VA 23061
Bulb growers since 1900

Bridgewood Gardens
P.O. Box 800
Crownsville, MD 21032
Hostas

Burnham Woods Nursery
6775 Hudoff Road
Bloomington, IN 47408
Flowering shrubs, uncommon perennials

Busse Gardens
17160 245th Ave.
Big Lake, MN 55309
Hard-to-find perennials; informative catalog

Carlson's Gardens
P.O. Box 305
South Salem, NY 10590
Northern-grown, acclimated native azaleas

Carroll Gardens
444 E. Main St.
Westminster, MD 21157
Shrubs, conifers, trees, bulbs, roses, perennials;
informative catalog

Coburg Planting Fields
573 E. 600 North
Valparaiso, IN 46383
Daylilies

Coenosium Gardens
4412 354th Street East
Eatonville, WA 98328
Unusual conifers

Cold Stream Farm
2030 Free Soil Road
Freesoil, MI 49411
Evergreen and deciduous trees, shrubs

Collector's Nursery
16804 N.E. 102nd Avenue
Battleground, WA 98604

Colorblends / Schipper & Co.
P.O. Box 7584
Greenwich, CT 06836
Bulbs in bulk, $50 minimum order

Conifer Garden (Bill Barger)
3200 Rohrer Road
Wadsworth, OH 44281

Cooper's Gardens
212 West Country Road
Roseville, MN 55113
Shade perennials

Cross Nurseries, Inc. (Wholesale only)
19774 Kenwood Trail
Lakeville, MN 55044
Conifers, trees, shrubs

Cunningham Gardens, Inc. (Wholesale only)
P.O. Box 37
Waldron, IN 46182
Ground covers and perennials

Dutch Gardens
144 Intervale Road
Burlington, VA 05401
Hardy and tender bulbs and perennials; catalog

Earthly Pursuits
2901 Kuntz Road
Windsor Mill, MD 21244
Grasses, perennials

Fancy Fronds
1911 Fourth Avenue West
Seattle, WA 98119
Wide selection of ferns

Feder's Prairie Seed Co.
12871 380th Avenue
Blue Earth, MN 56013
Seeds, wildflowers, grasses

Forestfarm
990 Tetherow Road
Williams, OR 97544
5000 varieties of woody natives, unusual plants,
trees, shrubs

Gee Farms
14928 Bunkerhill Road
Stockbridge, MI 49285
Trees, shrubs, conifers

Genesis Nursery
23200 Hurd Road
Tampico, IL 61283
Native plants

Girard Nurseries
P.O. Box 428
Geneva, OH 44041
Conifers, evergreens, azaleas, rhododendrons

Gossler Farms Nursery
1200 Weaver Road
Springfield, OR 97478
Hellebores, trees, shrubs

Greer Gardens
1280 Goodpasture Island Road
Eugene, OR 97401
Rhododendrons, conifers, Japanese Maples, rare
trees and shrubs, perennials, ferns, grasses

Hamilton Seeds and Wildflowers
16786 Brown Road
Elk Creek, MO 65464
Wildflowers, seeds, grasses, native trees

Heronswood Nursery
7530 NE 288th Street
Kingston, WA 98346
Conifers, trees, shrubs, vines, perennials;
extensive, informative catalog

Iseli Nursery (Wholesale only)
30590 S.E. Kelso Road
Boring, OR 97009
Dwarf conifers, conifers, Japanese Maples

J. F. New & Associates
128 Sunset Drive
Walkerton, IN 46574
Native plants, restoration

Jasper-Pulaski State Nursery
15508 W. 700 N.
Medaryville, IN 47957
Native trees

John Scheepers, Inc.
23 Tulip Drive
Bantam, CT 006750
Bulbs; colorful catalog

K. Van Bourgondien & Sons
P.O. Box 1000
Babylon, NY 11702
Bulbs; colorful catalog

Klehm's Song Sparrow Farm
13101 E. Rye Road
Avalon, WI 53505
Hostas, peonies, perennials; handsome,
informative catalog

Kuk's Forest Nursery
10174 Barr Road
Brecksville, OH 44141
Hostas

LaFayette Home Nursery, Inc.
1 Nursery Lane
LaFayette, IL 61449
Native plants from shoreline to timberline

Landscape Alternatives, Inc.
1705 St. Albans Street North
Roseville, MN 55113
Minnesota native woodland and prairie
wildflowers, grasses

Martin Brooks Rare Plant Nursery
235 Cherry Lane
Doylestown, PA 18901
Shrubs

Mary's Plant Farm
2410 Lanes Mill Road
Hamilton, OH 45013
Natives, shrubs, trees, ferns, shade-tolerant plants

McClure & Zimmerman
P.O. Box 368
Friesland, WI 53935
Bulbs; informative catalog

Mid-America Garden
P.O. Box 18278
Salem, OR 97305
Hostas, iris, daylilies

Midwest Groundcovers (Wholesale only)
P.O. Box 748
St. Charles, IL 60174

Miller's Manor Gardens
12788 E. 191st Street
Noblesville, IN 46060
Hostas, iris, daylilies, perennials, conifers

Minnesota Valley Wholesale, Inc. (Wholesale only)
14505 Johnson Memorial Drive
Shakopee, MN 55379
Shrubs

Minnesota Valley Garden Center
3232 West 150th street
Shakopee, MN 55379
Walk-in retail sales only; outlet for Minnesota Valley Wholesale, Inc.

Missouri Wildflowers Nursery
9814 Pleasant Hill Road
Jefferson City, MO 65109
Shrubs, grasses, wildflowers, plants, seeds

Mitsch Daffodils
P.O. Box 218
Hubbard, OR 97032
Rare and unusual daffodils; handsome catalog

Munchkin Nursery
323 Woodside Drive N.W.
Depauw, IN 47115
Woodland wildflowers

Naylor Creek Nursery
2610 West Valley Road
Chimacum, WA 98325
Hostas, epimediums, hellebores, and other perennials

Northwest Horticulture (Wholesale only)
14113 River Bend Road
Mount Vernon, WA 98273
Perennials

Odyssey Bulbs
8984 Meadow Lane
Berrien Springs, MI 49103
Unusual and hard to find bulbs

Old House Gardens
536 W. Third Street
Ann Arbor, MI 48103
Heirloom bulbs

The Oregon Garden
879 West Main Street
Silverton, OR 97381

Owl Ridge Alpines
5421 Whipple Lake Road
Clarkston, MI 48016
Alpine, woodland species

Peekskill Nurseries
P.O. Box 428
Shrub Oak, NY 10588
Ground covers, mail order only

Piccadilly Farm
1971 Whippoorwill Road
Bishop, GA 30621
Hostas

Plant Delights Nursery
9241 Sauls Road
Raleigh, NC 27603
Rare and unusual plants; delightful catalog

Possibility Place Nursery (Wholesale; retail by appointment)
7548 W. Monee-Manhattan Road
Monee, IL 60449
Native trees, shrubs, prairie plants

Prairie Moon Nursery
Route 3, P.O. Box 163
Winona, MN 55987
Native Midwest seeds and plants

Prairie Nursery, Inc.
P.O. Box 306
Westfield, WI 53964
Wildflowers, grasses, native plants, seeds; informative catalog

Prairie Ridge Nursery
9738 Overland Road
Mt. Horeb, WI 53572
Woodland, wetland, prairie species

Rice Creek Gardens, Inc.
11506 Highway 65
Blaine, MN 55432
3000 varieties of wildflowers, grasses, peonies, rock garden and alpine plants

Rich's Foxwillow Pines Nursery
11618 McConnell Road
Woodstock, IL 60098
Dwarf conifers, rare and unusual trees, hostas

Russell Graham
4030 Eagle Crest Road NW
Salem, OR 97304
Ferns, shade plants, and bulbs

Savory's Gardens, Inc.
5300 Whiting Avenue
Edina, MN 55439
Hostas, companion plants

Shady Oaks Nursery (Wholesale only)
P.O. Box 708
Waseca, MN 56093
Shade plants; excellent, well-written catalog

Sharp Bros. Seed Co.
Route 4, P.O. Box 237A
Clinton, MO 64735
Seeds only for wildflower, grasses

Shooting Star Nursery
444 Bates Road
Frankfort, KY 40601
Wildflowers, grasses, rushes, sedges, trees, woody vines, ground covers

Siskiyou Rare Plant Nursery
2825 Cummings Road
Medford, OR 97501
Rare and unusual plants, alpines, conifers; catalog

Soules Gardens
5809 Rahke Road
Indianapolis, IN 46217
Hostas, daylilies, companion plants; informative catalog

Spence Restoration Nursery (Wholesale only)
P.O. Box 546
Muncie, IN 47308
Native plants, restoration; handsome, informative catalog

St. Lawrence Nurseries
325 State Highway 345
Potsdam, NY 13676
Cold-hardy fruit and nut trees

Stanley & Son Nursery (Wholesale only)
11740 S.E. Orient Drive
Boring, OR 97009
Dwarf conifers, conifers, Japanese Maples
Retail sales: www.agardens.com

Tower Perennial Gardens
4010 East Jamieson Road
Spokane, WA 99223
Hostas, perennials plus; nice catalog

Trennoll Nursery
P.O. Box 125
Trenton OH 45067
Shade plants, hostas, ferns, native plants

Vallonia State Nursery
2782 W. County Road 540 S.
Vallonia, IN 47281
Native trees

Van Engelen Inc.
23 Tulip Drive
Bantam, CT 06750
Bulbs; informative catalog

Vans Pines Nursery, Inc.
7550–144th Avenue
West Olive, MI 49460
Grasses, trees, ground
covers, shrubs

Wade and Gatton Nursery
1288 Gatton Rocks Road
Bellville, OH 44813
Hostas, companion plants, trees, shrubs; extensive
catalog

Walden-West
5744 Crooked Finger Road NE
Scotts Mills, OR 97375
Hostas

Wavecrest Nursery
2509 Lakeshore Drive
Fennville, MI 49408
Japanese Maples, hollies, dogwoods

Wayside Gardens
1 Garden Lane
Hodges, SC 29695
Woody and perennial plants; handsome,
informative catalog

We-Du Nurseries
Route 5, P.O. Box 724
Marion, NC 28752
Trees, shrubs, wildflowers, ferns, grasses, bulbs,
aquatic and bog plants

Wetlands Nursery
P.O. Box 14553
Saginaw, MI 48601

White Flower Farm
P.O. Box 50
Litchfield, CT 06759
Lovely, informative catalog

Whitman Farms
1420 Beaumont Street
Salem, OR 97304
Unusual shrubs, trees, some natives

Wildtype
900 N. Every Road
Mason, MI 48854

Woodlander's
1128 Colleton Avenue
Aiken, SC 29801

A book is like a garden carried in the pocket.
—*Chinese proverb*

References

Adams, E. Blair. *Homescaping*. Laramie, Wyo.: Co-operative Extensive Service Bulletin B-951, College of Agriculture, University of Wyoming, March 1991.

Adams, George. *Birdscaping Your Garden: A Practical Guide to Backyard Birds and the Plants That Attract Them*. Emmaus, Penn.: Rodale Press, 1994.

Appleton, Bonnie Lee. *Trees, Shrubs and Vines*. Emmaus, Penn.: Rodale Press, 1993.

Armitage, Allan M. *Allan Armitage on Perennials*. New York: Prentice Hall Gardening, 1993.

———. *Armitage's Garden Perennials: A Color Encyclopedia*. Portland, Ore.: Timber Press, 2000.

———. *Armitage's Manual of Annuals, Biennials, and Half-Hardy Perennials*. Portland, Ore.: Timber Press, 2001.

Bailey, Liberty Hyde. *Standard Cyclopedia of Horticulture*. Vols. I, II, and III. New York: Macmillan, 1944.

———, and Ethel Zoe Bailey. *Hortus Third: A Concise Dictionary of Plants Cultivated in the United States and Canada*. Revised and expanded by the staff of the Liberty Hyde Bailey Hortorium. New York: Macmillan, 1976.

Bales, Suzanne Frutig. *Vines*. Burpee American Gardening Series. New York: Macmillan, 1995.

Barnard, Loretta, ed. *500 Popular Annuals and Perennials for American Gardeners*. Hauppauge, N.Y.: Barron's Educational Series, 1999.

Bartels, Andreas. *Gardening with Dwarf Trees and Shrubs*. Portland, Ore.: Timber Press, 1986.

Beaubaire, Nancy, ed. *Native Perennials*. Brooklyn, N.Y.: Brooklyn Botanic Garden, 1996.

Bennett, Jennifer, and Turid Forsyth. *The Annual Garden*. Buffalo, N.Y.: Firefly Books, 1998.

Bergman, Helene, ed. *Dwarf Conifers*. Vol. 21, no. 1. Brooklyn, N.Y.: Brooklyn Botanic Garden, 1980.

Bloom, Adrian. *Gardening with Conifers*. Buffalo, N.Y.: Firefly Books, 2002.

Brickell, Christopher, ed. *Encyclopedia of Garden Plants*. New York: Macmillan, 1989.

Britton, Nathaniel Lord, and Hon. Addison Brown. *Illustrated Flora of the Northern United States, Canada and the British Possessions*. New York: Charles Scribner's Sons, 1896.

Brooklyn Botanic Garden. *Gardening in the Shade*. Handbook #3. Brooklyn, N.Y.: Brooklyn Botanic Garden, 1972.

Brown, Emily. *Landscaping with Perennials*. Portland, Ore.: Timber Press, 1986.

Brown, Lauren. *Grasses: An Identification Guide*. New York: Houghton Mifflin, 1979.

Bryan, John, ed. *Manual of Bulbs*. Royal Horticultural Society. Portland, Ore.: Timber Press, 1995.

Burke, Ken, ed. *All about Ground Covers*. San Ramon, Calif.: Chevron Chemical, 1982.

Burrell, C. Colston, ed. *Ferns*. Brooklyn, N.Y.: Brooklyn Botanic Garden, 1995.

———, ed. *The Shady Border*. Brooklyn, N.Y.: Brooklyn Botanic Garden, 1998.

———. *Perennials for Today's Gardens.* Des Moines, Iowa: Meredith, 2000.

Coombes, Allen J. *Dictionary of Plant Names.* Portland, Ore.: Timber Press, 1994.

Cramer, Harriet L. *The Shadier Garden.* Avenel, N.J.: Crescent Books/Random House, 1997.

Cravens, Richard. *Vines.* Alexandria, Va.: Time-Life Books, 1979.

Cutler, Karen Davis, ed. *Flowering Vines.* Brooklyn, N.Y.: Brooklyn Botanic Garden, 1999.

Cutler, Sandra McLean. *Dwarf and Unusual Conifers Coming of Age: A Guide to Mature Garden Conifers.* North Olmsted, Ohio: Barton-Bradley Crossroads Publishing, 1997.

Darke, Rick. *Color Encyclopedia of Ornamental Grasses.* Portland, Ore.: Timber Press, 1999.

Davitt, Keith. "New Soil-test Kits Yield Reliable Results." *Fine Gardening* 64 (December 1998), pp. 32–35.

Deam, Charles C. *Trees of Indiana.* First revised edition. Publication no. 13. Indianapolis: Department of Conservation, State of Indiana, 1921.

———. *Flora of Indiana.* Indianapolis: Department of Conservation, Division of Forestry, 1940.

Dirr, Michael, and Charles Heuser, Jr. *The Reference Manual of Woody Plant Propagation.* Athens, Ga.: Varsity Press, 1987.

Dirr, Michael A. *Dirr's Hardy Trees and Shrubs.* Portland, Ore.: Timber Press, 1997.

Druse, Ken. *The Natural Shade Garden.* New York: Clarkson N. Potter, 1992.

———. *The Natural Habitat Garden.* New York: Clarkson N. Potter, 1994.

———. *80 Great Natural Shade Garden Plants.* New York: Clarkson N. Potter, 1997.

Easy Beauty with Annuals. Alexandria, Va.: Time-Life Books, 1996.

Ellis, Barbara, Joan Benjamin, and Deborah L. Martin. *Rodale's Low-Maintenance Gardening Techniques.* Emmaus, Penn.: Rodale Press, 1995.

Ellis, Barbara W. *Taylor's Guide to Growing North America's Favorite Plants.* Boston: Houghton Mifflin, 1998.

———. *Taylor's Guide to Annuals.* Boston: Houghton Mifflin, 1999.

Flint, Harrison L. *Landscape Plants for Eastern North America.* New York: John Wiley & Sons, 1997.

Foley, Daniel J. *Ground Covers for Easier Gardening.* New York: Dover, 1961.

Foster, F. Gordon. *Ferns to Know and Grow.* Portland, Ore.: Timber Press, 1984.

Gardening with Shade. Menlo Park, Calif.: Sunset Books, 1996.

Glimn-Lacy, Janice, and Peter B. Kaufman. *Botany Illustrated.* New York: Van Nostrand Reinhold, 1984.

Glimn-Lacy, Janice. *What Flowers When.* Indianapolis: Flower and the Leaf, 1995.

Greenlee, John. *Encyclopedia of Ornamental Grasses.* Emmaus, Penn.: Rodale Press, 1992.

Haggard, Ezra. *Perennials for the Lower Midwest.* Bloomington: Indiana University Press, 1996.

———. Trees, *Shrubs, and Roses for Midwest Gardens.* Bloomington: Indiana University Press, 2001.

Hallowell, Anne, and Barbara Hallowell. *Fern Finder.* Berkeley, Calif.: Nature Study Guild, 1981.

Halpin, Anne. *Gardening in the Shade.* Des Moines, Iowa: Meredith, 1996.

Harris, Wade. "Pruning Do's and Don'ts, and Some Conifer Tips." American Conifer Society's annual meeting, August 2000.

Harstad, Carolyn. *Go Native! Gardening with Native Plants and Wildflowers in the Lower Midwest.* Bloomington: Indiana University Press, 1999.

———. "Native Plants in Your Garden? Why?" *Wildflower, North America's Magazine of Wild Flora* 18, no. 3 (Summer 2002).

Hawthorne, Linden. *Gardening in Shade.* American Horticultural Society Practical Guides. New York: DK Publishing, 1999.

Hay, Roy, and Patrick M. Synge. *Colour Dictionary of Garden Plants.* London: Penguin Group, 1975.

Hebb, Robert S. *Low Maintenance Perennials.* Reprinted from vol. 34, no. 5 and vol. 35, no. 1 of *Arnoldia,* a publication of the Arnold Arboretum. Jamaica Plain, Mass.: Arnold Arboretum of Harvard University, 1974 and 1975.

Henderson, Carrol L. *Landscaping for Wildlife.* St. Paul, Minn.: Department of Natural Resources, 1981.

Herndon, William H. *Herndon's Lincoln.* Chicago: Belford-Clarke, 1889.

Hessayon, Dr. D. G. *The Tree and Shrub Expert.* Herts, England: pbi Publications, Brittanica House Waltham Cross, 1983.

Hogue, Marjorie Mason. *Amazing Annuals.* Buffalo, N.Y.: Firefly Books, 1999.

Holmes, Roger, ed. *Taylor's Guide to Ornamental Grasses.* Boston: Houghton Mifflin, 1997.

Hunt, Peter. *100 Best Shrubs.* London: Wyre & Spottiswoode, 1963.

Hyland, Bob, ed. *Shrubs.* Brooklyn, N.Y.: Brooklyn Botanic Garden, 1994.

Jackson, Marion T., ed. *The Natural Heritage of Indiana.* Bloomington: Indiana University Press, 1997.

Jelitto, Leo, and Wilhelm Schacht. *Hardy Herbaceous Perennials.* Vols. I and II. Portland, Ore.: Timber Press, 1985.

Jones, Samuel B., Jr., and Leonard E. Foote. *Gardening with Native Wild Flowers.* Portland, Ore.: Timber Press, 1990.

Keeler, Harriet L. *Our Native Trees and How to Identify Them.* New York: Charles Scribner's Sons, 1900.

King, Michael, and Piet Oudolf. *Gardening with Grasses.* Portland, Ore.: Timber Press, 1998.

Kingsbury, Noel. *Grasses and Bamboos.* New York: Watson-Guptill Publications, 2000.

Lawns and Ground Covers. Alexandria, Va.: Time-Life Books, 1989.

Lloyd, J. U., and C. G. Lloyd. *Bulletin of the Lloyd Library (29, 30, 31) of Botany, Pharmacy and Materia Medica.* Cincinnati, Ohio: Lloyd Library, 1931.

Loewer, Peter. *Rodale's Annual Garden.* Avenel, N.J.: Wings Books, 1988.

———, ed. *Ornamental Grasses.* Brooklyn, N.Y.: Brooklyn Botanic Garden, 1989.

———. *Tough Plants for Tough Places.* Emmaus, Penn.: Rodale Press, 1992.

———. *Ornamental Grasses.* Des Moines, Iowa: Better Homes and Gardens Books, 1995.

MacKenzie, David S. *Perennial Ground Covers.* Portland, Ore.: Timber Press, 1997.

Marinelli, Janet. "A Disease-Resistant Dogwood." Brooklyn, N.Y.: *Plants & Gardens News* 17, no. 2. Brooklyn Botanic Garden, Summer 2002.

McDonald, Elvin. *The 100 Best Bulbs.* New York: Random House, 1995.

Mohlenbrock, Robert H. *Ferns.* Carbondale: University of Southern Illinois Press, 1967.

Moody, Mary. *100 Plants for Easy to Maintain Gardens.* New York: Crescent Books, Random House, 1995.

Oakes, A. J. *Ornamental Grasses and Grasslike Plants.* New York: Van Nostrand Reinhold, 1990.

Obrizok, Robert A. *A Garden of Conifers.* Deer Park, WI: Capability's Books, 1999.

Ottesen, Carole. "When Good Plants Go Bad." Alexandria, Va.: *The American Gardener.* (American Horticultural Society). November/December 2001, pp. 44–48.

Patterson, Alan. *Plants for Shade.* London: J. M. Dent, 1981.

Peterson, Roger Tory, and Margaret McKenney. *A Field Guide to Wildflowers.* Boston: Houghton Mifflin, 1968.

Phillips, Harry R. *Growing and Propagating Wild Flowers.* Chapel Hill: University of North Carolina Press, 1985.

Phillips, Roger, and Martyn Rix. *Shrubs.* New York: Random House, 1989.

———. *Bulbs.* New York: Random House, 1989.

Pohl, Richard W. *How to Know the Grasses.* Dubuque, Iowa: Wm. C. Brown, 1954.

Poor, Janet Meakin, and Nancy Peterson Brewster. *Plants That Merit Attention.* Vol. II: *Shrubs.* Portland, Ore.: Timber Press, 1996.

Randall, John, and Janet Marenelli, eds. *Invasive Plants, Weeds of the Global Garden.* Brooklyn, N.Y.: Brooklyn Botanic Garden, Winter 1996.

Reinhardt, Thomas, Martha Reinhardt, and Mark Moskowitz. *Ornamental Grass Gardening.* Los Angeles: HP Books, 1989.

Rice, Graham. *A Handbook of Annuals and Bedding Plants.* Portland, Ore.: Timber Press, 1986.

Robinson, Benjamin. *Gray's New Manual of Botany.* New York: American Book, 1908.

Rockwell, F. F., and Esther C. Grayson. *The Complete Book of Bulbs.* Garden City, N.Y.: American Garden Guild & Doubleday, 1953.

Rose, Graham. *The Low Maintenance Garden.* New York: Viking Press, 1983.

Roth, Susan A. *Taylor's Guide to Trees.* Boston: Houghton Mifflin, 2001.

Sabuco, John J. *The Best of the Hardiest*. Flossmoor, Ill.: Good Earth Publishing, 1987.

Schmid, W. George. *Encyclopedia of Shade Perennials*. Portland, Ore.: Timber Press, 2002.

Shrubs & Trees (Best of Fine Gardening). Newton, Conn.: Taunton Press, 1993.

Simonds, Roberta L., and Henrietta H. Tweedie. *Wildflowers of the Great Lakes Region*. Champaign, Ill.: Stipes Publishing, 1997.

Snyder, Leon C. *Trees and Shrubs for Northern Gardens*. Minneapolis: University of Minnesota Press, 1980.

———. *Gardening in the Upper Midwest*. Minneapolis: University of Minnesota Press, 1985.

———. *Native Plants for Northern Gardens*. Chanhassen, Minn.: Anderson Horticultural Library, 1991.

Sperka, Marie. *Growing Wildflowers*. New York: Charles Scribner's Sons, 1984.

Stearn, William T. *Botanical Latin*. Portland, Ore.: Timber Press, 1998.

Sternberg, Guy, and Jim Wilson. *Landscaping with Native Trees*. Shelburne, VT: Chapters Publishing, 1995.

Swink, Floyd, and Gerould Wilhelm. *Plants of the Chicago Region*. 4th ed. Morton Arboretum, Lisle, Ill., Indianapolis: Indiana Academy of Science, 1995.

Taylor, Norman. *Taylor's Guide to Perennials*. Boston: Houghton Mifflin, 1987.

Tyler, Tom, and Jo Ellen Meyers Sharp. *Indiana Gardener's Guide*. Franklin, Tenn.: Cool Springs Press, 1998.

Vertrees, J. D. *Japanese Maples*. Portland, Ore.: Timber Press, 1978.

Viertel, Arthur T. *Trees, Shrubs and Vines*. Syracuse, N.Y.: Syracuse University Press, 1970.

Wasowski, Andy. "The Building Envelope." Alexandria, Va.: *The American Gardener* (American Horticultural Society). January/February 1997, pp. 26–33.

Wherry, Edgar T. *The Fern Guide*. Philadelphia: Morris Arboretum, 1961.

Wilson, Helen Van Pelt. *Successful Gardening in the Shade*. Garden City, N.Y.: Doubleday, 1975.

Wilson, Jim. *Landscaping with Wildflowers*. Boston: Houghton Mifflin, 1992.

Winterrowd, Wayne. *Annuals for Connoisseurs*. New York: Prentice Hall, 1992.

Yatskievych, Kay. *Field Guide to Indiana Wildflowers*. Bloomington: Indiana University Press, 2000.

Index

Page numbers in italics refer to illustrations.

Carolyn Harstad is author of *Go Native! Gardening with Native Plants and Wildflowers in the Lower Midwest* and is co-founder of both INPAWS (Indiana Native Plant and Wildflower Society) and the Indianapolis Hosta Society.

Jean Vietor graduated from Indiana University in Fine Art. She has exhibited mostly nature paintings for 33 years. Her mediums include watercolor, transparent acrylic, acrylic on canvas, computer art, and polymer clay art.